Educational Crisis and Reform

Perspectives from South Asia

Educational Crisis and Reform

Perspectives from South Asia

Edited By

ABBAS RASHID AND IRFAN MUZAFFAR

OXFORD

UNIVERSITY PRESS

OXFORD

UNIVERSITY PRESS

Oxford University Press is a department of the University of Oxford.
It furthers the University's objective of excellence in research, scholarship,
and education by publishing worldwide. Oxford is a registered trade mark of
Oxford University Press in the UK and in certain other countries

Published in Pakistan by
Ameena Saiyid, Oxford University Press
No.38, Sector 15, Korangi Industrial Area,
PO Box 8214, Karachi-74900, Pakistan

© Oxford University Press 2015

The moral rights of the author have been asserted

First Edition published in 2015

ISBN 978-0-19-940029-4

Typeset in Adobe Garamond Pro
Printed on 60gsm Book paper

Printed by VVP

In profound gratitude, to my parents Ahmad Hussain and Safia Hussain; to Farida, wife and friend; and to Zaair, Daanish, and Hooriya—may they live and prosper in saner times.

Abbas Rashid

In gratitude for their belief, commitment, and selfless devotion: to my mother Firdaus Jabeen and my wife Shamaila Qazalbash.

Irfan Muzaffar

To the teachers of South Asia who have the difficult but enviable task of being the dream keepers of our future generations and to the millions of out-of-school children who have waited too long for what should be theirs' by right.

Irfan Muzaffar and *Abbas Rashid*

Contents

Note on Contributors

Abbas Rashid is Executive Director, Society for Advancement of Education (SAHE) and a Coordinator of the Campaign for Quality Education (CQE) in Pakistan (http://www.cqe. net.pk). He works in the area of education policy research and advocacy. He has a number of research reports to his credit and contributes frequently in the media on issues related to education. His areas of special interest are language and learning, and citizenship education. Abbas holds a Masters degree from Columbia University, New York, USA.

Ajay Sharma is Associate Professor in the Department of Educational Theory and Practice, at the University of Georgia, Athens, USA. His current research centres on theoretical and ethnographic explorations of neo-liberalism's impact on education, and implications of Climate Change for science education. In his past research, Ajay Sharma has focused on understanding classroom discourse in K-12 science classrooms and science teacher education programmes from the perspectives of individual agency and equity. Before becoming a university based academic, Ajay Sharma worked in the Hoshangabad Science Teaching Programme in Madhya Pradesh, India, on middle school science curriculum and teacher professional development. He completed his doctoral studies in 2006 in the area of Curriculum, Teaching, and Educational Policy from Michigan State University, USA.

Amita Chudgar is Associate Professor of Educational Administration and Education Policy at Michigan State University. Her long-term interests as a scholar focus on ensuring that children and adults in resource-constrained environments have equal access to high-quality learning opportunities irrespective of their backgrounds. She has done PhD in Economics of Education from Stanford University, USA.

Anjum Halai is professor and an international education specialist with a Doctorate in Education from Oxford University, UK. She has worked in higher education in Pakistan and East Africa, teaching on graduate and post-graduate courses at the Aga Khan University Institute for Educational Development. Anjum has nearly twenty years of experience of leading international research and development projects in partnership with universities in the UK and Canada and has published widely in reputable global academic forums.

Ayesha A. Awan is an independent researcher who serves as a Senior Education Advisor to the Campaign for Quality Education in Pakistan (http://www.cqe.net.pk). She has extensive experience designing and conducting policy relevant research studies as well as advocating with government on key issues of educational reform in Pakistan. Areas of work have included student assessment systems, school effectiveness, citizenship education and early childhood education. She holds a Masters in Education (M.Ed.) in International Education Policy from the Harvard Graduate School of Education, USA.

Birgitte Refslund Sørensen is Associate Professor at the Department of Anthropology, University of Copenhagen. She has carried out extensive research on Sri Lanka and Denmark on issues such as development-induced displacement and resettlement, community and capacity building, post-conflict social reconstruction, humanitarian assistance and social recognition as social practice.

Faisal Bari is an Associate Professor of Economics at the Lahore University of Management Sciences (LUMS), and an Associate Research Fellow at the Institute of Development and Economic Alternatives (IDEAS). Dr Bari is an economist by training, however, education sector research has been an area of special interest for him for the last few years. He has done his doctorate from McGill University, Canada.

Fareeha Zafar is Professor, Graduate Institute of Development Studies at Lahore School of Economics, and Senior Advisor, Society for the Advancement of Education. She has worked as a consultant to various donors and as Technical Advisor to the Task Force on Education established by the Ministry of Education. She is also a founder member of Women's Action Forum (WAF) Lahore and served on the Board of Directors of the Pakistan Poverty Alleviation Fund, Punjab Education Foundation (PEF), and Leadership for Environment And Development (LEAD) Pakistan. Fareeha has taught at the University of the Punjab, Pakistan, for twenty-five years. She has also edited a book: *Women in Pakistan*. Fareeha has done her PhD in Geography from the School of Oriental and African Studies (SOAS), University of London, UK.

Irfan Muzaffar has a PhD in Curriculum, Instruction, and Education Policy from Michigan State University and a Masters of Arts in Mathematics Education from Teachers College, Columbia University. He has been working as a teacher-educator, campaigner, and as a researcher for the last twenty years. He is one of the founding members of the Campaign for Quality Education in Pakistan (http://www. cqe.net.pk), and Associate Fellow at the Institute of Development and Economic Alternatives. He has published his work in *Comparative International Review*, *Education Theory*, *Cultural Studies of Science Education*, and *Journal of Social and Policy Sciences*. He also contributes a bi-weekly column on issues of education reform in the English daily *The News* on Sunday.

James H. Williams is Associate Professor of International Education and International Affairs at the George Washington University. His research interests include: education and development, decentralization and administrative reform, education and health, cross-cultural organizational theory, education for marginalized and conflict-affected populations, and equity and achievement in large cross-national data sets. His recent publications include *Policy-Making for Education Reform in Developing Countries: Volume II, Options and Strategies*, co-authored with William Cummings. Dr William has done his Ed.D from Harvard University, USA.

Manasa Patnam is Assistant Professor of Economics at ENSAE-CREST, France. Manasa's research focuses on the economics of social interactions and spillovers. The broad theme of her research examines how non-market interactions, such as through social networks or geographical proximity, can affect economic outcomes, either by reducing transaction costs or through information sharing. She uses quasi-experimental settings, together with observational data, to study this issue in diverse contexts. Recent projects analyse cognitive and non-cognitive development amongst children, spatial spillovers of technology adoption in Africa, innovation in emerging economies, and consumer behaviour in the online marketplace. She has completed her doctoral studies from University of Cambridge, UK, in 2012.

Marie Lall is a Reader in Education and South Asian Studies at the Institute of Education, University of London. She is an honorary fellow at the Institute of South Asian Studies, National University of Singapore, a consultant member at the International Institute for Strategic Studies (IISS), and was an associate fellow on the Asia Programme at Chatham House till August 2011. She has held a number of short fellowships at world renowned universities in Australia, Germany, India and Pakistan. Dr Lall is a South Asia expert, specializing in geopolitical issues and education with specific regard to policy, gender, ethnicity and social exclusion issues, the formation of national identity and its close links with citizenship. She has written widely on these topics and is the author/editor of five books and a monograph. Lall received her M.Phil from Cambridge University in 1993 and her PhD from the London School of Economics, UK, in 1999.

Muhammad Farooq Naseer is Assistant Professor of Economics at the Lahore University of Management Sciences (LUMS) where he has taught econometric methods and development economics in the undergraduate and graduate programmes. His research interests lie in the field of development economics with a focus on education, vocational skills and labour markets as well as problems of political selection. He has received his PhD in 2007 in Economics from Yale University, USA.

Pervez Hoodbhoy is distinguished professor in the Department of Physics at Forman Christian College, Lahore. Dr Hoodbhoy has previously taught at the Quaid-i-Azam University and Lahore University of Management Sciences (LUMS), authored three books and over sixty-five research papers. He has written and spoken extensively on topics ranging from science in Islam to education issues in Pakistan and nuclear disarmament. In recognition of his contribution to his field of interest, he received the UNESCO Kalinga Prize for disseminating knowledge of the sciences, Abdus Salam Prize for Mathematics and the Baker Award for Electronics in 1984. Dr Hoodbhoy received his PhD in nuclear physics from the Massachusetts Institute of Technology, USA.

Reehana R. Raza is currently a Senior Human Development Economist at the World Bank. Previously she was Director of the Institute of Development and Economic Alternatives (IDEAS) and remains an Associate Fellow. She has over twelve years of experience in the areas of economics of education, institutional economics and public sector economics and governance. She has consulted for the World Bank in the Europe and Central Asian Human Development Unit in Washington, and worked for a four-year Department for International Development (DFID) funded research project on the Economics of Tertiary Education in South Asia. She has also consulted for the Asian Development Bank (ADB), the United Nations Development Programme (UNDP), US Agency for International Development (USAID), and other multilateral and bilateral agencies. Dr Raza has a bachelors' degree in International Relations from Mount Holyoke College, an M.Phil in Economics and Politics of Development, and a Doctorate in Economics from the University of Cambridge, UK.

Seher Ahmad is a doctoral student in Higher Education at the University of Pennsylvania with a Masters in Statistics from The Wharton School, USA. Her research interests include gender, education, stratification, and quantitative methods.

Sushan Acharya is an Associate Professor in the Education Planning and Management Department of Central Department of Education Tribhuvan University. She has also been supervising M.Phil theses of the School of Education, Kathmandu University. Dr Acharya has undertaken a number of research, evaluation, reviews, and consultancy projects in the field of education (both formal and non-formal) particularly with focus on social inclusion. She has published a number of articles on gender and social inclusion in the context of education. She holds an Ed.D in International and Non-Formal Education (1999) and Masters in International and Non-Formal Education (1994) from Center for International Education (CIE), University of Massachusetts (UMass), Amherst, USA; and Masters in English Literature (1984) from Tribhuvan University (TU), Kathmandu.

Wilfred J. Perera is Assistant Director General, Faculty of Leadership Development and Teacher Education at National Institute of Education, Sri Lanka. He is also affiliated with Centre for Education Leadership Development, Meepe. Some of his international publications include 'Decentralization of Education Management — the Sri Lankan Experience', and 'Changing Schools from Within: A Management Intervention for Improving School Functioning' published by the International Institute for Educational Planning (IIEP), UNESCO.

List of Abbreviations

ADB	Asian Development Bank
AEPAM	Academy of Educational Planning and Management
AKES	Aga Khan Education Service
AKF	Aga Khan Foundation
AKU	Aga Khan University
ASER	Annual Status of Education Report
B.Ed.	Bachelor of Education
BDI	Bangladesh Development Initiative
BICS	Basic Interpersonal Communication Skill
BRC	Block Resource Centre
CALP	Cognitive Academic Language Proficiency
CBMP	Cluster-Based Mentoring Programme
CDC	Curriculum Development Centre
CEDAW	Convention on the Elimination of all forms of Discrimination against Women
CPD	Continuous Professional Development
CQE	Campaign for Quality Education
CRC	Cluster Resource Centre
CRI	Children's Resource International
CT	Certificate in Teaching

DAI	Degree Awarding Institution
DDBF	Democracy and Development in Bangladesh Forum
DDEE	Divisional Directors of Education
DEO	District Education Officer
DFID	Department For International Development
DIET	District Institute of Educational Training
DNFE	Directorate of Non-formal Education
DPEP	District Primary Education Programme
ECED	Early Childhood Education and Development
EFA	Education For All
EPF	Education Production Function
ESDFP	Education Sector Development Framework & Programme
ESRA	Education Sector Reform Assistance
ETS	Educational Testing Service
FDE	Federal Directorate of Education
FRBMA	Fiscal Responsibility and Budget Management Act
GER	Gross Enrolment Ratio
GIKI	Ghulam Ishaq Khan Institute
GRE	Graduate Record Examination
HEC	Higher Education Commission
HFPS	High Fee Private School
ICT	Islamabad Capital Territory
IER	Institute of Education and Research

IIE	Institute of International Education
INFEP	Integrated Non-Formal Education Programme
IRT	Item Response Theory
KPI	Key Performance Indicator
LEAP	Learning and Education Achievement in Punjab Schools
LFPS	Low Fees Private School
LIFE	Literacy Initiative for Empowerment
LUMS	Lahore University of Management Sciences
MDGs	Millennium Development Goals
MHHDC	Mahbub ul Haq Human Development Centre
MHRD	Ministry of Human Resource Development
MLE	Multi Lingual Education
MOE	Ministry of Education
MOI	Medium of Instruction
MOPME	Ministry of Primary and Mass Education
MQM	Muttahida Qaumi Movement
MT	Mother Tongue
NAEP	National Assessment of Education Progress
NCED	National Centre for Educational Development
NCF	National Curriculum Framework
NCLB	No Child Left Behind
NEAS	National Education Assessment System
NFE	Non-Formal Education
NIE	National Institute of Education

NLM	National Literacy Mission
NPE	National Policy on Education
NRO	National Reconciliation Ordinance
NTS	National Testing Service
NUEPA	National University of Educational Planning and Administration
NUST	National University of Science and Technology
NWFP	North-West Frontier Province
OPT	Optional Practical Training
PAP	People's Action Party
PCST	Pakistan Council for Science and Technology
PDCN	Professional Development Centre North
PDE	Provincial Director of Education
PEDP	Primary Education Development Programme
PESRP	Punjab Education Sector Reform Programme
PIL	Public Interest Litigations
PISA	Programme for International Student Assessment
PITE	Provincial Institute of Teacher Education
PLCE	Post-Literacy and Continuing Education
PMSP	Punjab Middle Schooling Project
PPA	Past Pupils Association
PPP	Pakistan Peoples Party
PSI	Programme on School Improvement
PTA	Parent Teacher Association

PTC	Primary Teaching Certificate
PTSMC	Parent Teacher School Management Committee
QAU	Quaid-i-Azam University
RTE	Right to Education
SAFMA	South Asian Free Media Association
SAHE	Society for the Advancement of Education
SAP	Social Action Programme
SAT	Scholastic Aptitude Test
SBM	School-Based Management
SC	School Council
SDC	School Development Committee
SDU	Social Development Unit
SLEAS	Sri Lanka Education Administrative Service
SMC	School Management Committee
SMT	School Management Team
SSA	Sarva Shiksha Abhiyan
SSRP	School Sector Reform Plan
TAN	Transnational Advocacy Network
TLM	Total Literacy Movement/Mission
TTS	Tenure Track System
UEE	Universalization of Education
UGC	University Grant Commission
UIS	UNESCO Institute for Statistics
UNESCO	United Nations Educational, Scientific and Cultural Organization

UNICEF   United Nations Children's Fund
UPE   Universal Primary Education
USAID   United States Agency for International
          Development
VEC   Village Education Committee
VTE   Vocational and Technical Education
WSIP   Whole School Improvement Programme

List of Figures, Tables, and Maps

Acknowledgements—I

We are grateful to the South Asian Free Media Association (SAFMA) for supporting this effort as part of their series of publications on issues of regional concern, undertaken as part of their project under the South Asian Policy Analysis Network (SAPANA). The Society for the Advancement of Education (SAHE), and the Campaign for Quality Education (CQE), with which the editors are affiliated, welcomed the offer to collaborate with SAFMA as it meant an opportunity to engage a wider audience on these critical issues in education, through its media-related network in the region.

We also want to acknowledge our considerable debt to the Foundation Open Society Institute (FOSI) for getting us to start thinking about such a book, not least by supporting an international conference of educationists hosted by the Aga Khan University-Institute of Educational Development (AKU-IED). Some of the contributors to the book initially came together at the conference and had the opportunity to discuss and deliberate on issues of common concern in education.

We are deeply grateful to all our contributors who demonstrated patience and understanding through the long and sometimes trying process of the manuscript taking final shape.

Our thanks are also due to Ameena Saiyid at Oxford University Press Pakistan for taking special interest in the publication of this book and to Nadia Ghani in OUP's editorial team for working hard to bring this project to completion.

A special thanks to Ayesha A. Awan for her invaluable help in the task of editing and to Muhammad Azhar for diligently collecting basic country-level information on education-related indicators for South Asia.

Of course the editors are solely responsible for any gaps and errors that, doubtless, remain.

Abbas Rashid and Irfan Muzaffar
Lahore, 2014

Acknowledgements—II

We gratefully acknowledge permission by the authors as well as the concerned journals to include in this book, in their original form, two previously published articles.

Sorensen, Birgitte R. (2008), 'The Politics of Citizenship and Difference in Sri Lankan Schools', *Anthropology & Education Quarterly* 39 (4), 423–3.

Naseer, Muhammad F., Patnam, M. and Raza, Reehana R., (2010), 'Transforming public schools: Impact of the CRI programme on child learning in Pakistan', *Economics of Education Review*, 29 (4), 669–83. (A brief version drawn from this chapter is available at http://lums.edu.pk/mgshss/dprc/page.php/fac ulty-publications-dprc)

Introduction

Responding to the Education Deficit: A South Asian Perspective
—*Abbas Rashid and Irfan Muzaffar*

South Asia is a region that is blessed with abundant resources, both human and natural. It also has some unsavoury claims to fame. Among these: it is home to almost half the number of illiterate people in the world—approximately, 400 million (Mahbub ul Haq Human Development Centre, 2012). A comparable number of people in the region live below the poverty line. Public health expenditure in most South Asian counties is less than 2 per cent of GDP. The under-five years infant mortality rate in some South Asian countries such as India and Pakistan is particularly high at 61 and 72 per 1,000 live births, respectively (United Nations Population Fund, 2012). South Asian states have so far failed to deliver educational justice—which we may define loosely as an even distribution of quality education to various segments of the population. Therefore, only a fraction of South Asian youth can benefit from an increasingly globalizing world economy that is poised to reward those whose education has made them ready for gainful employment in a diverse job market. The resulting inequities in income are working as a fuel for the social and political conflicts in the region. An equitable opportunity to get a decent education for all children, among other things, is critical for providing individuals and society as a whole with means to alleviate poverty and reduce explosive inequities. Reforms aimed at ensuring educational justice for all children, therefore, assume critical importance.

This book looks at attempts to reform specific aspects of the education sector by the countries of the region. The idea of the book took hold towards the end of 2009 after a transnational dialogue held by the Campaign for Quality Education (CQE) in collaboration with the Institute for Educational Development—Aga Khan University (AKU–IED) on Education Quality in South Asia. So, while the volume is by no means a compendium of the proceedings of the dialogue, it does draw from them and the rich discussion at the meet served as a useful point of departure for many of the contributions. The book takes the position that the crises in education faced by different countries of the region differ in their nature as well as import. But notwithstanding the differences, there are also some common denominators such as, burgeoning populations and growth of private sector in mass education. The contributions in this volume aim at providing a deeper understanding of both the dimensions of the crises as well as responses to them. They also help us understand the nature of obstacles to reform, highlighting some of the attempts made and the measure of success achieved.

Published with the support of South Asian Free Media Association (SAFMA), this volume purports to be a source of information for the media, policymakers, and general public. Accordingly, the editors and contributors have sought to ensure that it remains accessible, in terms of its style and presentation to a non-academic audience. The hope is that this volume would thereby contribute to informed debate on critical issues relating to education reform in the countries of the region.

THE CONTEXT

More than one-third of all out-of-school children in the world live in South Asia (UNESCO, UIS, and UNICEF, 2005). While the South Asian countries have made considerable progress in recent years in addressing education-related issues, much remains to be done. Today, the region compares with sub-Saharan Africa in terms of the percentage of literate men and women as well as the share of national resources committed to education. The formidable challenges that governments in South Asia face have to do with both access to and quality of education. Nearly a third of all children between the ages 5–14 remain out of school (UNGEI, 2007). But many of the children who do find their way into schools do not stay the course. In other words, the dropout rates remain high (Hunt, 2008) transitions and equity. Further, even among many of those who finish primary schooling, the level of learning remains below par.

Public spending on education remains low across the South Asian region. Allocations to education over the decades hover around 2 per cent to 3 per cent of GDP with more states being closer to the former than the latter. Not many states in the region have managed to reach the minimum of 4 per cent of GDP for education recommended by UNESCO (2009) and World Bank (2010). Some say that improving education quality and access is even more a matter of political commitment than financial resources. And, this may well be so. There can be no doubt that available resources can be better utilised and a higher education budget is in itself no guarantee of a reformed or improved education sector. Having said that, we should keep in mind that the quantum of resources that a state chooses to allocate to a given sector is certainly one of the indicators of its measure of commitment to that sector. A rough comparison between the defence and education budgets of various states in the region is instructive in this regard (UNESCO, 2009). This takes on additional significance given that according to one estimate mentioned in Mahbub ul Haq Human Development Centre (1998) report, an additional 1 per cent of South Asia's combined GNP can ensure universal primary education (UPE) in the region.

It is a reflection of the complex and formidable nature of the challenges to education reforms that the commitments made by the governments of the region to ensure Education For All in Jomtien in 1990, more than two decades ago, are far from being realized (UNESCO, 2008a). Many observers think that education needs to become a political concern and that the political parties should be held to account by the citizenry in general and civil society in particular for their failure. Interestingly, a number of studies suggest that the demand for education is very high even among poor and illiterate households across the region. And yet, its articulation in ways that will generate sufficient pressure in the political realm has yet to happen for the most part (Dreze, 2004; Dreze & Sen, 2002). Education has yet to become the kind of political issue that can potentially shift the balance in terms of winning or losing elections. Equally, the problem can be seen in the perspective of the state elites' inadequate realization of its own self-interest in having the sort of populace that create and sustain a democratic polity as well as a knowledge economy, ensuring the social stability that is a prerequisite for individual and collective well being.

This volume has contributions from India, Pakistan, Bangladesh, Sri Lanka, and Nepal. Thus, not all countries of the South Asian region are represented in the volume. Yet, we believe that the issues discussed have relevance across the region.

WHITHER THE STATE IN EDUCATION?

The aspirations of a modern state inevitably entail commitments to universal basic education. Historically, this commitment to universal basic education has grown in tandem with the emergence of 'population' as a site for intervention and as a target for exercise of the power of state (Burchell, Gordon, & Miller, 1991). Taking care of a whole population, then, is the *raison d'etre* of the modern state. *Educating all* is, therefore, a commitment which characterises, even if on a rhetorical level, the claims to legitimacy of the state. The South Asian states too regularly reiterate their commitment to universal education in different forms. All countries from which contributions to this volume are drawn, mention the imperative for universal education in their constitutions: India, Pakistan, and Nepal regard education as a fundamental right, while Bangladesh and Sri Lanka list education under the directive principles of state policy. The constitutional commitments to universal education, however, are not matched by commensurate allocations to education sector. The constitutional pronouncements are not equalled by appropriate policies and plans to make universal access to quality education a reality for all South Asian school-age children. In practice, the state's commitment to providing access to quality education for all children is constantly thwarted by its reticence to take the necessary steps to realize this commitment. How does one explain this apparent disconnect between the word and the deed?

Marie Lall's contribution uses the case of India to respond to this question. The conduct of Indian state, Lall argues, is characterised by three main trends. The first of these is reflected in an increased spending of the Indian government on education and anti-poverty programmes. This, we believe, is in accordance with the constitutional commitments that we have alluded to earlier. The second trend is reflected in an apparent retreat of the Indian state from the actual provision of education services to assumption of the role of a contracting agency. This trend is, arguably, an instance of the so-called neo-liberal agenda, under which the state changes its role from a provider of public services to a being a financier and regulators of such provision by private contractors. Finally, Marie Lall directs our attention toward the emergence of a purely market-based system of education. This market of educational services seems to have emerged in response to an existing demand for them from the emerging middle and lower middle classes. When the children from these classes are enrolled in private schools, the state-run schools see a decline in their enrolments. Thus, a pattern of exit from the state-run schools is becoming increasingly palpable in India. We think that Marie Lall's description of a mass exodus from the state-run schools will resonate with the situation in other South Asian countries as well. For instance, in the case of Pakistan, the last two decades have witnessed a phenomenal growth in what are referred to as non-state or private schools: this sector grew by an estimated 68 per cent just between 2000 and 2005.

At present, this sector enrols 33 per cent of all school-going children and employs 44 per cent of all teachers in Pakistan. A similar situation prevails in Bangladesh where over 41 per cent of all enrolments are in the private sector schools.

The majority of private schools are characterised by a free relationship between private consumers and providers of education services. The states' efforts at regulating these schools are limited to their registration and to some require-ment pertaining to curriculum and assessment. Some private schools, such as some elite private school systems in the case of Pakistan, bypass the states' requirements for curriculum and assessment by having their students examined by the foreign secondary school examination systems such as the British O/A levels and University of Cambridge syndicate. In addition to these, the private schooling encompasses a growing number of *Low Fees Private Schools* (LFPS), that cater to the educational consumers from the poorer segments of South Asian population (Andrabi, Das, & Khwaja, 2008; Tooley, 2009; Tooley & Dixon, 2003).

This discussion of state's withdrawal brings us to a consideration of a framework offered by American economist Albert O. Hirschman for change in public and private organizations which has found a great deal of favour in explaining the change behaviour of public and private schools across the world. In his book *Exit, Voice and Loyalty*, Hirschmann (1970) argued that organizations undergo positive change either through a *political voice, exit, or loyalty*. The idea of loyalty is used largely in the case of organizations such as political parties whose affiliates would like to stick with them due to their party loyalty. *Voice and Exit*, however, are relevant and utilised by two contributions to this volume. We will describe them here briefly. Hirschman argues that public sector organizations do not respond per the expectations of those they serve; they change only in response to the *political voice*. Private sector organizations, however, change their conduct in response to the fear of losing their customers. This claim has an important implication for public schools. It implies that public schools are unlikely to improve their services even when they lose students to private schools. That is to say, they are not responsive to *exit*. They only change through exercise of political influence. This underscores the importance of the politics for reforms in public education sector, and of turning public education into a sufficiently political issue. The political deficit in education has also been seen as a problem by other scholars, notably Amartya Sen and

Jean Drèze who argue that education has not been sufficiently political in India (Dreze & Sen, 2002). Private schools, however, do everything they must to keep the consumers of their services from *exiting*. This implies that they will improve their services when faced with the fear of exit. Thus, this line of thinking leads us to think about the reforms in public and private schools in accordance with the dynamics of change in these sectors. At the risk of repeating, this dynamics consists of the following: the exit of students from public schools is unlikely to change their public endowments, while private schools are responsive to exit and can improve if faced with the prospect of flight of their customers.

Irfan Muzaffar and Faisal Bari use this framework to critique the current level of debates about education reforms in Pakistan. According to them, the ongoing division of education into large-scale public and private sectors has created possibilities of comparison of outcomes between the two kinds of schools, which have been readily seized by some policy entrepreneurs. Thus, numerous comparative studies of student achievement in public and LFP schools have also followed on the heels of the growth of private sector schools[1] (Andrabi, Das, Khwaja, Vishwanath, & Zajonc, 2007). These studies demonstrate that *ceteris paribus* the private schools outperform their public counterparts. Similar comparative studies leading to very similar findings have also been conducted in other countries of South Asia and are used to support policy proposals aimed at reducing the role of state in financing and provision of education.[2] Muzaffar and Bari, in this volume, argue that comparisons of public and private schools are barking up the wrong tree in the context of Pakistan. Their argument is hinged on the belief that both private and public schools are not doing well and need to improve. They follow Hirschman to suggest that both public and private schools will follow a different dynamic for reforms. While the state may regulate the private schools to preserve its stake in education and to ensure that their curricula are amenable to production of an informed, tolerant, and productive citizenry, it can leave them alone as far as their dynamic of change and improvement is concerned. They will change and improve in order to stay in business. The change and reform in the public schools, however, will require politicizing education in order to inject *voice* into the system. Their chapter explores ways in which political participation in issues of public education may be stimulated. They also suggest that the declaration of education as an inalienable human right through a recent constitutional amendment has provided new opportunities for reducing the political deficit in the matters of reform of public sector schools. Abbas Rashid and Ayesha A. Awan have also employed Hirschman's framework of *voice* and *exit* to make their case. They argue that the exit of the influential classes from the public schools has become central to the absence of *voice* in public schools. The state in seeking to pass on as much of its (constitutional) commitment to provide basic education to its citizens has sought not only to enhance the role of the market but also that of the community. They point to the greater state-directed community involvement in schooling in the form of PTAs, SMCs, or SCs that apparently aligns nicely with the democratic narrative of participation and subsidiarity.

They argue that this is of a piece with the larger pattern of state abdication in favour of the for-profit and the not-for-profit private sector at the cost of the state's own role in providing what are essentially basic rights to its citizens (Rashid, 2007). Taking Hirschman's arguments as a point of departure, Rashid and Awan contend that the more powerful/influential section of the community have effectively exited the public education system. With their children in private schools, they no longer have any real interest in improving the quality of public sector schools. The rest lack the *voice* or influence to hold the school or the education bureaucracy accountable. So even where such community organizations continue to function they do so at a low level of involvement with only a marginal ability to effect any changes. Rashid and Awan cite the experiment of participatory budgeting in Porto Allegro, the measure of success being an exception to the rule, to argue that only a politically mobilized community can provide the much needed leverage or *voice* to reform the public sector. There can be other exceptions, of course, as pointed out in their chapter. However, from a rights perspective, the state should not need much by way of leveraging to provide quality education to all.

While a growing private sector in education may be something of a norm in much of South Asia, the public sector is clearly dominant in Sri Lanka. And certainly with a literacy rate of over 90 per cent, it can claim a measure of success. However, as Perera's chapter makes clear all is not well with the system. The Programme on School Improvement (PSI) is an attempt at decentralisation of decision-making affecting schools.

It aims to encourage school-based decision-making with a greater role for zones and communities. Whether this effort at reform improves the quality of education in the long term or turns out to be an attempt on the part of the Sri Lankan state, in line with the Zeitgeist, to reduce its involvement in the education sector remains to be seen. Perera's chapter also brings up the issue of the community's role in school reform. He suggests, much as Rashid and Awan do in their chapter, that in the community-school relationship, it is the school that needs to provide an enabling environment for the community to play its role in supporting education reform.

Soresnson's chapter also on Sri Lanka brings the focus back on the state in the context of education. It takes up the vexed issue of citizenship education and the attempts by the Sri Lankan state to construct a narrative of citizenship through changes in curricula that is accommodative of multiple ethnic and religious identities. Sorenson argues that lived experience that incorporates everyday discrimination is likely to trump state-directed efforts in the realm of curricula and classroom. So the former needs to change before the latter can be rendered effective. Her chapter is a very useful contribution to the discussion on the role curricula and textbooks play in the construction of identity and citizenship. Clearly, education is an important site for intervention when it comes to internalized notions of citizenship. How far it can be effective is, in large part, determined by the context. At a minimum, though, it is reasonable to suggest that textbooks matter more than the curriculum and its stated guidelines. Further, the opinions and orientation of the teacher, the exposure to electronic and social media as well as the perspective and views of the larger community have a crucial bearing in shaping perspectives and the worldview of the school-going child. This is an important dimension of the process that is often ignored. In the emphasis on changing curricula and textbooks, the child appears to be locked into a uni-dimensional context with an implicit assumption that the curricula/textbook will render her/him into one kind of a citizen or another. This simplistic notion is strongly contested by Sorenson in her piece. The chapter is an important one inasmuch as it draws our attention to the imperative of citizenship education in addition to the other, more conventional, sought-after competencies.

Fareeha Zafar's chapter on girls schooling in Pakistan, in looking at the constraints suffered by girls with regard to education opportunities, points to the construction of a different kind of citizen through everyday lived experience distinguished by gender. The girls' middle school stipend scheme introduced by the government with the support of donor funding to increase girls' enrolment has been reviewed here by Zafar. She argues that while there is little doubt that it has increased enrolment, it is far from clear that the scheme has had any impact on the low levels of attainment and learning that are the bane of the education system as a whole. And while the gender gap is slowly narrowing, gender disparities persist. Still, the programme appears to be a successful intervention, given research showing that issues related to poverty contribute more than any other reason for children not attending school (Population Council, 2007).

There is clearly, then, a positive effect of the stipend on enrolment and retention. Counter-posed to this, however, is the rise of extremism that has emerged as a key challenge to the education of girls. The practice of exclusion, segregation, discrimination, and violence against women and girls shows an increase over the last decade. Girls schools have been targeted and blown in the tribal regions and other parts of the Khyber Pakhtunkhwa and threats to educational institutions that are coeducational, or only for girls, in other parts of the country are indicative of the further curtailing of opportunities for girls. Even otherwise, schooling seems to reinforce and strengthen the gendered identities and roles of the students. Texts and images that serve as the building blocks in this project of identity construction mostly go unchallenged or critically analyzed by the teachers and students. Similarly, Zafar argues, the media has reinforced the links between traditional social roles and expectations for women.

In recent years, the quality of education is also stated in terms of learner-centredness of the teaching and learning processes. Nearly all interventions aimed at changing the classroom practices privilege this approach but very few are rigorously evaluated to see the actual impact they may have had on the classrooms. Farooq Naseer, Manasa Patnam, and Reehana R. Raza's chapter fills this gap by examining an intervention in public schools through the Children Resources International (CRI) programme that resulted in improved learning among the students. It also underscores the need for nuanced evaluation of non-didactic methods of teaching that have gained greater currency in the last few years. Clearly, though, as Naseer,

Patnam, and Raza points out, much more work has to be done in the area of what works in terms of improving public sector education quality (Campaign for Quality Education, 2007) as the intervention was limited to a small number of schools in Pakistan's capital city. The CRI intervention included improved teaching through training as well as ongoing support by master trainers, provision of teaching and learning aids and the encouraging of parental engagement of at the classroom level. Clearly, the introduction of these elements of quality had a positive impact on student learning as demonstrated by Naseer, Patnam, and Raza's chapter. Identifying such elements and how they may combine to improve learning has important implications for policy. However, scaling up interventions of this nature in the context of the public sector at large remains a challenge at the level of governance underlining the need to address scarcity of human as well as material resources.

LANGUAGE AND LEARNING

As a point of departure, let us take note of the fact that there is widespread demand across the region for proficiency in English. Few parents, even among the poor and illiterate, doubt the usefulness of learning English as it is perceived as the language of social mobility and power. At the same time, there are numerous studies indicating that a child's cognitive ability is best developed at the earliest stages of schooling by the use of the home language or the mother tongue. A child of around five years of age, at the time of starting school, has a vocabulary of approximately 3,000 words in his home language (Ely, 2005). To build upon this resource in the initial stages of schooling means enhancing the child's capacity to learn. Far from being a zero-sum game between say the home language, the national language, and the global lingua franca, a start in school with the home language will subsequently enable the child—as a better learner—to pick up the latter two with greater ease (Rashid, 2011). There are exceptions to this rule, particularly where children are exposed to what constitutes the immersion method. Children from elite households, for instance, have far less of a problem learning English, not because they go to English medium schools (that is a part of the equation) but because outside the school they are immersed in an environment where English is effectively rendered the first language. But, we can well imagine how limited this number is across the region. On the other hand, teaching in the mother tongue at the primary level, as also recommended by UNESCO, entails a number of implementation issues (UNESCO, 2008b). The chapter by Sushan Acharya describes these issues in the context of Nepal. Demonstrating to parents as well as policy circles, the efficacy of teaching in the mother tongue, especially at the primary level, remains a difficult enterprise. Not least, because the practice is almost always accompanied by an absence of other elements of quality such as good teachers, infrastructure and textbooks. Further, the children in such schools are likely to come from poor households with little or no support at home in the context of learning.

TEACHING AND TEACHER EDUCATION

Educational systems consist of curricula, textbooks, assessment systems, teachers, and schools. They also include institutions that prepare teachers, researchers, and other individuals needed to provide educational services. Last, but not the least, they also consist of the ministries of education and other relevant departments, put in place by the state to support its education systems. However, the points of service in this elaborate and extended system are *the schools, and within schools, the teachers.* It is the school where the system engages with the young learner for a stipulated number of years. As such, state and society must ensure that every child has access to a school. This is the idea that animates the Millennium Development Goals (MDGs) related to the universal provision of education to all children.

Yet, when the state attempts to universalize access to quality education, the problem of providing access to quality teachers assumes politico-economic dimensions. Economics places a limit on the political aspirations to recruit, train, induct, and retain high quality teachers in the profession. The introduction of an agenda of free Universal Primary Education (UPE) in many countries, as set out in the first *Education For All* (EFA) framework in 1990, has increased the demand for trained teachers in proportion to huge increases in the student enrolment. The gaps between teacher demand and supply have resulted in huge shortages of qualified teacher in the developing countries. Teacher shortages plague many education systems in the developing world and often undermine the effectiveness of development interventions

aiming to improve student access to quality education
(Pandey, 2009). The countries of South Asia are also faced
with very high dropout rates, attributed largely to the poor
quality of education, most often in public schools. Thus,
both the need to enrol as well as retain an increasing number
of children is bringing teaching and teacher education under
increasing pressures.

In the face of these pressures, governments have adopted
some paradoxical stances. In Pakistan, for instance, one sees
a concomitant emphasis on professionalization and contractualization of teaching. On the one hand, initiatives have
been put in place that seek to increase the length of initial
teacher preparation programmes to as long as four years, thus
bringing them at par with similar induction programmes in
other professions such as medicine and engineering. There
are also efforts to develop professional standards as well as to
monitor teacher development through accreditation regimes
such as the one being put in place by the Higher Education
Commission (HEC). On the other hand, provincial
governments have also been encouraging the hiring of new
teachers on contracts. Different countries have had different
experiences with hiring teachers on contracts. However, the
objectives for doing so have been, more or less, the same—
cost cutting and more effective accountability of teachers
(Duthilleul, 2004). At least four characteristics of contract
teachers have been identified in the literature:

> They are hired on renewable contracts with no guarantees for
> renewal beyond the duration stipulated in the contract, they are
> typically less qualified than the regular teachers, they are paid

much less, and they are much more likely to be from the local communities (Muralidharan & Sundararaman, 2008).

In effect then, the policies aimed at professionalising teaching tend to be undercut by other policies aimed at cutting costs and improving accountability through short-term contracting. Ajay Sharma, in this volume, argues that the policies of hiring contract teachers are de-professionalising teaching. These policies are doing, he argues, a 'grievous harm' to the teaching profession by relegating teaching from a reasonably well-paid professional career to a low-paid, de-skilled contractual work. This process is debilitating and disempowering for teachers, both individually and collectively. Part of his argument against contracting draws itself from the need for longer and intensive initial teacher preparation, as is the case with most professions. Teachers must imbibe a core repertoire of professional practices and knowledge, that along with a shared professional ethos, helps maintain necessary and distinct professional standards. In bypassing appropriate teacher preparation, induction, and professional development, contract teaching is adversely affecting the work of teaching. Yet, South Asian countries must struggle with such dilemmas given the large number of teachers needed and given the need to hold teachers accountable for teaching their students to the best of their professional capacities.

The assumption behind Ajay Sharma's argument is that professionalization of teaching requires sound initial teacher preparation and a grounding and investment in a socially respected long-term teaching career. There is no agreement, however, amongst the teacher education scholars on the length and duration of initial teacher preparation. More recent scholarship on teacher education suggests the teacher preparation to be a continuum (Plessis & Muzaffar, 2010; Schwille, Dembélé, & Schubert, 2007). From a larger perspective, initial professional preparation of teachers is part of a *Continuum of Learning to Teach*, as illustrated in the figure below.

Fig. 1: Continuum of Learning to Teach

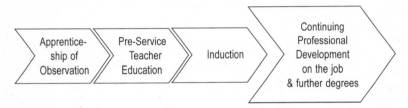

The pre-service teacher education programmes or 'initial teacher preparation' then is one, albeit foundational, part of this continuum. However, since teacher certification policies and standards may vary from one country to the other, pre-service programmes may also vary in duration and content. In some contexts, the continuing professional development programmes spread over a teacher's career may assume more importance, not least because they can potentially remediate the deficiencies in preparation left in the pre-service teacher education programmes. The chapter by Anjum Halai describes one such case in Pakistan.

Anjum Halai's description of an ongoing professional development programme recognizes that pressures of a rapidly expanding school system are resulting in recruitment of unprepared teachers—something that Ajay Sharma argues happens anyways in the case of contract teachers. Contract teachers or not, the pre-service programmes even for regular teachers, at least in the case of Pakistan, cannot respond to the increasing demand for professionally qualified teachers. We do not have the data for other South Asian countries, and Anjum Halai's chapter is not a comparative study. Yet, readers could draw from these cases to reflect on their own particular teacher education situations. Halai urges us to recognise that pressures to recruit teachers without adequate preparation can results in deficiencies in preparation that could potentially continue to persist if not identified and eliminated through appropriate continuous professional development. Halai describes a successful initiative, which is geared toward doing just that. As such, this description will be useful for teacher educators attempting to craft continuous professional development programmes.

In addition to the obvious, there are some crucial differences in these two aforementioned chapters on teacher education and teaching that merit mention. While Ajay Sharma is concerned about the state's adoption of practices of the private sector, namely short-term contracting of teachers, as detrimental to the profession and to the work of teaching, Anjum Halai is concerned with the direct effects of increased demands on teacher education programmes. Her emphasis on 'remedial' in-service and continuous professional development does not assume the existence of contract teachers, but rather emphasises that the initial teacher preparation is not doing a good job of preparing even the regular teachers.

We think that government, which remains the major employers of teachers in public schools, is also responsible for ensuring that all students get quality education. This is enough to justify the need for a robust and coherent teacher policy that must support the development of teachers as professionals throughout the countries of South Asia. Merely employing enough teachers to maintain a student teacher ratio of say 20 to 1 is not enough. Merely inducting them as regular teachers and giving them a relatively better salary than the contract teachers is not enough either. So governments cannot be content to be employers of teachers. A teacher development policy, therefore, must seek to find ways for the government to obtain maximum efficiency in employing, educating, and retaining high quality teachers for all students.

The quality of general college preparation of the entrants to teaching profession also has consequences for the form and content of teacher education. All of these factors demand a reconsideration of the role of teachers, their preparation, work and careers throughout the countries of South Asia.

HIGHER EDUCATION, LITERACY, AND RELEVANCE IN EDUCATION

The term higher education typically refers to research institutions in general including the universities as well as the post-secondary colleges. Literacy—which in the developing contexts is typically taken to be the ability to read and write—has no direct relationship with higher education. The need to imagine education in its relationship with the readiness and capacity of the society to put its educated human resources to optimal use also does not seem to be of direct relevance to the immediate issues of education reforms. However, quality basic education is not achievable without attention to reforms in each one of these areas. The teacher education programmes that Anjum Halai expounds on in her chapter would have been far more effective in preparing high quality teachers if the colleges had done a satisfactory job of equipping the would-be teachers with subject-matter knowledge. Holistic education reforms will need to focus also on determinants of quality education outside of the school, in the area of higher education, literacy, and relevance of education to society and economy. The contributions by Pervez Hoodbhoy, Amita Chudgar and Seher Ahmad, and Manzoor Ahmad and James H. Williams broach the issues, respectively, of quality in higher education, the lack of attention to adult literacy and the need for an educational development strategy in the context of South Asia.

Hoodbhoy uses the case of recent higher education reforms in Pakistan to point out that they are not adequately geared toward improving the quality of institutions. He proposes a higher education quality assessment index, a mathematical expression that pulls together various critical indicators of success. The use of this index, he argues, can help provide a clear direction toward, as well as accountability for, improvement in the quality of higher education institutions. In formulating such an index to assess the quality dimension of higher education institutions, Hoodbhoy is attempting something ambitious but at the very least the exercise can serve the valuable purpose of focusing attention on areas that are sadly being largely ignored in Pakistan's drive to make higher education accessible to much larger numbers. Hoodbhoy is fully cognizant of the difficulties involved in developing such an index for assessing quality across universities and disciplines. But, he argues, the task is unavoidable if we are to improve the quality of higher education institutions. He places the quality of teachers at the heart of the quality complex and suggests a dedicated apex institution for providing support to the faculty of higher education institutions in core subjects. In the context of higher education reform, he also points to the lack of attention and resources received by colleges as opposed to universities, presumably on the grounds that the former are not engaged in research. This is not a reasonable justification Hoodbhoy suggests, as there is not a whole lot of useful research being conducted by Pakistan's hundred odd universities either, barring few exceptions. We may add that improving the quality of education provided by colleges is critical also to the availability of better teachers at the school level.

Amita Chudgar and Seher Ahmad contribution draws our attention to research on both the prevalence as well as consequences of adult literacy in South Asia. The data presented by Chudgar shows South Asia to be home to over 400 million illiterates. Those adults who do become literate are also prone to a relapse into illiteracy for a variety of reasons. With a strong positive correlation between parental literacy and children's achievement, illiteracy thus presents itself as not an isolated issue, but one whose prevalence threatens to undermine investments in other determinants of quality education such as higher education and teacher education. A critical dimension of the issue of adult illiteracy is its prevalence particularly among the female population. Across the region, nearly half of all women are illiterate. This, Chudgar argues, has strong implications not only for children's enrolment but also school completion. Additionally, Chudgar (2009) and Chudgar (2007) showed that improvement in adult literacy levels at the community level also has strong positive associations with improved schooling outcomes of children. She goes on to assert that the benefits of adult literacy may even outweigh the benefits of reducing the family's poverty level. Consider, for instance, the fact that with respect to information about tuberculosis (TB), the numbers in India followed by Pakistan are the worst in terms of illiterate women; they are far less likely to be aware of TB compared to even women who can reads just parts of a sentence, and certainly far less likely to be informed than those who can read. And yet, in 2006, the Education For All (EFA) report identified literacy as 'one of the most neglected' EFA goals (UNESCO, 2005, 27). The report notes that literacy is 'not prominent in most education plans and typically accounts for only 1 per cent of public spending on education.' (UNESCO, 2005, 248).

Manzoor Ahmed and James William's contribution, though rooted in the context of Bangladesh, is a relevant reading for anyone seeking to make the connection between education and general well-being. Education—whether higher, basic, or adult literacy—is about assuming each human individual as a resource and developing it to improve the state of the individual as well as societal well-being. Ahmed and Williams in this chapter examine the current status, challenges and prospects for education in supporting a human resource centred development strategy encompassing quality, relevance, and equity in education. They reinforce the growing consensus, also reflected in other contributions to this volume described above, that basic education is a necessary but far from sufficient condition for national development. This is something that the authors regret Bangladesh ignored in its drive for meeting the objective of education for all. We believe that a rather exclusive focus of education reforms on basic education, while ignoring, higher education, adult literacy, and a focus on meaningful human resource development, is a problem that afflicts, to a varying degree, all South Asian countries. A focus on improving basic education with higher education seen as being a subsequent focus in a sequential strategy undermines also the effort to improve basic education. For, it is in the realm of higher education that the quality of key inputs to basic education i.e. teachers, textbooks, assessment systems, are developed. On the other hand, adult literacy has a strong bearing on the home environment, which becomes an important factor in the gains that a child is able to make at school. All of which is to say that effective and sustainable improvement in the education sector calls for simultaneity rather than sequencing of reform measures in adult literacy, basic education as well as higher education. Such a comprehensive reform initiative is obviously far from easy. But, it remains urgent and essential.

It is our hope that the contributions in this book spanning some of the central issues in education today will lead to a more informed debate on these issues. While most of the contributors have an academic background, it has been their endeavour to present their ideas in language that is accessible to a non-academic audience as well, particularly important from the point of view of generating consensus and influencing policy. To this end, the partnership between SAFMA with its region-wide outreach among media persons and policy makers and SAHE-CQE, which works with an extensive network of researchers on education in South Asia, should make for effective advocacy and mutually beneficial learning opportunities in terms of the possibilities of and obstacles to reform in the critical area of education.

REFERENCES

Andrabi, Tahir, Das, Jishnu, and Khwaja, Asim Ijaz (2008), A dime a day: 'The possibilities and limits of private schooling in Pakistan', *Comparative Education Review*, 52(3).

Andrabi, Tahir, Das, Jishnu, Khwaja, Asim Ijaz, Vishwanath, Tara, and Zajonc, Tristan (2007), 'Learning and educational achievements in Punjab schools' (LEAPS); Insights to inform the education policy debate', World Bank.

Bangladesh. Ministry of Education (2012), Education statistics. Retrieved 7 Dec. 2012, From http://www.moedu.gov.bd/index. php?option=com_content&task=view&id=300&Itemid=301

Burchell, Graham, Gordon, Colin, and Miller, Peter, eds. (1991), *The Foucault Effect: Studies in Governmentality*, Chicago: University of Chicago Press.

Campaign for Quality Education (2007), 'Education in Pakistan: What Works & Why?' Lahore: CQE.

Chudgar, Amita (2007), 'Looking beyond the household: The importance of community-level factors in understanding underrepresentation of girls in Indian education'. In M. A. Maslak, ed., *The Structure and Agency of Women's Education*, (Albany: State University of New York Press), 201–8.

Chudgar, Amita (2009), 'Does adult literacy have a role to play in addressing the Universal Elementary Education challenge in India?' *Comparative Education Review*, 53(4).

Dreze, Jean (2004), 'Democracy and right to food', *Economic and Political Weekly*, 1723–31.

Dreze, Jean, and Sen, Amartya (2002), *India: Developments and Participation* (USA: Oxford University Press).

Duthilleul, Yael (2004), 'International Perspectives on Contract Teachers and their Impact on Meeting Education For All: The Cases of Cambodia, India and Nicaragua', Paper presented at the Conference on Primary School Contract Teachers, Bamako, Mali.

Ely, Richard (2005). 'Language and literacy in the school years'. In J. B. Gleason, ed., *The Development of Language* (6th edition), Boston: Allyn & Bacon.

Hirschmann, Albert O. (1970), *Exit, Voice, and Loyalty: Responses to Decline in Firms, Organizations, and States* (Cambridge, MA: Harvard University Press).

Hunt, Frances (2008), 'Dropping out from school: A cross country review of literature', *Create Pathways to Access: Research Mongraph* (Consortium for Research on Educational Access, Transitions and Equity), 16.

Mahbub ul Haq Human Development Centre (1998). *Human Development in South Asia: The Education Challenge*, M. Haq. and K. Haq, eds. (Oxford University Press).

Mahbub ul Haq Human Development Centre (2012), 'Human Development in South Asia: Governance of People's Empowerment', M. Haq. & K. Haq, eds. (Lahore: Lahore University of Management Sciences [LUMS]).

Muralidharan, Karthik, and Sundararaman, Venkatesh (2008), 'Contract teachers: Experimental evidence from India'. Retrieved from http://econ.ucsd.edu/~kamurali/papers/Working%20 Papers/Contract%20Teachers%20(24%20May,%202010).pdf

Pandey, Saroj (2009), 'Barefoot teachers and the millennium goal EFA 2015: The dilemma of developing countries', *International Forum of Teaching & Studies*, 5(1), 52–61.

Plessis, Joy, and Muzaffar, Irfan (2010), 'Professional learning communities in the teachers college: A resource for teacher educators', Washington, DC: Educational Quality Improvement Programme 1 (EQUIP1).

Population Council (2007), Evaluation of the Punjab female school stipend programme.

Rashid, Abbas (2007), 'Revisiting Private Schools', *Daily Times*. Retrieved from http://dailytimes.com.pk/default.asp?page =2007\02\10\story_10-2-2007_pg3_2

Rashid, Abbas (2011), 'Mother Tongue or English: it is not a zero-sum game', *Daily Times*. Retrieved from http://www.dailytimes. com.pk/default.asp?page=2011\08\12\story_12-8-2011_pg3_2

Schwille, John, Dembélé, Martial, and Schubert, Jane (2007), 'Fundamentals of educational planning', in I. UNESCO, ed., *Global Perspectives on Teacher Learning: Improving Policy and Practice* (Vol. 84).

Srivastava, Prachi (2007), 'Neither voice nor loyalty: School choice and the low-fee private sector in India' (Vol. 134), New York.

Tooley, James (2009), 'The beautiful tree: A personal journey into how the world's poorest people are educating themselves', Cato Inst.

Tooley, James, and Dixon, Pauline (2003), 'Private schools for the poor: A case study from India'. Reading, UK: Center for British Teachers.

UNESCO (2005), 'Literacy for Life', EFA Global Monitoring Report 2006. Paris: UNESCO.

UNESCO (2008a), Education For All by 2015, 'Will we make it?' EFA Global Monitoring Report Paris 2008.

UNESCO (2008b), 'Mother tongue matters: Local languages as key to effective learning', Paris: UNESCO.

UNESCO (2009), Institute of Statistics, Retrieved from http://www.uis.unesco.org/Education/Pages/default.aspx?SPSLanguage=EN

UNESCO, UIS, and UNICEF (2005) 'Children out of school: Measuring exclusion from primary education', Montreal.

UNGEI (2007). United Nations Girl's Education Initiative: Regional Updates, *Girls Too! Education For All*, New York.

United Nations Population Fund (2012), 'By Choice not by Chance: Family Planning, Human Rights and Development', *The State of World Population,* (New York: United National Population Fund [UNFPA]).

World Bank (2010), 'Development and climate change', World Development Report, Washington DC: World Bank.

NOTES

1. See also Andrabi, T., Das, J., Khwaja, A. I., Vishwanath, T., and Zajonc, T. (2007). Learning and educational achievements in Punjab schools (LEAPS): Insights to inform the education policy debate: World Bank. Forthcoming, Oxford University Press, Pakistan.

2. For comparative studies on Indian private education sector, see also Srivastava (2007) and Tooley, and Dixon (2003).

1

India's Education Crisis: The Effects of Neo-liberal Policies on the Poor and the Middle Classes

—Marie Lall

INTRODUCTION

Today, India is witnessing three trends—the increased spending of the government on education and anti-poverty programmes, the adoption of a Neo-liberal agenda where services (including the same anti-poverty programmes) are contracted out to private service providers and the emergence of a parallel system of private education for the middle and lower middle classes who are buying out of the state system leading, in large part, to deterioration of public education. These three trends are the result of India's economic reforms and the effects of international globalization and policy trends affecting education sectors around the world.

In India, the 1991 economic reforms and the opening up of the domestic markets to international investment have led to increased disparities between the wealthy and the poor.[1] Despite high economic growth rates, the differences between the 'haves' and the 'have-nots' have never been greater. One consequence of India's growth is the rise of India's middle classes—a disparate group who cannot be put into one category, yet whose members have all benefitted from the economic policy changes and either have changed their consumption modes or aspire to do so. The economic and political power of the middle classes has also been on the rise. These changes have also left the urban poor and the rural population, who still make up over 70 per cent of the total population, mired in poverty and are becoming increasingly invisible in foreign and domestic media.

The rise of the middle classes has also had consequences for India's post-independence ideals, which privileged social justice and equality. Whilst still only representing 30 per cent of India's population, the middle classes no longer need the help of the state to provide them with public education and health, resulting in part in a withdrawal of the state from these services. Nowhere is this more visible than in the education sector. These changes have fundamentally altered the relationship between education and the state. The discourse of choice and the dominance of the markets by the middle classes has resulted in newly excluded groups (Lall & Nambissan, 2011). The state is playing a dual role in education today, both facilitating the process of *marketization* as well as addressing the disadvantage through specific policies and programmes in the context of the aspirations and demands from different social groups. Consequently, we are witnessing seemingly contradictory developments whereby the new trend is that of the withdrawal of the state from public services at a certain level, yet with increased state involvement at other levels, creating a sensation of a 'layered' state with no clear demarcated boundaries.

This chapter will first explore the crisis in public sector education looking in particular at issues of access and literacy. It then goes on to discuss various pro-poor programmes such as the mid-day meal scheme that have been put in place by the government in order to improve access, retention and quality of education for the poorer sections of society. The chapter will then discuss how the Neo-liberal agenda has resulted in government spending strengthening the non-government sectors and how despite these improvement measures, there has been a growth of private schools aimed mainly at the various sections of the middle classes. As India's new middle classes are seeking greater social mobility and looking at education options outside of the state system to achieve their aims, the state education system is experiencing the flight of the middle classes, resulting in a two-tier parallel system. This in turn will have long-term effects on India's democratic system.

EDUCATION IN INDIA

Historically, India has endeavoured to use education as a tool for increasing social equality, through developing both the primary, secondary and higher education sectors. However, despite big improvements such as significant expansion of rural schools as envisaged by the Kothari Commission, Universal Primary Education (UPE) was never achieved. The Indian Education Commission observed:

One of the important social objectives of education is to equalize opportunities, enabling the backward or underprivileged classes and individuals to use education as a lever for the improvement of their condition. (Thamarasseri, 2008, 190).

This of course can only be the case if all sections of society have equal access to schools where they receive an education of even quality. Indian policies seem to be aligned with this general objective.

Today, India is a signatory to the Millennium Development Goals (MDGs) and its constitution guarantees the right to elementary education up to the age of fourteen years. This constitutional commitment is relatively recent as the Right to Education (RTE) Bill was passed in the *Rajya Sabha* on the 20 July 2009 and on the 4 August 2009 in the Lok Sabha. The law was notified by the President on 3 September 2009 (India; Parliament, 2009). According to recent estimates, 73 per cent of children go to government schools, and 21.8 per cent of children between the ages of six and fourteen years are privately educated. Similarly, 10.7 per cent of government spending goes to education.[2]

Recent education figures paint a mixed picture on the ground: the Gross Enrolment Ratio (GER) from Classes I to VIII was 94.9 per cent and from Classes I to XII, 77 per cent in 2006, pointing to an improvement in access (India; Ministry of Human Resource Development, 2008). The figures recently collected by (Pratham, 2009), puts the out of schools figures at 4 per cent of children between the ages of six and fourteen and at 6.3 per cent between the ages of seven and sixteen.

However, for the country as a whole, the dropout rates from Classes I to X was 61.6 per cent. In the poorer states like Bihar, it was above 75 per cent. Among those who drop out, the percentage of children belonging to the Scheduled Castes across the country was 70.6 per cent; and of the Scheduled Tribes 78.5 per cent. In Bihar, the figure was close to 90 per cent for both these categories. The net result is that a sizeable percentage, as high as 30 per cent, of children in the school-going age are out of school; the percentage is as high as 50 per cent in the poorer states such as Bihar, mostly of the poorest sections of society.

As such, then, given its billion plus population, India has one of the largest number of out of school children in the world. According to the Demographic and Health Survey conducted by Huebler (2007), India has 21 million children out of school. In 2006, 83 per cent of children of primary school age were enrolled in school. Attendance in schools, both public and private, had increased by 13 per cent since 2000. But it still left a startling 17 per cent of children out of school. As a result of the increase in primary school attendance, the number of children out of school fell by almost one-third: from 30 million in 2000 to 21 million in 2006. This pattern has been observed for boys and girls, and for residents of urban and rural areas. However, disaggregation by household wealth reveals that one group of children did not follow the nationwide trend. Among the poorest 20 per cent of all households, the number of children out of school grew from 9.4 million in 2000 to 9.8 million in 2006. Although the primary school net attendance rate among children from the poorest households grew by 3 percentage points from 2000 to 2006, this increase was not strong enough to keep pace with population growth in the poorest segment of the Indian population. There is a strong link between poverty and education in India (Huebler, 2007). Even though education has increased by 20 per cent among the poorest in the country, the growth is not keeping pace with the population boom (Huebler, 2007).

The problems of quality, access, and retention are also reflected in the poor literacy rates across the country. According to the 2001 census data, nationwide average literacy rate was at 64.84 per cent, oscillating between Kerala's at 90.86 per cent and Bihar's at 47 per cent. Literacy rates are also gender dependent with female literacy at 53.63 per cent and male literacy at 75.26 per cent.[3] These census figures, however, have been contested by Pratham (2009) whose Annual Status of Education Report (ASER) checks the various levels of reading skills across the country and differentiates between children being able to recognise letters, words and read text, giving a much more nuanced image of literacy levels, especially in rural areas. Data collected by Pratham (2009) shows that illiteracy is much more widespread than the official figures would indicate.

Since the election of a Congress-led coalition in 2004, the government has been increasing its focus on anti-poverty initiatives. As the state has become richer, since 2003, government revenues have increased at the rate of 31 per cent per annum (Manor, 2012, 4), a huge array of redistributive programmes and anti-poverty programmes have been rolled out.[4] India's flagship pro-poor programme has been the Rural Employment Guarantee scheme—which guarantees every poor family hundred days of paid employment per year. A key programme in the education sector is the Sarva Shiksha Abhiyan (SSA),[5] which aims to universalise education for the children between the ages of six and fourteen. Under SSA, 155 new schools had already been opened until September 2009.

The Mid-Day Meals Scheme has been another flagship programme aiming at enrolling and retaining children in the schools. This programme involves provision of lunch free of cost to school children on all working days. The key objective of the programme is to increase school enrolment and attendance by offering families who cannot afford food an extra meal for their children. This is also meant to go a long way towards alleviating malnutrition and to improve concentration as hungry children cannot learn. Besides this, the scheme aims to improve socialization among children belonging to all different sections of society as well as helping social empowerment through the provision of employment to women. The scheme was first introduced in Tamil Nadu in the 1960s and now has been adopted by most of the states after a landmark direction by the Supreme Court on 28 November 2001. The success of this scheme is illustrated by the tremendous increase in the school participation and completion rates in the state of Tamil Nadu. Nearly, 120 million children are so far covered under the Mid-Day Meal Programme, which is also the largest school lunch programme in the world. Allocation for this programme has been enhanced from Rs. 3,010 crores to Rs. 4,813 crores (Rs. 48 billion) in 2006–2007.[6]

However, despite the staggering numbers of enrolments, such schemes are not without their problems and continue to be affected by the quality of hygiene and corruption issues. One example of the Mid-Day Meal Programme going wrong is the primary school in Bamhu (Bilaspur district, Chhattisgarh). The mid-day meal there is prepared in a 'soot-covered' classroom using a makeshift stove, next to the swarming pupils. According to the teacher, 'no teaching takes place after lunch as the classroom turns filthy. He wishes mid-day meals would be discontinued.' (Dreze & Goyal, 2003)

But quality and hygiene are not the only problem. Corruption too has played itself out. In November of 2008, *The Indian Express* along with a team of auditors carried out an inquiry on the scheme. The team of auditors appointed by the Comptroller and Auditor General (CAG) of India unearthed a Rs. 15.37 crores scam in Mid-Day Meal Scheme in the state. The team had carried out the inquiry in five districts (Ranchi, Chaibasa, Daltonganj, Gumla, Jamshedpur) and found that money was misappropriated by showing expenditure incurred in mid-day meals of those students who did not figure in records of the schools in these districts. As per the scheme, cooked food is served free of cost to students. Both the centre and the state government contribute towards the expenditure incurred. The auditors found that in these five districts, false records of students were maintained, and a large amount of the funds allocated for the free meal scheme were missing (Prasad, 2008). In March of 2009, *The Indian*

Express uncovered another scam in the Surendranagar district of Gujarat where those implementing the scheme had again maintained excess records of students to get more rations from the government (Service, 2009).

Beyond the Mid-Day Meals Scheme there are range of other education schemes and reforms the government has embarked on. Some are based exclusively in certain states, some are nationwide. The Education Guarantee Scheme in Madhya Pradesh is example of a state based education project aimed at increasing access and retention in schools.[7]

What is clear is that with increased revenues, the government of India has been able to develop large-scale programmes aimed at enhancing the enrolment and retention in India's primary schools in the public sector. Because of the socio-economic status of the population segments served by these schools, these expenditures are targeting the poorest sections of society. Yet, as discussed in the subsequent sections, the increase in numbers and power of Indian middle classes and their exit from the public schools create an enormous deficit in the ability of the public schools to deliver quality education that cannot be simply filled by the programmes such as the mid-day lunch.

THE 'NEW' NEO-LIBERAL AGENDA

But the Indian government is not only driven by what seems on the face of things a social democratic agenda. At the same time as increasing spending in the education sector, the government is also looking for increased private sector participation in education. In line with the effects of globalisation elsewhere around the world, the Indian state is changing its strategy with regard to public services from being less of a provider and more of a regulator. Whilst the various programmes have the right vision at heart, they have to be analysed in India's new economic, social, and political reality, which is heavily influenced by globalization and the logic of free market.

Globalization is associated with the increasing adoption of market forms for the delivery of public services, which were once organized by the state and financed through taxation (for example, education, health, and other welfare provisions). Many writers point to the increasing 'commodification' of these services and their penetration by a private sector ethos, either in provision or in sponsorship, or through the organization of services according to market principles by the introduction of consumer choice. Globalization has led to the restructuring of the education system at a global level, with the state increasingly taking a back seat, acting more as a regulator rather than a provider. Governments attempt to justify opening up education to corporate capital on the grounds that private sector management is more efficient, and that private entrepreneurs are needed to 'modernise' education for a globalized 'knowledge economy'. Following this trend, India has experienced increased market logic in its education system. This has resulted in growth of market-based education solutions, which target education of differential quality at clients with differential paying capacity. Therefore, the middle and upper middle classes are able to access private schools perceived to be more efficient and better. An affordable private school alternative has also emerged for the poorer parents. The high and low fee schools catering for different income groups imply that there is an issue of equity. Many scholars have pointed out that globalization has led to greater economic and social inequality (Kuisma, 2008; Rikowski, 2002; UNDP, 1999). Though educational access expands, it also becomes unequal in quality (Carnoy, 2000).

Since the 1990s, there has been an indiscriminate expansion of private schools across the country, which expanded the opportunities for the burgeoning middle classes. This increase does not accompany a proportional effort by the state to regulate the expanding private school sector. The private sector education offerings are, therefore, more in the nature of private shops.

> While education is critical for entry and upward mobility, for the large mass of people who have neither good quality education in the regional medium, and very small possibilities of working their way through English medium private schools and shrinking public sector—the future isn't very bright (Nambissan, 2010).

Though school education in India is free and universal, access to quality private schooling is denied or restricted to the economically weaker as the policy of reservations is not applied to school education. However, there have been demands from some civil society groups for a provision of access for deprived groups to elite private schools on the pretext that the state provides free land to private schools. Once the land is provided, schools ignore their commitment to the government to provide schooling for the poorer families in return. This has led to judicial intervention in certain states. In Delhi, for example, the state is now asked to implement a 20 per cent quota of seats in the private schools to provide quality schooling and infrastructure to underprivileged caste and social classes. The experience shows that in actual practice such a vision of egalitarianism is not accepted by the private schools as well as the parents of privileged backgrounds who send their children to those schools. The schooling delivered for those admitted on quota and for those from the privileged home backgrounds is entirely different. The timings of schools and teachers teaching these two groups of children are also different, with the less qualified teaching poor children and the better qualified teaching privileged children of the same school.

These inequities are further exacerbated by the demand for teaching and learning English, and the availability of capacity to do this well in only the schools servicing the privileged sections of the society. Even in the rural areas there is a demand for private English medium schooling because English is perceived as an emancipatory global language that can make them economically and socially mobile, and the private schooling is perceived to be of better quality in comparison to government schooling (Sarangapani, 2003). At the national level, the National Knowledge Commission envisaged introduction of English Medium at Class I itself, which encouraged some state governments such as Andhra Pradesh to formulate policies to make learning English mandatory at Class I:

. . . poor infrastructure, lack of basic amenities, and facilities, as well as adequate number of teachers is a feature of schools that Dalit children encounter as they enter government (local body managed) schools. In addition, curriculum is dominated by conventional pedagogy based on the textbook, chalk and talk and absence of relevant teaching aids. . . . This provides an unattractive learning environment for Dalit children (the majority of whom enter government schools) and contrasts with the quality of schooling in 'public-private' institutions enjoyed by the more privileged strata (Nambissan, 2006, p. 243).

In fact, it is paradoxical that, in India, the government on one hand made elementary education a fundamental right to be protected by the constitution; on the other, it falls in line with the demands of the market forces such as the Confederation of Indian Industry, Federation of Chambers of Commerce and Industry, which campaign for the withdrawal of the state. One important development in recent times is that India's Planning Commission (2004) has come out with a policy document to suggest an increased involvement of the private sector with the government contracting out services, limiting the government's role in education as opposed to increasing it. This is clearly a result of neo-liberal reforms as it is suggested that the anti-poverty programmes such as the Mid-Day Meals Scheme are contracted out to foundations or other service providers such as banks, the corporate sector or 'any person from civil society'. The Planning Commission (2004) expects such Public Private Partnerships to be more cost-effective, result in higher productivity and accelerated delivery.

All in all, the Indian government's increased spending on education is also benefitting the private sector, and these benefits accrue from partial commercialization of what used to be a state-run service, much on the same lines as what is happening in the UK and other western countries which have undertaken neo-liberal reforms (Ball, 2007).

THE ROLE OF EDUCATION AND THE MIDDLE CLASSES

The central concern in this whole discussion is the rising inequalities across society and the role of the middle classes. As mentioned earlier, India's economic reforms have led to the economic uplifting of around 30 per cent of its population. Unfortunately, the economic growth has not trickled down to all sections of society and the UNDP (2007) report notes that although India is rising economically:

> . . . [T]he bad news is that this has not been translated into accelerated progress in cutting under-nutrition. One-half of all rural children [in India] are underweight for their age—roughly the same proportion as in 1992 (25).

This clearly shows that economic reforms and the pro-poor programmes are not so far effectively helping India's most disadvantaged—and whilst the UNDP (2007) report focuses on rural India, the same is also true for the urban slums. The debate on how far inequalities are rising (or not) is fought out mainly by economists (Pal & Ghosh, 2007). Some argue that India's *Gini* coefficient of 36.8[8] is not that bad. However, in India the *Gini* coefficient is calculated based on the distribution of consumption expenditure as opposed to income data, skewing the figure as it does not take into account the savings of the rich. So despite 8–9 per cent economic growth, income inequalities are widening (Basu, 2007). Anecdotal evidence also shows that only certain classes of India's society are benefitting—weddings (a great social measure of wealth) have become increasingly lavish as the middle classes splurge on diamond, as opposed to gold, sets for their daughters and daughters-in-law. Needless to say that such luxuries are beyond the wildest dreams for those living on a few thousand rupees a month.

As the certain sections of Indian society are becoming richer, they are also able to 'buy out' of the government provision of health, education, and other public services. This in turn risks disintegration of a unifying system envisioned by Jawaharlal Nehru over sixty years ago. This also has an effect on the democratic structures as poorer sections of society are only able to access poorer quality public services and 'choice' is limited to the more affluent.

Whilst the functions of education include the promotion of social justice and the creation of a functional workforce, it is often forgotten that education is also a political tool to promote what Antonio Gramsci termed hegemony—'the power to establish the "common sense" of a society, the fund of self-evident descriptions of social reality that normally go without saying.'[9] This includes the power to establish authoritative definitions of social situations and social needs, the power to define the universe of legitimate disagreement and the power to shape the political agenda (Fraser, 1992,

53). In every country, one of the prime functions of education has been that of building a cohesive society—one held together by shared values, purposes and activities. Most education systems have been designed to more or less impose one culture—usually that of the elite: a dominant race, class, political party or colonial power. Determining and imposing a dominant culture from above is directly related to elite ambitions to control the wider population (Lall & Vickers, 2009). In post-independence India, education reflected the visions of the largely western educated and secular elites of the day. Today, the new middles classes set the agenda (Deshpande, 2003). They support the liberalization process and a pro-choice agenda for education. Their choice of private schooling means that as a consequence public education loses value in the eyes of the masses and even the poorer sections of society aspire to leave the public system.

So education—which had for decades played the role as a unifying force and was Nehru's way of creating a 'Gramscian' common sense of equality across India's many fault lines of caste, class, religion, and ethnic groups—has today fractured into two parallel systems. India's rising middle classes have started to 'buy out' of the state system and a vast array of new and private institutions offer their services at every level of affordability to the various groups. Whilst there has always been private education in India—this was reserved for the tiny elite and had little effect on the wider population. Government funded education has had many problems (e.g. access in rural area, teacher absenteeism etc.) but was for many years the only option, even for many of the middle classes.

Beteille (2001) has argued that the middle classes have long supported differentiated schooling which would equip their children with better credentials, thereby giving them an edge in the employment race. Middle class parents supplemented public schooling with tuitions and made sure their children accessed higher education. Varma (2007) goes as far as to say that in the past the educated elite enjoyed the 'scarcity value' their education gave them in a country with high levels of illiteracy. One could argue that before the emergence of the plethora of private schools, the main differentiating factor between the classes was the length of schooling and whether or not the child went to university.[10] However, public education was still a unifying factor, promoting a secular national identity and intending to provide equal chances for access to higher education. With the middle classes choosing to buy out, the poorer sections of society have no other option but to take whatever the state gives them. This has led to a trend in deteriorating public education institutions at school level, meaning more and more aspire to leave the system, creating a vicious circle.

India's *new* middle classes are largely understudied, yet increasingly important because of their role in creating hegemonic discourses, which legitimate only certain people, certain ways of being and behaving, and certain attitudes (Skeggs, 2004). Their behaviour affects the public sector and with it provision for poorer sections of society (Vincent & Menon, 2011). Today, neo-liberal policies encouraging an increased involvement of the private sector dominate the policy agenda.

Fernandes (2006) argues that the middle classes in India have 'increasingly resorted to privatized strategies designed to give individual benefits rather than through organized political pressure on the state'. (p. 131) She states that, 'everyday forms of privatization in arenas such as education and healthcare are part of the broader pattern of privatized middle class strategies designed to give upward mobility through the acquisition and deployment of various forms of social, cultural, and economic resources.' (p. 132). Choice is a big part of the new educational discourse and Waldrop (2004) found that parents research school reputation and base their school choice on their own priorities:

> What people in Delhi think of specific schools directly influences their reputation, and creates an image, partly based on their All-India exam results and, equally, upon rumours of the cultural taste of the families whose children are admitted there. The end result is a circular process of mutual symbolic capital exchange between the schools on the one hand, and pupils admitted and their families on the other (p. 208).

But choice is by definition limited to those with the social and cultural capital to exercise it. Lower class parents and those whose prime focus is to put a meal on the table do not necessarily have the background necessary to make strategic educational choices for their children. They have to hope that what the state provides is good enough. And if they chose low cost private provision they will again not necessarily be able to assess the quality of education their children are receiving, in effect taking great risks at high costs. Nambissan (2010) argues that:

[T]he upper tiers of the middle classes, have actively participated in the education system from a position of social and economic dominance that has allowed them shape the system, define what 'good education' is as well as the desirable cultural resources and manipulate capitals in order to ensure success. They have also been influential in policy making spheres in education and in that sense have defined notions of 'educational disadvantage' and ways to overcome it.

Education is therefore a central element in the middle classes' (and others) understanding of life chances and they will employ 'micro practices' to ensure the success of their children in an increasingly competitive system. (Nambissan, 2010; Vincent & Menon, 2011) The problem is that with the middle class flight from state education, those who are more disadvantaged also aspire to leave public education and try their best to copy that behaviour. Today, the private sector also offers education options for the poor and the very poor with private schools for profit emerging in Indian slums.[11] Most of these establishments are neither registered nor controlled for quality. Many close if they are not making enough profit, leaving their students to find another, similar school. This in itself creates a totally new set of problems that cannot be discussed here. The vicious circle leaves state education only for those who really cannot do differently and the state with less and less incentive to maintain quality.

CONCLUSION

Education provision in India is facing a complex situation whereby, despite increased state expenditure, the neo-liberal agenda and increased market logic have changed the nature of public provision beyond recognition. This is coupled with a flight of the middle and lower middle classes from the public system and their clear preference for private education. In effect, the Indian state is facing widening inequalities and a two-tier society emerging out of the reform process of the last twenty years.

The middle classes, who originally had the highest stake in the rights guaranteed through citizenship withdraw from the equation; the state's relationship is reduced to the second tier of largely poorer urban and rural Indians. Whilst still only representing 30 per cent of India's population, the middle classes no longer require the state to provide them with public education and health, resulting in part in a withdrawal of the state from these services and the strengthening of a neo-liberal agenda. Consequently, the question of rights and responsibilities is being eroded as state responsibility for providing public services is changing and with it affecting India's democracy. The discourse of choice and the dominance of the markets by the middle classes results in unequal access to public services both absolutely and in terms of quality.

India is experiencing nothing new as the similar policies and the same discourse can be observed globally across the middle classes. (Vincent, 2001; Vincent & Ball, 2007) The issue in India is more one of ensuring equality in light of maintaining a democratic system, where social inequalities do not become so entrenched that the gap becomes unbridgeable. In light of these complex and seemingly contradictory developments, the Indian government needs to rethink its policies and its pro-poor programmes. Rising inequalities in education provision are bound to translate in, and propagate, the social inequities that plague India. Stemming these inequities may be important for the future of India's democracy. A good common school system, rather than liberalization of educational provision, may be more likely to secure social and economic justice needed to provide a secure foundation to the Indian democracy.

REFERENCES

Ball, S. J. (2007), *Education Plc: Understanding Private Sector Participation in Public Sector Education* (New York: Routledge).

Basu, K. (2007), The pitfalls of the 'economy game', *BBC News*, Retrieved from http://news.bbc.co.uk/1/hi/world/south_asia/6365851.stm

Beteille, A. (2001), 'The Indian middle class', *The Hindu*. Retrieved from http://www.hinduonnet.com/2001/02/05/stories/05052523.htm

Carnoy, M. (2000), *Globalisation and Educational Restructuring* (Paris: International Institute of Educational Planning).

Deshpande, S. (2003), *The Centrality of the Middle Class Contemporary India: A Sociological View* (New Delhi: Penguin Books).

Dreze, J., and Goyal, A. (2003), 'The future of mid-day meals', *Frontline*. Retrieved from http://www.frontlineonnet.com/fl2016/stories/20030815002208500.htm

Fernandes, L. (2006), *India's New Middle Class—Democratic Politics in an Era of Economic Reform* (New Delhi: Oxford University Press).

Fraser, N. (1992), 'Rethinking the public sphere'. In C. Calhoun (ed.), *Habermas and the Public Sphere* (53) (Cambridge, MA: MIT Press).

Huebler, F. (2007), 'India has 21 million out of school', Retrieved from http://huebler.blogspot.com/2007/11/india-has-21-million-children-out-of.html

India, Ministry of Human Resource Development (2008), 'Educational statistics at a glance 2005–06' (New Delhi: Government of India).

India, Parliament (2009), 'The right of children to free and compulsory education act'. New Delhi: GoI. Retrieved from http://www.indg.in/primary-education/policiesandschemes/right-to-education-bill

India, Planning Commission (2004), 'Public private partnership: Report of the PPP subgroup on social sector' (New Delhi: Government of India).

Kuisma, M. (2008), 'Rights or privileges? The challenge of globalisation to the values of citizenship'. Citizenship Studies, 12 (6), 613–27.

Lall, M., and Nambissan, G. B., eds. (2011), *Education and Social Justice in the Era of Globalisation* (New Delhi: Routledge).

Lall, M., and Vickers, E., eds. (2009), *Education as a Political Tool in Asia* (Vol. Routledge Contemporary South Asia Series). (London: Routledge).

Manor, J. (2012), Did the central government's poverty initiatives help to re-elect it? In L. Saez and G. Singh, eds., *New Dimensions of Politics in India: The United Progressive Alliance in Power*, (Routledge), 13–25.

Nambissan, G. B. (2006), 'Terms of inclusion: Dalits and the right to education'. In R. Kumar, ed., *The Crisis of Elementary Education in India* (New Delhi: Sage Publications), 224–65.

Nambissan, G. B. (2010), 'The Indian middle classes and educational advantage: Family strategies and practices'. In M. Apple, S. J. Ball and L. A. Gandin eds., *The Routledge International*

Handbook of the Sociology of Education (London: Routledge), 285–95.

Pal, P., and Ghosh, J. (2007), 'Inequality in India: A survey of recent trends'. *DESA Working Paper* (Vol. 45), UN Department of Social Affairs.

Prasad, M. (2008), 'CAG unearths mid-day meal scam in five Jharkhand districts', *The Indian Express*, Retrieved from http://www.indianexpress.com/news/cag-unearths-midday-meal-scam-in-five-jhark/379881/

Pratham (2009), Annual Status of Education Report (ASER) 2009. Retrieved from http://pratham.org/file/National%20finding%20India.pdf

Rikowski, G. (2002), 'Globalisation and education'. A paper prepared for the House of Lords Select Committe on Economic Affairs (London).

Sarangapani, P. M. (2003), *Constructing School Knowledge: Ethnography of Learning in an Indian Village* (New Delhi: Sage Publications).

Service, E. N. (2009), 'Mid-day meal turns scam in Surendranagar village', *The Indian Express*, Retrieved from http://www.expressindia.com/latest-news/midday-meal-scheme-turns-a-scam-in-surendranagar-village/431035/

Skeggs, B. (2004), *Class, Self, Culture* (London: Routledge).

Thamarasseri, I. (2008), *Education in the Emerging Indian Society* (New Delhi: Kanishka Publishers).

UNDP (1999), Human Development Report 1999 (New York: UNDP).

UNDP (2007), Human Development Report 2007 (New York: UNDP).

Varma, P. K. (2007), *The Great Indian Middle Class* (New Delhi: Penguin Books).

Vincent, C. (2001), 'Social class and parental agency', *Journal of Education Policy*, 16 (4), 347–64.

Vincent, C., and Ball, S. J. (2007), 'Making up the middle-class child: Families, activities and class dispositions'. *Sociology*, 41(6), 1061–77.

Vincent, C., and Menon, R. (2011), 'The educational strategies of the middle classes in England and India'. In M. Lall and G. B. Nambissan, eds., *Education and Social Justice in the Era of Globalisation* (New Delhi: Routledge).

Waldrop, A. (2004), 'The meaning of the old school-tie: private schools, admission procedures and class segmentation in New Delhi. In A. Vaugier-Chatterjee', ed., *Education and Democracy in India* (New Delhi: Manohar-Centre De Sciences Humaines).

NOTES

1. The economic growth of the 1990s was a result of an expansion of goods and services. The increase in the variety of services led to an increase in consumption by the top quintile of the population and, ultimately, to a consumer-driven economic boom benefiting mainly those who were already well-to-do.

2. UNESCO Stats. http://stats.uis.unesco.org/unesco/TableViewer/document.aspx?ReportId=121&IF_Language=eng&BR_Country=3560

3. http://india.gov.in/knowindia/literacy.php

4. The money spent on these programmes is around $50 billion—but let's remember that the budget for the department for nuclear and Atomic energy is Rs. 2,474, 72 crores for 2009–10.

5. India, Sarva Shiksha Abhiyan. http://ssa.nic.in/and http://en.wikipedia.org/wiki/Sarva_Shiksha_Abhiyan

6. Wikipedia. *Mid-Day Meal Scheme*. http://en.wikipedia.org/wiki/Midday_Meal_Scheme [Accessed 12 Jan. 2010].

7. Education Guarantee Scheme: A Community-Government Partnership that Gets Millions into School in Madhya Pradesh. http://

info.worldbank.org/etools/docs/reducingpoverty/case/57/fullcase/India%20Educ%20Full%20Case.pdf

8. India, http://earthtrends.wri.org/text/economics-business/variable-353.html

9. Antonio Gramsci. http://beautifultrouble.org/theory/cultural-hegemony/and http://www.massey.ac.nz/~alock/theory/subpos.htm

10. This is also why reservations for Scheduled Castes (SC) and Scheduled Tribes (ST) was limited to higher education and not seen as relevant at school levels.

11. See work by Prachi Srivastava on private schooling in Indian slums.

2

Improving the Public Sector Schools in Pakistan: Strategies for Introducing Voice into the System

—Irfan Muzaffar and Faisal Bari

This chapter is concerned with the problem of improving public sector schools. We begin by reminding our readers of the three basic, and by now rather well-known, characteristics of the current educational landscape of Pakistan: the rise in growth of private sector schools; the concomitant decline in quality of public sector schools; and the abysmal learning gains by students in both. We then use this reminder to argue that the situation is ripe for a divisive and ultimately counterproductive educational sectarianism, with opinion polarized in favour of and against a laissez-faire policy toward private education. As a result, several recent and well-meaning comparative studies of Pakistani private and public schools, such as that of Andrabi, Das, and Khwaja (2008), are in danger of being interpreted along ideological lines by opposite camps on the private versus public school wars. Assuming education to be both a public and private good, we regard such interpretations to be counterproductive from a policy perspective. Given the low levels of academic achievement recorded for both sectors irrespective of marginal superiority of private schools, both sectors need support for improvement. Furthermore, we use Hirschman's typology of voice, exit, and loyalty as a starting point to argue that the challenge for improving public sector schools is much harder. Finally, recognizing the central importance of *voice* for the improvement of public sector schools, we examine the possibilities of reinsertion of a strong political *voice* for improvement of public sector schools in Pakistan.

THE DEBATES ON PUBLIC VERSUS PRIVATE EDUCATION

Beginning with the denationalization of state-run schools in 1979 and sustained by three decades of laissez-faire policy toward them, private schools have experienced phenomenal growth in Pakistan. Segmented and layered in ways that map the distribution of socio-economic status in our society, they range from schools charging very high fees (over Rs. 10,000 per month) to those with low fees (Rs. 100–300 per month). According to some estimates, one out of every three school-going children in Pakistan is enrolled in a private sector school (Pakistan. Bureau of Statistics, 2009). A large, thriving, and diverse private sector is now, in essence, an integral element of the education system in Pakistan. Of particular interest to the observers of this growth are Low Fees Private (LFP) schools. The LFP schools are portrayed as a dynamic education market place with several private commercially run schools competing to enrol children of parents belonging to low income households and disadvantaged groups. While the reasons behind parental choice are still being investigated, the evidence that parents prefer the LFP schools over public schools is thus far incontrovertible (Srivastava, 2007).

The evidence so far suggests that private schools are concentrated more in urban areas, in certain provinces (Punjab, urban KPK, and urban Sindh), and in certain markets (where supply of local female teachers is more and where parents show the capacity and willingness to pay the minimum level of fees needed to keep the LFPs in business). Even the LFP schools tend to screen out children from very poor backgrounds, suggesting the realization of market failures anticipated by some early observers of the late 1980s privatization drive in the education sector of Pakistan (Jimenez & Tan, 1987). As such, then, the public sector remains the largest education service provider for Pakistani children and one that is unlikely to be replaced by the private sector schools.

We do not have to belabour the point that the public sector education system has failed to deliver a decent education, a perception that is defied only by a handful of good public schools (Campaign for Quality Education, 2007). This perception is further strengthened by the recent comparative studies of student achievement in public and LFP schools in the province of Punjab (Andrabi, Das, Khwaja, Vishwanath & Zajonc, 2007a, 2007b). These studies demonstrate that *ceteris paribus* the LFP schools outperform their public counterparts. Such findings are not limited to Pakistan and have been reported for LFPs in many other developing countries including India (Tooley & Dixon, 2003), several countries in Africa (Tooley, Dixon, & Amuah, 2007; Tooley, Dixon,

& Olaniyan, 2005), and in Latin America (Naradowski & Andrada, 2001). However, we are more concerned here about the consequences of the response to these studies for educational debates in Pakistan.

Scholars concerned with the political economy of education have responded in ways that have rekindled the age-old debates that accompanied the development of the modern state and economy in the west. The expansion of education in western societies was necessitated by the emergence of democratic politics together with an expanding industrial economy. The rationale for universal education was threefold: survival, preservation, and reproduction of the society. For some, only state-run schools could do justice to this rationale. Then, as now, no one disagreed with the need for universal basic education. Rather, the debates raged over whether it was to be delivered through parental fees. Eventually, the nineteenth-century political economy in the then nascent democracies decided in favour of providing 'free' universal education, while also preserving the option of private schools to accommodate the dearly held value of individuals' right to choose. Western societies arrived at an equilibrium that preserved not only public and private forms of education but also the tension between them. Then the debates were between economists such as Adam Smith and John Stuart Mill, with the former a proponent of parental right to choose from market-based educational alternatives and the latter an advocate of state-based provision. The ghosts of Smith and Mill now haunt the current debates over provision of universal basic education in developing countries (Brighouse,

1998, 2004; Labaree, 1997; Tooley, 2003). We believe this longstanding educational sectarianism is not productive from a policy perspective. It does not help us to take both public and private sector schools as given elements of our educational landscape; it keeps us from developing the policy alternatives we need to reform both sectors. We wish to direct the attention of our readers away from a comparative perspective to one that may help us refocus the policy debate on improving the learning achievements in both public and private sector schools. To that end, we employ Hirschman's typology of *voice, exit* and *loyalty* as a starting point.

THE IMPORTANCE OF VOICE, AND ITS ABSENCE, IN PUBLIC SECTOR SCHOOLS

In his classic book *Exit, Voice and Loyalty*, Hirschman (1970) reported that organizations which were unable to meet the needs of their clients elicited either a *political* or an *economic* response from them. He termed the political and economic responses as the use of *voice* and *exit* respectively.[1] Responding with *voice* implied the use of political influence to arrest the decline of the affected organization—true for most public sector organizations as *exit* of clients does not create any incentives for their improvement. Responding with *exit* involved making an *economic* choice of ceasing to be the client of the declining firm—true for most private sector organizations with the possible exception of monopolies. Arguably, public and private schools fall neatly into these categories as responsive to *voice* and *exit* respectively (Labaree, 2000). As we all know, *exit* of students from public schools is unlikely to change their public endowments, and so exit per se does not constitute an incentive to improve. This is one reason that public-private comparisons are unwieldy from the viewpoint of policy. They are unlikely to help rejuvenate the public schools. In the case of a private school competing with other private and public schools in the vicinity, exit can play an important disciplining role. And even a real and possible *threat* of an *exit* could be an effective tool for instilling discipline. Private schools, thus, are responsive to exit, and can improve if faced with the prospect of flight of their clientele. The improvement in the case of the latter can be regulated usefully by the provision of accurate information about their performance to the consumers of their educational services.[2] At a minimum, curriculum and assessment standards in conjunction with regular assessments that are aligned with such standards may help generate a regulatory regime that involves the participation of citizen groups, consumers, as well as researchers. Routine reviews of learning achievements may need to be designed and used in ways that provide constructive feedback to both public and private sectors without feeding into a public versus private debate.

But in the case of public schools, information alone is not sufficient for their regulation and reforms. The situation is a lot more complex. Teachers, organized into unions and departments at the provincial level have their own interests, while bureaucracies working through educational departments have theirs. Teacher recruitment, promotion, firing, and reward structures, along with bureaucratic compensation and even resource allocations, are not likely to be influenced by client *exit.* The potential for parent intervention in this system is severely restricted as there is no clearly identified residual claimant and no accountability of other constituents through either market-based discipline or the political process. Hirschman (1970) tells us that public schools need political influence to improve. However, the *exit* from public schools, particularly in the case of Pakistan, has also implied elimination of *voice,* leaving behind the nexus of self-sustaining educational establishment alluded to above. With nearly all children of rich and influential parents attending private schools—and we can say that with some confidence in the case of Pakistan even without hard data—political economy has already been configured in ways that severely limit a potent political response in the face of declining standards of the public school system. What public system can improve in the absence of *voice?* Here, then, we are faced with a classic dilemma: we can neither eliminate public schools as there is just sufficient pressure to keep them going nor can we find a simple technical solution to improve them, for they can only be reformed through a combination of both political and technical means. One solution, and a simplistic one at that, could be to force the elite to send their children to public schools. But we know well that this is bound to fail, not least because it goes against the tenets of individuals' right to choose.

We now return to our original premise to reframe our objection to the public versus private debate. Education is both a public and a private good (Labaree, 1997). As a public good, it must serve the larger interests of social cohesion and inculcation of desirable social values in the populace, while as a private good it must help meet the needs of individual consumers. Irrespective of who provides the education, it must serve both goals well. Therefore, focusing the educational debate on private versus public obfuscates the real issues. Moreover, given the limits of the private sector and possible market failures, the public sector will continue to be the only source of formal education for the children of the poor, especially in more rural and less developed areas. Any serious debate in this matter requires an intensive and meaningful engagement with public schools.[3] While private schools respond to clients' exit, a better informed clientele can help keep them on their toes. It is in this context, we believe, that our resource and analytic energies need to focus on exploring innovative ways of reinserting the *political voice* to make public schools responsive to change and reform. If history is any guide, we have seen that technical reforms—teacher training, curriculum reforms, provision of physical facilities, and qualified teachers, etc.—have not succeeded in raising learning achievement. As the LEAPS (Learning and Educational Achievement in Punjab Schools) survey report put it, 'enrolment and learning are two completely different processes.'

While making vital information regarding quality of schools and child learning achievements available to parents could help in improving the private sector market, the same cannot guarantee improvement in public schools. Exit from public schools too has no influence on public schools. Yet, we cannot give up on public schools lest we wish to see the society collapse under the weight of resulting inequities. Given the nature of public sector education however, this can only be done if we strengthen the exercise of the voice option by clients in public sector schools. With the exit option frequently exercised by those who can afford it, finding alternative ways of strengthening voice or compensating for it is not going to be easy.

STRENGTHENING VOICE FOR THE PUBLIC SECTOR SCHOOLS

While *exit* as such, when overall enrolment in public schools still continues to be substantial, does not automatically signify decreasing articulation of '*voice*' for quality and/or reform in the public sector system. Nonetheless, if the more politically connected, educated, and articulate members of society continue to move their children from public schools to private, the ability of the people left behind to argue for and get change is bound to weaken. Where private options have allowed people to opt out of state-provided services, the quality of public provision is no longer a priority. As Khan (2011) states, especially in the case of education, apathy has become the norm:

> Like many others from my background I would complain about the state of the country but would not lift a finger to do anything about it. I was from that privileged class that was not affected by the general deterioration in the country. The schools we went to had an imported syllabus, so if education for the masses stagnated we were not touched by it (pp. 76–77).

The argument given above is neither new nor specific to Pakistan. In many countries, say Canada—where the government still creates substantial entry barriers for private providers in the school market, regulates them strictly, and exerts pressure on parents wanting to swap public for private schools—the rationale used to justify state policy is the same as above: if the elite are allowed to withdraw their children from the public education system, it will be hard for society to compel state schools to either improve existing or provide better quality of education.

Given that the state has announced repeatedly—despite including Article 25-A in the basic rights of the constitution—that it does not have the resources to provide quality education to all children in Pakistan and will need private sector help in order to do so, the option of shutting down and/or nationalizing all private schools to attract children to public ones, even if attractive, is no longer viable, given the inability of the state to offer effective governance in any sector it is currently involved in. Private schools are here to stay, and if recent trends are any indication, they are set to expand at a rapid rate for the foreseeable future. So, if having the children of the rich and the elite in the public sector is not an option, does this mean there is no other way for us to build pressure for reforms in the public sector education system? In the following sections we develop two separate, and sometimes competing arguments, both aiming at identifying the possibilities of developing a *politics of [and for] education*.[4]

INJECTING VOICE IN THE SYSTEM: THROUGH POPULAR DEMAND OR THROUGH LEGAL ACTIVISM

The first line of argument highlights the *role of legal activism* and a *progressive nurturing of public domain*—regardless of demand from the consumers of public education—as an approach toward inserting *voice*. The problem to be addressed is how to mobilise the elites to recognize and respond to the need for improving education for all children. There can of course be many approaches to address this problem. The line of thinking discussed in this section assumes that once the state's constitution has guaranteed that education is a fundamental right then public activism, though still possible, may be less wieldy than public litigations and legal activism. When we prioritise public demand in arguments about how to insert voice in the system, we may run the risk of providing the political elite with an alibi. Indeed, the politicians keep saying that we do not attend to education because our constituents do not push us enough. The line of thinking in this section also relies on a distinction between *education as a good/service* amenable to laws of demand and supply and *education as a basic right* amenable to political and legal analysis to suggest some further problems with the rhetoric of demand when articulated together with the idea of education as a basic right.

The logic of public demand in Pakistan entails an investigation into the ways in which particular arguments describe *agents* (or actors), their (potential) *actions*, the *purposes* and *means*, as well as the *scene* (or background) that contains them (Burke,

1969).[5] Let us begin by setting up the *scene*. The key features of the educational scene of Pakistan, both its supply and demand, are well presented in a policy brief by Andrabi, Das, and Khwaja (2010). The scene is described, as also mentioned in the beginning of this chapter, by the supply of drastically inadequate and low quality public education, a booming but credit constrained market of private schools, and a strong parental preference or *demand* for education. Here, though, demand is not articulated as *an act* but rather a desire and willingness to pay for education. It is seen as merely existing and playing an instrumental role in the expansion of the market of affordable private schools. In such a market situation, no one explicitly voices the demand. Instead, people express it by purchasing the goods and services offered by particular entrepreneurs. There is no need or grounds for collective action to access a good or service. The *scene* of the market does not require collective action, but rather, individual choice-making for its operation (Olson, 1971).

Thus, the market positions education as a private good or service, which is in high demand. This scene needs neither a *demander* nor collective public action to fulfil the demand. Surveys aimed to assess parental preferences may validate the existence of parental demand for education, but it is not paradoxical when said preferences do not turn into a source of public outrage. The market scene does not offer individuals the position of *citizens* or *activists* or *demanders* in the political sense of the term. Rather it only provides them with the choice to be, at the very best, an informed consumer.[5] This, we emphasize again, does not imply political action but rather an informed choice to consume a particular good or service. Political systems do not aggregate demands. Markets do. Demand articulation or aggregation is not necessarily about collective political action. Therefore, when the scene is *markets*, demand aggregation signals nothing more than an objective measure of total demand for particular goods and services. But when the scene is *democratic politics*, demand aggregation may signal political action. However, given the historical neglect of education as an issue in the electoral politics of Pakistan, it is very unlikely that it will. If public education has rarely ever been a staple of democratic politics, is it not rather naive to suddenly expect it to be so now? There is little scope for political action in this description of motives. Thus, there is nothing paradoxical if a large majority of parents do not show up on the streets demanding quality education for their children.

Let us consider the scene of public schools while still preserving the notion of education as a public as well as a private good, now to be supplied by the publicly funded education system instead of private education entrepreneurs. In this case, then, we are looking at a scene that, in addition to the children and parents, also consists of public servants and politicians. Let us also assume that the nature of demand for education is preserved under this transformation from the private school market to the public education system. Here we encounter the problem that has been worrying most policy-oriented thinkers in Pakistan: why does the demand for education—if it is indeed popular—remain unarticulated?

This palpable absence of strong public action does indeed appear to be paradoxical, however, when the anecdotal as well as survey evidence suggests the presence of a huge demand for education. If there is incontrovertible evidence for the presence of such high levels of demand for education across Pakistan—and there is—then why, worry the reformers, does it continue to simmer under the thick crust of political inaction? Why are there no government-shaking eruptions of this huge demand for education? If there was a way to aggregate the currently scattered demand and make the politicians more responsive, the requirement for *voice* will have been fulfilled. With *voice* injected into the system, public schools will, as Hirschman has foretold, improve. Politicians must somehow be roused into action. However, the rhetoric of demand articulation may in fact achieve the opposite.

The reason this rhetoric may not be responding to Pakistan's peculiar context is because it casts the ordinary 'citizens' in the role of inarticulate demanders, and politicians in the role of suppliers of education. Why this does not serve the purpose of injecting *voice* where it is most needed? This rhetoric assumes that the much needed political arm twisting of the public education departments will become a reality only when heavy salvos of public demand for education, fired by disadvantaged parents, will begin to challenge the politicians. Unless the demand for education is articulated by these parents, the politicians will not seriously attend to school improvement. Since it is the *politician's influence* that would ultimately change the schools for good and since it is not given a kick-start by the demanders, the status quo of abysmal failures is unlikely to change.

The worrisome consequence of the logic inherent in the demand/supply narrative when applied to public education is that the disadvantaged parents get the beating at both ends, firstly by being already deprived of quality education for her children and secondly for inadequately articulating her demand. Actors such as politicians are also constrained (and enabled) by local contexts, history, discourses, resources, institutions, structures etc. However, in this narrative, they are easily let off the hook simply because they are seen as *passive* responders to the public demand. However, as *active* politicians they are, like anywhere in the world, seeking re-election. Here it is pertinent to invoke the notions of *selectorate*—the set of people with a say in choosing leaders and with a prospect of gaining access to special privileges doled out by leaders—and the *winning coalition*—the subgroup of the selectorate who maintain the incumbent in office in exchange for special privileges (Bueno, A., Siverson, & Morrow, 2003). Bueno et al. (2003) argue that in the case of authoritarian states, the size of the *selectorate* and the *winning coalition* is too small. The implication of this, they argue, is that what appears to be a bad policy from a rational standpoint is actually good politics inasmuch as it helps keep the incumbents in power. We would argue that what Bueno et al. (2003) claims for autocracies also applies to fledgling democracies such as Pakistan. While the political office holders in Pakistan are responsive to the interests of a small *winning coalition* to keep them in the office, they find it useful to explain their inaction in terms of a lack of pressure on them from their constituents to improve the performance of public sector schools in their constituencies (Bari, 2011).

One way out of this dilemma is to work on the actors on both ends, i.e. by helping both the citizens to demand better and the politicians to recognize that educating the masses is in their own self-interest. This approach, then, introduces another actor into the scene that occupies the position of neither the citizen nor the politician but a mentor of sorts for both. The trouble with this approach is that it seeks to change the attitudes and behaviours of the *potential demander* and the *potential responder to the demand* without changing the objective conditions, which created their existing apathies in the first place. As we write this, we are aware of some innovative interventions that are attempting to help citizens articulate their demand for education and also help politicians and political parties become more responsive to them. We stand to learn a great deal about their effects with time.

Another way out of this dilemma is that politicians somehow develop a modicum of *enlightened self-interest*. This involves understanding that the positive externalities that follow from quality education for all citizens would eventually work in their favour, and that education for all leads to a win-win situation. Similar arguments were used by the reformers advocating universal education in the Western countries. As straight forward as this argument may sound, it may not easily influence the decisions of politicians especially because their children do not attend the same schools as the public in general. So what motivation can there be on the part of politicians, or the elite in general, to think about the education of the masses. This motivation could be either charity or enlightened self-interest. There is enough, actually a lot, of the former in Pakistan, as exemplified by the work of great many philanthropists. But there is little evidence of the latter.

Finally, let us revert to the distinction between *education as a good/service* and *education as a basic right* to reflect on the relevance of the idea of public demand to the reforms in public sector schools. The view of education as a good/service lends it for analysis in demand and supply terms. But when we view education as a *basic right* we can fruitfully examine it in political and legal, instead of merely economic terms. If the constitution of Pakistan has secured education as a (justiciable) basic right, then our efforts should be focused on mobilizing the legal and legislative means to ensure its delivery. Basics are demanded as long as they have not been constitutionally secured. After they have been politically secured, it makes little sense to demand them. Rather, the activism should focus more on finding legal and political ways of ensuring that the constitutional provisions are delivered in their letter and spirit. Therefore, it is important to ask whether we should invest our energies in stimulating demand by the 'poor' parent or in public litigations against the state if it fails to uphold the constitutional provisions.

To recapitulate, the line of thinking examined in this section argues that the logic of demand and supply works best when *the scene is market* and *parents are autonomous, self-contained, agentive, and individualistic consumers.* But when the scene is described by the constitution of the state and when education is a basic right, the logic of public demand and its articulation, the legal activism may be more effective. Basic rights are not goods, and politicians not suppliers. Once secured constitutionally, rights are no longer to be demanded, they are to be guaranteed and protected, just like any other provision of the constitution. Would it not sound contradictory to speak about education as a 'right'—which requires activism aimed at its protection through political and legal guarantees—and a 'good/service'—which is subject to the logic of demand and supply—in the same breath? What happens when, in our rhetoric, politicians implicitly assume the subject position of suppliers? It is only when they assume that subject position that they can turn around and tell us, 'Look, no one is knocking at our doors, so what do we do?' This response is appropriate if they are positioned as suppliers of education, but so if they are positioned as protectors of basic rights guaranteed by the constitution. Once positioned as protectors of basic rights they, as well as the institutions of state in general, need to be held accountable irrespective of demand or its aggregates.

The focus of analysis and action doesn't have to be on whether there is (or is not) enough demand for education and whether or not it is articulated or aggregated. The 18th Amendment provides the reformers with a single point agenda: make the state, its various institutions, and the political guardians of the constitution accountable for securing the provisions of the constitution. This requires a concerted, and focused, campaign by the *influential* elites, civil society organizations, and media. The *influential* in the preceding sentence is emphasized because it is a bit of a stretch to expect disadvantaged parents to collectively voice their demand for education. Some will argue that when people can mobilize to demand freedom and the rule of law, then why is it a stretch to expect the same for education? Such an objection assumes congruence between the (abstract) notions of freedom and education as potential motivators for political action. While there is ample historical evidence for the former as a motivator of political action, there is little for the latter.[6] Finally, by way of a positive proposal, we would like to follow Amartya Sen and Jean Drèze in saying that education is not a sufficiently political issue (1999). Sen and Drèze were concerned with this political deficit regarding education in India. As they put it:

> There is no question that, even in a country as poor as India, means can be found to ensure universal attainment of literacy and other basic educational achievements, at least in the younger age groups. There are important strategic questions to consider in implementing that social commitment, but the primary challenge is to make it a more compelling political issue. (p. 139)

Sen and Drèze argue that such was not the case in the pre-independence political movements, and they find it 'somewhat puzzling . . . the promotion of education has received so little attention from the social and political leaders in the post-independence period.' (p. 110) This deficit is even more pronounced in the case of Pakistan. Given the relatively small size of the *winning coalition* of our political office holders, there is little incentive for them to develop and implement sound policies to deliver quality education to the poorer segments of Pakistani society.

PROPOSALS

Provision of quality education to all children is a matter of *public interest*. As such it must be protected through appropriate actions. Based on the argument in this section, two broad strategies are proposed:

- **Legal Activism.** Public Interest Litigations (PIL)—the litigations to protect public interest—are indispensible strategies for social change. The concerned individuals and groups have used the mechanism of PIL to move the courts to protect the fundamental rights guaranteed under the constitutions of particular states. Furthermore, the PIL does not need to be filed by the aggrieved person but by any member of public. Thus, PIL are an effective strategy to insert voice for improvement of public sector schools by the influential members of the civil society on behalf of the aggrieved persons who may not possess the requisite social and economic capital to move the courts themselves. Needless to say, PIL can be used together with other advocacy strategies already in use by the civil society organizations.

- **Cultivation of Public Domain.** The political debates about proposals that seek to preserve public interest also ought to occur in a robust public domain. As Marquand puts it: 'Public domain is both priceless and precarious—a gift of the history, which is always at risk.

It can take shape only in a society in which the notion of a public interest, distinct from private interests, has taken root; and, historically speaking, such societies are rare breeds. Its values and practices also do not come naturally, and have to be learned. Where the private domain of love, friendship and personal connection and the market domain of buying and selling are the products of nature, the public domain depends on careful and continuing nurture.' (Marquand, 2004, 2)

Civil society organizations can play an instrumental role in nurturing the public sphere. However, in order to do that they will need to persevere in their advocacy. As Hannah Arendt (1998) argues that unlike architectural structures that continue to exist beyond the human *actions* that developed them in the first place, the public domain depends on constant nurturing and action. It disappears when the action that produced it is terminated.

PUBLIC ACTION FOR VOICE

The second approach to insertion of voice assumes that under suitable conditions, the Pakistani elites can be engaged in improving public education. Notwithstanding the absolute exit of elites from the public sector schools, there are certain points to be made here. There is plenty of evidence (empirical, too) to suggest that the same people and the same classes can behave very differently at different times, and under different circumstances. The involvement of the urban middle and upper classes, including students (especially from private sector universities), in the lawyers' movement of 2007–08 surprised many political pundits. Where many had been critical of the apathy of the Pakistani youth and middle classes throughout the 1990s and early 2000s, the myth was forcefully questioned by their participation in the lawyers' movement. Similarly, the involvement of the elite in the 'Arab Spring' has also surprised many commentators.

But there are good explanations for this contingent response. Simply put, people's preferences change over time. And sometimes the changes in preferences occur for many at around the same time and in the same direction. This can be driven by factors that are, or have been, affecting them all in more or less the same manner. Hirschman (1982) explains how people might shift between pursuing private interests almost exclusively during some periods of their life to the exclusion of public interests and participation in public actions, and, in later periods, the opposite extreme. Was the participation of the middle class a sign of such a shift having taken place over the years previous to the lawyers' movement? Was the same thing happening to large numbers of people in Arab countries as well, only becoming evident once the movements started? Irrespective of whether the lawyers' movement and/or the Arab Spring represent such shifts, Hirschman convincingly shows that such shifts can and do occur. The elite can get involved in public action. The issue has more to do with the right kind of environmental and contingent factors.

DIGGING DEEPER

In a way, creating the conditions conducive to elite involvement leads one back to a classic problem of governance: how is the gap between the ideal government and the actual government to be mediated? In a democratic system, elections are supposed to fill this gap. Representatives offer themselves periodically for election and their performance determines if they are to be re-elected. But this is not a complete solution to the problem. Elections may be rigged, restrictions may be placed on those eligible, or the political system may have other flaws that make elections an imperfect way of mediating the gap between the ideal and the actual government. Various political philosophers have proposed specific solutions to the issue. Hobbes (2009) argued that the law-giver himself could resolve the issue. The only problem with this solution is the self-interest of the law-giver. In Pakistan, we have repeatedly witnessed benevolent military dictators assume power in the name of reforms, only to be reduced fairly quickly to undermining governance to ensure personal longevity and other interests. Most recently, we saw this with General Musharraf, starting with his presidential referendum and other constitutional amendments in 2002 to retain his dual office, all the way up to the National Reconciliation Ordinance (NRO) in late 2007 to keep himself in power.

John Locke suggested that the ultimate power lay with the people and they had the right to revolt if they felt that their representatives were not protecting their civil rights (1988). But this too is not an easy option to exercise. The costs of a popular revolt, if one does get organized, are significant, and there is no guarantee that post revolt/revolution, the incoming order will be any better at reducing the gap between the ideal and the real government.

Though Immanuel Kant is not known for his work in political theory, some recent literature has pointed out that he had a very innovative idea for his time for filling the governance gap. Kant postulated that the gap be filled by civil society (Ellis, 2005). His rather inclusive understanding of civil society captured the public space that was being created, enhanced, and enlarged during his lifetime. It included what was produced in newspapers, periodicals, journals, and other spaces of public debate by intellectuals, academics, and public figures.

But given his own ethics, Kant demanded that the output considered should represent the public interest. This is also linked to the demand for universality in Kantian ethics (Kant, 1784). Though Kant allowed for the fact that the solution he was proposing favoured order over chaos and, in some cases, might lead to a slower approach to change compared to, say, the revolt/revolution option that Locke postulated, he felt his way provided a much better opportunity for progressive change towards reducing the gap between the ideal and the real government. This also ensured that there could be a continuous tracking of the actual government so that, given the reality of living in an uncertain world, there could be a continuous dialogue between governance ideals and actual government performance.

A lot has changed in the notion of 'civil society' and 'public space' since Kant's time. But the Kantian notion could be used to create demand for reform in the education sector. The proposal is generalizable to other sectors and services too.

A PROPOSAL

The problems seem obvious. Children, parents, and communities are not articulating their demand for education into a priority for political representatives. When constituency-level politicians are not pressurised, they do not pass on any pressure to the political leadership either. Using the Kantian notion of civil society, and making use of the changes that have taken place in both public space since Kant's time and communication technology, one might be able to find better ways of narrowing the gap between the ideal and the real.

GENERATION AND DISSEMINATION OF REQUISITE INFORMATION

Parents and communities need to know what their children are learning and how the schools that their children go to are performing, compared to other schools in the area as well as on an absolute basis, in order to set minimum standards of learning and education. University research departments or research institutes can collect, package, and design the information that needs to be disseminated. Local civil society organizations can not only collect this information, they can also help disseminate it to communities. Local media, whether it is local newspapers or FM radios, can be used for dissemination of information and for getting feedback from parents and communities.

CREATING ACCOUNTABILITY NETWORKS

The number of children out of school in any area and the performance of local schools need to be presented to local representatives and officials. One way to think about this problem is in terms of creating effective competition and/ or contestability at the local level. Given that every level of society has elected representatives, for both incumbents looking to make a comeback and those who are desirous of entering the arena of local politics for the first time, it should be possible to not only make children's schooling records and performance a political issue, it should also be possible to create over time some traction for parental and community involvement. This may lead to the beginnings of accountability of representatives on the basis of the performance of education-related variables and outcomes of schools in their constituency. The same process, structured at higher levels, could potentially allow society to bridge the gap between the ideal and the real. By potentially creating some competition and/or contestability amongst various subcategories of the political elite, the problem of elite involvement could also be challenged while allowing for the fact that it might not be possible at present to create direct involvement of the elite through enrolment of their children in the state-provided education sector.

CONCLUSION

This crux of our proposal is that mechanisms are available to improve public schools in the face of a monumental growth in private schools. Giving up on public schools is simply not an option. The acceptance of education as a fundamental right has opened up possibilities of legal activism in addition to the traditional opportunities for the role that can be played by civil society. The approaches to address the problem of public action for school reforms may vary but their intended effect does not. Civil society activists are already putting in practice some of the proposals outlined in this chapter. The viability of other strategies such as PILs is being explored. The salience being given to education in the last election campaign is another healthy sign that a politics of education is finally coming of age in Pakistan.

REFERENCES

Andrabi, Tahir, Das, Jishnu and Khwaja, Asim Ijaz (2008), 'A dime a day: The possibilities and limits of private schooling in Pakistan', *Comparative Education Review*, 52(3), 329–55.

Andrabi, Tahir, Das, Jishnu, Khwaja, Asim Ijaz, Vishwanath, Tara and Zajonc, Tristan (2007a), Learning and educational achievements in Punjab schools (LEAPS), Report (Forthcoming) (Washington: World Bank).

Andrabi, Tahir, Das, Jishnu, Khwaja, Asim Ijaz, Vishwanath, Tara and Zajonc, Tristan (2007b), 'Learning and educational achievements in Punjab schools (LEAPS): Insights to inform the education policy debate' (Washington: World Bank).

Bari, Faisal (2011), 'Enlightened self-interest', *The Daily Times*. Retrieved from http://pakistan policyideas.wordpress.com/ 2011/08/02/enlightened-self-interest/

Brighouse, Harry (1998), 'Why should states fund schools?' *British Journal of Educational Studies*, 46(2), 138–52.

Brighouse, Harry (2004), 'What's Wrong With Privatising Schools?' *Journal of Philosophy of Education*, 38(4), 617–31.

Bueno, D. M. B., A., Smith, Siverson, M. R., and Morrow, D. J. (2003), *The Logic of Political Survival* (Cambridge: MIT Press).

Burke, Kenneth (1969), *A Grammar of Motives* (Chicago-Illinois: University of California Press).

Campaign for Quality Education (2007), 'Education in Pakistan: What works & why?' (Lahore: CQE).

De, Anuradha, Dreze, Jean, Noronha, Claire, Pushpendra, Rampal, Anita, Samson, Meera, . . . Kumar, Shiva (1999), *Public Report on Basic Education in India* (New Delhi: Oxford University Press).

Ellis, E. (2005), *Kant's Politics: Provisional Theory for an Uncertain World* (New Heaven-Connecticut: Yale University Press).

Gladstein, M., Justman, M., and Meier, V. (2004), *The Political Economy of Education* (Cambridge-Massachusetts: MIT Press).

Hirschman, Albert O. (1970), Exit, voice, and loyalty: Responses to decline in firms, organizations, and states (Cambridge: Harvard University Press).

Hirschman, Albert O. (1982), *Shifting Involvements: Private Interests and Public Actions* (Princeton-New Jersey: Princeton University Press).

Hobbes, T. (2009), ed., Peterborough: Broadview Press.

Jimenez, Emmanuel, and Tan, Jee P. (1987), 'Decentralised and private education: The case of Pakistan', *Comparative Education*, 23(2), 173–90.

Kant, I. (1784), 'An answer to the question: What is enlightenment?' Retrieved from http://www.english. upenn.edu/~mgamer/Etexts/ kant.html

Khan, I. (2011), *Pakistan: A Personal History* (London: Bantam Press).

Labaree, D. (1997), 'Public goods, private goods: The American struggle over educational goals'. *American Educational Research Journal*, 34(1), 39.

Labaree, D. (2000) ed. 'No exit: Public education as an inescapably public good', *Reconstructing the common good in education: Coping with intractable American dilemmas* (Stanford, California: Stanford University Press).

Locke, J. (1988), *Two Treatises on Government* (3rd edn.) (Cambridge: Cambridge University Press).

Marquand, D. (2004), *The Decline of the Public: The Hollowing Out of Citizenship* (Cambridge: Polity Press).

Muzaffar, Irfan, and Bari, Faisal (2010), 'Educational debates in Pakistan: Barking up the wrong tree?' *Social Science and Policy Bulletin*, 1(4), 2–6.

Naradowski, M., and Andrada, M. (2001), 'The privatization of education in Argentina', *Journal of Education Policy*, 16(6), 585–95.

Naseer, M., Patnam, M., and Raza, R. (2010), 'Transforming public schools: Impact of the CRI programme on child learning in Pakistan', *Economics of Education Review*, 29(3), 669–83.

Olson, M. (1971), *The Logic of Collective Action: Public Goods and the Theory of Groups* (Cambridge-Massachusetts: Harvard University Press).

Pakistan. Bureau of Statistics (2009), 'Pakistan Social and Living Standards Measurement Survey (2008–09)' (Islamabad: Government of Pakistan), Retrieved from http://www.

statpak.gov.pk/fbs/content/pakistan-social-and-living-standards-measurement-survey-pslm-2008-09-national-provincial

Srivastava, Prachi (2007), *Neither Voice nor Loyalty: School Choice and the Low-Fee Private Sector in India*, Vol. 134 (New York).

Tooley, James (2003), 'Why Harry Brighouse is nearly right about the privatisation of education', *Journal of Philosophy of Education*, 37(3), 427–47.

Tooley, James, and Dixon, Pauline (2003), *Private Schools for the Poor: A Case Study from India* (Reading, UK: Center for British Teachers).

Tooley, James, Dixon, Pauline, and Amuah, I. (2007), 'Private and public schooling in Ghana: A census and comparative survey', *International Review of Education*, 53(4), 389–415.

Tooley, James, Dixon, Pauline, and Olaniyan, O. (2005), 'Private and public schooling in low-income areas of Lagos State, Nigeria: A census and comparative survey', *International Journal of Educational Research*, 43(3), 125–46.

NOTES

1. We have intentionally avoided a discussion of *loyalty* as we do not regard it to be as applicable to public and private schools as *voice* and *exit*.

2. The role of government as an information provider is also proposed by the LEAPS reports. See on p. vii in, Andrabi, T., Das, J., Khwaja, A., Vishwanath, T., and Zajonc, T. (2007).

3. Rigorous evaluations have already shown that some interventions improve learning significantly even in the public schools. See, for example, Naseer, Patnam, and Raza (2010).

4. The two lines of arguments about various approaches to rejuvenate a politics of education in Pakistan are based on conversations between the two authors. They have also been shared with public earlier as two separate articles in the Social Sciences and Policy Bulletin. See for example, Muzaffar and Bari (2010).

5. As Kenneth Burke puts it: 'Any complete statement about motives will offer *some kind* of answers to these five questions: what was done (act), when or where it was done (scene), who did it (agent), how he did it (agency), and why (purpose)'. (Burke, 1969) xv.

6. Some may argue that the conception of market used here belongs to the neoclassical or the Walrasian conception of the market and that within the field of 'political economy', voter preferences, collective action, and political demand articulation are considered important determinants of the delivery of public goods and services. Caution, however, is needed in using the political economic models concerning the behaviour of voter-consumer developed in liberal democratic contexts to think about the problems of education in countries with different political arrangements. See, for example Gladstein, Justman, and Meier (2004).

7. As an aside, some have even argued in personal correspondences with the author that higher literacy in the Arab world has played a significant role in fomenting the so-called 'Arab Spring'.

3

School Management Committees in Pakistan: Mobilizing Communities for Education?

—Abbas Rashid and Ayesha A. Awan

INTRODUCTION

The crisis in Pakistan's education has to do with access as well as quality. As donor assistance rose in the 1990s, the notion of community involvement in school improvement steadily gained ground. The idea of community involvement in schooling has travelled far, not least courtesy of the World Bank, which in tandem with providing loans, places a high premium on its set of prescriptions for reform. The World Bank, while funding public education, has also promoted the idea of public-private partnership. This may take the form of governments providing funds to private sector schools. Alternatively, organizations or individuals from the private sector may 'adopt' public sector schools. Another form of 'partnership' is community involvement or support in improving the school. The latter mode of partnership will be the focus of this paper.

A review of Pakistan's national education policies almost from the time of independence shows the government's inclination towards seeking partners to shoulder the 'burden' of providing education to all. The burgeoning private sector that has emerged over the last two decades is seen by the government as a strong partner, well on track for making up for the deficiencies of public sector education. Parallel to this trajectory, donors are seen as partners helping to make up the resource gap in the education budget. Not least, the community has been nominated as a partner for enhancing quality and increasing enrolment in public sector schools. One look at the dismal figures on out-of-school children, dropout rates, student outcomes or other relevant indicators would be enough to reveal that these 'partnerships' have not resulted in bringing Pakistan anywhere close to the objective of providing children with schooling commensurate with even minimum standards.

In this chapter, we will examine the notion of community-school partnership, embodied in the institution of the School Management Committee (SMC) or School Council (SC),[1] much favoured by international NGOs and donors, and widely embraced by the government. This chapter contests the idea that the SMC can play the role envisaged for it in the context of school improvement in Pakistan, barring exceptional circumstances. Moreover, it argues that the community, manifest at the local level in whatever form, is not in a position to play a decisive role in school improvement.

The chapter will first explore the theoretical perspectives on community participation and the politics of empowerment.

It will then review the objectives, roles, and responsibilities of SMCs in Pakistan as well as research on their performance. It will then highlight three cases of community participation in Pakistan from a multi-case study. Finally, in light of these findings, it will discuss how the relationship between the school and the community can help improve the quality of education in public sector schools.

COMMUNITY PARTICIPATION AND POLITICS OF EMPOWERMENT

What do we understand by community participation? Participation has its degrees and levels depending on the context (Shaeffer, 1994). Communities can be *involved* in providing services, contributing resources or money, attending meetings, and even consulting on particular issues. However, these are largely passive activities. They can also actively participate in delivering services, decision-making, identifying options, and judging feasibilities. Similarly, Arnstein (1969) devised a participation typology in the form of a ladder in which each rung of the ladder represents one of eight levels of participation. The first two rungs of the ladder, *manipulation* and *therapy*, essentially involve putting citizens on committees to 'educate' them or to get their support rather than changing social structures, whereas the last three levels, *partnerships, delegated power and citizen control*, entail redistribution of power through negotiation between citizens and power holders. Certain kinds of involvement in schooling are of limited value in the context of quality, 'there is little evidence to suggest that parents' involvement in *governance* (emphasis added) affects student learning in the school, although there may be other benefits and indirect effects.' (Fullan & Stiegelbauer, 1991, 237). We contend in this chapter that community participation through the SMC framework in Pakistan conforms to a low level of participation and is unlikely to either impact the delivery of education or improve its quality.

So why does the SMC continue to remain popular as a vehicle for improvement of schooling quality? In the context of Pakistan, apart from the longstanding proclivity of the government to seek partners in what should be a core state obligation of educating its citizens, the 'staying power' of the SMC may also have something to do with the travelling reform paradigm. According to Burde (2004a), 'whether or not they work, PTAs provide a vehicle for INGOs to claim increased local participation in poverty alleviation and social mobilization programmes.' (p. 176) So, even though educational transfer implies isolating education from its political, economic and cultural context, it serves the purpose of providing a participatory and democratic façade, if nothing else.

The import and modification of the SMC format epitomizes what Ritzer terms, the 'irrationality of rationality' (cited in Steiner-Khamsi, 2004, 206) in that the poorest, least educated and thereby least empowered sections of the community are supposed, by virtue of this 'participatory' mechanism, to improve and monitor education delivery at school. The well-off section of the community, barring exceptions, is not represented on the council or at any rate will not be active, given that such parents will almost invariably be sending their children to private schools. Given this crucial 'exit of voice' (Hirschmann, 1970) from the council, the nominated parents can only play a limited role in relation to the school. In the context of Hirschman's formulation, the parents who cannot afford a private school for their children have no choice except to continue with the public sector school. Those with means have a choice between 'exit' and giving 'voice' to their concerns with regard to the deteriorating quality of education being delivered and hope that their concerns are addressed but are likely to choose exit given that it is the easier option. And even parents who have a sense of 'loyalty' towards the school, for whatever reason, are likely to only defer the decision to exit if there is no real improvement in quality.

So, it is a relatively disempowered community that may, potentially, engage with the public sector school. Such engagement, in exceptional cases, is in evidence when the school is performing reasonably well and the teachers appear to be making a real effort, which is to say that community support is triggered in response to the dynamic of a school seen to be making the necessary effort, rather than the other way round. Several studies suggest that the initiative has to come from the school. A study by Dauber and Epstein asserts that, 'data are clear that the *schools practices* to inform and to involve parents are more important than parent education, family size, marital status and, even grade level in determining whether inner city parents stay involved in their children's education through the middle grades.' (cited in Fullan & with Stiegelbauer, 1991, 234).

In any case, in the absence of *political* engagement, promoting 'community participation' in managing social services may be of limited value. While it aligns nicely with the narrative of equity and democracy, the rhetoric of community participation runs the risk of engendering complacency or worse: 'rather than the vibrant civil society it is meant to produce, community participation promoted with uncritical enthusiasm in the field of educational development and education in emergencies, runs the risk of leaving disillusioned and disempowered communities in its wake.' (Burde, 2004b, 73) *Participation*, sans the *political*, invariably means that the power to set and sustain the agenda rests elsewhere and the community, with its low-level participation, acquires little by way of agency.

Abers (2006) comments insightfully on the politics of participation with regards to the successful Porto Allegro experiment in participatory budgeting, 'The reason that the PB was so successful in Porto Alegre was not so much that it was a "good model". The capacity of the PB to promote both democratization and civic organizing grew directly out of the fact that the design of that model fit into an alternative *political* (emphasis added) strategy. Thus, thinking about how to replicate the Porto Alegre experience requires focusing less on how to "copy the model" than on the art of politics.' (Abers, 2006, 89). A decontextualized emphasis on 'community' and its 'participation', on the other hand, comprehensively disregards the political notion of empowerment and the 'voice' that becomes audible because of it. Undeniably, the community can be mobilized but not in the absence of a political process; one that would ensure their genuine involvement in decision-making (Friere, 1970).

What we find then is that, regardless of impact, the emphasis on a greater role for the community conveniently lends itself to an implicit alignment with the discourse of democratization, local empowerment, decentralization/devolution, and school-based management. As such, SMCs are seen as the vehicle for ensuring community engagement in the process of school improvement, not least in Pakistan.

Community or parent participation committees exist in each province of Pakistan. These committees consist of local education stakeholders, usually parents, head teachers and schoolteachers, community members, government representatives, and in some cases students. The composition of the committees has continued to change over the years, for example, more recently, in Punjab, 'notables' have been added to the list of members.

For the most part, such committees are expected to accomplish some or all of the following: motivate communities to send their children to school and reduce dropout rates; monitor student and teacher attendance; monitor performance of teachers and staff; plan and execute school infrastructure improvement; purchase furniture, equipment, and books; raise local resources, and 'develop mutual confidence and trust' between teachers and parents. Taking the example of Punjab, any issues with regard to SMC functioning must be reported to officials who are part of the district bureaucracy, and financial oversight of the SMC is carried out by office bearers of the Department of Education (as opposed to members of the community). Both in terms of formation as well as accountability then, the SMC enterprise is rendered hierarchical, employing a top-down process, rather than a community-led horizontal one (as illustrated in the case studies described later).

Community involvement through SMCs as the primary engine for school-based improvement and reform underpins many a government policy formulation. In the Punjab alone, since 1994, the SMC has undergone at least five rounds of reconstitution and capacity building, each time seeking to address the perennial issue of efficacy. The first organized form of community participation appeared in 1994 under the Social Action Programme (SAP) consisting of twelve members tasked with motivating parents to enrol their children in school, monitoring teacher attendance and participating in school management and finance. In 1998, the SMC was reconstituted to include nine members, mostly parents and teachers, with similar expectations; again it remained ineffective due to lack of capacity. In 2000, the SMC was reconstituted and renamed the School Council (SC), composed of eleven members this time consisting of teachers, students, two retired government servants, and a revenue officer for financial assistance. Under the Punjab Education Sector Reforms Assistance Programme (PESRP), in 2003–04 it once again resurfaced with 50 per cent parents' representation and the authority to spend up to Rs. 400,000 on the school. In 2005–06, a capacity-building programme for the SCs was initiated in partnership with the Rural

Support Programmes. And as of 2008, assessments by the government indicate that the SMCs still require 'capacity building'.

Alongside reform projects, substantial funding has been allocated to SMCs regardless of their capacity to absorb that funding. In Punjab, the 2007–08 budget for SMCs of Rs. 772 million was revised to Rs. 53 million, indicating that only 7 per cent of the budgeted amount was spent—yet allocation for 2008–09 was increased to Rs. 1,022 million. Similar sums have been allocated in Sindh. Despite such substantial funding and continuous attempts towards improvement, the SMC remains unable to perform as expected.

A number of research studies conducted over the years on SMCs and their performance point to several key issues. A study exploring community participation through SMCs as far back as 1999, Khan (2003) looked at a sample of 149 government and NGO schools across all provinces of Pakistan. It found that in government schools, parents and communities were usually oblivious to the existence of the SMC and only one of the 43 government schools had a functioning SMC. Over half of the SMCs met less than once a month and the focus of activities was repair and maintenance. The majority of members were teachers, not parents. Generally, teachers viewed parents' involvement as a threat and an interference in their affairs. Parents felt that they lacked the time, resources and ability to play a role in the school, particularly with respect to monitoring quality. The role of the teacher was seen to be beyond the purview of the community.

More recent studies, such as the community stakeholder consultations of the Punjab Education Sector Reform Programme (PESRP) in three districts of southern Punjab also found similar issues (Zafar & Mashallah, 2006). First, the study found that community members were often informed rather than consulted on decisions by the head teacher and SMC proceedings were often dominated by the head teachers or district education officers. Secondly, it found that community involvement at a certain level often existed prior to the formation of the SMC as well. Finally, despite the support of district education officials, it had not been possible to improve the attendance and teaching performance of teachers in most cases.

This perception of SMC ineffectiveness is, on occasion, echoed by donors as well. A study report on devolution in Pakistan by several donors, says, 'For their part, SMCs . . . operate with varying degrees of effectiveness. Most are still largely controlled by head teachers who continue to select members, and school management remains de facto with the staff. Most SMC members, moreover, know little if anything about their roles and responsibilities.' (ADB DFID World Bank, 2004, 8). And another report on decentralization of education in Pakistan says, 'In reality, the school management committees have no functional role except for some involvement in school finance. The SMCs are not clear of their roles and responsibilities.' (UNESCO, 2006, 32).

In summary, these studies and reports point out that despite the fact that SMCs are dominated by school-based staff, teachers nonetheless resent parent or SMC interference in school matters, while the SMC has limited power to improve the school since it lacks the authority to address issues such as teacher absenteeism. It appears then that participation through the SMCs in Pakistan is largely limited to passive involvement and is actually a form of tokenism, where community members have no real opportunities to effect change.

UNDERLYING ISSUES WITH SMCs

What then seems to be the issue with the SMC? There is substantial funding for SMCs, and reform projects make continuous attempts to address their capacity issues. However, it appears that these attempts are missing the point. The way in which the SMC has been conceptualized is itself problematic, starting with the notion that the SMC represents the community.

Instead of emerging as an organically developed community organization, the SMC is a bureaucratically created, officially notified and often NGO-assisted community forum. In this scenario, the SMC is subject to written rules of conduct; it is formally notified by the district authorities; its expenditure is subject to scrutiny by district education officers, and the lines of accountability run not to the community, but rather, to the district government. This raises the question as to whether SMCs are, in effect, an organizational construct for the channelling of community energy, or quite simply, the rule-based and government-funded lowest implementation tier of the district education bureaucracy.

Similarly, the decentralization of schooling in Nepal via community management hinges on an active, if not central role for parents and local stakeholders, yet this is being dramatically curtailed (Carney, 2009). Firstly, the ministry has secured a management structure that assures its control of decentralized provision. Whilst the committees comprise significant numbers of local community members, the District Education Officer (DEO) and a district-appointed 'focal person' ensure that the decisions taken by the committees are in line with the government's broad policy agenda. At all stages, the DEO reserves the right to intervene with respect to SMCs; to appoint members where needed; and to overturn 'democratic' decisions. In all community schools new sub-committees are in the process of being established—for example 'project monitoring committees' and a 'social audit committee'—with the DEO driving the agenda.

At best, communities may seek to support schools, but the kind of participation suggested by the SMC calls for a more energized, proactive approach. To that end, there is an underlying assumption that the community, as represented on the SMC, has the 'voice' to effect changes such as curbing teacher absenteeism and improving education delivery. However, the reality is that the SMC usually consists of community members who are the least empowered and thus least likely to accomplish the tasks assigned to them.

School Management Committees (SMCs) are expected to take on a wide array of roles and responsibilities to improve school quality. However, when most schools conform to a very low quality baseline in terms of infrastructure, teaching, or leadership, how is it possible for an SMC—lacking voice and leverage—to accomplish these goals? Studies have shown that where community organizations are effective there is usually some level of existing quality within the school; something the community can work with to improve.

EXCEPTIONS TO THE RULE: COMMUNITY PARTICIPATION IN PAKISTAN

Here we explore some exceptional cases of community participation to identify a few of the factors underlying motivation and success. The cases are a part of a multi-case research study of 43 schools, in public and private sectors, spanning 8 locations across Pakistan (Campaign for Quality Education, 2007). As one of its themes, the study examined the nature of community participation in the relatively better schools.

CASE ONE

In a rural girls' school in Gwadar, Balochistan, we find a dynamic head teacher: Begum. She demonstrates a deep and abiding interest in all aspects of the school. She is concerned about her students memorizing facts instead of comprehending them; she is uncomfortable with a lack of application of pedagogical skills that could help kids really learn; above all she is concerned about the department of education's lack of capacity to address her concerns. Begum spends most of her day interacting with her teachers and students; visiting teachers during trainings to evaluate and support their classroom practice, while also supporting them as they become equipped with new methods of teaching their students better. She engages in school improvement planning by collaborating with the SMC to develop and implement plans. As a motivator, she works from a position of trust that she has been able to generate in her students, teachers, and school community. Her judicious spending of funds is demonstrated by the transformation of the school from a two-room primary school to a thriving secondary school in less than ten years.

As a consequence of this dynamic leadership at the school level, we find increased community responsiveness and a proactive SMC. When a major donor-funded programme wanted to provide some already decided upon input to the school, the SMC pushed back and secured assistance more in line with school and community needs. Members of the community also protested on numerous occasions when the department tried to transfer Begum, thus demonstrating their commitment to protecting the interests of the school.

This case is illustrative of how dynamic school leadership can make a difference. A school may gain the trust of the community through efforts to improve itself, if it takes the lead in developing a strong relationship with the community.

CASE TWO

For seventeen years, a government boys' school located in rural Sialkot (Punjab) was a poorly performing school characterized by dilapidated infrastructure, inadequate teaching staff and teacher irregularity. In 1999, this all began to change. A well-regarded landowner with political connections and linkages to the education department, who happened to be part of a not so active school council, began taking a keen interest in the school. This special interest of a few members ensured that the school council effectively utilized grant money to add on rooms, construct a boundary wall and purchase furniture. Immediately that year there was a huge jump in enrolment: from 25 to 150 students. The council then set its sights on increasing the teaching staff by lobbying with the department, eventually the number of teachers were increased from three to five.

In 2002, the landowner, via the council, took a bold step and forced the aged head teacher, with his traditionalist mindset to step down. As a replacement, they chose Hassan, a hard-working junior teacher perceived to be a better leader, one who recognized the value of new teaching methodologies. This move quickly bore fruit. Upon becoming head teacher, Hassan began to involve teachers in planning and making key decisions. He created a system of delegation of duties so that important functions continued to be performed even when he himself or one of his teachers were not present in the school. Teachers responded to his efforts by regularly seeking guidance from him. Over the next two years, the school's reputation began to improve. The school received awards at the local level for best school and students received awards in extracurricular competitions. The school attracted another 100 students including children from neighbouring villages and 40 girls. Parents were more willing to send their daughters to this boys' school located just outside the village rather than the girls school inside the village, due to what they felt was an obvious difference in quality.

Motivated by the positive improvements within the school, the school council along with Hassan stepped up their efforts. They conducted extensive fundraising with local philanthropists and political representatives. They were able to raise 10,000 rupees from the local elected officials, and for school furniture needs, they were able to raise close to 38,000 rupees, ensuring that all students had chairs and desks.

This case exemplifies how a motivated member of the community used the SMC to help bolster school leadership which then transformed the school and drew greater community support, building on a relationship of trust between community and school resulting from improved school quality.

CASE THREE

In the tight-knit Ismaili community of the Northern Areas —a sect renowned for the value they place on education and community service—we find a school with staff and community in harmony with each other, both respectful and appreciative of each others' role in improving quality. The school has received a variety of inputs and support. During 1990s, the Aga Khan Education Services, Pakistan (AKES,P) upgraded the school to a middle school, provided technical support and engaged the community. In 2004, the Whole School Improvement Programme (WSIP) was initiated focusing on several aspects, including community involvement, as part of the effort to improve the school. Both teachers and the community throughout have demonstrated a dedication to improving the school.

We find strong leadership amongst the head teacher and teachers. Teachers demonstrate their dedication by providing extra coaching to students over vacations, and daily, after prayers at the *Jamaat Khana* (community centre). School achievement is apparent from the successful entry of many of the school's students to the best high school in Gilgit, while a teacher from the school has been honoured with the Best Teacher Award for Gilgit. The Village Education Committee (VEC) commends the commitment of the teachers and points out that because the local community has a very positive image of the school, they have no hesitation in extending their support and cooperation to it. As the chairman put it, 'You cannot clap with one hand. In the success of our school there are many people who have made their contributions. Most of all, however, we are grateful to our teachers for their unwavering commitment. . . .'

As a consequence of this, and partly as a result of its somewhat unique community ethic, we find that the VEC has consistently contributed to the school over the years. It works with the school to hire teachers for vacant positions and monitors teacher attendance. It also constructed twelve classrooms, with each household not only contributing a specific amount of money for construction, but also participating in the manual work of the project. Most of the teachers at the school appreciate the role and contributions of the VEC. They like the idea of selecting the VEC members from amongst the parents of their students, because, as one teacher commented, their own children are at the school therefore they take a genuine interest in school performance. Teachers also appreciate the fact that the committee members always assisted them whenever they requested to meet parents to resolve their children's issues.

In this case, again, the community participates and is effective, not least because of the school-based leadership and the general perception within the community that the school and its staff are making a real effort to improve the quality of education. However, in this case there is an additional factor at work. The mobilization of the Ismaili community is also given an impetus by an important extra-local factor: the pronounced emphasis on education of their spiritual leader, the Aga Khan that encourages members of the community to look more earnestly for ways to meaningfully engage with the school.

In the examples above, there are clearly elements beyond the rule-based organizational framework of the SMC that ensure community participation and its contribution to school success:

i. School leadership through the head teacher;
ii. Individual leadership within the community; and
iii. A cohesive community mobilized within an ethos of community service.

The mere insertion of an SMC does not appear to be of major consequence. Therefore, while effective means must be employed to ensure community engagement, the government, by way of policy reform, needs to work harder to ensure the availability of *motivated teachers, including the head teacher,* as the key instrument for improving school quality.

CONCLUSION

What is clear from the foregoing is that SMCs, at least in Pakistan's public education sector, have not been able to meet expectations in supporting schools or improving education delivery. Among the underlying issues: the SMCs are not organically developed from the bottom up as part of a broader political process aimed at mobilizing communities; poor communities lacking organization and 'voice' are in a weak position to monitor or bring about change at the level of the school and most schools lack even the minimum quality that would encourage the community to meaningfully engage with the school and contribute to it.

As such, parental involvement through the SMCs is limited and often resented by school-based staff that views SMC efforts to monitor or question the way the school is being managed as unnecessary interference. So, when the school representatives come to dominate the SMC, which happens often, they have little interest in making the SMC a viable entity. However, in those cases, where the school staff itself is interested in engaging the community, the results are more likely to be positive. Of course, in exceptional cases the community may play a key role in establishing a productive relationship with the school, but that is more likely where the community is already mobilized and has little to do with the formation of an SMC.

While ways need to be found to encourage community participation, government policies must focus on investing in school leadership through careful identification of good teachers and head teachers, by motivating them and ensuring their professional development. Implicit in such a policy framework would be the assumption that in school-community relations the initiative can as easily, and perhaps to better effect, rest with the school rather than the community. For the community to take an interest in the school the latter must be seen to improve or at the very least demonstrate a potential to do so. What is crucial then is for the state to continue to focus on and invest in the elements of quality that go into making a better school.

We do need to remind ourselves that education is a public good of great import. It must therefore remain a paramount concern and responsibility of the state. This is not to deny or minimize the role of the community or the parents, or indeed any other stakeholder in the critical pursuit of making quality education accessible to all. However, in the context of a neo-liberal discourse that seeks to minimize the role of the state, other stakeholders are being assigned greater responsibility to this end—even as budgetary allocations are maintained at a certain level and formal legislation facilitating universal basic education is put in place. In Pakistan, community participation and SMCs have received increasing attention in the context of improving quality and access in education. In a way, the communities are being told that they are essentially responsible for the education of their children, which also enables the state to give up its responsibilities.

In a similar vein, the role of NGOs has been highlighted as adopt-a-school programmes have been tried out. Not least, Low-Fee Private Schools (LFPS) have been held up as a panacea in terms of both access as well as quality. Public funds, in fact, are now diverted to such schools through the Punjab Education Foundation. What emerges then is a picture in which the state is curtailing its own role in delivering this critical public good and attempting to pass on the responsibility to parents, community, the not-for-profit private sector and in particular to the for-profit private sector. Viewed in this broader context, it is easier to comprehend the role that the SMC has been assigned, one that is flawed not only in implementation but also by way of design.

REFERENCES

- http://pide.org.pk/pdr/index.php/pdr/article/viewFile/2643/ 2610
- A brief version drawn from this chapter is available at http://lums.edu.pk/docs/dprc/10-SSPB-Autumn-2011.pdf
- Brief versions drawn from this chapter are available at http://www.cqe.net.pk/pdf/Education%20Debate%20in%20 Pakistan%20Barking%20up%20the%20Wrong%20Tree.pdf, http://lums.edu.pk/docs/dprc/4-SSPB-Spring-2010.pdf, http://www.academia.edu/1440490/Educational_Debates_in_ Pakistan_Barking_up_the_Wrong_Tree, http://www.opensociety foundations.org/briefing-papers/education-debate-pakistan-barking-wrong-tree, http://pakistanpolicyideas.wordpress.com/ page/23/

Abers, R. (2006), Porto Alegre and the participatory budget: Civic education, politics and the possibilities for replication. Building local and global democracy (81–94): Carol Institute. Retrieved from http://fimforum.org/en/library/Porto_Alegre_and_the_ Participatory_Budget.pdf

ADB DFID World Bank (2004), Devolution in Pakistan: Overview of the ADB/DFID/World Bank Study.

Arnstein, S. R. (1969), A ladder of citizen participation, *Journal of the American Institute of Planners*, 35(4), 216–24.

Burde, D. (2004a), 'International NGOs and best practices: The art of educational lending'. In G. Steiner-Khamsi, ed., *The Global Politics of Educational Borrowing & Lending*, New York, NY: Teachers College Press, 173–87.

Burde, D. (2004b), Weak state, strong community? Promoting community participation in post-conflict countries. *Current Issues in Comparative Education*, 6(2), 73–87.

Campaign for Quality Education (2007), 'Education in Pakistan: What works & why?' (Lahore: CQE).

Carney, S. (2009), *Negotiating Policy in an Age of Globalization: Exploring Educational 'Policyscapes' in Denmark, China and Nepal* (Denmark: Roskilde University).

Friere, P. (1970), *Pedagogy of the Oppressed*, New York: Continuum.

Fullan, M., and Stiegelbauer, S. (1991), *The New Meaning of Educational Change*. New York: Teachers College, Columbia University.

Hirschmann, A. O. (1970), *Exit, Voice, and Loyalty: Responses to Decline in Firms, Organizations, and States* (Cambridge, MA: Harvard University Press).

Khan, S. R. (2003), Participation via collective action in government and NGO schools in Pakistan, *Development in Practice*, 13(4).

Shaeffer, S. (1994), 'Participation for Educational Change: A synthesis of experience', Paris: International Institute for Educational Planning (IIEP).

Steiner-Khamsi, G. (2004), Blazing a trail for policy theory and practice, In G. Steiner-Khamsi, ed., *The Global Politics of Educational Borrowing and Lending* (New York, NY: Teachers College Press), 201–20.

UNESCO (2006), Decentralization of Education in Pakistan in Country Report at the UNESCO Seminar on EFA Implementation: Teacher and Resource Management in the Context of Decentralization (Islamabad: UNESCO).

Zafar, F., and Mashallah (2006), Community stakeholder consultations on Punjab Education Sector Reforms Programme (PESRP) in 3 southern districts of Punjab (Lahore: SAHE).

NOTE

1. School committees involving parents have gone by different names over time and across the provinces, for example, School Council (SC) in Punjab, Parent Teacher School Management Committees (PTSMC) in Balochistan, and previously Parent Teacher Association (PTA) in several provinces.

4

The Programme on School
Improvement: A Participatory as
Opposed to a Bureaucratic Approach
—Wilfred J. Perera

INTRODUCTION

THE EARLY DAYS

Democratic Socialist Republic of Sri Lanka has a recorded history that stretches from 600 BC. to the present day. The civilization and culture of the Indian subcontinent had considerable influence on the ancient Ceylon and the country's education received much of its impetus from the Buddhist fraternities. Learning and education were primarily a function and duty of royalty. Some Kings were great scholars themselves. Gradually, education was primarily imparted in village or temple schools. The teachers (Guru), guided by the needs of the community, determined the curriculum. Education was greatly honoured. Learning, without the guidance of a teacher was unthinkable. The teacher-pupil relationship was intensely personal and mutual with the teacher influencing the formation of pupil's character. Teacher most generously imparted the knowledge to the pupil. During this period, decision-making was highly decentralized and 'institutional' based.

THE COLONIAL PERIOD

A succession of outside powers starting from the Portuguese in 1505, then the Dutch and the British ruled the country until it gained independence in 1948. The colonial rulers geared the education policies to meet the political, economic, and social needs of their interest. Many writers argue that the education system created by the colonial powers was class based both in structure and spirit (Premaratne, 1991).

> The colonial rulers, whether they were Portuguese, the Dutch or the British, naturally were averse to anything that would strengthen the unity and solidarity of the native population The foreign rulers worked on the elements that would contribute to the weakening of the solidarity of the majority of the population, and to the creation of a class loyal to the foreign rulers only. (p. 4)

With the occupation of colonial powers, the formal schools were established and this was an imposition rather than a natural emergence. The educational administration became highly centralized preventing the locals from actively participating in educational affairs.

EFFORTS TOWARDS DEMOCRATIZATION OF EDUCATION

However, the country fares favourably with other countries in the region in enrolment rates at primary and secondary levels, mainly due to an educational policy adopted in the last six decades that emphasizes education as a right of every citizen. Three steps initiated by the first Sri Lankan minister of education in 1944 were almost revolutionary for the period. They were the introduction of a system of free education (from *Kindergarten* through *University*), and making the mother tongue the medium of instruction in all primary classrooms and opening of government central schools in rural areas to provide secondary education in English medium. These moves were aimed to remove the privileges and prejudices of education through equalization of educational opportunities and resulted in a large expansion of the school-going population. The democratization of education is pertinently expressed by Jayasuriya (1987, 4–5):

i. to make available to all children a good education free of charge, so that education ceases to be a market commodity purchasable only by the urban affluent;

ii. to make the national languages the media of instruction in place of English so that opportunities of higher education and lucrative employment open only to the microscopic number of the urban affluent would become available to others as well;

iii. to rationalize the school system, so that educational provision is adequate, efficient, and economical;

iv. to ensure that every child is provided with instruction in the religion of his/her parents and is not taught any other religion except with the concurrence of parents;

v. protect teachers from exploitation by managers of schools in as much as the profession of teaching has to be accorded due respect if schools are to be well-staffed with dedicated teachers; and

vi. to make adequate provision for adult education.

The 1944 initiatives was later followed from time to time with other measures, namely the provision of financial aid to the pupils of low income families who pass the Grade 5 scholarship examination; free text books, free uniforms, free mid-day meals, and subsidized travel with the intention of providing equal opportunities. The constitution of the country (1978) affirms the right to universal and equal access to education at all levels. Compulsory education became a priority in the 1990s with compulsory education regulations (Sri Lanka, Parliament, 1997). The report of the National Education Commission (1992) drew attention to the need for such legislation. Regulations 'made in furtherance of the National Policy of the State to provide education for all children' were enforced by a Gazette notification in November 1997 and came into operation on the 1 January 1998.

Anecdotal evidence reveals that non-enrolment rates in 1994 were 10.6 per cent for boys and 10.5 per cent for girls in the 5–14 age groups (Sri Lanka, Department of Census and Statistics, 1994). Data from the annual school census have indicated that dropout rates have declined rapidly since 1998. Retention rates in 2001 were 97.6 per cent at the end of primary education (96.9 per cent boys and 98.3 per cent girls), and 83.0 per cent at the end of junior secondary education (79.1 per cent boys and 86.3 per cent girls). Micro studies have found that out-of-school children in Sri Lanka are concentrated in low-income urban neighbourhoods, disadvantaged and remote villages and plantations. The reasons for non-attendance of children to school or reasons for leaving the school prematurely can be categorized either as school-related factors or as non school-related factors (L. Perera, Perera, & Wijeratne, 1997, 40):

School-Related Factors:
  i. Lack of teachers or teacher absenteeism
  ii. Lack of individual care
  iii. Poor quality in teaching
  iv. Non-qualified primary teachers teaching in primary grades
  v. Inability of the school to provide pleasant learning experiences
  vi. Rejection of admission by the schools for not having a birth certificate
  vii. Rejection of admission by the school for being overage
  viii. Harassment by other pupils
  ix. Lack of empathy on the part of (some) principals and teachers or harsh punishments

Non School-Related Factors:
  i. Economic difficulties
  ii. Family problems, which also make them work at home
  iii. Disabilities or ill-health of pupils
  iv. Students in the lower grades seek employment
  v. Absence of both parents and single parent
  vi. Distance to the school from home
  vii. Displacement

The positive measures stated above were not sufficient for the country to attain equity in education, as there are serious economic imbalances among families, as well as regions. The imbalances in respect of physical and human facilities in schools also have inhibited achieving the goal of equity in education. Deficiencies in the infrastructure of some schools and the problems regarding deployment of teachers in the school system have caused difficulties to achieve this target. The disparities among schools have widened and the education authorities were unable to arrest it. Sri Lanka's National Education Commission Report (2003) states that, the quality of education deteriorated due to disparities:

> The inequitable allocation of available resources widened disparities among ever expanding urban schools, rural schools and small schools that met the educational needs of disadvantaged communities, thereby reinforcing the social exclusion of the poor and resulting in the virtual extinction of many small schools in the 1990s. (p. 13)

The effective implementation of compulsory education regulations and the sensitization of officials, principals, and teachers of the right of every child to education, irrespective of socio-economic background, will make it possible to achieve the universalization of education. Lack of sustained economic growth resulted in a reduction in expenditure on education almost, limiting financial allocation to the maintenance of the system. A major proportion was for salaries of educational personnel. The expenditure for other quality inputs to enhance the learning-teaching processes, and creating learning environments, were proportionately negligible.

The Special Committee on Education in its proposals made in early forties envisaged the role of education as an instrument to reduce socio-economic inequalities (Ceylon, 1943). The proposal emphasized the need to 'weld the heterogeneous elements of the population into a nation' and to develop individual personality and character for effective living. The idea of social relevance thus declared by the then leaders of education we have failed to hold on to. We got to stress the need for committing to equality of educational opportunities. The economies of scale have resulted in the closure of the small disadvantaged schools. On the other hand, polarization of schools has occurred, the larger schools becoming large and smaller schools becoming smaller. The closure of schools has deprived some of even basic education. There is a continuing need for the policymakers and implementers to target extra attention for schools with concentrations of low socio-economic students as part of their responsibility. The government has declared its commitment to do so. This perspective raises a long-standing concern in which many sociologists of education have been interested: that of the relationship between education and social/economic inequalities. Though education was envisaged as an instrument to reduce socio-economic inequalities, it has only been able to eliminate extreme forms of inequalities, but not inequalities.

The over emphasis on the examinations and the way that schools are monitored and evaluated, do create competition within and between institutions. Such competition is increasingly becoming a significant characteristic of the present educational system. Within the present system, there are both winners and losers. On the other hand, too much academic emphasis and examination biased education does not help to create a natural environment. It was way back in the early eighties that the Education Proposals for Reform, stated the following as one of the four major weaknesses in the Sri Lankan education system (Sri Lanka, Ministry of Education, 1981):

> Schools have become more a medium for competition than institutions imparting sound education. Excessive emphasis on examinations has led to an impoverishment of the content of learning inside the class room and diminution of the importance of the most valuable outcomes that accrue from co-curricular activities. In serving primarily the scramble to reach the top, the needs of the majority who cannot get there are neglected. (Sri Lanka, Ministry of Education, 1981, ii)

As Udagama (2001) identifies, the situation did not improve; even after two decades the school system in Sri Lanka is highly structured and its curriculum is designed to cater to the 2 per cent who enter the universities.

> Our text book knowledge at the school level is geared only to higher education in a limited number of subjects in isolated divisions as arts, science, humanities, etc. is out-dated, limited and sterile. (p. 324)

The National Education Commission (2003) argues how narrow the educational thinking and implementation had been.

From a human development perspective, quality has facets other than academic excellence. The curriculum development process from the 1960s focused on what was perceived to be a democratic process of providing a minimum knowledge base and basic competencies for all students, through uniform curriculum materials presented in 'pre-packaged' courses and the state monopoly of textbooks distributed to all schools. Regrettably, this well-intentioned policy has resulted in the bureaucratization of curriculum development, the reinforcement of a traditional weakness in the education system of rote learning and lack of space for the expression of teacher and student initiative and creativity.

Acquisition of information became a paramount consideration, relegating to low priority the promotion of personality attributes such as critical thinking, problem solving, decision-making, team work, responsibility and human values that are essential to ensure effective performance in the work place as well as a multifaceted quality of life. Little was done widely to counter the examination dominated, competitive ethos of the learning environment through the curriculum and co-curricular activities. The juxtaposition of an examination oriented curriculum and an excessively competitive ethos and ineffective management within the school and the education system spawned also a private tuition industry which has become a parallel structure from primary to senior secondary education that militates against the development of a holistic educational process and the quality of education and living. (pp. 14–15)

The heavy bias on 'performance', which only takes the 'mental intelligence' into account not only undermines the value of education but also deprives a majority of students to be treated as equals. Schools are run on a factory model. In such a model, you exclude many because they do not fit that model. Under the factory model, schools set standards for grade levels; this emphasizes producing a standard product. If students are not up to the standards, then you have to put them aside. If education cannot shape or mould the future then it is of less value. One cannot accept the reality as it is but needs to alter it. Neill (1967), founder of one of the earliest 'progressive' or 'free discipline' schools stated that,

> In all countries, schools are built to educate the young. All the wonderful labs and workshops do nothing to help John or Peter or Ivan surmount the emotional damage and the social evils bred by the pressure on him from his parents, his schoolteachers, and the pressure of the coercive quality of education. (p. 139)

Are we aware of the market forces already in force that oppose the equality of opportunities? Those who promote market forces believe that competition leads to the enhancement of standards and the absence of competition to inefficiency and wastefulness. Here competition within and between institutions has become an increasingly significant characteristic of the present educational system. The marketization of education has been justified by its proponents on several grounds. These include that such changes will both enhance schools' performance and make them more accountable; that parents will be given more choices and be better informed; and that the overly bureaucratic and levelling-down tendencies of the former system will be removed and the value for money will be established as a major principle of funding, planning and curriculum development and innovation throughout the educational system. Most academics argue that managerialism, consumerism and marketization are essentially negative forces sustaining social inequality. There is a continuing need for educational systems to target extra attention for schools with concentrations of low socio-economic students as part of their responsibility.

DECENTRALIZATION OF EDUCATION AND ITS CONSEQUENCES

DECENTRALIZATION OF EDUCATION

In order to maximize efficiency and effectiveness of educational administration, the government restructured and reorganized its educational administrative machinery on several occasions by the creation of layers between the central ministry and the schools, but the efforts did not produce the desired outcomes. The process of decentralization was mainly carried out by establishing layers between the central ministry and the school. By doing this, it was expected to bring management closer to the schools. Though the geographical units of administration shifted from centre to the middle, the way the schools function, remained virtually unchanged.

By 1994, the layers above the school had increased to five, namely, the central ministry, provincial ministry, provincial department, zonal office, and the divisional office. In some areas, a sixth layer had been created, the district education office. The multiplication of layers had created problems for the school. Several studies have identified many issues (Cabral, 1989; K. G. Kulasena, 1989; Manoharan, 1988; W. J. Perera,

1987; W. J. Perera and Palihakkara, 1997; Silva et al., 1993, Sri Lanka, Staff College for Education Administration, 1986):

- Multiple controls of schools by the different layers, i.e. different offices issued different instructions on the same subject.
- Principals were called for meetings by two or three layers the same day.
- The officers, who were responsible to help schools to function better, themselves lacked skills and work ethics.
- Lack of coordination between the different layers.
- The layer closest to the school, the division, was overlooked by principals. Schools preferred to be controlled by the higher layer, ignoring one closest to them.
- Administrative procedures had become longer. There was duplication. The different layers often increased the work of the principals.

FUNCTIONS OF THE LAYERS ABOVE THE SCHOOL

The role and functions of each of these layers, stated in the documents, are as follows:

CENTRAL MINISTRY

The responsibility for education in Sri Lanka is shared by the central government and the provincial councils. The Ministry of Education (MoE) is the central government agency vested with the executive authority for implementation of policy in education. The Central Ministry supported by national agencies such as the National Institute of Education (NIE), Department of Examinations, Department of Educational Publications and the National Library Services Board, is responsible for:

- Laying down of national policy in education
- Monitoring the maintenance of standards in educational institutions
- Formulating the national curriculum and training of provincial/zonal trainers
- Managing of specified schools designated as national schools
- Teacher Education
- Public Examinations
- Development and delivery of educational material
- Development of libraries

The secretary to the ministry is the chief executive officer and is accountable to the minister of education. The secretary is closely supported by the additional secretaries, the directors, and the heads of departments.

PROVINCIAL MINISTRY

The Provincial Council Act of 1987, enacted on the Thirteenth Amendment to the Constitution, led to an island-wide devolution of political and administrative functions. There are nine provincial councils coterminous with the provinces and each has a provincial ministry of education with a minister in charge of the subject of education. The

Provincial Councils had come into being with very strong muscles of devolved power. The provincial secretary is the chief executive officer. The provision of facilities to all schools other than specified schools, appointment of principals to the provincial schools, implementation of non-formal education programmes, construction and maintenance of buildings, libraries, play grounds, procurement and distribution of educational aids and furniture are provincial functions.

PROVINCIAL DEPARTMENT

The schools in the province other the national schools are managed by the provincial departments of education, which is headed by the Provincial Director of Education (PDE). The provincial education office constitutes the apex of the provincial educational development structure. With the establishment of the provincial ministry, the role of the provincial education department and the provincial director were automatically reduced. The provincial director was made accountable to the provincial secretary.

ZONAL EDUCATION OFFICE

Considering the largeness and its multiplicity of functions, the provinces were divided into zones. The zones were established for the purpose of better administration and quality development. The zonal director is the chief executive officer of the zone and is supposed to strengthen the vital linkages and play a pivotal role in coordinating educational development. The zonal director has to directly liaise with the PDE, Divisional Directors of Education (DDE) and the schools and through the PDE with the NIE, MoE and other related agencies. He/she is assisted by a specialist team of Sri Lanka Education Administrative Service (SLEAS) officers. The zonal office is responsible for general administration of the schools in the zone. A zone generally consists of approximately 100 schools though there are exceptions. For instance, the Dehovita Zone, the zone with the largest number of schools has 217 schools, and the Mahaoya Zone has only 33 schools. The main functions of the of the zonal organization is to,

- Maintain, supervise and enhance the quality of teaching/ learning process at school level
- Coordinate and implement the in-service teacher training programmes in collaboration with the MoE, NIE, Department of Examinations, other departments and Universities
- Utilize effectively limited specialized personnel involved in Science, Mathematics, Technical subjects, English, and Inclusive Education
- Coordinate activities of foreign funded projects
- Coordinate teacher establishment activities
- Coordinate co-curricular, cultural, and library activities
- Collect and disseminate information

DIVISIONAL EDUCATION OFFICE

The Divisional Education Office established under the zone has the control of about 40 schools. Supervision of schools is entrusted to the DDE in charge of the divisional education office. He/she is primarily a field officer and is required to carry out school supervision, collect and disseminate information, and guide the master teachers in quality improvement activities. He/she will have a group of master teachers (ISAs).

THE CONSEQUENCES

The multiplication of layers resulted in more complex procedures and confusion about administrative responsibilities. The lack of clarity in roles and functions and the lack of a strong 'work ethic' in newly established layers hindered rather than supported school improvement. School practices and functioning remained almost unchanged though administrative authority was transferred from the centre to the periphery. The decentralization process has not increased the participation of principals, teachers, parents and members of the community in the decision-making process. The rigid bureaucracy and officialdom in the layers above the schools have often led to frustration, hostility, lack of enthusiasm, and suppression of creativity among principals and teachers (W. J. Perera, 2009).

Reluctance to move away from the centralized traditions that is in place for decades prevents the education system from responding to individual and local needs. Frequent changes in policies and programmes, ambiguity in objectives, cultural and social constraints, and lack of resources have all impeded the decentralization process. Diversifying the curriculum by adding pre-vocational subjects; introducing cluster schools; introducing school development boards were some of the other measures that were taken to decentralize education. In spite of all these moves, the government's stated intention to improve the education system through greater participation by local communities has rarely been met.

MOVE TOWARDS SCHOOL AUTONOMY

The Sri Lankan educational authorities had realized, even as far back as 1979, that schools can do better if they are not imprisoned by national directives. The 1979 report of the Education Reform Committee stated:

> There is no denying that some of our schools possess wide variety of talents and excellence. The uniform application of policy in all schools alike, however, has tended to heighten rather than heal the imbalances between the developed and under-developed sections of the system, while national standards in management, discipline and quality of education have remained stagnant. . . . The prescribing of uniform curricula, text books and examination standards on all-island scale has had adverse effects. It has succeeded not in educating all the children of the nation but in driving large numbers of children out of school long before they could achieve anything worthwhile from their education. Teachers, however sympathetic and understanding of the individual differences and capabilities of their pupils, have little freedom to deviate from the official examination requirements which at best will benefit only about 10% of the candidate population. (Sri Lanka, Ministry of Education, 1982)

The National Education Commission outlined the government's vision to give schools more autonomy.

School-based management has been accepted as an effective tool in the management of schools. It should specifically state the power, authority and responsibilities of the principal and the senior management group of the school. There shall be a council of management for each school comprising the principal, representatives of the staff, parents, past pupils and well-wishers and a departmental nominee to assist the principal in the formulation of policy and preparation of development plans and monitoring the implementation thereof. (Sri Lanka, National Education Commission, 1997, 27)

Several arguments were used to promote school autonomy in Sri Lanka (W. J. Perera, 1997, 1999, 2006; W. J. Perera, 2000). Here is a quote from W. J. Perera (2006):

First, the schools are submerged in a sea of macro programmes and tend to blindly follow the script sent from the centre. Although housed on school campuses, principals remain representatives of upper layers of the hierarchy. Secondly, the majority of schools have not identified the reservoir of potential energy, both human and physical, and hence these resources go under-utilized. They hardly attempt to develop their infrastructure or generate new resources. Thirdly, only a handful of schools attempt to link themselves with outside institutions to improve the quality of curricula. Schools need to take the initiative to provide more interesting and relevant curricula. Fourthly, there is a need to involve the school in school planning and resource management. Lastly, teacher development programmes currently focus on the skills of individual teachers rather than school-wide programmes and practices. Through school-based staff development programmes, congruence between staff development and school needs can be achieved. (p. 219)

In Sri Lanka, several schools proved that given the opportunity, they can achieve much. These achievements were strong enough to convince those who were either opposing or indifferent to the school autonomy movement to think otherwise. Though it is worth mentioning the achievements of many schools, in this paper we will present extracts from five cases (Walasbedda, Meegasthenna, Pushpadana, Pallethalavinna, and Isipathana) here.

1. **Walasbedda School** (remote village school in the Uva Province with 210 students and 12 Teachers)

For a time, Walasbedda had no drinking water as the school sits on a hill. Authorities studied the site and allocated Sri Lankan rupees 50,000 (USD 443) for a water project. Workers started digging 40 ft. below the ground, but they soon hit a rock, which eventually caused the engineers to abandon the project. One day Mr Ratnayake (the principal of the school) saw a child drinking muddy water from a water puddle. He was determined to find drinking water, so and with the help of a few parents, he started drilling the rock. There was more discouragement than encouragement, but the team did not give up. They continued to drill the rock, and weeks later, they found water about 60 ft. from the mouth of the well. Today, water is distributed to meet the needs of people and vegetation in the school premises. (W. J. Perera, Wijesinghe, and Wijethunge, 2007, 30–1)

2. **Meegasthenna Maha Vidyalaya** (remote village school in the Sabaragamuwa Province with 205 students and 19 Teachers)

The teachers normally work 33 to 38 periods (the maximum is 40 per week) a week. In addition, other duties are delegated to them. Furthermore, the staff attends to the in-service seminars and they also involve themselves in many community affairs. There are three associations in the village called.

  i. Village Development Society;
 ii. Temple Development Society; and
iii. Youth Society.

Most of the teachers are members of at least one of these. The principal is the chief adviser and the deputy principal is the President of the Village Development Society. They are mainly concerned with the development of infrastructure facilities in the village. The Temple Development Society attempts to create a religious environment in the village through many activities. The principal is the chief adviser in the Youth Society. The dedication and self-motivation of teachers is evident from the examples below:

  i. A teacher brought her sick child to the school and allowed him to rest in the staff room and worked in the classes so that the school children were not deprived of their lessons.

 ii. A pregnant teacher has visited a child who has not come to the school for many days, on the way to the school in the morning. She managed to bring two children to the school who had been absent.

iii. Most of the teachers stay after the school for extra work on their own until evening.

According to a parent: 'These teachers are Gods; we can talk about anything with the teachers. We work as a family, when there is a national festival they come to our places with sweets and parents. If there is funeral in the community, the school staff participates. (W. J. Perera et al., 2007)

3. Pushpadana Balika Maha Vidyalaya (Large city school in the Central Province with 1,718 students and 100 teachers)

The work in the school is delegated. Two deputy principals support the principal in finance administration academic, extra-curricular and hostel management. There are also three assistant principals. Daily functioning of the school is well organized and is smoothly carried out. Morning assembly is conducted by the students. The communication system is effective and announcements are delivered thrice a day: in the afternoon in Sinhala. The teachers make the announcements and the principal makes only special announcements. An exemplary supervision programme is implemented internally, which supports the daily functioning of the school smoothly.

The management committee consists of the principal, assistant principals, deputy principals, sectional heads and prefect of games. It meets once a month to discuss school activities. There are other committees established for various activities. The parents and the teachers can be committee members. There are several committees to improve areas such as: sports, hostel, school management, discipline, uniforms, special projects, canteen, aesthetics, entertainment, technical, agriculture, environment, vehicles, bands, religious activities, sewing, languages scholarships, photography buildings etc. Once a year members change, generally every teacher must sit on at least one committee. Parents and students are also members of some committees. (W. J. Perera et al., 2007)

4. Pallethalavinna School (Village school in the Central Province with 18 teachers and 648 students)

The link between school and the community is very high and effective. There is a major community contribution towards school development. Parents and other well-wishers have provided many facilities to the school. The principal has built very close relationship with the community and he made them aware about the school vision, mission and objectives. They know the school targets and help the school to achieve those targets. The strategies, which are used to get community support, could be seen through some initiated activities and are given below:

- S. D. S. official committee consists of 15 parents (one parent from each class) and the principal, two deputies and one teacher (as treasurer).

- This committee participates in the decision-making in internal school management.

- Once a month they meet and discuss school matters.

- Sometimes the committee suggests some activities and principal listens to them. If it is in congruence with the school annual plan or development plan then the school takes up that idea and implements it. The parents have suggested that the class circles should be held once a month, rather than once a term, and this is now being done.

- The items, which are included in the annual plan, are organized by the parents in the given class.

- Class circles conduct discussion on students' progress, children's learning difficulties, classroom development, special projects for student development and school development.

- The principal also participates in every class circle.

- There is a special society called 'parents' welfare foundation. Its role is to conduct the Teachers' Day, take a actions to start new Grade 6, organize a health clinic, maintain the children's park, the aesthetic unit and sound system, provide equipment for the administrative unit, maintain water supply system etc. (W. J. Perera et al., 2007)

5. Isipathana College (City school in the Western Province with 4,296 students and 100 teachers)

The principal appreciates autonomy because he is able to do things easily and quickly to accomplish the aims of the school. The principal is of the opinion that for school development the school must have freedom to take decisions. Now a days, schools are deprived of development, as principals have no authority to work freely. Principals, deputy principals, school development societies take decisions on financial matters. Administrative and academic decisions are taken by the principal, deputy and the senior management team. The principal, deputy principals, SDS, and physical resource management committee take decisions on resources.

In this school, teacher recruitment decisions are taken by the principal. There is a circular on teacher recruitment and teacher allocation issued by the MOE. If a school recruits a teacher, beyond the given cadre, the principal has to pay for that teacher. (W. J. Perera et al., 2007)

The move towards school autonomy in Sri Lanka was influenced by four main factors. First, by the performance of Sri Lankan schools that were already demonstrating the above characteristics, especially in the rural sector. They were making changes from within. Second was the government's commitment to empower grassroots. Third was the conviction professionals. And fourth was the influence of the international School-Based Management (SBM) movement coupled with appreciation from donor agencies.

The World Bank (2005) through the Education Sector Development Programme supported and promoted the Programme on School Improvement (PSI) movement. In its project appraisal document, World Bank (2005) highlights PSI as a key policy initiative and identifies it as a balanced control model of SBM.

> Devolving power and responsibility to the school level, through the adoption of a balanced control model of school-based management called the Programme for School Improvement (PSI) is a key policy reform. . . . The balanced control model spreads administrative power evenly between principals, teachers and members of local communities. The model will be pilot tested in selected zones . . . and if successful scaled up to the national level later. (p. 55)

In a subsequent mission in 2009 at an evaluation meeting, the institutionalization of Programme on School Improvement (PSI) is appreciated in the following way:

> It was proposed at the meeting that a sense of ownership, based on a realization that PSI was not something imported but was a response to the needs of Sri Lankan schools, would contribute to the institutionalization and sustainability of the programme. Specific activities to support strengthening of the PSI concept identified at the meeting included the development of networks of school principals and a more dynamic role for the zonal officers. (World Bank, 2009, 55)

Programme on School Improvement (PSI)

The Programme on School Improvement (PSI), the Sri Lankan version of school-based management was introduced to schools of eight zones in 2006, to schools of another nine zones in 2007, schools of further eighteen zones in 2008, schools of ten more zones in 2009 and schools of another seventeen zones in 2010. It is to be expanded to schools of the rest of the zones in the country in 2011 (Sri Lanka. Ministry of Education, 2010). PSI undoubtedly, is the most ambitious and widespread organizational reform in educational administration in the recent times in the country. In the PSI, schools are given a degree of autonomy in the areas of planning, teaching-learning process, co-curricular activities, staff development and the maintenance and development of the school plant. The emphasis of PSI will be to increase flexibility in the internal functions of the school, increase efficiency in the school's use of resources and make the school more responsive to the potential of each child so that they will become useful citizens. PSI acknowledges that genuine renewal can be achieved only if schools make a conscious effort to diagnose their organizations and initiate essential organizational changes. The PSI promotes:

- involving community representatives in school planning and encouraging schools to respond effectively to the needs of parents and the demands of the community thus strengthening the partnership between teachers and the school community; schools to use resources efficiently to design development plans to achieve school objectives with more focused attention on the aims of education;

- a coherent and coordinate approach to all aspects of planning and to deliver school development programmes more effectively;
- academic independence of schools;
- congruence between staff training and school needs thus improving staff development which leads to higher student achievement; and
- innovation and change.

In the long term, PSI will result in greater transparency of what is going on in schools and there will be more equity in the distribution of resources. If schools are to work with more autonomy, it is believed that several functions carried out by the layers above the school need to be delegated to the school level.

It is clearly anticipated that standards of education in schools will rise as a result of the introduction of PSI as it enables them to implement the curriculum through approaches best suited to their resources and students. Considerable progress has been made by Sri Lanka in its efforts to support school autonomy movement in the recent times. In order to achieve equity and improve quality, the Ministry of Education (MoE) introduced a policy framework, namely the 'Education Sector Development Framework & Programme (ESDFP)' for a period of 2006–10 (Sri Lanka, Ministry of Education, 2006b). Several steps were taken by the MoE to improve quality in the teaching-learning process. Autonomy was given to schools in the procurement of educational quality inputs and disbursement of funds for higher-order processes (Sri Lanka, Ministry of Education, 2002). Special programmes, projects, and activities for 'higher-order processes aiming improvement of the quality of primary and secondary education have indeed revitalized the teaching learning process. Moreover, schools are empowered to access supplementary financial allocations (Sri Lanka, Ministry of Education, 2006a). School also receives funds for school-based staff development. Staff appraisal will enable the school to identify the strengths to be developed and weaknesses to be addressed and to negotiate personal and professional development needs. Positive, committed parent-school relations play a significant role in student outcomes. Under PSI, procedures are being established and practiced to involve parents actively.

School-Based Management (SBM) is to be introduced to the schools through the creation of a School Development Committee (SDC) and a School Management Team (SMT).

CONSTITUTION OF THE SDC

The SDC (School Development Committee) would consist of teacher/parent/past pupil representatives and a representative of the education authority. The principal shall function as the chairperson of the SDC throughout his/her period of office in the school. The deputy principal (the person who heads the school in the absence of the principal) will be the deputy chairperson. In schools where there are three or less than three teachers, all staff shall constitute the SDC. In other schools, the number in the SDC will be decided according to criteria given below.

No. of teachers 4 to 10:   3 teachers (including the head and the deputy)

No. of teachers 11 to 80:   4 teachers (including the head and the deputy)

No. of teachers above 80:   5 teachers (including the head and the deputy)

The SDC will have three to five parent representatives according to the student population.

No. of students less than 500:   3 parents
No. of students 501 to 1,000:   4 parents
No. of students more than 1,000:   5 parents

In addition, there are three past pupil representatives and a representative of the education authority in the SDC.

SELECTION OR APPOINTMENT OF/TO THE SDC

- **Teacher Category:** The members of the SDC other than the principal and the deputy will be elected at a staff meeting held for this purpose. The principal shall convene and supervise the election process. The quorum of the above meeting shall not be less than two-third of the total number of teachers. A teacher member once transferred to another school ceases to be a member.

- **Parent Category:** Three parents shall be elected to represent the parents in the SDC at the annual general meeting of the School Development Society (SDS). Members of the academic staff of the school shall not be eligible to be elected as parent representatives. The principal shall supervise the election process. A parent ceases to be a member when he/she is no longer a parent of a student of that school.

- **Past Pupil Category:** Three past pupils shall be elected to represent the Past Pupils' Association (PPA) in the SDC. No members of the academic staff of the school shall be selected to represent the PPA. The principal shall supervise the election process. When there is no established Past Pupils Association (PPA) in the school the principal shall summon a meeting of the Past Pupils of the school, giving fourteen days prior notice of such a meeting, and select the representatives.

- **Representative of the Education Authority:** The zonal director will identify and allocate one member of the zonal staff, to each of the provincial schools within the zone and the secretary, central ministry of education, in consultation with the provincial directors of education will allocate one officer to the national schools, thus making strong links to improve communication, transparency and accountability. This officer will visit schools regularly, participate in the SDC meetings and in the school affairs, identify areas of strength and weakness and provide support to the school as required. He/she will be the link between the school and the educational authority. In allocating this representative to the school his/her authority, ability, and acceptance will be considered. One officer may be made responsible to a number of schools depending on the availability of officers in the zone.

ELIGIBILITY FOR SELECTION TO THE SDC

The following persons will not be eligible or will disqualify from being selected, elected, nominated, or continue to function if he/she,

- is a member of parliament/provincial council/local political authority;
- is less than eighteen years of age;
- is declared to be of unsound mind, under any law;
- is declared insolvent or bankrupt;
- is a person on whom a sentence of imprisonment, including suspended sentence imposed by a court of law for a period of more than six months;
- is absent from three consecutive meetings of the SDC without a valid reason.

TERM OF OFFICE OF MEMBERS OF THE SDC

The term of office of the members of the SDC other than the principal, the deputy, and the representative of the education authority will be three years. They may be re-elected only twice. Members of the SDC other than the principal, the deputy and the representative of the education authority may resign from his/her membership at any time giving fourteen days prior notice. The principal shall function as the chairperson of the SDC throughout his/her period of office in the school. The deputy principal will be a member as long as he/she does so. The representative of the education authority will be a member as long as he/she is authorized to be so by the appointing authority. If a member of the teacher category or parent category or past pupil category disqualifies to be a member of the SDC, the principal may get appropriate bodies to nominate a representative until those bodies formally select a member.

MEETINGS

The SDC shall meet at least once a month. In its first meeting, the SDC will select a secretary. The secretary will maintain records and correspondence. When the occasion demands more, frequent meetings may be held. One of the regular meetings may be held as the annual general meeting to sanction plans, annual accounts, approve the annual budget, and review progress. A special meeting may be summoned by the secretary of the SDC on the request of the principal or on a written request of the one-third of the members of the committee given one-week notice. The quorum of the SDC meetings shall be two-third of the members of the committee.

SCHOOL MANAGEMENT TEAM (SMT)

This is a team established within the school. All the school-staff members of the SDC, the other deputy principals, assistant principals, and sectional heads will constitute the SMT.

FUNCTIONS OF THE SDC AND SMT

There will be delegation of authority to the SDC in identified areas now held by the zonal office. SMT will work very closely together with the SDC. The SDC in consultation with the SMT may appoint any other subcommittees for school improvement and decide upon tasks according to the requirements of the school. These subcommittees may consist of teachers, parents, past pupils, and resource persons drawn from the community.

EXPECTED OUTCOMES OF PSI

a. Schools are required to prepare a five-year school development plan and an annual operational plan. Planning offers schools the opportunity to take initiatives, to develop an identity and to ensure a more secure future. Development of the five-year school development plan and an annual operational plan is operational from 2006. The schools were given a booklet, 'Instructions for School Level Planning.' (Sri Lanka, Ministry of Education, 2006c) The plans are submitted to the zonal office by the provincial schools and to the central ministry by the national schools. A zonal team/central ministry team reviews the plan and resources are allocated to each school, based upon a needs analysis against previously identified criteria.

b. Schools will carry out a wide range of curricular and co curricular activities and specific programmes for personality development of children. It is clearly anticipated that standards of education in schools will rise as a result of the introduction of PSI as it enables them to implement the curriculum through approaches best suited to their resources and students. The schools have to develop mechanisms to better utilize the quality input grants. PSI schools are encouraged to engage in a wide range of curricular and co-curricular activities.

Increasing the range and quality of co-curricular activities will improve performance of students. Improved interaction with the wider community could result in the inclusion of field trips, guest speakers, and work visits. Former pupils and current parents may have the expertise and knowledge, which could contribute to the co-curriculum. Careful planning of the timetable is essential to the learning process when each day provides a balanced and varied experience of academic, aesthetic, practical, and physical activities. In the preparation of the school time-table, national standards have to be maintained, for example the total number of teaching hours in each subject and the minimum number of teaching hours per teacher, whilst ensuring sufficient flexibility to accommodate the particular needs of students and reflect local needs and employment opportunities.

c. There will be more congruence between school needs and teacher development. Staff appraisal will enable the school to identify the strengths to be developed and weaknesses to be addressed and to negotiate personal and professional development needs. Since schools will identify areas for development, both individual and collective staff training needs, the congruence between staff professional needs and those of the school will improve, to the benefit of student achievement.

d. Schools will proactively involve themselves in the maintenance and development of the school plant. The schools may initiate construction work and repairs as deemed necessary for the development and effective functioning of the school. The significance here is that schools will move the emphasis from crisis management to planned management of the school plant. Medium and long-term developments to the infrastructure will be reflected in the 5-year school development plan.

THE PRESENT SCENARIO

Before the zones were established two to three decades ago, the Sri Lanka education system was quite different.

1. First, the gap of professionalism between the school personnel (teachers and principals) and officers in the above layers have reduced remarkably. Teachers are more qualified than they were twenty years ago. A fair number have even obtained Masters qualifications.

2. Second, the revolution in communications has made the traditional flow of communication from upper layers to the school less meaningful, as access to information is possible through websites etc.

3. Third, Specific projects that focus on the development of selected schools have become less effective and ethically questionable. There is a growing belief that all schools need attention; all children be given fair chances.

4. Fourth, the local people/officers have less passion with the nationally driven programmes.

The zonal education office is at the frontline of management of public schools. They are responsible for ensuring that the school meets the minimum service standards. They have a role in identifying schools' strengths and areas to be improved including teacher development and teacher establishment. They are supposed to supervise and advise schools. This implies that all the zones need to have the capacity to identify school standards and performance. The zones need to have the staff with necessary skills to provide technical support and the management capacity to organize and support teacher establishment and development. Capacity of the zones to support school quality improvement differs from zone to zone depending on the leadership, available cadre, and professional skills of the officers. Not all zones have equal capacities in doing so. Especially those in remote and difficult areas do not have the sufficient cadre.

CHANGES IN THE STRUCTURE AND ROLES

Any major reform needs to build in appropriate structures. As identified by the studies, the layers above the schools were not providing the kind of support that was needed. This raised the need for the policy makers to look at the issue more closely and suggest the necessary structural changes as appropriate. The evidence elsewhere shows that where structures are simple, responsibility and accountability become clearer and there is less confusion. Therefore in PSI, structures are kept simple. In examining as to how the zonal officers support and guide the schools in improving themselves in an environment where schools are given a fair degree of autonomy also calls for the consideration of changes in organizational structures at different levels, the cultural values, and strategic imperatives. The zonal officers and school staff are expected to become associates and join together to transform the school to provide quality education. For schools to improve their quality, the zone has to play an active and creative role. They have to trust, empower, support, encourage, and enable the school to realize its optimum potential. While doing so, they also have to make demands on the school. Support without pressure might let the schools float; while pressure without support will alienate the schools from the zone. There is continuous dialogue as to how we could achieve this desirable educational change. We are aware that this organizational change has to be viewed in the broader context of societal change. At present whatever proclaimed by the layers above the school has to be absorbed and implemented by schools. Innovations and changes, are created and nurtured outside the school and then introduced to schools.

The approaches of SDCs are expected to be anagogical. It builds on using already acquired knowledge and experience. It is self-motivated and self-directed. It is based on applying learning to real life situations, thus finding solutions to issues and problems. It is based on team work, mutual understanding and as such, consistency and coherence to development work. The members while working together in implementing changes may learn and identify further insights and better ways of doing things. The SDCs in almost all the cases consist of heterogeneous groups. The committee has conceptual thinkers, practitioners, young and old, men and women, rich and poor. This heterogeneity may be advantageous for improved performance as highlighted by Kakabadse, Ludlow, and Vinnicombe (1987).

Heterogeneous groups have members whose backgrounds, experiences, values, and beliefs are diverse. Those groups are likely to be able to make higher quality decisions, which have greater acceptance among those affected by them. They are likely to display greater creativity and innovation and possess, inherently in their composition, the characteristics necessary to produce enhanced group performance. Whether or not creativity materializes is a function of the members' commitment, willingness to manage internal conflict, the application of their technical and interpersonal skills and ability—in fact, the group dynamics which occur as a result of members, interactions (p. 158).

Talking, deliberating, and working together create constructive networks and commitments grow. Lieberman and Grolnick (1998) are of the view that networks of people build commitment.

Networks build commitment in direct proportion to the extent to which members feel they have a voice in creating and sustaining a group in which their professional identity and interests are valued. The ways in which people are brought together affects the interplay between participants' developing relationships with each other and with the ideas that will form the basis of their work. Collaborative relationships build trust, essential to the development of ideas, and ideas build network interest and participation as they themselves are transformed by the participants (p. 715).

At present school effectiveness seemed to have a narrow approach without penetrating to the point of impact. The school-based team has to re-conceptualize what is meant by a successful school. The school and the office have to engage in the growth of mutuality. The quality of dialogue has to mark the genuine empowerment of teachers. The zonal office is to perceive that they are working with schools and not on them. Very often teachers are told and not heard. They are seen as a part of the problem but they are in fact the solution. The team is not simply a group that reflects but who systematically review, evaluate, and improve. This involves a serious commitment to the task of deliberating, identifying, challenging and contributing to the renewal of what schools do. The development of whole-school policies is necessary for wider development. It entails continuous dialogue and debate between staff, learning to listen and respect one another. Schools need to have the right climate and adequate opportunities to talk issues through.

The initiators have been concerned on the sustainability of PSI at zonal and school level. The reform involves a shift in purpose, structure, and the nature of work—functions—of the zonal office/officers. Small-scale studies reveal that, SDC members (mainly the teachers, parents, and past pupil members) lack understanding of the concept, the authority, and the functions of the SDCs (Nedungamuwa, 2009). Though the architects of PSI expect the principal and zonal members to educate the other members, the cascade model has not been effective. Once zones are selected by the provincial authorities to introduce PSI, the funder fathers visit the zone and spend three days. The principals in all the schools are met as a group for one full day and all the officers of the zone for one full day. Schools have varied characteristics. While interviewing and sharing with principals and local educational administrators it was evident that the success of the reform or lack of it, heavily depend on the attitudes of the personnel. In the PSI, the SDC members will meet once a month, the zonal representative in addition to her/his participation at the SDC meeting will spend a day or more in a given month in the school. Participation rate of members at SDC meetings were not satisfactory.

There has to be constructive dialogue in which all parties are free to voice their fears concerns and hopes. Parents are often the driving force to motivate school staff. Welcoming parents into a classroom and school is vital to having them to be part of the team for school improvement. The Sri Lankan teachers were hesitant to accept the involvement of community and to give them ownership. This attitudinal and cultural aspect may take time to change. It is also difficult to change this from outside and change has to come from within. School-based concepts have not yet been well perceived and understood. The support and supervision services provided by zones to the schools has been continuously investigated in detail using multiple approaches. Exactly how zonal offices provide services to their clients, primarily teachers, and principals is a key concern. A collaborative partnership between the zonal authorities and the school community will enable school improvement efforts sustain. The participation of the stakeholders in the school improvement process enables development projects to be tailor-made to the specific context of the school. The need for multiple involvements and specially of families, in school reform is thus presented by Nieto (1998).

It is becoming increasingly clear that substantive changes in education will occur only through reformation of the entire learning environment. This includes not only curriculum and materials, but also institutional norms, attitudes and behaviours of staff, counselling services, and the extent to which families are welcomed in schools (p. 431).

REFERENCES

Cabral, L. M. C. (1989), *Kegalle After Management Reforms in Education*.

Ceylon (1943), *Report of the Special Committee on Education: Sessional Paper XXIV of 1943* (Colombo: Government of Ceylon Press).

Jayasuriya, J. E. (1987), 'The democratization of education', Contribution of Dr C. W. W. (Kannangara Maharagama: National Institute of Education).

Kakabadse, A., Ludlow, R., and Vinnicombe, S. (1987), *Working in Organizations* (London: Penguin).

Kulasena K. G. (1989), 'A study of introducing educational innovation through management practices', A preliminary draft presentation of the Ratnapura District (Maharagama: National Institute of Education).

Lieberman, A, and Grolnick, M. (1998), 'Educational reform networks: Changes in the forms of reform', in A. Hargreaves, A. Lieberman, M. Fullan and D. Hopkins, eds., *International Handbook of Educational Change: Part Two* (Great Britain: Kluwer Academic Publishers), 710–29.

Manoharan, S. S. (1988), Decentralization in the Baticaloa district.

Nedungamuwa, D. M. D. K. (2009), 'A Study on the Operational Behavior of School Development Committees at the Initial Stage of Implementing the Programme for School Improvement', (PGDEM Dissertation), CELD, NIE, Meepe.

Neill, A. S. (1967), 'Summerhill education vs standard education', In L. Jackson and M. Jackson, eds., *Message and Medium: A Course in Critical Reading* (London: Hodder and Stoughton), 137–9.

Nieto, S. (1998), 'Cultural differences and educational change in a socio-political context', in A. Hargreaves, A. Lieberman, M. Fullan and D. Hopkins, eds., *International Handbook of Educational Change: Part One* (Great Britian: Kluwer Academic Publishers), 418–39.

Perera, L; Perera, Wilfred J., and Wijeratne, S. U. (1997), 'The management of teachers: Improving primary teacher provision through better management, the Sri Lankan experience'.

Perera, Wilfred J. (1987), 'Move towards decentralization: The Sri Lankan experience in educational administration'.

Perera, Wilfred J. (1997), 'Changing schools from within—A management intervention for improving school functioning in Sri Lanka', (Paris: IIEP/UNESCO).

Perera, Wilfred J. (1999), 'Move towards school autonomy: Can Sri Lanka to achieve it through school based management', *Economic Review.*

Perera, Wilfred J. (2006), 'Efforts towards decentralization: Ideology vs the reality—The Sri Lanakan case', in C. Bjork, ed., *Educational Decentralization—Asian Experiences and Conceptual Contributions* (Springer), 211–23.

Perera, Wilfred J. (2009), 'How Can the Administration Help School Functioning Move from Bureaucracy to Collegiality?', Paper presented at the ANTRIEP seminar on successful education systems for a changing world: Monitoring and evaluating the effectiveness of education systems' (Shanghai Normal University): Shanghai.

Perera, Wilfred J. (2000), 'School autonomy through school-based management' *The Case of Sri Lanka Improving School Efficiency: The Asian Experience* (Paris: UNESCO, IIEP), 33–74.

Perera, Wilfred J., Wijesinghe, K. T., and Wijethunge, I. W. (2007), Successful school management—A series of training modules and case studies prepared by ANTRIEP (Paris: IIEP-UNESCO).

Perera, Wilfred J., and Palihakkara, H. (1997), 'Decentralization in education: The Sri Lankan experience', In R. Govinda, ed., *Decentralization of Educational Management—Experiences from South Asia* (Paris: UNESCO, IIEP).

Premaratne, B. (1991), 'Free Education redefined: Education in defense of freedom', Dr C. W. W. Kannangara (Maharagama: National Institute of Education).

Silva, G. N., Ginige, L., Gunasekara, S., Perera, Wilfred J., Ranasinghe, R. H. H., and Balasooriya, A. S. (1993), 'Decentralization in education: A study problem rising out of a new provincial set-up' (Maharagama: NIE).

Sri Lanka, Department of Census and Statistics (1994), Demographic Survey (Colombo: Sri Lanka).

Sri Lanka, Ministry of Education (1981), 'Education Proposals for Reform—in Collaboration with Ministry of Higher Education & the Ministry of Youth Affairs and Employment' (Colombo: Government of Sri Lanka).

Sri Lanka, Ministry of Education (1982), 'Towards Relevance in Education: Report of the Education Reforms Committee—1979' (Colombo: Government of Sri Lanka).

Sri Lanka, Ministry of Education (2002), *Circular no. HRD/ PPM/2002/30* (Colombo: Government of Sri Lanka).

Sri Lanka, Ministry of Education (2006a), Circular no. ED/3/37/12/16 (Colombo: Government of Sri Lanka).

Sri Lanka, Ministry of Education (2006b), Education Sector Development Framework & Programme, (2006–2010)', (Colombo: Government of Sri Lanka).

Sri Lanka, Ministry of Education (2006c), 'Instructions for School Level Planning', (Colombo: Government of Sri Lanka).

Sri Lanka, Ministry of Education (2010), Circular No. 2010/35—'Programme on School Improvement: A Supplement', (Colombo: Government of Sri Lanka).

Sri Lanka, National Education Commission (1992), 'The First Report of the National Education Commission', (Colombo: Government of Sri Lanka Press).

Sri Lanka, National Education Commission (1997), 'Reforms in General Education', (Colombo: Government of Sri Lanka Press).

Sri Lanka, National Education Commission (2003), 'Envisioning Education for Human Development: Proposals for a National Policy Framework on General Education in Sri Lanka', (Colombo: Government of Sri Lanka Press).

Sri Lanka, Parliament (1997), 'Compulsory Education Regulations —1997' (Colombo: Government of Sri Lanka Press).

Sri Lanka, Staff College for Education Administration (1986), 'An Impact Evaluation of the Pilot Project on the Decentralization of Regional Administration of 1984 in Kegalle, Chilaw and Matara Districts in Sri Lanka: A Case Study', (Maharagama: Government of Sri Lanka).

Udagama, P. (2001), 'Colonialism globalization and education in reforming education', (Maharagama: NIE).

World Bank (2005), 'Project appraisal document: Education sector development project', (Colombo: World Bank, 15 Nov. 2005).

World Bank (2009), 'Education sector development framework and programme supervision and implementation support mission, Aide Memoire', (Colombo: World Bank, Aug. 2009), 10–21.

5

The Politics of Citizenship and Difference in Sri Lankan Schools

—Birgitte Refslund Sørensen

Sri Lanka has for the past three decades been undergoing fast and profound economic, political, social, and cultural transformations caused by globalization and violent conflicts between the government and various political groups. These processes affect the constitution of Sri Lanka as state, nation, and society with implications for how different population groups can imagine and identify themselves and others, and for the rights and duties of different groups. The formation of citizens in response to new challenges and opportunities takes place in many institutional and social settings. Sri Lanka has made huge investments in the construction of schools and training of teachers to make education available and accessible to all children regardless of socio-economic background and region of residence.

Today the net enrolment in primary education is close to 100 per cent, and children spend many hours every day in school, attending private tuition classes, and doing homework. This makes the school a fundamental institutional site for the ongoing cultural formation and disciplining of children as citizens.

There are several questions regarding education in Sri Lanka: What kinds of citizens are created in the schools? What kinds of skills and knowledge are learned? What kind of social and moral values are taught? What views of diversity and difference are produced in the schools today? This chapter explores what kinds of citizens the Sri Lankan nation-state has attempted to create through education and how school children belonging to Sri Lanka's two largest minorities: the Tamils and the Muslims, construct their citizenship in the school environment, where they are concurrently exposed to the often contradictory official discourses of textbooks and the social memories and interests of their communities. Underlying this inquiry is a concern about whether education in Sri Lanka is a positive and constructive force contributing to social development and peace, or whether it is a largely negative and destructive force that fosters growing inequality and social conflicts (Bush & Saltarelli, 2000; Davis, 2006; Smith & Vaux, 2003).

My use of the terms *citizen* and *citizenship* is inspired by recent anthropological explorations of the subject, which share a critique of state-centred, legal definitions of citizenship as the basis for social analysis. In political science, citizenship is commonly treated as a relationship between the state and the individual, and emphasis is on the individual's political and civil rights as a member of a nation-state. The anthropological perspective instead considers citizenship a notion or idea that is ascribed different meanings and significance in particular historical, cultural, social, and political contexts, and that is evolving in response to changing worlds (Jeffery, 2005; Kabeer,

2005; Stewick & Levinson, 2007). The anthropological perspective often also assigns particular importance to its construction from below, captured in concepts such as 'cultural citizenship' (Rosaldo, 1994), 'societal citizenship' (Kabeer, 2005), and 'folk paradigms of justice.' (Fraser, 2003) The advantage of this approach is that it connects an abstract concept to people's concrete experiences, concerns, and aspirations as they emerge. They are given meaning and expressed within particular social worlds. However, for it to remain useful as an analytical term it is necessary to define its core content that crosscuts the many localized versions. On the basis of ethnographic research in different parts of the world, Kabeer (2005) identifies certain values that all people associate with citizenship, and she suggests that these may therefore serve as a way of delineating the concept. One value is 'justice', which focuses on when it is considered fair to treat people equally and when decisions should be based on differences. The second value is 'recognition', which addresses both the intrinsic worth of all human beings and the respect for their differences. The third value is 'self-determination', which deals with people's ability to exercise some degree of control over their own lives. Finally, there is 'solidarity', which considers the capacity to identify with others and to act in unity with them in their claims for justice and recognition. Kabeer (2005) suggests that the four dimensions of citizenship are often interrelated in people's lives, but she does not elaborate further on this.

Departing from a similar preoccupation, Fraser (2003) argues that virtually every experience of subordination and injustice contains elements of both redistribution and recognition, which should be united in a single theoretical framework that stresses their inter-relationship and interpenetration. Thus, she proposes a 'perspectival dualism' in which the two categories exist as co-fundamental and mutually irreducible aspects of justice (Fraser, 2003, 3). Fraser's perspectival dualism can help us better comprehend how education generates complex experiences of justice and injustice and enhance our understanding of how notions of citizenship emerge and develop within the educational field.

Ong (1996) likewise advocates for an anthropological approach to citizenship that recognizes the concept's social embeddedness. According to Ong (1996), this implies that definitions of citizenship inevitably take place within asymmetrical relations of power and are objects of continual contestation. With inspiration from Foucault, Ong defines citizenship as 'a cultural process of "subject-ification", or subject-making, which entails the dual dimensions of "self-making" and "being-made".' (1996, 737) Constructions of citizens, in other words, are never the direct result of nation-state projects or of the subjects' own efforts, but are mediated outcomes. In continuation of her problematization of uni-dimensional analyses that tend to exaggerate the agency and control of either state or subject, Ong (1996) suggests that attention be paid to the role of civil institutions and social groups as part of a wider governance structure. (p. 738)

The social setting for the formation of citizenship in Ong's view is not simply a context, nor is it just a container of localized meanings of citizenship. The social setting is a complex constellation of actors with vested interests and uneven access to power that engage actively and vehemently in the production of citizens. The above theoretical conceptualizations of citizenship constitute my starting point for exploring what kinds of citizens are created within Sri Lankan schools today.

The chapter is divided into three parts. The first part discusses the development of Sri Lanka's education policies and priorities from a historical perspective and shows that although Sri Lanka has been effective in building up a mass-education system that provides every child with basic literacy and numeracy skills, education has not resulted in a more even distribution of resources and hope, nor has it succeeded in uniting children of different backgrounds and identities under the umbrella of an inclusive national identity. Instead, education has become a contentious issue that mobilizes many in search of better futures and in political and even violent struggles for justice. The section concludes with a discussion of the most recent educational reforms, which attempt to address this particular challenge of growing social disparity and disruptive violence by giving increased attention to citizenship education.

The second part of the chapter builds on ethnographic research with school children and teachers in minority schools in North-Western Sri Lanka. In this section, I explore how school children are continuously *being made* and are *self-making* through their engagement with teachers and authorities, the consumption of official textbooks, and through a reading of their school's relative standard and a

commitment to the community's social memory. As I show in
the following section, community members do not passively
accept when their schools receive insufficient resources and
support, but mobilize available social networks to improve the
availability and quality of education and through this their
position as citizens.

EDUCATION POLICY AND SINHALESE NATION-BUILDING

Sri Lanka's transition from colony to independent nation-
state in 1948 was remarkably peaceful.[1] In less than a decade,
however, the unity and harmony was broken and replaced
by political struggles that eventually escalated into violent
conflicts on several fronts from the 1970s. What is little
recognized is that shifting education policies played a decisive
role in establishing this antagonistic environment. In 1944,
the British government established a commission to consider
necessary constitutional reforms in Sri Lanka, and in its
final report it emphasized that the relationship between the
Sinhalese majority and the different minority groups posed a
serious challenge. The constitution of 1945 safeguarded the
basic rights of linguistic, religious minorities, but in 1956, the
newly elected nationalist government adopted a new language
act that made Sinhala, the language of the Sinhalese majority
the only official language of the country. At the same time
a process of government takeover of schools was initiated,
which served to reduce the influence of missionary schools,
nationalize the school system, and to make education available
to all children (Angela Little, 2003, 92–4; Nissan, 1996, 34–7).

The last goal emerged in response to growing pressure from Sinhalese voters to improve opportunities for the Sinhalese youths who were dissatisfied that the Tamil minority dominated the public sectors because of privileged access to education under colonial rule. To achieve mass education English was replaced with *Swabasha*, the vernacular languages, as the medium of instruction. The switch to teaching in the vernacular was perceived to facilitate learning for all children and, moreover, it signalled a political break with the colonial heritage. However, the policy had damaging repercussions for inter-ethnic relations and contributed to a segregation of education on ethnic and linguistic grounds—a division that still prevails. Although children of a Sinhalese background generally benefited from the government's policy, the policy had long-term negative consequences for Tamil-speaking children, as their access to public-sector jobs was restricted, because proficiency in the Sinhalese language was now required as a result of the Sinhala Only Act.

The Tamils experienced further marginalization a decade later, when new policies for university admissions were approved. All students had previously participated in the same competitive examinations to gain entrance to the university, but from 1971 access to university became regulated on the basis of language and this meant that Tamil-speaking students required higher marks. A year later, a district quota system was adopted to compensate for the fact that children in the rural areas did not have access to the same quality education as children in the urban areas. The end result was a dramatic decrease in the number of places for Tamils at universities.

In some disciplines, especially science-based disciplines, the Tamils' admittance dropped by up to two-thirds, whereas the number of Sinhalese students increased significantly (Matthews, 1995, 80; Nissan, 1996, 13; Ponnambalam, 1983, 176–7). Together these alterations of education policy constituted a major blow to the status and future prospects of the Tamil population, and experiences of discrimination in education were highly contributory to their growing self-consciousness as an ethnic group and a minority, and became increasingly entrenched in their fight for self-determination.

According to Perera, in one study a Tamil informant even claims that 'discriminatory education policies were the single most important reason which led them to guerrilla activities.' (Nissan, 1996, 12)

If we return to primary education, there are still many unresolved and controversial issues. Tamil advocates direct strong accusations against the government of unequal distribution of financial and human resources, which results in poorly equipped and understaffed Tamil medium schools. They also question the noticeable underrepresentation of Tamils in institutions responsible for policymaking, curriculum preparation and textbook production, and the political appointments of principals. Finally, Tamil-medium teaching material is criticized for its poor quality and strong Sinhalese cultural bias. I return to these issues in the second part of this chapter. Education remains the official responsibility of the Sri Lankan state, also in the Liberation Tigers of Tamil Eelam (LTTE) controlled areas.[2] However, the LTTE has slowly built up its own parallel state institutions—including a LTTE Department of Education that provides special education to children in the areas under its control (Liberation Tigers of Tamil Eelam [LTTE], 2006; Stokke, 2006). The education provided by the LTTE directly challenges the authority of the Sri Lankan state to define the Tamil nation and the Tamil person, by offering an alternative social imaginary. The foreword of a history textbook issued by the LTTE explains:

> The history textbooks by the Sri Lankan government that are taught in the schools are not based on true history, but have exaggerated the Sinhalese community, concealed the greatness of the Tamils and has been twisted in a manner to demean the Tamils. . . . By teaching Tamil translations of Sinhala works, written by and for the Sinhalese, the Tamil students are taught Sinhalese history, which says that this Sinhala-Buddhist country is only for them and that their history is the history of Eelam. (Sambandan, 2004)

Subsequent chapters account for the historic development of Tamil Eelam, the Tamil national anthem, and their red flag with the roaring Tiger, and aim to give the Tamil children pride in their cultural identity and make them sympathetic to the struggle. Awareness of a shared cultural heritage is also created through special cultural and language programmes. In its fight for self-determination, the LTTE can be seen as proposing and practicing 'cultural citizenship' as an alternative to the government's idea of national citizenship (Rosaldo, 1994).

Somewhat surprising perhaps, the education policies of the 1950s to the 1970s were also contributory to the political mobilization of Sinhalese youths. As argued above, a growing number of Sinhalese youths in the rural areas had benefited from the education reforms and many had even made it into university (Gunaratna, 1990).

Having invested their hopes in education, they were now looking forward to receiving their rewards in the form of employment and social mobility. However, these benefits failed to materialize for most. Instead, they witnessed how privileges continued to be bestowed on a small, mainly urban and westernized elite, whereas the majority of the rural youths were still trapped in an intensifying rural poverty or struggling along in urban centres where they lived under miserable circumstances searching for a better life that seemed increasingly unreachable (Gunaratna, 1990, 65).

Inspired by socialist class struggles elsewhere in the world, the socialist People's Liberation Front (Janatha Vimukhti Peramuna, or JVP) was founded in 1965 with the aim of staging a socialist revolution. JVP regarded the universities and other institutions of learning as prime sites for the reproduction of abusive neocolonial power relations, and they became a significant venue for the enactment of their political protests and recruitment of cadres who were taken to special education camps for political re-socialisation.

Describing the situation at one university in the late 1980s, Bruce Matthews writes: 'Mass rallies and show trials, public humiliations, and even floggings and executions were standard features of what remained of university life.' (1995, 82). The JVP was behind a countrywide ferocious insurrection to overthrow the government and combat capitalism and international interference in 1971 and in the late 1980s, but was eventually defeated. Today the JVP is part of mainstream politics, but they continue to have many supporters among Sinhalese university students, who are still involved in violent ragging and political mobilization. Most recently, JVP-led university students condemned the government for abandoning the deep-rooted principle of free education at all levels and surrendering to global capitalist forces (The Island, 28 Feb. 2008). The universities, in other words, remain politicized spaces where fierce competition for power and social recognition along class and ethnic lines takes place, which has turned the educated person into a highly ambiguous figure. The Muslim population constitutes the second largest minority in Sri Lanka. Historically, the Muslims have been living dispersed throughout the country, where they have developed tight economic relationships with neighbouring Sinhalese and Tamil communities.

The Muslims' political leaders have mostly been drawn from the urban economic elite and have sought to obtain influence and access to resources by supporting the Sinhalese-dominated government, rather than claiming an independent political identity. Yet, as O'Sullivan (1999) shows, the economic policies and the growing ethnification of politics from the 1970s resulted in the emergence of a separate Muslim ethnic and political identity, which culminated in the formation of the Sri Lankan Muslim Congress (1999).

According to O'Sullivan (1999), education was involved in this development in more ways. The liberalization of the economy exposed the Muslims to growing competition, as other groups, especially the Sinhalese, took up business and trade as a livelihood strategy. As Muslims were generally lacking behind in education, this was soon identified as a crucial area for improvement if the Muslim minority should succeed in protecting its interests. As O'Sullivan puts it, 'Muslim businessmen began to consider education as an important element of success both in terms of unlocking new opportunities and maintaining competitiveness with the enlarged number of business rivals.' (p. 257)

As the Sinhalese government sought to marginalize the Tamil minority, and furthermore benefited from Muslim political support, the Muslim elite managed to make the government give certain concessions. Muslim training colleges and a new category of Muslim government schools were established, and subjects related to Islam developed (O'Sullivan, 1999, 255). Next, the university admission rules discussed above also benefited the Muslims, whose access to university education went significantly up and enabled them to enter the competition for attractive public sector jobs (O'Sullivan, 1999, 257, 261). As education became increasingly vital for the socio-economic status and mobility of the Muslim minority, it also became a vital political issue. Contrary to the Tamils, who emphasized aspects of recognition and self-determination over redistribution, the Muslims stressed redistribution and were less adamant on issues regarding recognition and identity.

Sri Lanka's protracted political conflicts have multiple causes and what is considered the most contentious and critical concern shifts over time. Yet as I have shown education is enmeshed in complex ways in all of the country's most consequential conflicts (S. Perera, 2006; Selvarajah, 2003). The debates and struggles about education are tied to issues of social justice, recognition, self-determination, and solidarity, Kabeer's (2005) four-core elements of citizenship, and Jeffery's assertion that in India 'contemporary debates about education reflect struggles over the normative domains of citizenship and identity' also appears applicable to neighbouring Sri Lanka (p. 23).

As the discussion shows, questions of access to primary and higher education and medium of instruction, are not neutral policy measures to achieve a higher national level of learning, but are instrumental in defining children's and youths' particular place in society, in terms of their identity, social status, and rights. In postcolonial Sri Lanka, it has been the Sinhalese population that has benefited the most from education policies, as their language and religion (Buddhism) were naturalized as the country's official and as their access to better employment and income improved considerably. Therefore, the government's policies have been bitterly contested and criticized for not recognizing and respecting the culture of the minorities and for failing to achieve a just redistribution of resources.

EDUCATION REFORMS AND THE NEW IMAGINATIONS OF A NATIONAL CITIZENSHIP

The ties between education and social unrest and conflict in Sri Lanka are complex and are not yet fully accounted for and understood, but there is wide recognition that the link does exist. In the following section, I discuss how this knowledge has been incorporated into new education policies. In 1989, a Presidential Commission on Youth was established with a mandate to examine the causes of youth unrest and provide recommendations. The report presented by the commission in 1990 was to slightly alter the focus of future educational policy making. The investigations suggested a causal link between the performance of the education system and the emergence of rebellious youths among both Sinhalese and Tamils. This turned conflict into an issue that the school system could no longer ignore, and one it was obliged to assist in solving. Influenced by this change in thinking, the National Education Commission that had been appointed in 1991 identified 'the achievement of national cohesion, national integrity and national unity' and 'establishment of pervasive patterns of social justice' as important national goals (Angela Little, 2003). More initiatives were taken to reach the goal, among them the introduction of 'peace education', but observers generally agree that the initiatives were largely unsuccessful (Ginige, 2002; Matthews, 1995, 84; L. Perera, Wijetunge & Balasooriya, 2004, 393, 410).

In 1997, the government introduced a new education reform, which it had engineered in consultation with international educational agencies and under the influence of an emerging global agenda for education.[3] New planning tools and management structures were introduced (Angela Little, 2003), and new institutions were established to conduct policy-relevant research and advise the government. L. Perera et al. (2004) describe the reform as a milestone in the development of a national education policy that would address the country's major problems (p. 397), and that as the Ministry of Education (2005) phrases it, would be 'enhancing life competencies and upholding the value of peace and social cohesion.' (p. 6) Concrete changes include a new language policy, which prescribes that all children in government schools shall be taught the two national languages, Sinhalese and Tamil (L. Perera et al., 2004, 402).

In addition, a comprehensive process has been launched to reorganize and improve the content of the most contested and controversial subjects (history, religion, and social studies), which are moreover to be systematically monitored for any ethnic, religious, gender, and poverty bias (Wickrema & Colenso, 2003, 11). Entirely new subjects that aim to 'develop the total personality of the child' including the ability to build positive interpersonal relationships and accept diversity, have also been introduced (L. Perera et al., 2004, 400; Sri Lanka, National Institute of Education, 2006b).

One example is the subject of 'citizenship education' for grades 6–9, which aims to create 'citizens full of competencies and good virtues' who will 'admire the culture multiplicity and develop competencies and positive attitudes towards national integration.' (Sri Lanka, Department of Education,

2005, vii). The textbook for Grade 7 illustrates the visions and values behind the subject. It is divided into three sections, which briefly deal with the individual's rights, duties, and obligations in the context of 'the family', 'our society', and 'our culture', respectively. Sri Lanka's diversity is mainly addressed in the section on 'our culture', where it is stated that 'there are five races in Sri Lanka, namely, Sinhala, Tamil, Muslim, Burgher, and Malay. They follow the religions Buddhism, Hinduism, Islam, Christianity, and Catholicism.' (Sri Lanka, Department of Education, 2005, 30). This introduction is followed by brief descriptions of the major religious festivals of each community, which makes each group appear as having essentialised and separate cultures.

The text attempts to incorporate the different groups into a common imagined national community by stressing that all groups made significant contributions to the struggle for independence, that all are Sri Lankan citizens, and that Sri Lanka is their common motherland (Sri Lanka, Department of Education, 2005, 29, 34). A separate section on human rights likewise intends to stress children's commonalities across ethnic divides and their inclusion in Sri Lanka as a democratic country where 'all of us get the opportunity of enjoying several rights' according to the country's legal framework (Sri Lanka, Department of Education, 2005, 26). These rights include: 'the right to criticize the ideas of other children and citizens,' but not the 'right to humiliate them or speak in a manner that will harass them.' (Sri Lanka, Department of Education, 2005, 28)

For Grades 10 and 11, the newly introduced subject 'civics and governance' creates the potential for an even more direct address of Sri Lanka's contemporary political predicaments. The 2007 syllabus for Grade 10 students includes sessions on democracy, decentralization, and devolution; the multicultural society; economic systems and relations; and conflict resolution in a democratic society, whereas Grade 11 students study law and justice, government, human rights, environmental problems and sustainable development, and international relations (Sri Lanka, National Institute of Education, 2006a, 2006b). The new reforms, in other words, outline a new social imaginary in which the prior national identity defined on the basis of Sinhalese cultural values is replaced with a multi-ethnic national identity that makes all citizens equal and that aims to inculcate a new culture of tolerance.

As the implementation of the new syllabus is still in its inception, it is premature to make any evaluation, but a few remarks of caution are in place. The reform relies heavily on curriculum change and on the written textbook as the agent of change in regard to reaching the particular objective of 'national integration and unity' (Angela Little, 2003; L. Perera et al., 2004).

According to Wickrema and Colenso (2003),

> [T]he textbook is very much the central component of the teaching-learning process, with teachers making little reference to the syllabus, to broader pedagogical resources, and to the development of broader competencies beyond the remit and

content areas of textbooks. The historical monopoly of textbook production, combined with the reluctance of teachers and students to deviate from the textbook, has made the content of the single textbook that much more critical and contentious. (p. 3)

The prevalence given to the textbook can be linked to Sri Lanka's educational culture that stresses rote and exam-oriented learning, and the teacher is considered an authority figure whom you can ask questions, but not question (S. Perera, 2006, 22). As Stewick and Levinson (2007) suggest, however, new civic values of democracy and tolerance cannot be taught and internalized by students solely through abstract texts, but need to be firmly anchored in the social structure and practices of the school and this may pose one big challenge for the recent reforms. Anthropological studies conceptualize education as an evolving social practice and the school as a vibrant and contested arena. The priorities outlined in educational policies, and concepts and values introduced in textbooks are significant aspects of the way in which children are 'being made' as citizens, because they have authority. However, their real effect on children's self-perception can only be assessed by examining their implementation and appropriation in concrete social environments, where other actors introduce competing values and truths.

THE NEGOTIATION OF A RESEARCH METHODOLOGY

The empirical data for this chapter stem from a field study that is part of a larger research project on education, conflict, and post-conflict reconstruction in Sri Lanka. The field study took place during February and March 2006 in and around Puttalam town in the North-Western Province, an area I am familiar with from earlier research and humanitarian work on war-related internal displacement and social reconstruction. Puttalam town has always had a sizeable Muslim population, whereas the district's rural areas have been dominated by the Sinhalese. In October 1990, the LTTE expelled all Muslims from the north, and many ended up in temporary refugee camps close to Puttalam town or with resident relatives. The district's Muslim population thus went from 9.9 per cent in 1981 to 18.8 per cent of the population in 2001, and 67.5 per cent of Puttalam town's 40,967 inhabitants are today Muslims (Sri Lanka, Department of Census and Statistics, 2001). Population growth has generated fierce competition over scarce resources between the host and refugee populations (Hasbullah, 2004; Sørensen, 2001).

The field study involved five Tamil medium schools (Grades 6–13), of which one is Roman Catholic, one Hindu, and three Muslim.[4] I had planned to use participant observation in classes and staff meetings in two schools as my main methodology to collect data on the everyday formation of citizenship in schools, but a number of incidents forced me to revise my research strategy and methodology. First, the local authorities were powerful 'gatekeepers'; they demanded that I obtain their approval for each activity I wanted to carry out with teachers and pupils, which made more open-ended, participatory research incredibly difficult. Second, the crisis emanating from the publication of defamatory drawings of the Prophet Muhammad (PBUH) in a Danish newspaper had also reached Sri Lanka and made the Muslim community acutely alert to outsiders and their overt and possible covert agendas. Next, local elections were impending, and political meetings involving school staff frequently interrupted everyday routines in the schools. In some cases, this meant that research became a less urgent activity for my informants, whereas in others it contributed to exposing the sensitivity of the research topic. In consultation with educational officers and principals, I developed a research methodology consisting of questionnaires and focus group interviews with teachers and pupils, individual interviews with educational officers and principals, group interviews with representatives of school development societies and old pupils' associations, thematic workshops, photo and essay assignments with smaller groups of pupils, participation in public school events, and to a lesser extent casual conversations with pupils.

I also interviewed all NGOs in the area that had a child focus, and some of the major private tuition centres. In illustration of the sensitivity and significance of my research topic, activities with children in some cases took place under close supervision and direct interference of a gatekeeper appointed by the school or mosque, whereas in others the staff were engaged, helpful, and constructive facilitators of the research process. In my field diary, I repeatedly noted that the research was far more complicated than any other research project I had carried out in Sri Lanka in terms of getting access to informants.

Because of my empirical research focus on the school, children were being categorized as school children and turned into subjects of the state to be surveilled and controlled, which is testimony of the extreme politicization of education in Sri Lanka.

The change in methodology contributed to a slight change in research objectives from how citizenship is taught in class through the curriculum to how the school as an institution produces and conveys messages about citizenship through its organization and its position in the community (Bush & Saltarelli, 2000, 21). As the field research proceeded, this turned out to be a fortunate change in focus, which resonated well with the viewpoints and experiences expressed by most informants and that contributed with new insights about the interrelationship between aspects of recognition and redistribution that a focus on the content of textbooks alone could not bring forward.

THE EVERYDAY FORMATION OF CITIZENS

Although the notion of citizenship is nearly universal, what it means and how it is experienced is not. The narratives of my interlocutors stressed two distinct but related dimensions of citizenship: access to resources and development; and cultural recognition and self-determination. These were expressed and defined in relation to my informants' vertical relationship with the nation-state and its representatives, and as part of their horizontal social relationships of solidarity (Kabeer, 2005). My preparations for the field research had been informed by arguments in the scholarly literature and the public debate in Sri Lanka regarding the relationship between education and nation-building in conflict situations (Bush & Saltarelli, 2000; Davis, 2006). This had led me to expect that informants would talk excessively about the content of teaching material. The issue did occur, but in most cases concerns regarding the availability of resources were fore-grounded, and I argue that the particular exposition and explanatory linking of issues contain instructive lessons regarding the conceptualization and experience of citizenship in Sri Lanka.

DEFINITION THROUGH ABSENCE

In each school, I asked pupils to produce a descriptive portrait of their school in text, drawings, or photos. Going through the presentations, I was struck by the fact that despite the evident differences in size and standard between the selected schools, the presentations were remarkably similar in both focus and content. With no exception and little variation they all concentrated on the defects and deficiencies of their schools, whereas more positive aspects were only given scant attention. Regardless of whether the school consisted of permanent, well-maintained brick buildings or it was located in a dilapidating and more humble construction, whether it had many or few teachers, well-equipped libraries and science laboratories or none at all, the students consistently tried to document the complete lack or insufficient availability and low standard of their school's facilities.[5]

When the children took me on a grand tour of their school, they guided me to overcrowded classrooms, sparsely furnished, with little more than a ragged chair and desk for the teacher, and classrooms that were unusable because of leaky roofs and cracked floors. They showed me outdoor classes with small children sitting uncomfortably on the hot sand under a tree, following the soothing shade that demarcated the boundaries of their classroom, and they led me to shelters made from palm leaves (cadjan), which only gave the studying children minimal protection from the blazing sun and the torrential monsoon rains. The inadequate classrooms were not the only thing that concerned the pupils. In all the schools, pupils complained about libraries with empty shelves or outdated literature and poorly equipped science labs. Moreover, the pupils were troubled by the poor standard of sanitation that constituted a serious health hazard and contradicted all they had learned about good health.

Their photo essays illustrated the prevailing situation with countless photos of garbage piled up in the school ground; wells where the water surface was covered with plastic shopping bags, paper, and other rubbish; and stinking filthy latrines. Complaints over the lack of a school fence, which gave easy access for stray animals and other trespassers, were also frequent. The children's perception was widely shared among the staff and management, who matched the pupils' documentation of absence with detailed, meticulously prepared lists of what was needed, in what numbers and amounts.

Experiences of neglect were not only expressed in relation to infrastructure and facilities. On more occasions, principals and teachers complained that their school did not receive the regular visits from the educational office where deficiencies would be recorded and useful professional support provided. Although the staff was obviously not interested in excessive interference of external authorities, the infrequent visits of officials prevented communication and were interpreted not only as misconduct but also a strong indicator of the school's and the whole community's low public status. In a similar vein, I was informed of several incidents, where no action was taken by the authorities when the school management reported criminal acts such as illegal encroachment or theft of computers and other valuables from the school.

To see how these identifications and expositions of missing or deplorable facilities and absent or non attentive authorities relate to the formation of situated notions of citizenship, it is necessary to explore how pupils and staff themselves interpreted and explained their situation. The children's reflections regarding the standard of their school are interesting as they imply an objectifying, comparative gaze. The children's negative evaluation of their school made implicit reference to an idealized cultural image of how a school ought to be, and explicit reference to Sinhalese majority schools and to national schools that receive direct funding from the government. Both were perceived to have a surplus of resources and to be closer to the ideal. In several cases, however, the schools of neighbouring villages belonging to the same ethnic community, were also perceived to be better off. In both cases, differences in access to resources were typically explained to be the direct result of politics.

As scholars examining the development of the modern Sri Lankan state have pointed out, the introduction of a representative form of government and universal suffrage in 1931 resulted in growing attention to the needs and grievances of their constituencies, and even before independence, the provision of welfare had become a central—and costly—feature of the Sri Lankan state (Brow, 1996; Hettige, 2004; Jayaweera, 2007; Richardson, 2004). As I have argued elsewhere (Sørensen, 2008), the authority and legitimacy of the Sri Lankan state is today highly dependent on its provision of welfare to its citizens, and the population claims a principled right to development. Apart from contributing to material and social welfare, the provision of resources also serves as a symbolic recognition of the receiving group's inclusion in the national community as citizens. Conversely, the lack of development can be regarded as testimony of a group's exclusion or marginalization from the national community. The relative absence of the state in the minority schools symbolized in the lack of classrooms, the absent or broken furniture, and the shortage of teachers is, as I see it, as powerful a communication about the nature of the Sri Lankan nation-state as is its presence through flags, anthems, and textbooks, which is typically in focus in studies of education and nation-building. When my informants showed me the missing facilities, they were evoking not only an image of the archetypical Sri Lankan school but also their social imaginary of the state.

My informants' accounts of absence, I argue, serve an argument of state-based discrimination against minorities, not unlike that inherent in analyses of how the nation-state imposes itself symbolically through textbooks or social ceremonies. But whereas the state's strong symbolic presence provokes alienation, resistance, or at least distance, focus on its relative absence appears instead to function as a tactic for claiming a position as rightful Sri Lankan citizens and an attempt to compel the state to recognize its moral obligation to deliver welfare and take proper care of all its citizens. The teachers and pupils, in other words, practiced what (Jackson, 2002) Jackson calls a 'politics of storytelling' (2002) when they voiced what in their view were legitimate expectations toward the government and politicians to provide appropriate facilities for learning.

Their expectations were repeatedly echoed in my conversations with parents and teachers. As one principal expressed it, 'Of course we would like to get the assistance from the government. But we do not get [it], so we approach other possible sources of funding. But even when the assistance of NGOs is considerable, they can only help with buildings and our material needs. The real problem here is teaching and the lack of teachers, and only the government can—and should—solve that.' (interview, 6 March 2006) I suggest then that what at first appeared simply to be depressing accounts of schools in a deplorable state could also be interpreted as unassuming, but insistent claims for recognition and inclusion in the political and moral national community as citizens with equal rights and opportunities. The social imaginary of equal citizenship contained in the previously discussed textbook for citizenship education in other words finds resonance among teachers and children, but contrary to what the textbook explains, they know that inclusion has to be continuously worked for, at least when you do not belong to the Sinhalese majority or enjoy the benevolence of a powerful patron. In the following, I explore further how staff and pupils perceived the logics of politics to work, and how that formed their experience of citizenship.

MULTIPLE ORDERS OF MARGINALIZATION

Citizenship refers to both rights and entitlements, and to a sense of identity and belonging (Fraser, 2003; Kabeer, 2005; Ong, 1996). Although pupils in all schools and of all ages expressed their grievances over the poor physical conditions at their school in similar ways and agreed that the main reason was political, significant patterns of difference emerged, when I explored the existing explanations of this inequality.

In the Hindu school, the older pupils, who were entering a more demanding and decisive phase of their education, were particularly outspoken on the issue. From their perspective, the gravest problem was the acute shortage of qualified teachers and the lack of good learning materials, as this directly affected their education, exam results, future career opportunities, and social positioning. As mentioned earlier, the large number of vacancies in Tamil-speaking schools has for several years been a hot issue repeatedly brought up by Tamil politicians and educationists. Although the authorities seek to explain away this problem by referring to the warlike situation prevailing in large parts of the Tamil region, my student informants did not hesitate to diagnose it as a result of discrimination, which evidenced that they were not fully recognized as a minority.

For the students, the shortage of teachers had dire consequences, as they missed out on important classes, which reduced their chances of passing exams. Many families tried hard to raise money to send their child to private tuition classes, but it was costly and could be risky too, as this account by an A-level male student reveals, 'You see, in our school we don't have any math teachers for A-level, so I have to travel to Colombo once a week to take extra classes. I want to go to university.' After a pause he continued, 'but I'm scared to travel, because if something happens, it can be dangerous to be a young Tamil boy, especially if you come from Jaffna.' (interview, 16 Feb. 2006) In a workshop with this young student and his classmates, the discussion fell on learning material. 'Very often our textbooks are several months late, and that makes it difficult for us to cover the curriculum in time to prepare for exams,' one boy informed. A classmate took over, explaining that this delay was partly because of the fact that most textbooks are first written in Sinhalese and then translated into Tamil and distributed to Tamil-medium schools.

Moreover, the translations are frequently of poor quality, as exemplified by another student. 'We find it very difficult to read the texts and understand the questions [for exams], so we spend too much time understanding them and then we have less time to answer them.' And his conclusion, uttered with a mixture of disdain and self-pity, was disturbing: 'This is done to make us Tamils look more stupid than the Sinhalese!'

To support their friend's conclusion, others quickly added that education programmes on television were also only targeting Sinhalese students, again reducing the opportunities for Tamil students to do well in the competition for access to higher education and good jobs (workshop, 16 Feb. 2006).

Echoing the elder students' concern and their allegations of state-sponsored discrimination against them as a minority, the management and senior staff revealed their utmost frustration that official meetings and written documents and letters from the authorities were most often in Sinhalese, a language in which most lacked proficiency.

After having explained how translations of circulars, regulations, letters, and other documents occupied much of his own and the secretariat's time, and how humiliated he felt at meetings when having to explain his situation in a language that was not his mother tongue, the principal of one school stated, 'It makes me feel like a second-rank citizen in my own country.' (interview, 16 Feb. 2006) Although such comments undoubtedly emerged from lived experiences, they were clearly also embedded in and nourished by the collective narrative of the Tamil minority's grievances and struggles for cultural recognition and self-determination.

The Muslim schools of the study included two newer schools that mainly catered for the children of displaced families, and one older school in an impoverished neighbourhood in the town periphery. Unlike the Tamil informants, the Muslim teachers and pupils here did not evoke their religious identity or minority position as explanatory factors per se when commenting on their educational situation. But how then did the Muslim teachers and pupils explain what they nevertheless perceived to be acts of discriminate distribution within the educational field?

In the two schools for children of internally displaced parents, strong emphasis was being put on the traumatic and disruptive experience of displacement, which had entered social memory and become part of the community's social identity. One group of pupils concluded their written account of the difficulties they faced in school, with the following words. 'Displacement is the reason for that. Our property, education rights, everything was destroyed when we were displaced from our native place in the Vanni by weapon-holding Tigers.' The narratives of displacement called to mind memories of the prosperous and successful schools that had been left behind and stressed that education had turned into a struggle hard to win, because resources were fewer and competition greater. Inclusion in the humanitarian category of internal refugees, however, not only signalled a separation from territory, property, and possessions but also spelled a restriction in the internally displaced people's ability to participate in politics. This was important because the majority of schools and other social services are funded by the provincial government, and gaining access to funds in many cases was dependent on being able to build effective patron-client relationships.

The displaced Muslim population remained registered in the province they had been forced to flee, and hence could not cast their votes for politicians in the province of their residence and in this way turn their concerns into publicly recognized political priorities. At the same time, there was little chance that votes for the politicians in their home province would have any effect either, as they were unlikely to be willing to transfer resources to another district (Hasbullah 2004). As one informant phrased it, 'Votes, not needs, determine what you get,' and he thereby stressed that ordinary politics had replaced humanitarian practice, and that because of their unresolved situation of prolonged displacement, the Muslim community was prohibited from participating in both the humanitarian and the political game. The experience of lack of political rights was accentuated by the daily experience of stigmatization by the host community, which made them feel out of place as evidenced by this extract from an essay written by a young boy: 'I suffer like a person sunk in floods . . . I will wait for the day that erases the label of refugee.'

The third Muslim school, established in 1971, was situated in a poor neighbourhood. Most families depended on low-paid casual labour in local salt pans and fisheries, and the community suffered from a wide range of poverty-related social problems such as alcoholism, drug abuse, crime, fighting, malnutrition, illiteracy, and health problems.

Education was also affected with long-term absenteeism and a high dropout rate, lack of support from parents, and irregular presence of teaching staff. According to the School Development Society (SDS), they had approached many politicians and NGOs for support and assistance, but had in most cases been disappointed. Some politicians had made visits and delivered speeches that promised to improve the school and bring development, only to neglect the community afterward. According to the SDS, the community was neglected because it did not support the government, and because the community was considered backward, rude, hostile, and of little prestige. This reflected on the image of school, which was publicly referred to as a 'punishment station', in which only principals of the 'wrong' political observation or with a blemished record would be appointed, and that teachers would do their best to escape. The NGOs did not provide an alternative solution, because they mainly focused on children of displaced families, and there were only a small number of displaced families in the community. The pupils of this school did not point to a single factor (ethnicity), or a single event (displacement) as the cause for their misfortune, but instead conceived of themselves as belonging to an impoverished and hard-pressed group, who had to battle exploitation and exclusion on several fronts, including from within, and whose identity had largely been conflated with its socio-economic position.

The Roman Catholic school had been established under colonial rule, but later been moved to a new locality outside town. Its present principal was Roman Catholic, but its teachers and pupils included many Muslims and Hindus from the area. The community it supported was poor, largely dependent on low-paid seasonal work, living dispersed on different small islands and coastal villages. The accounts of the pupils of this school were less concerned with finding an explanation for the lack of facilities and more focused on past achievements and future challenges. This may be because of their younger age, them coming from more remote areas, or the strong discipline and compassionate atmosphere that prevailed at the school. Whenever they voiced some critical reflections these were more often directed at themselves and their own community, and concerned problems related to labour migration, the difficult position of girls, or the temptations of consumerism.

The principal and teachers, however, soon introduced the topic of politics in our discussion about the school. Being a small Tamil-medium school, they generally felt less privileged, and time and again they had experienced how their arguments and requests for support fell on deaf ears, whereas the neighbouring Sinhalese school received excessive support from the authorities. Moreover, the principal had experienced how her family's close connections to the political opposition had been used against her. Contrary to the other schools, however, such experiences did not appear to have mobilized a strong collective narrative of blame, nor had it generated a claim for cultural citizenship. Instead, the situation seemed to have given rise to a strong sense of communal solidarity and united them in a dedicated struggle to slowly, but surely improve the children's and the community's socio-economic situation through an education based on respect, tolerance, and discipline.

The experiences of the different schools in this section remind us to be apprehensive of how the formation of citizenship as a political process may employ numerous and shifting categories of differentiation, intertwining aspects of redistribution and recognition. In this section, I have exemplified how authorities through their interventions in education contributed to defining and positioning teachers, pupils, and their families as citizens. Despite the official policy that all are equal citizens, none of my informants expressed a sense of full recognition and inclusion, and in the next section I analyze in more detail how their experience of 'partial citizenship' affects their acts of 'self-making'.

THE CREATION OF PERIPHERAL CITIZENSHIP

The perception of deprivation and of partial citizenship that existed in schools resulted neither in apathy nor in actual resistance, but, rather, in innumerable activities to reduce its negative effects. As I shall show, these activities were insistent acts of self-making (Ong, 1996) that creatively exploited possibilities in the prevailing system to regain a sense of pride and control and define meaningful forms of membership and belonging.

At the time of my fieldwork, political campaigns, and meetings preceding local elections were frequent. Although there was little confidence in politics among my informants, most principals and senior teachers would nevertheless partake in meetings organized by the authorities and contesting parties with the vain hope that they would receive gifts for the school or succeed in forcing promises of future assistance.

And even when they did not receive anything at most meetings, not being present could easily be interpreted as offensive and strain relationships. The schools, however, developed several alternative strategies to improve their situation, and these were expressive of and contributory to forming their citizenship from below. The strategies from below concentrated on mobilizing social networks of different kinds, and contrary to the political relationships that were framed by the logic of resources in return for votes or other kinds of reciprocal exchange, these networks, I argue, rested on moral notions of commonality and expressed citizenship as horizontal solidarity (Kabeer, 2005).

The kinds of social networks that different schools were capable of mobilizing to buttress support varied a great deal, as did their resources and capacities. All schools in Sri Lanka have a School Development Society (SDS) with teacher, parent, and pupil representatives. Their task is to facilitate the relationship between a school and the community and to assist the school in solving emerging problems, and they were typically a strategic player in addressing lack of resources. For instance, they would initiate social activities in the community to generate money to pay voluntary teachers or smaller infrastructure projects. In one of the schools, situated in a community of displaced Muslim families, the SDS had been more ambitious and rented a van to go on a grand fund-raising tour from their village to Colombo to raise money for the replacement of a temporary shelter with a permanent brick building. Their main targets were the many successful Muslim businessmen who had established their enterprises along the main road and who, according to the SDS, had a moral obligation to support their community. Another target was a Muslim politician who had succeeded in becoming a national minister, and whose family shared the experience of displacement. Even though his ministry's mandate did not directly match the school's concerns, there was wide agreement that he too had a special obligation to support his community, which he did on several occasions. So although the Muslims generally complained over their lack of political representation in the area, they were not without initiative and repeatedly demonstrated that their extended social networks possessed considerable resources and willingness to step forward in support of the community.

Students at the Hindu school expressed a similar doubt about the support of politicians. One group of students wrote in their essay: 'There will be so many politicians coming and going. They will say so many things and create so many ideas in our minds, but they don't fulfil even 1 per cent.' And therefore they too had to rely on their own resources. The Hindu school's social network reflected the Tamils' traditional pursuit of careers as lawyers, engineers, doctors, and university professors. The most important network was the Old Boys' Association (OBA) that counted more than three hundred members in Sri Lanka and abroad.

Over the years, the OBA had repeatedly demonstrated its indisputable loyalty when it had helped raise money for land purchase, a proper school gate, the construction of a Hindu shrine, and a science laboratory. Members also helped to improve teaching at the school by volunteering to give lectures of interest and relevance to the pupils. The worth of the OBA was widely acknowledged, and the students did not hesitate to ascribe the success of their school to the commitment and loyalty of former students. A group of students wrote, 'The present situation of this school is achieved by the Old Boys' Association. They have helped the school a lot,' and the students anticipated that they too would remain supportive of their school. 'We will do as much as we can for our younger brothers and sisters.'

Contrary to what could be expected from a policy that promises free education, a substantial part of the schools' activities and investments were in fact covered by the schools themselves and their social networks. This meant that the two schools that served poorer and largely illiterate communities were in fact doubly marginalized, because they did not have a resourceful network to mobilize. The main point I want to draw from these examples, however, is that the work of the SDSs and OBAs has a significance that goes well beyond its economic aspects in that it contributes to shaping the children's sense of who they are. Every time the SDS or the OBA contributed something to the school, it was interpreted and praised as 'our own achievement' as opposed to something allocated by the state or some other external agent.

Hence, the achievements of the SDS and the OBA served to reinforce identification with and pride in the school and the local community. Appadurai's (1998) distinction between 'neighbourhood', which refers to situated communities, and 'locality', which is a property of social life, are useful here. According to Appadurai (1998), neighbourhoods exist in opposition to the nation-state's social imaginary of a homogenous population, and constitute 'a perennial source of entropy and slippage,' (p. 191) because they are concerned with their own reproduction, for which they depend on the

production of 'local subjects'. (p. 179) The pupils' tribute
to the SDSs and OBAs was clear evidence of the schools'
attempts and success in producing loyal local subjects, and
so was the pupils' unequivocal view that the purpose of their
education was to enable them to 'do good for the community'.

Ironically, the segregated national school system can be
argued to support this process that entails a real or potential
contestation of the nation. Contrary to the argument
regarding the national socialization of pupils through the
invasion of the school space with national symbols, I found
that the symbolic space and daily routines of the schools were
far more expressive of the community's own religious and
cultural values than of their incorporation into a national
space. The Muslim schools all had a small mosque or prayer
room for staff and pupils, and the school flags, emblems,
mottos, and school anthems all established unambiguous
links between Islamic virtues and education. Offices and
classrooms were decorated with posters from Mecca or quotes
from the Quran, and the community's cultural identity
was inscribed on bodies through a particular dress code
and temporal structuring of the day. At the Hindu school,
a statue of the goddess of speech, wisdom, and learning,
Saraswathy, welcomed teachers, students, and other visitors
at the gate, and just inside was a Hindu shrine, which to
the principal's regret still needed some work before it could
be used for religious functions at the school and become a
natural rallying point for the Hindu community. The school
secretariat was decorated with posters of Hindu gods and
goddesses, ceremonial oil lamps, and other religious and

cultural paraphernalia. And the walls in the library were decorated with framed pictures of Indian notabilities such as Jawaharlal Nehru, Indira Gandhi, and classic Indian writers and thinkers that accentuated the importance of language and traditional arts and culture and the Indian roots of Tamil culture. The particular configuration of the social spaces of the Muslim and Hindu schools, I argue, effectively challenged the nation-state's attempt to impose its own order on the schools. According to Fernandez (2000), there exists 'a mode of knowledge on the periphery, which is to invert the boundary relationship; to conceptualize itself as central and the putative centre as remote, inept, peripheral to its own essential values.' (p. 12) In all the schools, politics was perceived to have a major impact on education, and that instead of producing equal citizenship, it resulted in inequality and mis-recognition. The schools that appeared most successful in countering this labelling and its ramifications were those that managed to 'invert the boundary relationship,' to use Fernandez's expression (2000, 12) and to make a centre of itself, or to produce what could be termed peripheral citizenship, where both recognition and redistribution to a large extent stemmed from internal sources and solidarity.

CHANGING POLICIES OR POLITICS?

In recognition of the fact that education plays a significant role in the socialization of pupils as citizens and that education in conflict and post-conflict situations has become a site of intervention of growing importance, I shall conclude by briefly reflecting on the policy relevance of my analysis. Like many other governments, the government of Sri Lanka has decided to combat conflicts and foster social cohesion through education. A key strategy has been to eliminate discriminatory contents from learning material and to develop a new curriculum including subjects related to peace, tolerance, and citizenship. Leaving aside the many difficulties pertaining to effective implementation of the strategy, the question remains as to whether it is likely that an improved curriculum will deliver a significant change in attitudes and behaviour and hence to contribute to peace and social cohesion. As my analysis suggests, there are several reasons why this is indeed doubtful.

Even though many of my informants at some point mentioned the need to better accommodate the histories, values, and viewpoints of different communities in school textbooks, they were generally far more concerned with the uneven access to quality education. The appointment of principals and teachers; the allocation of resources for buildings, equipment and facilities; the distribution of books; and the engagement of relevant authorities were repeatedly brought up as examples that contradicted the notion of equal citizenship that was contained in textbooks, and replaced them with a sense of partial citizenship. The main reason for this was to be found outside the school and classrooms, in the extreme influence of politics on education. The decentralization of government and resources in Sri Lanka has generated a political structure based on patron–client relationships, where recognition and resources are exchanged for votes or other favours. As shown in the discussion, political patronage first of all operates on the basis of ethnic distinctions, which put the Sinhalese majority at the apex and opposes it to the ethnic minorities. However, other distinctions such as occupation, legal status, and political affiliation are also frequently put to work and created their particular experiences of inclusion and exclusion, and as argued they also paved the way for constructions of an alternative local, peripheral citizenship.

Reflecting on the limitations of the curriculum as an agent of change in conflict situations, Bekerman (2005) asserts that 'only that which is done is learned . . . only that which is done through sustained effort and is able to echo in multiple contextual social settings stands a chance to enter memory and be acted upon so as to become part of the social fabric.' (p. 240) My analysis similarly suggests that more attention must be paid to children's total experience of going to school, and these are structured by the wider society in general and the political system and political culture in particular. In other words, it is the political system—its manner of distributing resources and hope, its way of generating material and mental categories of differentiation—that needs to undergo change. As long as children experience deprivation and discrimination and see these as the result of a system where 'politics and not policies count' as one informant phrased it, then they are unlikely to induce the notion of equal Sri Lankan citizenship with any credibility and will instead turn to ethnic and other local notions of citizenship that can guarantee them some degree of security.

REFERENCES

Appadurai, Arjun (1998), *Modernity at Large: Cultural dimensions of Globalization*, Vol. 1 (Minneapolis: University of Minnesota Press), 178–99.

Bekerman, Zwi (2005), 'Are there children to educate for peace in conflict-ridden areas? A critical essay on peace and coexistence education', *Intercultural Education*, 16(3), 235–45.

Brow, James (1996), *Demons and Development: The Struggle for Community in a Sri Lankan Village* (Tuscon: University of Arizona Press).

Bush, Kenneth and Saltarelli, D. (2000), 'The two faces of education in ethnic conflict: Towards a peacebuilding education for children', (Florence: UNICEF Innocenti Research Centre).

Davis, Lynn (2006), 'Education for positive conflict and interruptive democracy', in H. Lauder, P. Brown, J. A. Dillabough, and A. H. Halsey, eds., *Education, Globalization and Social Change* (Oxford: Oxford University Press), 1029–37.

Fernandez, James (2000), 'Peripheral wisdom', in A. Cohen, ed., *Signifying identities: Anthropological Perspectives on Boundaries and Contested Values*. (London: Routledge), 117–44.

Fraser, Nancy (2003), 'Social justice in the age of identity politics: Redistribution, recognition, and participation', in N. Fraser and A. Honneth, eds., *Redistribution or Recognition?* (London: Verso), 7–109.

Ginige, Indira Lilamani (2002), 'Education research for policy and practice: Secondary education reforms in Sri Lanka', *Educational Research for Policy and Practice*, 1(1), 65–77.

Gunaratna, Rohan (1990), *Sri Lanka: A Lost Revolution? The Inside Story of the JVP* (Kandy: Institute of Fundamental Studies).

Hasbullah, S. H. (2004), 'Justice for the dispossessed: The case of a forgotten minority in Sri Lanka's ethnic conflict', in S. H. Hasbullah and B. M. Morrison, eds., *Sri Lankan Society in an*

Era of Globalization: Struggling to Create a New Social Order (New Delhi: Sage), 221–40.

Hettige, Siri T. (2004), 'Economic policy, changing opportunities for youth, and the ethnic conflict in Sri Lanka', in D. Winslow and M. D. Woost, eds., *Economy, Culture, and Civil War in Sri Lanka* (Bloomington: Indiana University Press), 115–30.

Jackson, Michael (2002), *The Politics of Storytelling: Violence, Transgression and Intersubjectivity* (Copenhagen: Museum Tusculanum Press).

Jayaweera, Swarna (2007), 'Schooling in Sri Lanka', in A. Gupta, ed., *Going to School in South Asia* (Westport, CT: Greenwood), 167–94.

Jeffery, Patricia (2005), 'Introduction: Hearts, minds and pockets', in R. Chopra and P. Jeffery, eds., *Educational Regimes in Contemporary India* (New Delhi: Sage), 13–38.

Kabeer, Naila (2005) ed., *Inclusive Citizenship: Meanings and Expressions.* (London: Zed).

Liberation Tigers of Tamil Eelam (LTTE) (2006), 'Caring for the children in Tamileelam'. Press release released on the Children's Day on 1 Oct. 2006. http://www.ltteps.org/?view=1622and folder=2

Little, Angela (2003), *Education for All: Policy and Planning Lessons from Sri Lanka* (Sevenoaks: DFID Education Publications).

Little, Angela (2003), *Labouring to Learn: Towards a Political Economy of Plantations, People and Education in Sri Lanka,* (Colombo: Social Scientists' Association).

Matthews, Bruce (1995), 'University education in Sri Lanka in context: Consequences of deteriorating standards', *Pacific Affairs,* 68(1), 77–94.

Nissan, Elizabeth (1996), *Sri Lanka: A Bitter Harvest* (London: Minority Rights Group).

O'Sullivan, Meghan (1999), 'Conflict as a catalyst: The changing politics of the Sri Lankan muslims', in S. Gamage and I. B. Watson, eds., *Conflict and Community in Contemporary Sri Lanka, 'Pearl of the East' or the 'Island of Tears?* (Colombo: Vijitha Yapa Bookshop), 253–78.

Ong, Aihwa (1996), 'Cultural citizenship as subject-making, Immigrants negotiate racial and cultural boundaries in the United States', *Current Anthropology*, 37(5), 737–62.

Perera, Lal, Wijetunge, S, and Balasooriya, A. S. (2004), 'Education reform and political violence in Sri Lanka', in S. Tawil and A. Harley, eds., *Education, Conflict and Social Cohesion* (Paris: UNESCO, International Bureau of Education), 375–433.

Perera, Sasanka (2006), 'Sri Lankan education system as a reflection of society's ruptures: A conceptual and theoretical exploration', (draft), http://www.education.gov.lk/nec/documents/nec_rs_007.pdf

Ponnambalam, Satchi (1983), *The National Question and the Tamil Liberation Struggle* (London: Zed).

Richardson, John M. (2004), 'Violent conflict and the first half decade of open economy policies in Sri Lanka: A revisionist view', In D. Winslow and M. D. Woost, eds., *Economy, Culture, and Civil War in Sri Lanka* (Bloomington: Indiana University Press), 41–72.

Rosaldo, Renato (1994), 'Cultural citizenship in San Jose, California', *Political and Legal Anthropology Review*, 17(2), 57–63.

Sambandan, V. S. (2004), 'History from the LTTE', *Frontline*. Retrieved from http://www.frontlineonnet.com/fl2103/stories/20040213000206000.htm

Selvarajah, M. (2003), 'Education in the conflict areas in Sri Lanka: A case for capacity building at local schools in Batticaloa', in M. Mayer, D. Rajasinghan-Senanayake and Y. Thangarajah, eds., *Building Local Capacities for Peace. Rethinking Conflict and Development in Sri Lanka* (New Delhi: MacMillan), 288–304.

Smith, A., and Vaux, T. (2003), 'Education, conflict and international development', (London: DFID).

Sørensen, Birgitte Refslund (2001), 'Sri Lanka: Developing new livelihoods in the shadow of war: Displaced, relocated and resettled Muslims), in B. R. Sørensen and M. Vincent, eds., *Caught Between Borders* (London: Pluto, 172–202).

Sørensen, Birgitte Refslund (2008), 'Humanitarian NGOs and Mediations of Political Order in Sri Lanka', *Critical Asian Studies*, 40(3), 89–113.

Sri Lanka, Department of Census and Statistics (2001), Census on population and housing, http://www.statistics.gov.lk/PopHouSat/PDF/Population/p9p8%20Ethnicity.pdf

Sri Lanka, Department of Education (2005), 'Citizenship Education: Grade 7', (Battaramulla: Government of Sri Lanka).

Sri Lanka, Ministry of Education (2005), 'Education for Economic Development and Prosperity', (Colombo: Government of Sri Lanka).

Sri Lanka, Ministry of Human Resource Development Education and Cultural Affairs (2004), 'School Census 2003 Preliminary Report', (Battaramulla: Government of Sri Lanka).

Sri Lanka, National Institute of Education (2006a), 'Civics and Governance: Syllabus Grades 10 and 11', (Maharagama: Government of Sri Lanka).

Sri Lanka, National Institute of Education (2006b), 'Life Competencies and Civic Education: Syllabus Grade 6', (Maharagama: Government of Sri Lanka).

Stewick, E. D. and Levinson, B. eds. (2007), *Reimagining Civic Education. How Diverse Societies Form Democratic Citizens* (Plymouth: Rowman and Littlefield).

Stokke, Kristian (2006), 'Building the Tamil Eelam state: Emerging state institutions and forms of governance in LTTE-controlled areas in Sri Lanka', *Third World Quarterly*, 27(6), 1021–40.

Wickrema, Ariya, and Colenso, Peter (2003), Respect for diversity in educational publication—The Sri Lankan experience. Retrieved from website://siteresources.worldbank.org/EDUCATION/ Resources/27800-1121703274255/1439264-1126807073059/ Paper_Final.pdf

NOTES

1. Sri Lanka was known as Ceylon until 1972, but for the sake of simplicity I use its current name for all historical periods.

2. Tamil Eelam is the name of the independent state to which the LTTE aspire.

3. Although interesting, it is beyond the scope of this chapter to discuss the influence of globalization and international aid on Sri Lanka's education system.

4. Sri Lanka's schools are segregated according to medium of instruction. 68% of the schools are Sinhala-medium, 29% Tamil-medium, 0.5% Sinhala and Tamil 45, 1.8% Sinhala and English, 0.5% Tamil and English, whereas 0.2% teach in Sinhala, Tamil, and English. The corresponding figures for Puttalam's 343 schools are: Sinhalese-medium (78%), Tamil-medium (20%), Sinhala- and Tamil-medium (1%), and Sinhala- and English-medium schools (1%; see Sri Lanka, Ministry of Human Resource Development Education and Cultural Affairs (2004)). Schools are moreover categorized according to religion and there are Buddhist, Hindu, Muslim, Roman Catholic, and Christian schools (L. Perera et al., 2004, 396).

5. I want to stress that my research does not disclose whether or to what extent my informants' views were substantiated by hard facts, but as Richardson (2004) argues, 'in an ethnically conflicted society . . . it is perceptions of relative deprivation rather than abstractions crafted by economists that matter.' (60)

6

Reforming Gender Inequities in Education: Pakistan's Girls Middle School Stipend Programme
—Fareeha Zafar

Government has in general failed in ensuring adequate quality provision and enrolment of girls beyond primary education. Issues of shortage of girls' schools, dysfunctional schools, lack of female teachers, quality of teacher performance, shortage and delay in provision of textbooks, and relevance of the curriculum are some of the key factors in the perpetuation of poor quality education. Girls and women endure additional constraints due to their restricted mobility, lack of control over resources, limited autonomy and decision-making, and a low level of awareness of their civil rights. It is now an accepted fact that girls who have been to school for a significant amount of time often become drivers for positive social change and when they are able to work are more likely than boys to invest most of their earnings in their families.

This chapter explores several dimensions of the crisis of girls' education in Pakistan and looks at some of the initiatives taken by government including a review of the female middle school stipend component of the Punjab Education

Sector Reform Programme (PESRP) since 2003.[1] Research shows short- and medium-term impact of the intervention as being highly successful especially, as in Pakistan this is the stage where most girls drop out of school. The evidence thus suggests that there appears to be a greater retention in girls' schooling in areas receiving the stipend and the gender gap is less in stipend areas as girls are catching up. The initiative has been appreciated by teachers, parents, and communities.

DIMENSIONS OF GENDER INEQUITY IN EDUCATION

Notwithstanding constitutional guarantees and official pronouncements, gender issues in education stem from political, economic, social, and cultural factors. Pakistan has one of the highest rates of out-of-school children in the world. Of the approximately 6.5 million out-of-school children at the primary school level, more than half are girls. At the primary level, net enrolment of children of the relevant school age is 66 per cent. Furthermore, almost half the children who join school do not complete primary education and a significant proportion of those who do complete are neither fully numerate nor literate. Not only is the situation much worse in the rural areas of the country, interprovincial differences are extremely disturbing as well. There is little difference between rural Sindh and Balochistan, and with the exception of the Punjab province, and that too in only a few districts, girls participation lags behind in all provinces. Similarly, transition rates from one level of education to the next are extremely low for both sexes but more so for girls.

Only half the children who complete primary school move on to middle schools, that is eight years of schooling and only a quarter have access to secondary education. With the majority of the population exposed to less than eight years of schooling and a miniscule number with ten years of education, the shortage of potential teachers is acute; rural areas are particularly vulnerable to the paucity of human capital (Pakistan, Bureau of Statistics, 2007).

In general, state policies and laws tend to complement and reinforce patriarchal structures in societies that are traditional and feudal. A symbiotic relationship exists between women's subordination resulting in dependence on male relatives and the need for adequate social services such as education. Thus, girls are more likely to be left out from school, in all age groups and in both low and high literacy areas. Inequities at the primary level result in even greater gender disparity at higher levels in combination with low transition rates to middle level and increased dropout rates before completion. With more than one-third of the population living below the poverty line in Pakistan, the performance of women/ girls is responsive to the stereotyped expectation of families and social cultural settings; and contributes to the higher out-of-school and dropout rate among girls. Rural girls from poor and illiterate families inevitably are the most deprived of education. Poverty is clearly an outcome of hierarchies of power but it is also multidimensional. In socio-economic and political systems dominated by men, poor girls come out the worst. Girls are taken out of school to ensure the households' survival. Many programmes that look primarily at school provision leave issues of gender and poverty inequalities untouched.

Education of girls is seen as a challenge to the male breadwinner role within the most established institution that of the patriarchal family. However, once parents accept the need to educate girls then facets of gender socialization show positive outcomes. Research shows that girls are willing to carry the double burden of homework and housework, they exhibit greater discipline, and there is less violence and fewer conflicts in girls' schools. Consequently, girls are out-performing boys at all educational levels.

Another factor is the better performance of female teachers particularly due to their use of innovative, activity based teaching methodologies in retaining girls in school. Furthermore, communities view female teachers as better role models for girls. Teacher recruitment policies have changed in response including the option given to female teachers to apply for jobs in schools of either sex so that currently 51 per cent of public school teachers are female. However, their ability to perform effectively is hampered by policy gaps relating to appointment of substitute teachers against teachers on maternity leave and issues of mobility. Research conducted in the prosperous district of Faisalabad in the Punjab province of Pakistan shows teacher shortages in different subjects compounding the problem in government schools. Private and community schools are able to address this issue by employing local women and training them on a continuous basis. Furthermore, qualification is not a bar in private and community schools.

SYSTEM RESPONSE TO THE CRISIS

Government has opted for more girls schools, upgradation of primary schools, construction of girls community model schools that go up to the elementary level, provision of free textbooks, stipends to girls to continue their education beyond primary, preference for female teachers, and incentives for private sector. These have become part of the political agenda, but, in the absence of systemic change, progress is slow and while the gender gap is slowly narrowing, gender disparities persist.

Projects initiated during the 1990s in Pakistan took note of two realities: the need to create additional seats for the increased number of students projected to complete primary school; and the importance of elementary education with a special focus on girls' education. Thus special initiatives were needed to ensure that more girls were in the system. Poverty and the lack of female teachers were seen as major impediments to the transition of girls from primary to middle schooling.

In 1992, the government of Pakistan requested the assistance of the Asian Development Bank (ADB), DFID and the World Bank to analyze issues, strategies, and options relating to expanding and improving middle-school education, and to prepare a project proposal to address identified issues. The government confirmed its priority for the project to the 1993 Country Programming Mission and requested that ADB assistance be limited to the provinces of Balochistan, North-West Frontier Province (now Khyber Pakhtunkhwa), and

Sindh. This initiative materialized under a loan from ADB from 1994 and 2001 (Asian Development Bank, 2004). The project focused on three areas:

a. under access and participation upgrading primary schools to middle schools, stipends to rural girls to complete middle school, and stipends to rural female matriculates to become middle school teachers, as well as studies for private sector participation;

b. as part of quality improvement curriculum review and restructuring, in service training of teachers, piloting a middle school achievement testing system and support to provincial governments for reviewing and supervision; and

c. for institutional strengthening studies to be conducted for school management organization, planning, monitoring, evaluation, and involvement of communities.

The project was rated as partly successful on completion, as despite the school upgrading programme and provision of substantial training inputs, enrolments did not increase as intended. Many schools were not adequately staffed and many facilities provided were not effectively utilized. Also, the impact of quality components was not readily apparent. Increase in private sector participation and number of female teachers could be attributable to the project. The Project Completion Report (PCR) identified poor governance as the primary cause of the project's overall poor performance.

In the Punjab province, the Punjab Middle Schooling Project (PMSP) was undertaken through Official Development

Assistance (ODA) support during the same period. Although it did not focus specifically on gender as the ADB one, the consultancy team from Cambridge consultants addressed gender and other equity issues in all project components, monitoring systems were improved and the project undertook impact evaluation studies and published the research results. These efforts helped the Punjab to introduce new and more effective practices. The project addressed equity issues in education through key interventions of quality components in the areas of training and material development. As such in all training programmes at least one session was allocated to *gender issues in education.* By the middle of 1999, 132 titles of fiction and non-fiction supplementary reading materials were published and gender audit of the first 84 supplementary readers was carried out, and shared with the teams responsible for developing supplementary readers. The Social Development Unit (SDU) of PMSP contributed towards the editorial process and writing activities for the supplementary readers in order to address the gender bias in readers (Khalid & Mujahid-Mukhtar, 2002). The success of the programme can be judged from the lasting impact of the training on teachers as has emerged from studies undertaken in the recent past (AKU-IED & SAHE, 2003; Society for the Advancement of Education, 2009). The PCR cites relevancy of materials, cost effectiveness, gender supportive materials, and teacher training as the main reasons. However, shortcomings point to lack of interest among teachers and library personnel, lack of maintenance funds, one time nature of the intervention, no ownership of the project, lack of consonance with the curriculum and examination system, failure to integrate intervention with the syllabus, lack of training of supervisory staff, and failure to provide related materials.

A SUCCESSFUL INTERVENTION: PUNJAB FEMALE SCHOOL STIPEND PROGRAMME

Conditional cash transfer programmes are now being widely used in Latin America, the Middle East, and Africa to give money either to mothers or families on condition that children attend school. These programmes are showing some positive results in improved rates of girls' enrolment and attendance at school (World Bank, 2010).

The Punjab Education Sector Reform Programme (PESRP), financed via World Bank lending, has three pillars:

a. public finance reforms to realign expenditures at the provincial and district level toward education and other pro-poor expenditures;
b. devolution and public sector management reforms; and
c. education sector reforms to improve quality, access, and governance of the education system.

Within the education sector, the reform programme has introduced a number of interventions: distribution of free textbooks, upgraded/new school infrastructure, recruitment of regular and contract teachers, increasing entry qualifications of teachers, female stipend programme, providing greater authority to school councils, NGO, and community management of school councils. The female middle-school stipend component is part of a package of reforms under which the Government of Punjab is responding to gender gaps in education by providing rupees 200 per month to girls enrolled in Classes VI, VII, and VIII in government schools, in 15 poorest districts of Punjab conditional on 80 per cent attendance during the school year.[2] The districts in which the stipend has been administered were selected from the bottom developmental rankings of the Punjab districts thus targeting the more rural areas.

EFFECTIVENESS AS PART OF A PACKAGE OF INPUTS

As in the case of previous interventions aimed at increasing access of girls to education beyond primary, the middle school stipend for girls was envisaged as one of a number of interventions targeting schools. It is the combination of inputs such as free textbooks, a stipend, recruitment of contract teachers with higher qualifications and physical inputs including extra classrooms, boundary walls, latrines etc. that households identify as contributing to girls' education. The stipend was first implemented in February 2004 and has continued since then under PESRP-II.

INCREASE IN ENROLMENT

An evaluation of the Punjab Female School Stipend Programme, Population Council (2007) shows that issues related to poverty contribute more than any other reason for children not attending school. Domestic responsibilities are imposed on girls more so than on boys, irrespective of area. This is also a manifestation of poverty where more helping hands are needed at the farm or home. Of those girls whose parents reported having ever received a stipend from schools, 80 per cent were currently in school. At ages 11–12, 94 per cent of girls who received a stipend were in school; correspondingly 83 per cent and 65 per cent were in school at ages 13–14 and 15–17. Of those girls whose parents reported having ever received a stipend from schools, 80 per cent were currently in school. At ages 11–12, 94 per cent of girls who received a stipend were in school; correspondingly 83 per cent and 65 per cent were in school at ages 13–14 and 15–17. There is clearly a positive effect of the stipend on enrolment and retention even though the sample that received stipends is very small. To some extent, boys' enrolments in middle school in the experimental areas also show improvements, depicting a possible spill over effect of the stipend scheme influencing household behaviour.

Communities also associate the increase in enrolment in middle schools with the government's stipend policy. Even in small and remote villages where a middle school is accessible, the stipend has resulted in higher enrolment even though all the people are not fully aware of a policy directive. However, communities with just primary schools tend to fall outside the ambit of the stipend scheme as few girls are able to move to cities to avail of this opportunity (Zafar & Mashallah, 2006).

Districts selected for the stipend programme present stark differences between private and public schools in material resources: in public schools almost a quarter of the schools did not have toilet facilities, and only about one-half of the classes had partial furniture when compared to private schools where almost all schools had toilets, and more than three-quarters of the classes had the requisite furniture. For a start, this confirms that the stipend programme has been correctly targeted towards the most neglected districts. The very different situation of schooling availability meant that girls and boys traversed much longer distances to reach school. Most definitely this is a deterrent against school attendance. Distances to school are much longer for girls in stipend areas compared to non-stipend areas. As the school level rises so does the distance travelled to reach the school also increases, for both boys and girls in both areas. There is also little evidence of switching from private to public schools in the stipend areas, supporting the fact that public schools remain the dominant and preferred (and possibly the only) choice in these districts. In the more developed districts not only are there more schools, the distance to school is also less. Head teachers tend to be more permanent in the more developed districts as well. There are fewer private schools in the less developed districts (Population Council, 2007).

While there is a clear positive effect of the stipend on enrolment and retention quality remains unaffected. Literacy and numeracy tests at the household level shows that there are small differences in learning quality between stipend and control districts (learning levels are slightly lower in stipend districts, however, the difference is insignificant).[3] This finding is also supported by qualitative research (Zafar & Mashallah, 2006).

DEMAND FOR HIGHER EDUCATION

The stipend scheme has also had an impact on girls access to higher education opportunities especially in large villages. The concurrent provision of resources in the schools—financial, physical, and human—has contributed to the increased enrolment of girls.[4] Education of girls is not necessarily linked to work options in the minds of communities who view the absence of secondary schools as prohibiting girls access to opportunities for higher education. Not only middle schools but elementary and high schools for girls have also been improved. Even small remote villages welcome the up gradation of the local primary school though security issues remain a concern. Women in general are very keen to give education to their girls and want the stipend to continue till matriculation. Mothers recognize and appreciate the addition of missing facilities, which, according to them, is the government's responsibility and not that of the community. The concern for incomplete work, inadequate provision of school furniture and other facilities remains.

EMPOWERING GIRLS

In feudal or conservative communities, girls are at liberty to spend the stipend. This has improved their status in the family and with reference to boys. Girls are also feeling more empowered as they are free to use it as they wish. In one community, the father of a girl asked her to lend him the money of the stipend but she refused to do so.

OBSTACLES TO REFORM

Despite numerous projects, gender seems a tokenism rather than a political will among development agencies and government.

THE POLITICAL ECONOMY OF GENDER

Systems of education—public, private, non-formal, and madrassa (religious schools)—are symptomatic of a political economy resting on tribal and feudal power structures where patronage, kinship (*biradari*), and constituency concerns continue to provide a rationale for providing less and low quality education to the poor, females, and minorities. While patriarchy is systemic and identifies governance systems, its relationship with class is highly significant. Poor women and girls are discriminated against more than those of other classes. This is most evident in the case of access to basic education and health services. The extended family system prevalent in rural areas continues to exert a negative impact on girls' access to education (Farah & Shera, 2007, 19). Feudal styles of patronage and manipulation operate despite an emerging industrial sector. However, economic power provides women more space and the means to challenge a patriarchal culture. Middle-class women bear the brunt of the gendered division of labour, upholding training, and increasingly joining the labour force—mostly in the informal and service sectors. Low-income and poor women suffer from the gendered division of labour in the family/society and violence despite selling their labour. Sale of women also has a poverty/class dimension.

Economic constraints direct parental choices to favour sending their sons to school rather than their daughters. Even if there is a minimal tuition fee charged in schools, expenditures on uniform, textbooks, school funds, and other materials, in addition to the opportunity cost of sending daughters to school, serve as constraints. Opportunity costs increase when children grow up and become more useful in the family's income-earning and/or domestic activities. In Pakistan, children in poor and even low-income families contribute substantially to the household income, directly through working with their parents in the fields, and this is common to both boys and girls, and as domestic labour. In addition, girls in particular help their mothers in household chores and in looking after their siblings. The large family size contributes to the need for the labour of girls. This also helps to explain the higher school dropout rates among grown up girls. It has also been observed, that where mothers go out of the house to work, school going girls are kept out of school to do the housework. Issues related to poverty contribute more than any other reason for children not attending school. It is clear that poverty remains the biggest obstacle for both boys and girls in all areas. Domestic responsibilities are imposed on girls more so than on boys, irrespective of area. This is also a manifestation of poverty where more helping hands are needed at the farm or home (Population Council, 2009).

THE PATRIARCHY-FUNDAMENTALISM NEXUS

The low status of women in Pakistani society ensures the existence of gender disparity in the availability of food, education, health, and employment facilities for women. Women's poor health status, caused by excessive child bearing and high level of illiteracy, is the result of their lower socio-cultural standing. For lack of information pertaining to different methods of family planning, social pressure to produce sons and often the permission of the husband or other influential family members, male and female, women are unable to fully utilize family planning facilities.

Of particular concern are security issues emerging from the prevailing feudal culture that feeds on the vulnerability of girls, who become victims of feudal-based and ethnic conflicts. Furthermore, sectarianism and fundamentalism impact on the enrolment of girls, functioning of schools, availability of female teachers, and education in general. Schoolgirls have become targets of kidnapping, acid throwing, and other acts of violence, as frequently reported in the press. Many forms of violence against women, such as *Karo Kari* or honour-killings, are associated with the community or family's demand for sexual chastity and virginity. The perpetrators of these crimes are mostly males and family members of the murdered women, who go unpunished or receive a reduced sentence. Violence against women is the most powerful mechanism used by the family, society, and state to silence the voices of resistance to the existing gender related social relations of production and reproduction, and their subordination. Such crimes, more often than not, are committed against women/girls from the lower and poorer classes, and mostly in rural areas.

Religious extremism has emerged as a key challenge to the education of girls. The practice of exclusion, segregation, discrimination, and violence against women and girls shows an increase over the last decade. In recent years, a key target of the worst forms of violence such as rape has increased as girls venture out of their homes and on the way to school. The targeted blowing up of girls' schools in the tribal regions and other parts of the Khyber Pakhtunkhwa (formerly, North-West Frontier Province) and threats to educational institutions that are co-educational, or only for girls, in other parts of the country are indicative of the further curtailing of opportunities for girls.

EQUITY NOT EQUALITY

Most global education policy has drawn on the Millennium Development Goals' emphasis on parity, focusing on 'what works' to get girls in school. Such an approach, which has often employed instrumental arguments about the economic returns to educating girls, rather than emphasizing rights in and through education and the transformation of gender relations, has often discouraged women's rights activists from engaging in education campaigns.

In some contexts, an exclusive focus on girls' education has also led to confusion about gender equality goals. Thus, when, as for example in a country like South Africa, more girls than boys are in school, officials come to think they have 'done' gender, although issues remain concerning economic, political and social rights, violence, and ideas about masculinity and femininity that undermine equality concerns. In short, gender issues come to be viewed in terms of enrolment numbers in schools and these are often considered as separate to concerns around equality in society as a whole (Unterhalter, North, & Parkes, 2009). In the Punjab province the focus on reducing gender disparities in primary and middle education has identified similar trends (Society for the Advancement of Education, 2010).

DISCONNECTED SOCIAL POLICY

An artificial separation of the school from wider social processes has also led to a failure to adequately address the ways in which issues of gender equality in schools interact with issues relating to poverty, health, large family size, housing, and work. In Pakistan, enrolment of girls compared to boys is lower at the primary level with the gap increasing with each successive grade. Studies show the gender gap to be greater from grade three onwards. In the absence of compulsory education, children tend to enter school at an older age especially in rural areas; this affects girls more as their height and onset of menarche are key determinants of their participation in education. The most critical grade is class three, the level at which the curriculum becomes more difficult, the girl requires special attention as she is reaching adolescence, and gender biases become institutionalized (Zafar & Malik, 2004). Girls more than boys tend to have responsibilities such as caring for younger siblings and the extended family, housework, farming, and piece-work, that keep them from having sufficient time to do school work. This may lead to their early withdrawal from education or may prevent them from attending school altogether. Early marriage is another area of concern especially in the dropout of girls before completing primary/middle school (UNICEF, 2011).

THE CRITICAL ROLE OF QUALITY OF EDUCATION

Illiteracy among poor and rural people is common. The most marginalized group deprived of education is the rural girls from poor and illiterate families. Parents' education has a strong influence on children's education. In Pakistan, mother's education appears to have a greater impact than father's education on children, particularly on the enrolment of girls. Given the high rate of illiteracy among women, their attitude to educating girls is quite encouraging, provided the girl is learning something in school.

A key aspect of patriarchal structures is the social assigning of men as the heads of families. In the absence of other support systems parents prefer to invest more on a son's education, because they are considered most likely to provide some return on their investment. In a study conducted on female teacher's and girl's access to primary school in rural areas of Pakistan, parents agreed that basic education was important for both boys and girls, but insisted that boys education must be a priority as their old age social security was attached with better economic ability of their sons (Zafar, 2004).

Women suffer additional constraints due to their restricted mobility, lack of control over resources, limited autonomy and decision-making, and a low level of awareness of their civil rights. There is minimal questioning of the role of the family, community, society, and educational institutions including the school, in promoting and sustaining stereotyped roles and images of girls and women. Textbooks and their content play a central role in the learning process especially with regard to cognitive development and the learning of life skills.

Language use is central to the construction and depiction of gender relations, specifically women in school texts, and has a direct bearing on what students learn to perceive as 'normal' and 'natural' vis-à-vis women's role and status in society, as well as on the value systems they internalize (Society for the Advancement of Education, 2010). With economic compulsions forcing women into the formal and non-formal market, their vulnerability to traditional social and cultural norms has increased. Female teachers are no exception to the pressures faced by women.

FROM EQUITY TO EQUALITY: CHALLENGING SOCIAL DISCRIMINATION

Whether the stipend scheme is viewed as income transfer or incentive payment by households, its contribution in increasing girls enrolment beyond primary school cannot be undervalued. Questions still remain regarding whether these programmes are adequate to address improved attainment at school, unequal gender relations within households and communities, and improvements in women's access to longer-term resources (Unterhalter et al., 2009).[5] Global and national education policies have drawn on the MDGs' emphasis on parity, focusing on 'what works' to get girls in school. Such an approach, which has often employed instrumental arguments about the economic returns to educating girls, rather than emphasising rights in and through education and the transformation of gender relations, has often discouraged women's rights activists from engaging in education campaigns (Unterhalter et al., 2009). The media has played a key role in reinforcing the links between traditional social roles and expectations for women. An artificial separation of the school from wider social processes has also led to a failure to adequately address the ways in which issues of gender equality in schools interact with issues relating to poverty, health, large family size, housing, and work.

For a long time strategies to improve access of girls were based on a rather narrow understanding of gender issues in education. Amongst these, the most common was construction of schools. Country-level research indicates the need to include interventions both at the demand and supply side of education. Strategies need to be based on a comprehensive understanding of the many factors involved, and deeper levels of analysis of how different communities in Pakistan take decisions about enrolling their boys and girls in school.

The importance of understanding transitions in girls' educational lives, from not only primary to secondary school but also from school to work, and the need to interrogate the quality and role of private education cannot be underrated. Strategies for gender equality must start with transforming the quality of teachers, the local school environment, and educational institutions. Despite reform of curricula and school textbooks, gender inequalities continue to be perpetuated in the classroom as negative female stereotypes still perpetuate. Classroom practices, such as a teachers' language and pedagogy, are still far from encouraging girls› self esteem and educational achievements. Pre-service education and training, and teachers in training need to be given opportunities to examine the way schools and schooling practices reproduce and reinforce gender distinctions and inequalities. If a long-run objective of the stipend programme is to increase the supply of female teachers particularly in low literacy and relatively poorer regions of Punjab not only do the Bachelors, Masters, and professional degrees currently required for teaching at the middle level need revision; the recruitment and posting of teachers based on these qualifications for teaching specific subjects also requires attention.

Classroom observations, textbook analysis, and interviews have revealed that schooling reinforces and strengthens the gendered identities and roles of the students. The national identity construction through the official curriculum offer the traditional roles of women and men as the history, language and literature, and ethics/moral education disciplines differentiate the roles of women and men in the traditional culture and such texts and images are not challenged and critically examined by the teachers and students. The rise of violence, mainly among boys and men, indicate that masculinity is constructed around violence (Society for the Advancement of Education, 2010).

Teachers fail to recognize that their practices are gender-biased and their language is sexist. However, if asked their practices differentiated the female and male students and imposed gendered expectations, they tend to ignore the effects of their everyday organization of classroom, activities, their talk, assessment, attention, and discipline. Change is needed in the ways that women are represented in the discursive field. But these changes need to move beyond the merely cosmetic. If the stranglehold of gendered roles and behavioural patterns are to change, women need to be restored to visibility in multiple areas of life. The need to be seen, not as 'relative creatures' whose identity is shaped by their relations to men, but as independent human beings whose contribution to society, like that of men, occurs at multiple levels of social and economic productivity in the private and public spheres of life (Society for the Advancement of Education, 2010).

Although the overall picture is discouraging, there is room for optimism. Educated girls marry later, want smaller families, and use contraception, thus, providing evidence for the centrality of girls' schooling in development as provided by the rapid fertility decline necessary for replacement levels. The demographic dividend, thus, rests on full enrolment of girls in primary school with female employment especially in non-agricultural activities essential to hike up employment rates. Moreover, educated households especially those with female earners are more likely to save and invest financially and in education. Regardless of the empirical methodology adopted, there are a number of consistent findings. Firstly, the estimated marginal returns to additional years of schooling are significantly higher for females than for males. Secondly, returns increase with higher levels of education, pointing to convex education-earnings profiles. Finally, the labour market differentially rewards males and females with relatively low education levels. Women with middle schooling are rewarded substantially more as compared to women with primary education. This is not true for males (Aslam, 2007). The receipt of the stipend does have a notable impact on attendance in school, and on retention, in comparison to those girls who did not receive the stipend pointing towards the need to expand the scheme to ensure wider impact. Rated as a wonderful programme for helping parents in educating their girls beyond primary, extension of the stipend scheme to private schools makes eminent sense (Society for the Advancement of Education, 2010).

Pakistan is obliged by its constitution and ratification of international treaties to ensure free education up to the secondary level and a respect for women's human rights and fundamental freedoms. The Convention on the Elimination of all forms of Discrimination Against Women (CEDAW) requires that all government departments ensure the rights to life and security of the person of all individuals in their jurisdiction of any kind, including sex. It is the responsibility of the state to guarantee equal status of women in all spheres including education.

REFERENCES

ADB DFID World Bank (2004), Devolution in Pakistan: Overview of the ADB/DFID/World Bank Study.

AKU-IED & SAHE (2003), 'Effectiveness of in-service teacher training programmes of the university of education Punjab', Aga Khan University Institute of Educational Development.

Asian Development Bank (2004), PCR: PAK 22091—Project completion report on the middle school project (Loan 1278-PAK[SF]) in Pakistan, Nov. 2004.

Aslam, Monazza (2007), Rates of return to education by gender in Pakistan (GPRG-WPS-064).

Farah, Iffat, and Shera, Seher (2007), 'Female education in Pakistan: A review', in R. Qureshi and J. Rarieya, eds., *Gender and Education in Pakistan* (Pakistan: Oxford University Press), 3–40.

Khalid, Humala Shaheen and Mujahid-Mukhtar, Eshya (2002), 'The future of girls' education in Pakistan: A study on policy measures and other factors determining girls' education', UNESCO.

Molyneux, M. (2008), 'Conditional cash transfers: A Pathway to Women Empowerment', Retrieved from http://www.pathways ofempowerment.org/Pathways_Brief_5.pdf

Pakistan Bureau of Statistics (2007), Pakistan Social and Living Standards Measurement Survey (2006–07) (Islamabad: Government of Pakistan).

Population Council (2007), Evaluation of the Punjab female school stipend programme.

Population Council (2009), Pakistan's demographic transition in the development context.

Rawlings, L. B. (2005), 'Evaluating the Impact of Conditional Cash Transfer Programmes', *World Bank Research Observer*, 20(1), 20–55.

Society for the Advancement of Education (2009), Situation Analysis of the Primary School Libraries Project (Lahore: SAHE).

Society for the Advancement of Education (2010), 'Situation analysis of gender disparities in primary and middle education in the Punjab', Case studies of Khanewal and Rawalpindi districts, GEPSP Punjab.

UNICEF. (2011), 'Adolescence: An Age of Opportunity', *The State of the World's Children 2011* (New York: UNICEF).

Unterhalter, Elaine, North, Amy, and Parkes, Jenny (2009), 'Gender equality and women and girls' education, 1995–2010: How much is there a space for hope?' Paper for UNESCO 15-Year Review of the Beijing Platform of Action.

World Bank (2010), 'Do conditional cash transfers lead to medium-term impacts?' Evidence from a female school stipend programme in Pakistan by IEG.

Zafar, Fareeha (2004), 'Gender review of education in the Punjab' (Lahore: SAHE).

Zafar, Fareeha, and Malik, Mirrat (2004), 'Why girls dropout from school: Findings of a survey in the Punjab' (Islamabad: UNESCO).

Zafar, Fareeha, and Mashallah (2006), Community stakeholder consultations on Punjab Education Sector Reforms Programme (PESRP) in 3 southern districts of Punjab Lahore, SAHE.

NOTES

1. For further details about the programme visit PESRP site: http://pesrp.edu.pk/activity_03.aspx
2. Ibid.
3. Impact of the Punjab Female School Stipend Programme: Triangulating the Analysis using Primary and Secondary Data Sources (2008).

4. In a Government Girls Elementary School in one village, a boundary wall has been constructed, roof repaired, wall chalking done, water tap, footpaths between lawns and classrooms built, whitewash, cupboard, teaching learning boards. The water pipe and bricks for raising the boundary wall were provided by the community. The school grant in 2005 was PKR 51,000 and total available at present is more than PKR 106,000. There is an HT and seven teachers. Although the one contract teacher appointed in 2004 left because of transport problems.

5. See for example, Molyneux (2008) and Rawlings (2005).

6. Pakistan has also introduced Article 25-(A) into the Constitution that stipulates free and compulsory education up to the secondary school level for all children between the ages of 5–16 years.

7

Transforming Public Schools: Impact of the CRI Programme on Child Learning in Pakistan

—Muhammad Farooq Naseer, Manasa Patnam, Reehana R. Raza

INTRODUCTION

Classroom innovations are rare in public sector schools in Pakistan. An extensive system of formalized examinations and cultural norms that value hierarchy ensures that classroom teaching remains didactic. Classes are teacher-led, have limited teacher-child interaction, and are focused on maximizing skill transfer—often through rote learning, with little exploration outside the government-determined curriculum. Limited resources mean that few initiatives are taken to visualize concepts or experiment with tools, providing little space for children to explore ideas outside the realm of their textbook. Teachers have limited incentives to experiment in classrooms and often do not have the necessary skills. There are also broader challenges facing the school administrators, which make issues of instructional approach almost secondary. This includes lack of teachers, lack of physical infrastructure, and in some cases, lack of children.

One recent exception has been an intervention that seeks to make classrooms child-friendly in public sector primary school in Islamabad. This intervention has taken place due to a Public Private Partnership (PPP) between the Federal Directorate of Education (FDE) and Children's Resource International (CRI) Pakistan, a non-profit training and education organization that is engaged in improving the quality of education in public sector schools in Pakistan.[1] The focus of CRI Programme is to democratize the learning environment, encourage children to take initiative and make active choices. It is introduced into government-run primary schools under existing management structures. The philosophy behind the programme is that children develop best when they are actively involved in their own learning process.

Hence the goal is to create a classroom environment where children feel confident to drive the learning process which is open-ended and is overall a fun place to learn. Rigorous evaluations of education sector reform are few in Pakistan, although increasingly becoming a norm internationally. The recent emphasis on rigorous evaluations of experimental interventions has led to number of evaluations of experimental design currently in process.[2] Moreover, few evaluations[3] exist of the numerous PPP interventions that have been implemented since 2003, which are outside the purview of experimental design. Building up a solid database of preliminary results of these existing programmes has immeasurable value for future policy design. This chapter by undertaking a rigorous evaluation of an existing PPP intervention makes a contribution to this effort. The focus of this evaluation is to determine the composite impact of a PPP that seeks to modify the classroom environment. Transforming classrooms to be 'child-friendly' encompasses a number of inputs including teacher training, improving family literacy and encouraging family involvement in the classrooms, and providing material inputs. Isolating the impact of each individual factor that together contributes to making a classroom child-friendly would be fruitless. Therefore, no attempt is made to isolate the effect of specific inputs of the CRI intervention on learning achievement. Although the decision to focus on the net effect of the CRI intervention is driven by the researchers' interest in child-friendly classrooms, problems with identification of individual variables in the Education Production Function (EPF) approach also preclude its usage. A number of criticisms have been made of empirical studies, which are based on the EPF approach. Meta-analyses which examine the empirical literature on inputs and school effectiveness find that there is little consensus on which inputs actually have significant impacts on school effectiveness (Fuller & Clarke, 1994; Glewwe P., 2002; Hanushek, 1986; Krueger, 2003). Such contradictions in results have limited value for policy-makers trying to optimize school performance (Glewwe P., 2002). Second, positive analysis of actual policy and budgetary decision-making processes reveals that inputs into the education production function are not optimized ex ante as predicted by theory. Rather, input choice seems inordinately influenced by educators and their preferences (Filmer & Pritchett, 1999). Last, the singular focus on inputs fails to capture the more complex process of education delivery where different local conditions determine how pedagogy affects achievement (Fuller & Clarke, 1994). However, attempts to measure local context and its impact on achievement through pedagogy is extremely difficult and few rigorous studies exist which capture this impact.

We compare learning outcomes and attendance among children in Programme schools with similar children in non-Programme schools using propensity score matching. The results indicate a positive and significant effect of child-friendly classrooms on learning; the combined effect across three subjects; English, Urdu, and Maths is found to lead to an improvement of up to 11 percentile in class ranking. This effect is robust to alternative estimators and selection on unobservable. Moreover, the effect is consistent when disaggregated by gender. The rest of the chapter is organized as follows. Section 2 reviews this policy intervention by situating it in the local context. It also examines the relevant literature and provides important details on the CRI Programme, which determine our empirical methodology as outlined in Section 3. Section 4 provides a description of the data while Section 5 discusses the results on the Programme's impact. Section 6 concludes.

BACKGROUND

RELATED ISSUES

Schools remain important for improvements in learning achievement. Schooling, whether public or private, continues to be the dominant factor in explaining learning achievements in developing countries. This is unlike developed countries where socio-economic characteristics outweigh school effects in determining learning achievement (Heyneman & Loxley, 1983). Recent evidence from rural Punjab in Pakistan presented by the Learning and Education Achievement in Punjab Schools (LEAPS) project also indicates the importance of school effects on learning outcomes.[4] The project indicates that for districts in Punjab 50 per cent of the variation in learning achievement can be explained by the variation in schools. Adding district and village variables increases this to 60 per cent for certain subjects while further addition of covariates for child and household characteristics only marginally improves the total explained variation to 68 per cent (Tahir Andrabi, Das, Khwaja, Vishwanath, & Zajonc, 2007; Das, Pandey, & Zajonc, 2006).

Public schools also remain important despite the recent growth of private schools in Pakistan. First, private schools are not more successful in all areas of the economy. Tahir Andrabi, Das, and Khawaja (2002a) show that private schools have expanded successfully in Punjab but in Balochistan and Sindh, they have been less of a presence. The evidence suggests that despite the success of private schools, market failures may continue to exist. Private and social returns may not equate and public schools have to deliver where private schools fail to go. And although the evidence of learning achievements in rural Punjab indicates that private schools out-perform public schools, there is great variation in public school performance with top government schools performing close to top private schools in mathematics. This indicates that there is a possibility of improvement in public schools

(Das et al., 2006). One means of doing this may be through Public Private Partnerships (PPPs), which can offer new resources, pedagogical approaches, and if accompanied with new institutional arrangements, different incentives for better performance.

Public Private Partnerships are a popular instrument through which governments across the world are seeking to address the ills of education delivery. By introducing non-government actors, through different contractual arrangements, the objective has been to increase quality, cost effectiveness, and access to schools. Pakistan has been no exception. The Government of Pakistan (GOP) has been a forerunner in experimenting with PPPs in the education sector. A new initiative was launched in 2001 under the Education Sector Review (Pakistan, Ministry of Education, 2001) giving special emphasis to PPPs. The GOP recognized the government's limitation in managing the education sector and advocated a much larger role for PPPs for the purpose of both: (i) mobilizing financial resources; and (ii) designing, executing and monitoring education activities (Pakistan, Ministry of Education, 2001). The GOP's goal as stated in the ESR was to sign on 26,000 partnerships by 2005. As of 2003, the government already had 6,240 schools upgraded through PPPs in Punjab and NWFP—renamed Khyber Pakhtunkhwa (Ministry of Education, 2004). Despite this breadth of experimentation with PPPs in Pakistan, few evaluations exist of these interventions.[5]

Moreover, little is known about different classroom environments and their impact on learning in Pakistan. With the exception of Children's Resource International (CRI) intervention in the public schools, adoption of child-friendly classrooms is usually limited to private schools. Even internationally, the empirical literature on outcomes under non-didactic approaches is limited and mostly draws on the US experience. The overall evidence from a number of longitudinal studies in the US favours child-friendly approaches for children of lower income groups in specific subject areas (Stalling & Stipek, 1986). Other studies have found that socio-economic status matters in determining whether child-friendly classrooms affect learning achievement. Studies that examine the introduction of this approach in middle-class children see no significant difference in learning achievement between these two approaches (Hirsh-Pasek, Hyson, & Rescorla, 1990).

The literature on learning achievements in developing countries is even sparser and mostly limited to post-primary schooling. Lockheed and Zhao (1993) highlight that more child-friendly approaches correlate negatively with science and math achievement in the Philippines. Fuller, Hua, and Snyder (1994) find that open-ended discussion of subjects like Maths by teachers undermine students' performance. Other studies that have compared didactic to non-didactic classroom environment find that children do better on achievement tests in classrooms where more didactic approaches are followed (Lockheed & Komenan, 1989).

INTERVENTION

The Children's Resource International (CRI) Programme was adopted in 2002 in the ICT schools as part of a larger strategy of the GOP to establish Islamabad Capital Territory (ICT) as the model school region in Pakistan. With USAID funding and the aid of its parent organization, Children Resource International Washington, CRI (Pakistan) was established in 2002 to implement the programme starting with 25 schools in Islamabad. An additional 10 Islamabad schools were added in 2003. From 2006, the CRI programme has been extended to 300 plus schools in Islamabad essentially covering all public schools involved in teaching from Kindergarten to Grade VIII in the country's capital.

The intervention supports a number of the Government of Pakistan's (GOP) objectives outlined in the ESR (2001–2005) including universal primary education, improving quality of education through teacher training and national literacy. Following Patrinos (2006), the Children's Resource International (CRI) intervention can be classified as a government contract for management and professional services.[6] In the CRI case, the government has contracted out for a package of inputs that introduces a new instructional approach based on making classrooms more child-friendly and teacher-facilitated rather than teacher-led. The intervention infused new pedagogical ideas and resources into the existing school system without changing the institutional environment or salary incentives. The CRI programme was introduced in yearly steps, starting with Kindergarten/Grade I teachers in 2002, with teachers of each subsequent grade being introduced to it every year. By September 2006, teachers in all grades between I and V in the 25 schools had been trained in child-friendly instructional approaches. Thus by June 2007, the cohort of Grade V children were the first to have completed their whole primary education (KG/Grades I–V) in child-friendly classrooms. A number of inputs contribute towards making a CRI classroom child-friendly. This includes teacher training, parent literacy and parent involvement in classrooms, and provision of material inputs to classrooms. We provide details on each of these aspects below.

Teacher Training

Teacher training is an important component of the CRI's goal of transforming classrooms. The adopted teaching methods aim at training teachers in interactive methods of learning. These methods were used to encourage children to be more creative and independent, take responsibility, and develop critical and independent thinking. Teacher training is offered at the start of the academic year when a teacher/classroom is introduced to the CRI approach. Training is offered twice for five days each, once at the beginning of the programme and once in the middle of the year. Teachers are subsequently supported by technical assistance offered to teachers and their schools throughout the academic year. This takes the form of regular visits by master trainers who support and review the biannual training already offered. Overall, between 2002 and 2006, the number of teachers trained was 788 including 173 head and deputy head teachers.

Parent Literacy and Family Involvement

A second component of making a CRI classroom child-friendly is improving parent literacy and encouraging family members to participate in their children's classrooms. The family literary component involves offering parents (and other family members) an opportunity to improve their literacy levels. The literacy component involves a hundred lessons offered in two sessions by CRI trained teachers. The programme however was not universally offered in all CRI pilot schools.

In total 2,300 individuals attended the programme over the 2002–06 period in the pilot schools.[7] Parent involvement is the second component of this programme, which encourages family members to be involved in their children's classrooms to assist teachers and occasionally share their insights or teaching experience.

Material Provisions

A critical component of transforming classrooms is establishing activity centres to help children interactively explore their lessons. In each CRI classroom, a number of activity centres were established including: mathematics, science, literacy, art, and dramatic play. To activate these centres, CRI provides classrooms with a number of teaching and learning aids, including furniture and other materials inputs such as basic building blocks, prisms, magnifying glass etc.

Children's Resource International (CRI) classrooms are distinguished from non-CRI classrooms by a number of activities, which make learning fun. These include morning meetings, choice times, book making, and author chair time. For example, in the morning meeting, children sit in a circle, share books, celebrate birthdays, and share any other concerns they have. During book-making time, children make their own stories and share them with their classmates. All these components together contribute towards transforming these classrooms from being teacher-led to being teacher-facilitated and child-friendly. This evaluation captures how this transformation of the classroom affects the learning outcomes of students.

METHODOLOGY

It has to be noted that while the selection for the CRI programme was restricted to schools, our objective is to compare individual test score differences. Thus, our identification strategy hinges on a two-stage matching procedure. We first construct a comparison group of schools who have not received the CRI programme (non-CRI schools, henceforth) but are most similar in characteristics to the set of schools who have received the CRI programme (CRI schools, henceforth). We then pool the student level information from both the treatment and control schools to subsequently match the children across these schools in order to compare their performance. The comparison, in the final analysis, is between matched groups of CRI and non-CRI children.

IDENTIFICATION STRATEGY

The chapter employs a two-stage matching procedure to estimate the ATT estimator. In the first stage, we undertake school level matching and in the second stage, we match children within the matched CRI and non-CRI schools in our sample.

School-level Matching

Twenty-five schools were selected for the CRI programme in 2002 by the Federal Directorate of Education (FDE). These comprise our treatment group for estimation. The comparison group of schools was then constructed from the remaining population of Islamabad schools. The FDE had provided us with a detailed description of the school attributes on which the initial school selection was based. Important criteria for selection included the location of school, whether it was in the rural or urban area, the type of school and its language of instruction.[8] Thus, our matching strategy relied in large part on finding a good match for CRI schools along these dimensions using pre-programme school information from a census conducted in 2002–03. After incorporating these variables, we arrived at the following specification for our school selection equation:

$$(1)\ Pr(y_S = 1) = A\,(\alpha_1 + \beta_1 K_s + \psi)$$

Where K_S is the vector of school quality covariates and ψ represents location specific effects—is the cumulative distribution function for a standard logistic variable. Based on the above selection equation, we were able to select a sample of 67 comparable Islamabad schools including the initial set of CRI partner schools. The schools were then stratified into various blocks—which we will term as school level blocks—based upon the similarity of their propensity scores (p-scores). Finally, we check whether our matching procedure is able to balance the distribution of the relevant variables in both treatment and comparison schools in each block. For the blocks to be balanced, the average estimated p-score as well as the mean of each variable in the selection equation should not be statistically different across CRI and non-CRI schools within each block. Ensuring that the balancing properties have been satisfied will imply that the assignment to treatment can be considered random within each block under the ignorability of unobservable assumption.

Child-level Matching

We use a similar procedure to match CRI children to non-CRI children. However in this case we estimate the p-scores employing a logistic regression of participation within each school level block, which was defined previously by school-level matching. Thus we have:

$$(2) \quad Pr(y_s = 1) = A \left(\propto_2 + \beta_2 C_i + \varphi T_s \right)$$

Where y_i is whether the child has been recipient to the CRI programme (being in a CRI school at the time of testing) or not; C_i is a vector of all child covariates and T_s consists of teacher attributes. Based upon this, children are further stratified into blocks. As stated earlier, we restrict our observations within the common support region as well as test for the two balancing properties. It has to be noted that each school-level block is further stratified into various child level blocks. The final blocks, the child-level blocks that have been created are balanced not only on child-level covariates but also on school level covariates.

Estimation

Within each block, in which both CRI and non-CRI children are present, we will compute the difference between the average outcome of the treated units and the control units. Following Becker and Ichino (2002), we compute a weighted average of the difference within blocks as our estimator of programme impact, where the weight for each block is given by the corresponding fraction of treated units in that block.

SELF-SELECTION AND SENSITIVITY ANALYSIS

A convincing non-experimental evaluation of some existing programme is an empirical challenge. However, in the absence of experimental data, using non-experimental methods has value, provided one tests the underlying assumptions of such methods in the given context (R. Dehejia & Wahba, 1999; Heckman & Hotz, 1989).[9] Recently, a series of papers have reviewed different non-experimental evaluation estimators with a view to find conditions under which they perform well relative to the experimental estimators of the treatment effect (R. Dehejia, 2005; Smith & Todd, 2001). They conclude that the reliability of non-experimental estimators varies widely depending on the quality of data as well as the correct specification for the propensity score. Factors such as having a richer set of controls, geographical proximity of treatment and control units and using the same source of data for the two groups (with consistent definitions and measurement) as well as using a specification that satisfies the balancing property and is robust to small changes greatly improves the performance of a non-experimental estimator. As stated in Sections 4 and 5 below, the above conditions are satisfied for our chapter. In addition, we perform a range of robustness analyses to determine the reliability of our estimates. In the first instance, we consider alternative estimators for the treatment effects by comparing the results from stratified matching to those obtained by using various other propensity score-based matching techniques viz. spline and kernel-based matching. We also present results from the bias-corrected matching estimator proposed by (Abadie & Imbens, 2006).

Secondly, we consider the sensitivity of our estimates to selection-on-unobservables bias. Here, we make use of the bounding approach proposed by Rosenbaum (2002) to determine the extent to which the unobserved factors must influence treatment selection to affect our results. The bounds on the odds ratio that either of the two individuals receive the treatment is given by:

$$(3)\ \frac{1}{e^\gamma} \leq \frac{P_i(1-P_i)}{P_j(1-P_j)} \leq e^\gamma$$

The Rosenbaum bounds calculate at each value of e^γ, the significance level for the null hypothesis that treatment effect is equal to zero. This cut-off point should be large enough to place confidence in our estimates against the presence of unobservable selection bias.

DATA

The chapter uses two primary sources of data: the Federal Directorate of Education (FDE) database on school-level attributes and information collected through tests and surveys administered to individual Grade IV children and their teachers in selected sample schools. The FDE database contained detailed information on all Islamabad schools from a census conducted in 2003.

This data was used to select matching non-CRI schools on the school attributes that were used to choose pilot schools for the CRI Programme. This was discussed extensively with the Director Training of FDE, and our specification was based on the criteria highlighted in that meeting. We examine the impact of the CRI programme on five outcomes of interest: the total score obtained by a child on the test as well as the score in English, Urdu, and Mathematics along with his rate of class attendance. The child testing instrument, which had three sub-sections on Urdu, English, and Mathematics comprised of 48, 51, and 44 questions respectively.

The language sections tested children, among other things, on their reading comprehension and simple sentence creation abilities, and the Mathematics test included arithmetic operations like multiplication, division, LCM etc. The questions ranged in their difficulty level and were appropriate for the curriculum being taught in the schools for Grades III–V. To maintain reliability of the test outcomes, the testing instrument was kept strictly confidential from the school authorities in both CRI and non-CRI schools.[10] In addition, we obtained school attendance records of children for the months of January, February, and March 2007. The survey also provided us with detailed information on children and their parents' occupation, education, as well as household asset and demographics using a child questionnaire which was administered on the same day to all children who took the test. Relevant information was also collected on class teachers in the sample schools.

Table 1: Descriptive Statistics

Variable	CRI		Non-CRI		Difference	
	Mean	SE	Mean	SE	Mean	SE
Child						
Male[a]	0.51	0.03	0.5	0.02	0.01	0.03
Age in years	9.74	0.05	9.97	0.05	−0.23**	0.08
Mother went to school[a]	0.68	0.02	0.63	0.02	0.06+	0.03
Father is professional[a]	0.62	0.03	0.59	0.02	0.02	0.03
Father is entrepreneur[a]	0.16	0.02	0.15	0.01	0,00	0.02
Number of siblings	3.42	0.09	3.75	0.08	−0.34**	0.12
Number of older siblings	1.86	0.09	1.91	0.07	−0.05	0.11
Asset Index	0.44	0.11	0.24	0.08	0.20	0.14
Child height	137.2	0.43	137.5	0.38	−0.35	0.6
Child weight	61.7	0.78	64.8	0.76	−3.10**	1.14
Teacher						
Teacher academic Qual[a] (FA/FSc. Or above)	0.07	0.01	0.84	0.01	0.13**	0.02
Teacher experience (years)	9.82	0.36	6.75	0.27	3.08**	0.44
School						
English medium[a]	0.88	0.09	0.67	0.09	0.21	0.14
Isl. Model College[a]	0.25	0.11	0.23	0.08	0.02	0.13

Variable	CRI		Non-CRI		Difference	
	Mean	SE	Mean	SE	Mean	SE
F.G. Model School[a]	0.63	0.13	0.4	0.09	0.23	0.15
Boys School[a]	0.13	0.09	0.13	0.06	−0.01	0.11
Co-educational[a]	0.63	0.13	0.63	0.09	−0.01	0.15
Urdu score	24.51	0.43	22.57	0.33	1.94[b]	0.54
Math score	21.76	0.35	21.1	0.27	0.67	0.44
English score	31.66	0.37	28.65	0.35	3.01**	0.53
Total score	77.93	1.03	72.31	0.88	5.61**	1.38
Urdu score (IRT)	27.09	0.29	25.1	0.25	1.99**	0.39
Math score (IRT)	24.6	0.21	23.18	0.18	1.42**	0.28
English score (IRT)	31.96	0.31	29.87	0.26	2.09	0.41
Total Score (IRT)	83.6	0.81	78.2	0.69	5.50**	1.08
Average attendance	0.86	0.00	0.87	0.00	−0.01[+]	0.006
Number of Observations	**378**		**608**			

Notes: This simple comparison of means is done after pooling observations from all the different blocks together. Thus, as expected, CRI and non-CRI children are not evenly matched along several dimensions as indicated by significant differences in the mean values of covariates.
[a]Dummy variable.
[+]Significant at 10% level.
**Significant at 1% level.

In the following analysis, we restrict our attention to those children who received all of their primary schooling in the same school and were thus exposed to the CRI programme for at least a total of four years (we allow children who entered school in Grade I rather than kindergarten). Originally, the children in Grade IV who undertook the test also included those who were lateral entrants into CRI and non-CRI schools.

Fig. 2: Propensity Score Matching Blocks, CRI and non-CRI

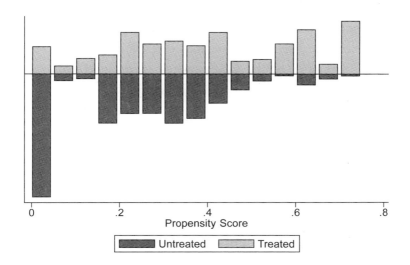

Their inclusion in our analysis presents a potential problem of self-selection. We understand that there may be limitations to analysing only the restricted sample as it is possible that the students leaving CRI schools were in fact the ones not affected by the programme. In the absence of any tracking information on children who left a school, we do not have information to address this particular concern but we expect a large majority of school switches to arise from unrelated migratory flows in the city because of the centralized admission policy in ICT and the general norm restricting school transfers under ordinary circumstances.[11]

Be that as it may, there is an additional advantage to focusing on the restricted sample which comprises children with (at least) four years of CRI exposure. If one believes that learning effects accumulate over time, then including children with different levels of exposure to the programme would dampen the overall estimate of the programme's effect due to the heterogeneity of individual level treatment effects. Thus, irrespective of any selection bias, we would expect more reliable estimates of the CRI's overall learning effect over a four-year period from this restricted sample.[12]

Our first set of results use the simple aggregate score on the test as the outcome variable. However, such an approach has a serious shortcoming in that it does not account for differences between the individual questions on the test. Moreover, two individuals with the same aggregate score on the achievement test might still differ in their latent cognitive ability.[13] In order to account for both the difficulty level of individual questions and the student's latent ability, we use Item Response Theory (IRT), to readjust the aggregate scores. We specify a three parameter logistic model for the probability of a correct response by an individual to the different test questions. The IRT adjusted score is then, essentially a sum of the probabilities of providing a correct answer to each question on the test. Table 1 reports descriptive statistics on all those Grade IV children who took the test and compares the means of different variables across treatment and comparison groups.[14] Several variables have a significant difference across the two school groups. But that is to be expected since the table is comparing the average children in CRI and non-CRI schools after pooling together the data from all the different blocks. Our two-stage matching yielded several blocks where CRI and non-CRI children were matched as shown in Fig. 1. A better comparison is to look at CRI and matching non-CRI children within a block defined on child attributes. Figs. 2 and 3 do such a comparison by depicting the mean assets and age of children within blocks. Overall, the children in the treatment and control group are reasonably well-matched on wealth within these blocks.

Fig. 3: Mean Asset of Children by Blocks, CRI and non-CRI

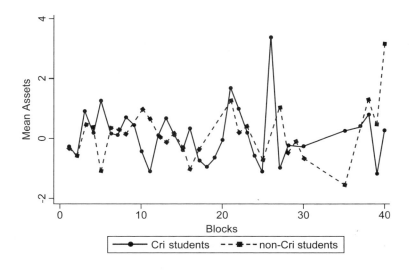

We also rigorously tested the balancing property for match quality as mentioned earlier in Section 3. We also compare the distribution of obtained propensity scores between CRI schools and non-CRI to verify that they are similar. The two sample Kolmogorov–Smirnov statistic, under the null that the two distributions are equal, is 0.37. We are unable to reject the null at the 5 per cent level of significant; in effect confirming that the propensity scores obtained for CRI and non-CRI schools belong to the same distribution.

RESULTS

The final sample of matched children contains data on 986 children from 46 schools. We plot the distribution of exam scores for the children in the two groups. Fig. 4 shows that the overall distribution of scores for CRI lies to the right of the scores obtained by non-CRI children. Thus, without controlling for individual heterogeneity, there is a marked difference in scores in the favour of CRI children.

Fig. 4: Mean Age of Children by Blocks, CRI and non-CRI

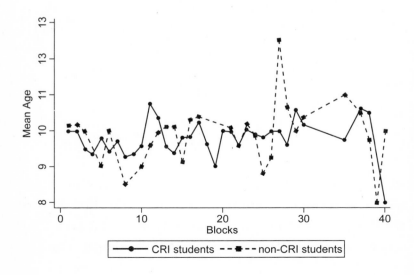

After having matched children in the CRI schools with similar children in the non-CRI schools, we proceed to obtain estimates of the average CRI effect on a student's exam scores. Table 2 reports the average treatment effect on the treated using both the total test score as well as the IRT-adjusted score. Given our specification for the propensity score we were able to match 362 children in the treatment (CRI) schools with 173 children in the comparison schools.[15]

Table 2: School and Child Selection Prohibits

Dependent Variable	CRI	
	(a) School level (cluster F.E.)	(b) Child level (school block F.E.)
F.G. Model School	−0.646 (0.67)	−
Islamabad Model College	−1.497+ (1.74)	−
English medium	2.613* (2.42)	−
Co-educational	−1.520* (2.17)	−
Boys school	−0.428 (0.55)	−
Male	−	0.167+ (1.68)
Age in years	−	−0.130** (2.63)
Mother went to school	−	0.045 (0.39)
Teacher academic qual.	−	1.563** (7.76)

Dependent Variable	CRI	
	(a) School level (cluster F.E.)	(b) Child level (school block F.E.)
Teacher experience (years)	–	0.081**
		(9.37)
Father is professional	–	0.043
		(0.37)
Father is entrepreneur	–	0.012
		(0.080)
Number of siblings	–	–0.086*
		(2.48)
Number of older siblings	–	0.056
		(1.49)
Asset index	–	0.01
		(0.38)
Child height	–	0.029**
		(4.06)
Child weight	–	–0.016**
		(4.27)
Observation	77	986

Note: Absolute value of z statistics in parentheses.
⁺Significant at 10% level.
˙Significant at 5% level.
˙Significant at 1% level.

The balancing requirement for the propensity score was met after the children were divided in 17 blocks of matching CRI and non-CRI children. The table reports the ATT estimate for each of the three subject components of the test as well as the overall test score and average rate of attendance during the period January–March 2007.

Table 3: Average Treatment Effect on the Treated: Stratified Matching

	Total Score	IRT Score
Urdu	1.579	2.441**
	(1.63)	(3.08)
Math	1.059	1.747**
	(1.33)	(3.77)
English	3.378**	2.576**
	(2.78)	(3.36)
Total Score	6.026*	6.764**
Average attendance	0.014	0.014
	(1.49)	(1.49)
	Treatment	**Control**
No. of Observations	362	173
Child height	–	0.029**
		(4.06)
Child weight	–	−0.016**
		(4.27)
Observation	77	986

Note: Absolute values of bootstrapped t-statistics in parentheses. The first column reports total marks on the test and the second column is the effect on a weighted aggregate computed by using a 3-parameter item response model.
+Significant at 10% level.
*Significant at 5% level.
**Significant at 1% level.

Column 1 in Table 3 shows that the estimated treatment effect is positive for all of the outcomes and significant for the total test score, i.e. CRI children perform better than matching children who have not received exposure to the CRI programme, overall as well as in English. CRI children also attend school more often. The difference is larger in magnitude for the two languages as opposed to mathematics. The IRT-adjusted score accounts for the difficulty of individual items on the test and is significantly different for the two groups on all sections of the test. The CRI programme seems to have the greatest effect on a child's reading and writing skills as compared to simple numeric abilities. The effect on all subject areas is statistically significant at 1 per cent.

Fig. 5: Kernel Density Distribution of Scores, CRI and non-CRI

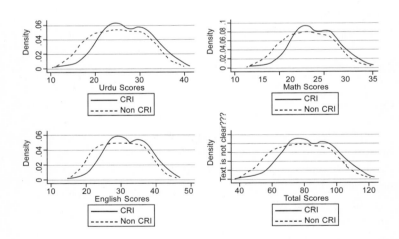

The effect of the CRI programme on a student's overall performance on the test is to increase the average score by 6.8 marks. The attendance rate over the last three months has been greater by 1.4 percentage points for CRI children as compared to non-CRI children, a difference which is statistically significant at 10 per cent in a one-sided significance test.

Table 4: Sensitivity Analysis

	Kernel matching (1)	Abadie-Imbens (2)	Spline matching (3)
Urdu	0.634	1.504**	1.47**
	(1.409)	(3.61)	(4.31)
Math	0.477	1.066**	1.06**
	(1.391)	(3.61)	(4.10)
English	0.66	1.592**	1.56**
	(1.038)	(3.60)	(3.63)
Total Score	1.771	4.161**	4.09**
	(1.232)	(3.61)	(4.20)
Avg. attendance	0.021*	−0.007	−0.0097
	(2.086)	(0.91)	(1.10)
# Treatment	341	378	281
# Control	181	608	608

Notes: 1. The difference in the number of observations for Abadie–Imbens and Spline matching arises due to the difference in the underlying matching approach. 2. For the Abadie–Imbens estimator, we report the heteroskedasticity robust analytical *t*-statistics for sample ATT. For the rest, absolute values of bootstrapped *t*-stats are reported in parentheses.
⁺Significant at 10% level.
˙Significant at 5% level.
˙˙Significant at 1% level.

An effect of this magnitude on student test scores is quite big. One has to keep in mind that while the actual size of the learning effect varies from individual to individual, the above estimates capture the average effect on child's learning over a period of four years. Given the distribution of IRT-adjusted scores among sample children, the above effect translates to an improvement by 0.4 standard deviations. To put this in context, a difference in expected IRT-adjusted score of 3.0 implies an increase in the student's rank by about 5 percentiles at the mean of student score distribution. Therefore, assuming percentile grading where there is a grade change at every 10 percentiles above 60, this effect would imply an improvement of about one letter grade due to the CRI Programme.[16]

SENSITIVITY ANALYSIS

Next we examine the robustness of these results by using alternative estimators of the treatment effect on IRT-adjusted scores in Table 4. The first estimator (kernel matching) matches the treated children with a weighted average of all un-treated children with weights that are inversely proportional to the distance between their propensity scores, while spline matching performs spline-smoothing matching by first fitting a natural cubic spline on the propensity score to outcome. Thus, these estimators create a many-to-one match for each treated individual on the sample thereby increasing the number of matched observations but potentially reducing the overall quality of the match. In addition, we also use the nearest-neighbour matching estimator proposed by Abadie and Imbens (2006), which does not use the propensity score but matches the treated and control units based on the distance between covariates and computes a bias corrected estimator. The estimated effect is similar in magnitude and statistically significant for the last two estimators.[17]

Table 5: Rosenbaum Bounds

Gamma	Urdu	Math	English	Total Score
1	3.80e–06	3.10e–06	4.60e–06	3.90e–06
1.05	0.000021	0.000017	0.000025	0.000022
1.1	0.000095	0.000079	0.000113	0.000097
1.15	0.000353	0.000299	0.000412	0.000361
1.2	0.001110	0.000951	0.001278	0.001132
1.25	0.003018	0.00262	0.003432	0.003072
1.3	0.007223	0.006349	0.008123	0.007341
1.35	0.015451	0.013741	0.017191	0.01568
1.4	0.029928	0.026912	0.03296	0.03033
1.45	0.053084	0.048236	0.05790	0.053724
1.5	0.087077	0.079911	0.094117	0.088018
1.55	0.133267	0.123445	0.142810	0.134548
1.6	0.191785	0.179215	0.203868	0.193414
1.65	0.261351	0.246236	0.275730	0.263298
1.7	0.339396	0.322225	0.355567	0.641595
1.75	0.422443	0.403923	0.439711	0.42480
1.8	0.506630	0.487585	0.524216	0.509041
1.85	0.588262	0.569515	0.605408	0.590621
1.9	0.664240	0.646516	0.6803	0.666459
1.95	0.732339	0.716194	0.746834	0.734349
2	0.791284	0.777075	0.803926	0.793043

Table 6: ATT by Gender

	Stratified matching	Kernel matching	Abadie-Imbens
A. Girls			
Urdu	2.26**	1.33+	2.04**
	(3.49)	(1.87)	(1.08)
Math	1.62**	0.98*	1.46**
	(3.80)	(2.24)	(3.11)
English	2.40**	1.39*	2.18**
	(3.65)	(2.08)	(3.10)
Total Score	6.28**	3.71*	5.68**
	(3.21)	(2.40)	(3.10)
Average Attendance	−0.005	0.024*	0.014
	(0.386)	(2.50)	(1.29)
# Treated	176	180	180
# Control	131	154	209
B. Boys			
Urdu	2.87**	3.55**	2.08**
	(3.28)	(4.01)	(3.55)
Math	2.07**	2.56**	1.49**
	(4.56)	(3.30)	(3.61)
English	3.01**	3.70**	2.19**
	(3.42)	(3.61)	(3.51)
Total Score	7.95**	9.81**	5.76**
	(4.07)	(3.25)	(3.55)
Average Attendance	−0.031+	−0.009	−0.034**
	(1.98)	(0.78)	(2.92)
# Treated	141	198	198
# Control	270	248	307

Note: The total number of observations used in computing a non-parametric estimator of the treatment effect varies depending on the number of individuals that match on observable attributes.

+Significant at 10% level. *Significant at 5% level. **Significant at 1% level.

Table 7: ATT by Wealth

	Stratified matching	Kernel matching	Abadie-Imbens
A. Top 35% of the wealth distribution			
Urdu	2.41*	2.42*	0.51
	(2.82)	(3.42)	(0.61)
Math	1.73**	1.75**	0.34
	(2.62)	(3.05)	(0.57)
English	2.56*	2.56*	0.54
	(2.29)	(2.58)	(0.60)
Total Score	6.70**	6.74*	1.39
	(2.70)	(2.92)	(0.59)
Average Attendance	0.014	0.010	−0.016
	(0.61)	(0.82)	(0.98)
# Treated	101	109	129
# Control	83	81	154
B. Bottom 35% of the wealth distribution			
Urdu	2.06*	2.19**	1.30*
	(2.15)	(2.64)	(1.94)
Math	1.45**	1.56**	0.92*
	(2.26)	(2.76)	(1.94)
English	2.19*	2.31**	1.37*
	(2.09)	(3.33)	(1.92)
Total Score	5.70*	6.06**	3.58*
	(2.50)	(2.74)	(1.93)
Average Attendance	−0.011	−0.002	−0.014
	(0.26)	(0.06)	(1.15)
# Treated	94	95	95
# Control	93	110	188

Note: The total number of observations used in computing a non-parametric estimator of the treatment effect varies depending on the number of individuals that match on observable attributes.

⁺Significant at 10% level. *Significant at 5% level. **Significant at 1% level.

The kernel matching estimates show no significant impact on learning even though the estimate for attendance is positive and significant. But the point estimates are positive for each subject and generally lower than the stratified matching estimates reported earlier. Taken together, the estimated effect of the Programme from the three different estimators ranges in value from 1.77 to 4.16 and is significant for two out of the three methods used. In addition, we observe an increase in the IRT-adjusted score of CRI children of between 0.63 and 1.50 for Urdu, 0.48–1.07 for Mathematics and 0.66–1.59 for English. Of these, the effect on Mathematics is the smallest in magnitude compared to the other subjects. On balance, we conclude that there is a positive and significant effect of CRI Programme on the overall learning of children with four years of exposure.

SELECTION ON UNOBSERVABLES

Of course the above analysis is constrained by then on-experimental nature of our data. So far, we have invoked the *Ignorability of Treatment* assumption standard in the matching literature, to assume that the attributes used in the propensity score matching are sufficient determinants of an individual student's selection into the treatment group. To what extent are our results robust to a potential imbalance in the unobservable factors across matching blocks of observations? We attempt to address this question by computing the Rosenbaum bounds for the estimated average treatment effects. We compute the bounds for the spline estimates that produce the smallest yet significant estimates for the CRI effect.[18]

Table 5 reports the different levels of unobservable imbalance across the two groups captured by the gamma values. For each gamma value, columns 2–5 report the significance levels (or p-values) for the null hypothesis of no treatment effect in test scores based on the stratified matching estimator.

Using the restricted sample, we find that the treatment effect for Urdu continues to be significant at 10 per cent level for gamma values up to 1.50 and it stops being significant in between 1.50 and 1.55 indicating that the cut-off gamma value lies in this interval.[19] This means that the unobserved factors would have to increase a child's odds of receiving CRI treatment by a factor of 1.50 or more than 50 per cent before it would alter our conclusion that exposure to CRI treatment improves the Urdu of a student. The same interpretation applies to the other test scores (see Table 5).

There is no clear consensus yet as to what qualifies as a small enough cut-off point that would undermine the results of estimation. Watson (2005) notes that while in health sciences, the cut-off point for the odds ratio are found to be quite large (greater than 6), the same estimates appear to be much lower in social science (as low as 1.1). In that sense, and given that we have controlled for several key factors that determine school selection, our results may be viewed as relatively robust to bias arising from unobserved effects driving school selection.

Table 8: Summary of Interventions

Source and country	Intervention	Effect on learning outcomes	Cost-effectiveness
Adding additional inputs *Banerjee, Cole, Duflo, and Linden (2007)*, India	A computer-assisted learning programme focusing on Maths.	Increased Maths score by 0.47 SD in the second year.	The computer programme cost approximately $15.18 per student per year.
Contracting extra teachers *Banerjee et al. (2007)*, India	Remedial education programme that hired young women to teach students lagging behind in the basic literacy and numeracy skills.	Increased average test scores by 0.28 SD in the second year.	Remedial Education Programme cost approximately $2.25 per student per year.
Duflo, Dupas, and Kremer (2009), Kenya	Intervention included (i) hiring contract teachers and subdividing classes between regular and contract teachers; (ii) he above with the addition of training school based committees to monitor teachers.	With contract teachers test scores increased by 0.18 SD but the result petered out. Contract teachers in combination with better school based management increased test scores by 0.21 SD and almost the same.	Not available.

Incentive-based scheme for teachers *Duflo, Hanna, and Ryan (2007)*, India	Camera-based monitoring as well as bonuses for teacher performance.	Increased test score by 0.17 SD.	Camera plus bonus for attendance cost $6 per student per year.
Muralidharan and Sundararaman (2008), India	Performance-based bonuses to teachers on the basis of average improvements in test scores of their students	Increases test score by 0.19 SD in Maths and 0.12 SD in language and the average treatment effect was 0.15 SD.	Performance-based bonuses, compared to the other intervention (of smart inputs) delivered 0.06 SD higher score for the same expenditure.
Glewwe, Illias, and Kremer (2008), Kenya	Teachers received prizes for above average school test scores.	Increased test score by 0.14 SD on those tests that were linked with no incentives.	Not available.
Parental Involvement in Learning *Banerjee, Duflo, Glennerster, and Khemani (2008)*, India	Three prolonged intervention, of information about (i) school quality and local leaders' responsibility (ii) The above and parents trained to test children and (iii) The above (i) and (ii) and training of volunteers to teach children to read in camps.	Interventions (i) and (ii) has no effects. Intervention (iii), under which 8% of the students attended camps had the following impacts: 22.3% were more likely to read letters; 23.2% more likely read a word or paragraph; 22.4% more likely to read a story.	Not available.

GENDER AND WEALTH

We also examine the variation in our results by gender and wealth (Tables 6 and 7). The point estimates of the Programme's impact are positive and significant for both boys and girls but slightly higher in magnitude for boys. Again, the effect on math skills is the smallest in magnitude and holds true across the two genders. In addition, the CRI effect is positive for both wealthy and poorer children in the sample—a typology that was created by looking at the top and bottom terciles of the asset distribution. The effect on poorer children is more robust but in the two cases where both sub-samples have a significant CRI effect, the magnitude of the effect is larger for wealthier children than it is for children coming from poorer families. We posit that this may be due to differential resources and home environments.[20]

CONCLUSION

The CRI programme has been working for the last five years to improve the learning environment in Islamabad government schools by making classrooms child-friendly. We have found that there is a significant positive learning impact of the CRI programme on all the curricular components— Urdu, English, and Mathematics—which may be explained by its effect on the classroom environment. Grade IV children in CRI schools perform better on average; exposure to the CRI programme improved student's tests score by 0.4 standard deviation, improving the average student's ranking by 4–11 percentiles about his/her current standing vis-à-vis other students in the cohort. Table 8 presents results from recent randomized interventions in the education sector which have focused on improving outcomes, specifically test scores.

Comparatively, the cumulative impact of the CRI intervention of 0.4 SD in test scores, is significantly better than many other recent interventions that have looked at improving learning outcomes in developing countries. Desegregation of results by gender and wealth indicates a slight learning advantage in favour of boys. We show that this causal relationship between the CRI programme and greater learning achievement is sufficiently robust to the presence of unmeasured confounding variables. However, we qualify our results by placing them in the Pakistani context where schooling process is widely held to be associated with tedium and apathy. In such a setting, interventions which attempt to change the very nature of these public school classrooms by making them interactive, child-friendly and fun, can indeed provide one solution to the problem of quality in Pakistan's public schools. What limited evidence we have on cost-effectiveness further supports the view that programmes like CRI may be possible solution to the malaise in public sector classrooms.

In a recent USAID evaluation of the CRI Programme, the annual unit cost of pre-Grade I student and Grade I student were calculated to be US$8.90, for Grade II it was calculated to be US$7.90, while for Grades III and IV it was US$8.20. Relative to other interventions (see Table 8), the CRI intervention is more costly than the introduction of remedial teachers (Banerjee et al., 2007) and even the camera based monitoring/teacher bonuses scheme (Duflo et al., 2007) but is of lower cost than the computer assisted learning programme used in India (Banerjee et al., 2007), which delivers an almost equivalent impact in terms of learning outcomes.

Few studies exist that examine the impact of non-didactic approaches in developing countries. This reflects the lack of experimentation with pedagogy in the developing country context as well as the lack of impact evaluations of such initiatives if they exist. Interventions that focus on making classrooms child-friendly are gaining ground in donor dialogues with developing countries.

Children Resources International Washington itself has a presence in Morocco, Tunisia, India, Afghanistan, South Africa, and Mongolia among others. Other organizations like The Open Society Institute and The Aga Khan Foundation are also pushing for similar approaches at the early childhood level. Rigorous evaluations of existing and future programmes will add to our knowledge of the impact of non-didactic methods on learning achievement in the developing countries. Overall, our results present a contrasting picture to previous analyses that examine non-didactic learning approaches and child learning outcomes in a developing country context. There are two possible explanations. Firstly, it may be down to the fact that the CRI Programme introduces child friendly pedagogy early in a child's learning experience, i.e. through the primary years of schooling. This could prevent CRI children from becoming dependent on more hierarchical transfers of knowledge that tend to be based on rote learning and teacher led delivery. Secondly, this chapter captures the cumulative effect of the CRI intervention over a four-year period. Four years of exposure to non-didactic methods may allow children to gain confidence in this learning method, potentially improving learning outcomes. Of course more research is required before these propositions can be firmly established.

APPENDIX A

Table A.1: Number of Teachers Trained under CRI in Islamabad (2002–06)

Teachers trained (2002–2006)	Grade	Number of trained
Teachers	KG to III	304
Teachers	IV	142
Teachers	V	169
School heads and deputy heads	All school	173
Total number of teachers trained		788

Table A.2: Distribution of Children by the Grade of the Current School

First Class	Non-CRI	CRI	Total
0	23 (2.3%)	9 (1.3%)	32 (1.9%)
1	663 (65.6%)	501 (72.5%)	1164 (68.4%)
2	94 (9.3%)	45 (6.5%)	139 (8.2%)
3	101 (10.0%)	70 (10.1%)	171 (10.0%)
4	129 (12.8%)	66 (9.6%)	195 (11.5%)
Total	1010 (100%)	691 (100%)	1701 (100%)

Table A.3: Verifying the balancing property

Dependent Variable	CRI	
	(a) Within school blocks	(b) Within child blocks
F.G. Model	0.054	-
	(0.12)	
Islamabad Model	0.121	-
	(0.32)	
Whether boys school?	0.082	-
	(0.24)	
Whether Co-ed school?	−0.083	-
	(0.21)	
Male	-	0.022
		(0.47)
Age of child (in years)	-	−0.003
		(0.15)
Mother went to school	-	0.014
		(0.31)
Teacher experience	-	0.006+
		(1.69)
Whether father is a professional?	-	−0.008
		(0.18)
Whether father is entrepreneur?	-	−0.004
		(0.07)
Number of siblings	-	0.001
		(0.10)
Number of elder siblings	-	−0.002
		(0.14)
Asset index	-	0.000
		(0.03)
Child height	-	0.002
		(0.66)

| Dependent Variable | CRI | |
	(a) Within school blocks	(b) Within child blocks
Child weight	-	−0.002
		(0.92)
Observations	46	511
Number of matching school blocks	4	-
Number of matching child blocks	-	20
F-test for x-variables: p-value	0.99	0.98

Notes:
1. Absolute value of t-statistics in parentheses.
2. Regression (a) includes cluster i.e. geographical controls for different areas within Islamabad.
+Significant at 10% level.
*Significant at 5% level.
**Significant at 1% level.

REFERENCES

Abadie, A., and Imbens, G. (2006), 'Large sample properties of matching estimators for average treatment effects', *Econometrica*, 74(1), 235–67.

Andrabi, T., Das, J., and Khawaja, A. (2002a), 'The rise of private schooling in Pakistan: Catering to the urban elite or educating the rural poor', (World Bank & Harvard University).

Andrabi, T., Das, J., Khwaja, A. I., Durya, F., and Zajonc, T. (2002b), 'Test feasibility survey Pakistan: Education sector', *Harvard Kennedy School Working Paper* (Cambridge, MA: Harvard University).

Andrabi, T., Das, J., Khwaja, A. I., Vishwanath, T., and Zajonc, T. (2007), 'Learning and educational achievements in Punjab schools (LEAPS): Insights to inform the education policy debate', World Bank.

Andrabi, T., Das, J., Khwaja, A. I., and Zajonc, T. (2008), 'Do value-added estimates add value?' Accounting for learning dynamics, BREAD Working Paper, Vol. 170.

Banerjee, A., Cole, S., Duflo, E., and Linden, L. (2007), 'Remedying education: Evidence from two randomized experiments in India', *Quarterly Journal of Economics*, 122, 1235–64.

Banerjee, A., Duflo, E., Glennerster, R., and Khemani, S. (2008), 'Pitfalls of participatory programmes: Evidence from a randomized evaluation in education in India'.

Barnett, W. S., and Nores, M. (2009), 'Benefits of early childhood interventions across the world: (Under) investing in the very young', *Economics of Education Review*, 29(1).

Becker, S. O., and Ichino, A. (2002), 'Estimation of average treatment effects based on propensity scores'. *The Stata Journal*, 2(4), 358–77.

Chaudhury, N., and Parajuli, D. (2006), 'Conditional cash transfers and female schooling: The impact of the female school stipend programme school enrolment in Punjab, Pakistan', *World Bank Policy Research Working Paper'*, Vol. 4102.

Crump, R., Hotz, V. J., Imbens, G., and Mitnik, O. (2009), 'Dealing with limited overlap in estimation of average treatment effects'. *Biometrika*, 96(1), 187–99.

Das, J., Pandey, P., and Zajonc, T. (2006), 'Learning levels and gaps in Pakistan', *World Bank Policy Research Working Paper*, Vol. 4067.

Dehejia, R. (2005), Practical propensity score matching: A reply to Smith and Todd. *Journal of Econometrics*, 125, 355–64.

Dehejia, R., and Wahba, S. (1999), 'Causal effects in non-experimental studies: Reevaluating the evaluation of training programmes', *Journal of the American Statistical Association*, 94(448), 1053–62.

Duflo, E., Dupas, P., and Kremer, M. (2009), 'Additional resources versus organizational change in education. Experimental evidence from Kenya'.

Duflo, E., Hanna, R., and Ryan, S. (2007), 'Monitoring works: Getting teachers to come to school', NBER Working Paper, Vol. 11880.

Filmer, D., and Pritchett, L. (1999), 'What education production functions really show: A positive theory of education expenditures', *Economics of Education Review*, 18(2), 223–40.

Fuller, B., and Clarke, P. (1994), 'Raising school effects while ignoring culture? Local conditions and the influence of classroom, tools, rules and pedagogy', *Review of Educational Research*, 64(1), 119–57.

Fuller, B., Hua, H., and Snyder, C. W. (1994), 'When girls learn more than boys: The influence of time in school and pedagogy in Botswana', *Comparative Education Review*, 38(3), 345–76.

Glewwe P. (2002), 'Schools and skills in developing countries: Education policies and socio-economics outcomes', *Journal of Economic Literature*, 40(2), 436–82.

Glewwe, P., Illias, N., and Kremer, M. (2008), 'Teacher Incentives: National Bureau of Economic Research'.

Hambleton, R., and Swaminathan, H. (1985), *Item Response Theory: Principles and Applications* (The Netherlands: Kluwer Academic Press).

Hanushek, E. (1986), 'The economics of schooling: Production and efficiency in public schools', *Journal of Economic Literature*, 24, 1141–77.

Heckman, J., and Hotz, J. V. (1989), 'Choosing among alternative non-experimental methods for estimating the impact of social programmes: The case of manpower training', *Journal of the American Statistical Association*, 84(408), 862–74.

Heyneman, S. P., and Loxley, W. A. (1983), 'The effect of primary school quality on academic achievement across twenty-nine high-and-low income countries', *The American Journal of Sociology*, 88(6), 1162–94.

Hirsh-Pasek, K., Hyson, M. C., and Rescorla, L. (1990), 'Academic environments in preschool: Do they pressure or challenge young children', *Early Education and Development*, 1(6), 401–23.

Krueger, A. B. (2003), 'Economic considerations and class size', *The Economic Journal*, 113(485), 34–63.

Lockheed, M. E., and Komenan, A. (1989), 'Teaching quality and student achievement in Africa: The case of Nigeria and Swaziland', *Teaching and Teacher Education*, 5(2), 93–113.

Lockheed, M. E., and Zhao, Q. (1993), 'The empty opportunity: Local control of secondary schools and student achievement in the Philippines', *International Journal of Educational Development*, 13(1), 45–62.

Muralidharan, K., and Sundararaman, V. (2008), 'Teaching incentives in developing countries: Experimental evidence from India'.

Pakistan Ministry of Education (2001), 'Education Sector Reform Action Plan 2001–2005', (Islamabad: Government of Pakistan).

Pakistan Ministry of Education (2004), 'Public Private Partnerships in the Education Sector: ESR action plan 2001–2005', (Islamabad: Government of Pakistan).

Patrinos, H. A. (2006), 'Public–private partnership: Contracting education in Latin America', World Bank.

Rosenbaum, P. R. (2002), *Observational Studies* (New York: Springer).

Smith, J. A., and Todd, P. (2001), 'Reconciling conflicting evidence on the performance of propensity-score matching methods',

American Economic Review: Papers and Proceedings, 91(2), 112–18.

Stalling, J. A., and Stipek, D. (1986), 'Research on early childhood and elementary school teaching programmes', in M. Wittrock, ed., *Handbook of Research on Teaching* (New York: Macmillan).

Watson, I. (2005), 'The Earnings of Causal Employers: The Problem of Unobservables' (Conference proceedings).

NOTES

1. The Federal Directorate of Education is a department of the Ministry of Education responsible for implementing the education policy in Islamabad Capital Territory (ICT). The name of the non-profit organization involved in this intervention has since been changed to Children's Global Network Pakistan (CGNP).

2. The World Bank is currently financing impact evaluations of conditional transfers being used to incentivize private schools to attract students and improve learning through the Punjab Foundation Assisted School Programme and the Sindh Education Foundation pilot Promoting Private Schools in Rural Sindh.

3. One exception is Chaudhury and Parajuli's (2006) working paper on conditional cash transfers to encourage female enrolment in public schools in Punjab.

4. The LEAPS project is funded by World Bank and is a multiyear study that examines impact of varies policies intervention in public and private schools in three districts in Punjab (Attock, Faisalabad and Rahim Yar Khan) through testing Urdu, English, and Math Skills. The LEAPS testing instrument was also used for the CRI evaluation.

5. See Strauss, Bowes, Marks, and Plesko (2000) for an excellent overview of the obstacles facing teacher quality reform in the US.

6. Patrinos (2006) outlines different types of contracting that exist under different PPPs in education. Governments contract out for either (i) management and professional services (input), (ii) operational services (input), (iii) education services (output), (iv)

facility availability (input), and (v) facility availability and education services (input and output bundle).

7. Rough back-of-the-envelope calculations indicate that these constitute 18.5% of all those parents whose children were in CRI pilot schools over this four-year period.

8. The selection of CRI pilot schools can be loosely described as stratified (non-random) sampling where the schools were first stratified by type: the 25 pilot schools had 5 Islamabad Model Colleges, 15 FG Junior Model Schools, and 5 FG Primary Schools (of which the first two types of schools had English as the medium of instruction and the last categories had Urdu). In addition, the schools were also stratified by location. All of the 25 pilot schools except 2, were located in the urban area of FDE jurisdiction—the Islamabad city. Within the city, the schools were picked from different residential sectors. The reason stated by the FDE Director for selecting pilot schools from different sectors was to make these schools, and the children receiving the CRI treatment, somewhat demographically representative of Islamabad city given the different socio-economic features of these sectors.

9. We verify that the balancing property is satisfied within school and child blocks by testing for the joint significance of covariates within these blocks. The results are produced in Table A.3 in Appendix A.

10. The testing instrument used in this study was borrowed from another large-scale school research project, LEAPS. For more details on the testing instrument, refer to (Tahir Andrabi, Das, Khwaja, Durya, and Zajonc, 2002b).

11. For the centralized admission policy, see the FDE website at: http:// fde.gov.pk/TheFunctions.htm. We present the aggregate trends on the in-coming students across CRI and non-CRI schools in Appendix Table A.2.

12. In addition, there had been a reassignment of teachers between CRI and non-CRI schools that occurred in the last year of the pilot phase (2006–2007) with the expansion of the programme to all Islamabad schools. We drop schools with reassigned teachers from the final analysis. The full sample estimates are consistent with the findings presented here and are available from the authors upon request.

13. For example, consider two students who scored 'n' marks on Maths and correctly answered the same set of 'n-1' questions. The only difference was that student A correctly answered a one-digit addition whereas student B got that question wrong but correctly answered a more complicated two-digit addition with carry. Hambleton and Swaminathan (1985) is a classic treatment on item response theory.

14. The child questionnaire, administered to each student, recorded the quantity of each asset (about 20 different types) present in the household of the child. We were able to combine this information into an asset index by the method of principal components.

15. As mentioned in Section 3, each estimator uses a different technique to match subjects receiving treatment with those who did not. Thus, the number of observations in each group varies, depending on the estimator used.

16. Tahir Andrabi, Das, Khwaja, and Zajonc (2008) point out that the problem with a static value-added specification of child learning is that it fails to account for the dynamic nature of achievement gains, wherein individual level heterogeneity entering in each period interacts with the achievement level in the past period. Intuitively, this would mean that the treatment effect of any short term intervention is likely to fade out in the long run. However, since the CRI intervention is a sustained programme directed towards the treated students in each school year, it would be fair to conclude that the improvement in learning was of the magnitude 0.4 SD over the treatment period. There is little discussion in the literature on the sustainability of education related interventions. Recently though, Barnett and Nores (2009) review evidence of over 30 early childhood interventions that impact child cognitive, behavioural, health, and schooling outcomes and show that the effects were sustained over the longer run.

17. We also checked the sensitivity of the Abadie–Imbens estimates by trimming the sample of all those 63 observations where the propensity score was outside the [0.1,0.9] interval (Crump, Hotz, Imbens, & Mitnik, 2009). The estimates from the trimmed sample (not reported) were very similar to those reported in column 2. We thank the referee for suggesting this robustness check.

18. However, this may not completely stack the board against finding an effect because the spline estimates, though smallest in magnitude, happen to be statistically quite significant.
19. The 'Gamma' reported in Table 5 is the same as the e^{γ} in Section 3.
20. We also split the sample by mother's educational attainment and found positive and significant effects for the children of the least educated mothers across all subject. For the sub-sample with most educated mothers (matric or above), the learning achievement is no different in CRI children relative to non-CRI, except a positive CRI effect on mathematics.

8

Situating Multilingual Education in Nepali Context

—Sushan Acharya

INTRODUCTION

Language plays a critical role in shaping the quality of the teaching and learning process. Countries with a great deal of linguistic diversity, such as Nepal, stand to benefit from the use of Multilingual Education (MLE Research & Expert Team) policies. Gradual changes in language policies and provisions have been observed in this respect since the restoration of multiparty system in 1990. However, the effectiveness of reform attempts to address this issue have been compromised by interlocking factors that influence quality as a whole. Thus, there are tensions between the promise of MLE and the challenges of its implementation. Language reform policies must take into account these tensions.

This chapter begins with an overview of the role of MLE, discussing the international research literature on its positive contribution to quality. It is followed by an overview of the linguistic scenario in Nepal. Then it goes into the Nepali state's response to linguistic diversity including one reform programme on MLE. In light of this programme and research on MLE in Nepal, the chapter analyses the challenges to implementing MLE in Nepal, contrasting the promise with the tensions. Finally, it provides recommendations on how to move forward.

ROLE OF MLE

To cater to the learning needs of all children irrespective of their languages, MLE has been introduced in several countries. In MLE, teaching and learning begins in the child's first language, which is often their mother tongue (MT). After an initial three to four years in MT instruction, children are gradually transitioned to second and third languages. The rationale behind this method is to relate classroom material in a language of their MT in order to augment their comprehension. Through such methods, the understanding of abstract concepts is easier as teachers are able to provide appropriate scaffolds. In addition, teaching in MT can encourage communication between the students and the teachers, boosting children's confidence as well as enhancing their knowledge about the subject matter. This can lead to a strong foundation, decreasing the chances of dropout, grade repetitions, and under-achievement.

Through different pedagogical methods, MLE has the potential to fulfil the learning needs of every child who enters the school. Even when students use a variety of different languages, instructions can be arranged in groups according to specific MTs (UNESCO, 2003). This is usually carried out through multi-grade teaching method, which has been in practice in formal education. In instances where grouping is not possible, as when students are few, a language that is most common among the students can be used for instruction and extra support provided for those that find it difficult to understand (UNESCO, 2003).

MLE EXPERIENCES IN DIVERSE CONTEXTS

International research exhibits the positive impact of using MT as medium of teaching and learning both in terms of equity and student performance. For example, a UNESCO (2008) study on bilingual education programmes carried out in Mali, Peru, Papua New Guinea, and the USA found students in bilingual education excelling in terms of overall academic achievement as compared to their counterparts from a monolingual second-language system.

Saikia and Panda and Mohanty (2009) as cited by Awasthi (2004) also found, in the case of *Bodo*-speaking community of Assam, a positive impact of bilingual competence in the achievement of minority children in primary school. The positive impacts on access and internal efficiency, including learning outcomes seen in some Latin American and French-speaking African countries, World Bank (2005) has also confirmed the long term benefits of MLE. The findings show that, with the use of students' MT, teachers were able to use multiple activities in the classroom, and parents' involvement in their children's learning also enhanced. Legitimization of parent's and community's language in children's schooling and their ability to understand what was taught or learned at school, strengthened their sense of inclusion (World Bank, 2005).

Another version of MLE, a culturally-rooted holistic approach named 'MLE Plus' introduced in Orissa, India aims at empowering the community and students for simultaneous growth at both ends, has been found more fulfilling than general school based MLE. The assumption is 'the growth of one is integrally linked to the growth of the other' (Panda & Mohanty, 2009, 306). In a comparative study of student achievement in the subjects of language, mathematics, environmental science, and drawing, MLE plus school children did far better than students from just the Oriya medium school and also MLE schools (Luykx et al., 2007; Panda & Mohanty, 2009). Moreover, bilingual education, a foundation of MLE, made classroom teaching more comfortable for female students, thereby showing positive effects on girls' enrolment, retention and performance (UNESCO, 2005). D'Emilio (2009) also found girls benefiting most from bilingual programmes. These studies observed enhanced participation and confidence among the learners including improved status of gender equality. Regarding costs, which are always a major issue in education, the international studies assure that although the initial cost is high, the bilingual programme is more cost-effective in the long run, because it increases internal efficiency.

The research indicates that overall quality is still a limitation. In Mali, Peru, Papua New Guinea, and US it was realized that changing the medium of teaching/learning alone may not produce significant outcomes, if the overall quality of education is poor (UNESCO, 2008). Therefore in Mali 'Pedagogie convergente' a modality for interactive teaching/

learning in MT while making children functionally bilingual, was developed because without new methods and materials for teaching, a positive outcome was not possible (UNESCO, 2008). All four bilingual programmes examined by UNESCO (2008) showed the need of linking pedagogy and curriculum while applying MT in teaching/learning. This point will be explored further with regards to the MLE pilot in Nepal.

LINGUISTIC SCENARIO AND MEDIUM OF INSTRUCTION IN NEPAL

Linguistic diversity has always been a significant feature of Nepali life. Languages belonging to Sino-Tibetan, Indo-European, Austro-Asiatic, and Dravidian language families are all spoken in Nepal (Yadav & Turin, 2005) and there are other languages whose genetic affiliation has yet to be confirmed. Although different sources propose different figures, Yonjan-Tamang (2009) estimates that 125 to 200 languages are spoken in the country. Some languages of Nepal have a rich writing tradition while others lack a script. Therefore, the languages of the country lie in extreme ranges in terms of their use and life chances. Languages with a written tradition and/or are spoken by significant number of people are known as 'developing' (e.g. Nepali, Maithili, Bhojpuri, Awadhi) and those that do not have a written tradition and/or are spoken by limited number of people (e.g. Santhal, Danuwar, Chepang, Jhangad, Sanpang) are in danger of extinction. Yonjan-Tamang (2006) has grouped the languages of Nepal into four categories, according to his scale, 'almost dead' languages are highest in number, followed by languages grouped under 'endangered' and 'highly endangered' categories, and only 4 to 15 languages respectively fall under the 'safe' and 'almost safe' categories respectively.

Additionally, language communities and indigenous nationalities of Nepal are very unlikely to be concentrated in one geographic location and with that school catchment area. Consequently, 'linguistic features tend to converge from one language to another. As a result, a single language under the influences from other languages differs greatly.' (Nepal. National Language Policy Recommendation Commission, 1994, 9)

In Nepal, *Khas* Nepali language, which for the purpose of this chapter has been called Nepali language, is the official language and the medium of school education. In spite of the use of Nepali as a medium, MLE has long been practised in the classrooms. At times, when Nepal had to use textbooks written in Hindi for school education the medium of instruction and interaction was carried out in Nepali. But the southern part of the country, where most of the languages had high level of intelligibility with Hindi, used Hindi as a medium of instruction. Use of local languages in classroom interaction/instruction replaced Hindi after Nepali language textbooks were brought into the system.

National Education Plan for Nepal (1955) advocated for the use 'national Nepali language' from Grade I with initial support in MT in order to explain the topic or terminologies if needed. The legacy of such practices continued. Subsequently,

MLE continued to be practiced informally in two forms. In one form, teachers use local mother tongue to deliver the entire lessons. This happens mostly in the case of well-developed languages like Maithili, Bhojpuri, Awadhi, and some languages, which have high levels of intelligibility with Nepali such as *Tharu*. Classroom interaction between teacher and students might also occur in the same language. In another form, teachers translate some portions of the lessons or terminologies into the local mother tongue and used Nepali for the rest of the lesson. Both the practices have been known as teaching in 'local language'.

In the above scenario, schools of Nepal are likely to deal with three or more mother tongues (MT) or mixed languages. While this linguistic diversity is an asset, managing diverse classrooms and providing equal learning opportunity to all is also a challenge. Many children who come to classrooms with local languages as their MTs have inadequate skills in the teaching language, which is often the national language used in their classrooms. Many children may struggle to learn because the nature of the classroom communication differs from social communication (Cause, 2010; Sadovnik, 2001). Although unaware of this distinction, traditionally many teachers have been practicing different and sometimes ad hoc methods to help students who are not skilled in the language used in the classroom. These practices are found more common in developed languages and languages that have high compatibility with Nepali. From these efforts, some have benefitted while others have not as children with local languages as their MTs struggle not only to understand the means of communication but the content of communication simultaneously.

Although the classroom practice and interaction are undertaken in local languages, the exam papers are still prepared in Nepali language and students are expected to respond in the same. In this situation, although students comprehend the lessons many of them do not comprehend the questions and thus cannot respond. This happens even if the children's MT has high level of intelligibility with Nepali language (Awasthi, 2004).

STATE'S RESPONSE TO LINGUISTIC DIVERSITY

Children's inability to comprehend the language used in classroom teaching has long been recognized as one of the major factors affecting children's cognitive development and their overall response to education. In Nepal, prior to the 1990s, institutionalizing one language in the name of establishing harmony and unity was still a national agenda and the ruling class and their associates viewed the development of different languages and cultures as a threat to the national identity (Jim Cummins, 2001). The successive education policies, provisions, statutory frameworks, and recommendations of the national commissions could not depart much from the legacy of the 'one language policy' promulgated by the National Education Plan (Nepal, National Education Planning Commission, 1955; Sharma, 2002). The assimilation approach continued, which, according to Cummins (2009), is actually exclusion, because rather than recognizing and utilizing indigenous people as resources, it hides languages and cultural differences. It was only from 1990s when the political regime was changed that a shift in language related policies and provisions began. Hence a clause about MT as a medium of instruction and a provision for primary level education in MT was inserted in the 5th Amendment 1992 of the Education Act of 1971 (Khanal, 2003).[1] Then, the provision to fund MT teaching at the primary level by the local government was included in the Local Governance Act of 1999 and Regulation, 2000 (Nepal, Parliament, 1999, 2000). Likewise, the interim constitution of Nepal (Nepal, Parliament, 2007) further granted 'the right to get basic education in mother tongue as provided for in the law' (Article 17). The School Sector Reform Plan (2008b) and National Curriculum Framework (2007) have also made provisions for MLE. In this way, the country has gradually opened up avenues for the implementation of MLE.

Attempts have been made to redress the situation and respond to these legal provisions. Translating some textbooks of lower grades and developing supplementary materials in some local languages have been the major responses. Challenges still exist in aligning the various provisions and documents. Nevertheless, it is part of this reform effort that the 2007 Multilingual Education (MLE) pilot project was implemented.

NEPALI EXPERIENCE OF MLE

MLE PILOT PROJECT

The MLE pilot project, a two-and-a-half-year joint initiative of the Government of Nepal and the Government of Finland implemented between 2007 to 2009, sought to enhance the quality of education for all through the provision of bilingual education (Finland, Ministry for Foreign Affairs, 2006, 4). In order to achieve this overarching objective, the programme specifically aimed to generate modalities to facilitate non-Nepali speaking children's learning, to develop the capacity of duty bearers at different levels of school education, and to recommend policy options for the implementation of MLE. The project was also expected to support the social and cultural rights through quality education (Finland, Ministry for Foreign Affairs, 2006). For the pilot, eight languages from six districts were selected. Seven schools from the selected six districts were identified in consultation with the District Education Office, district level branch of concerned linguistic communities, and the local chapter of the federation of the indigenous people's organizations. Major activities of the pilot included supplementary reader and curricular material development; capacity development; and an attempt to institutionalize the pilot activities.

The programme first dealt with the perceptions of MLE amongst key stakeholders. At the initial stage a stakeholder consultation was held at the school level to assess parents' concerns about mother tongue teaching and learning. In this consultation, parents requested that three languages, i.e. the mother tongue, *Khas* Nepali, and English be taught. Followed by this, school-level orientations were organized. Dialogues on the concept of mother tongue education and the role of local government were organized with stakeholders such as the District Development Committee and district level representatives of political parties.

READING AND CURRICULAR MATERIAL DEVELOPMENT

The development of supplementary reading materials in MT through a participatory approach involving local knowledge holders and students was a unique aspect of the project. Student groups comprising of third to fifth graders were formed in all the seven selected schools. Meanwhile, local knowledge holders skilled in the selected language/s were also identified. The local knowledge holders and the student groups worked together. The local knowledge holders narrated stories, poems, and jokes in their respective language/s, which were illustrated in pictorial forms by the students groups. Along with students' illustrations, oral presentations of the local knowledge holders were also scribed and published. The books and posters produced were used by teachers, students, and parents/guardians.

The pilot project mobilized teachers to develop curriculum and textbooks in MT as a subject, and develop and adapt the textbooks written in Nepali into the selected languages. The development and production of the mother tongue language textbooks of Grade I and II in all eight selected languages was completed at the end of the project. In some languages, Grade III textbooks were also produced. As an offshoot of the project, materials including a teacher's guidebook on

Nepali as a second language was developed in a book form and shared with concerned stakeholders.

CAPACITY DEVELOPMENT

Capacity development for mother tongue teaching was one of the main objectives of the project. Teachers from the pilot schools were provided with training on MT teaching. A six-day long MLE training book for the implementation of mother tongue based MLE was developed. A training of trainers for teachers from fifteen different mother tongues was organized in collaboration with the National Centre for Educational Development (NCED). Teacher training manuals in seventeen different mother tongues including English and Nepali were also produced. Self-learning material in all fifteen mother tongues were also developed. Besides formal training, the involvement of central, district and sub-district level, Ministry of Education/Department of Education (MOE/ DOE) staff and other stakeholders in the pilot programme processes, and their exposure visits to India were also part of the capacity development.

INSTITUTIONALIZATION OF PROJECT ACTIVITIES

In order to institutionalize and scale-up the programme, several steps were taken. MLE pilot project review and consultations with experts led to the development and approval of a 'Guideline for Implementing Multilingual Education Programme (2009)'. Towards the end of the pilot programme, each of the pilot school adopted two neighbouring schools to implement MLE. At present, there are twenty-one MLE schools spread across the originally selected six districts. In those additional MLE schools, DOE provided orientation to the teachers.

The pilot project was successful in ensuring several elements of MLE at input level. For example, development of teacher training materials, integration of MLE teacher training in the system, curriculum development, and textbook adaptation at the school level, development and approval of the MLE Guidelines are some key achievements made by the project. However, the extent of achievement made with regards to the stated objective could not be measured partly because the design of the project did not have provisions for systematic baseline information collection to compare the outcome after the completion.

RESEARCH ON MLE IN NEPAL

As mentioned earlier, since no baseline study was undertaken, the changes that occurred in the student learning outcome after the MLE pilot intervention could not be determined. Several studies and evaluations carried to examine the changes brought by MLE found that use of local mother tongue (MT) has been able to create friendly or conducive learning environment for students who came with non-Nepali MTs (Acharya & Giri, 2009; MLE Research & Expert Team, 2009; Weinberg, 2009a). Some anecdotal information derived from those studies indicates the potential of MLE in addressing the language related barriers encountered in children's education. Such observations have made people presume that MLE would help enhance student performance.

Although, there are still not enough research evidences to clearly relate the medium of instruction with low internal efficiency, that is dropout, repetition, survival, low performance, and so on, children with *Khas* Nepali MT are found doing better in education than children with other MTs (Acharya & Giri, 2009; Awasthi, 2004; Karki, 2002). Dropout and repetition is also high among non *Khas* Nepali speaking children in Grades I and II (Acharya & Giri, 2009). However, the tendency to compare the internal efficiency aspects alone and seeking satisfaction within it might further side line the larger issues of quality education observed in most government aided schools, where the children with Nepali as their MTs are also the victims of poor quality education.

There is a dearth of systematic studies that establish relationship between language of instruction and students' learning achievement in Nepal. Often studies that compare children's ethnicity and/or language with the achievement scores obtained by them in certain subjects show children from non Nepali MT comparatively doing worse than those with Nepali MT (Acharya & Giri, 2009; Karki, 2002). A study done in schools where *Tharu* language was partially used in classroom practice, showed no significant difference in the achievement of third graders but dropout and repetition was higher among *Tharu* speaking children in lower grades (Acharya & Giri, 2009). The reasons for dropping out were multiple. Some children were moved to private schools; some dropped out because of the need to assist their families economically, and so on. This study was based on the national achievement test result of Grade III conducted by the Department of Education, which was then supplemented by empirical study. But in a *Tharu* MLE school where Grade II exam was administered in *Tharu* language, *Tharu* students scored as equal to Nepali speaking students which was not the case in the previous exams in that school. (Weinberg, n.d.-c) This showed that MLE intervention at lower grades seemed more effective. In the same community, a head teacher of a school where a NGO has been implementing MLE observed that, 'the overall quality of learning and teaching has improved in our school' (KC, 2009, 5).

When the concept of MLE was promulgated, the culture and language development, and preservation movement had already gained currency. MLE, therefore, provided a forum to further promote the cause of language and culture conservation. Many MLE programmes thus emerged as a result of the nation's response to the challenges of linguistic diversity in education, as well as language and culture preservation movement, which had already taken off the ground. Such programmes have been implemented in government-aided as well as private schools. Primarily non-government organizations, in collaboration with language communities have been supporting most of these programmes.

One such MLE programme launched through a private initiative and has been successful in establishing itself as a good practice is the Modern Newa English School. Preservation of the *Newari* language and quality education are the stated objectives of the school, which was started in 2003 in the heart of Kathmandu city. The founder has no intention to upgrade the school from its pre-primary level. In playgroup and nursery, *Newari* is used as a medium, whereas in Lower Kindergarten (LKG) and Upper Kindergarten (UKG) English is the medium—*Newari* and Nepali are taught as subjects. The school has been using *Devanagari* script to teach *Newari* writing but plans to switch to Newari scripts in the future. (Weinberg, n.d.-a) Students in Modern Newa English School are predominantly Newars with some belonging to other language groups including Nepali. All communicate in both Nepali and Newari languages (Weinberg, n.d.-a). The graduates of this school have been joining other regular private schools. A network of Newa pre-primary schools has also been established. Modern Newa English School provides training and support to teachers and administrators of the new schools at the initial stage, and seven such schools have already been established within Kathmandu valley (Weinberg, n.d.-a).

While most MLE programmes are getting entangled within two broader interests—language and culture preservation, and preference for languages that are occupationally and economically benefitting some (e.g. a MLE pilot school in *Rasuwa* and a *Tharu* MLE programme in Dang districts), are functioning better than the others. Teachers who are competent in local mother tongue (MT) and their positive attitudes towards MT teaching and enthusiasm have been ascribed for this situation (Weinberg, n.d.-c).

CHALLENGES SURROUNDING MLE IN NEPAL

Multilingual Education (MLE) is a part of a system. It directly and indirectly interacts with different but equally important aspects of the teaching learning processes. Therefore, it cannot be isolated from other aspects of a child's schooling. MLE has to function within competing realities which often create tension in its implementation. It is influenced in one way or the other by overall education quality related factors as well as socio-political and economic factors. When there are conflicting interests over MLE, people tend to utilize it to serve varied objectives. For some, it is a vehicle to establish a so-called standard form of their languages, whereas for others it is a tool to conserve and develop their languages and cultures. The tension in determining a child's MT further adds another layer to the challenge already created by multiple language settings. The challenges and issues emerged in MLE programmes in general and MLE pilot in particular are discussed below.

DETERMINING A CHILD'S MT/FIRST LANGUAGE

To a larger extent, the issue related to the identification of a child's mother tongue (MT) is the manifestation of the contesting perspectives regarding MLE. For example, whether the MT should be considered as a language that a child speaks at home to communicate or the language that her/his parents speak that the child does not necessarily comprehend. From pedagogue and educationists' perspective, the language that a child uses to communicate at home should be her/his MT. But from the perspective of language activists, irrespective of the language that a child uses for communication, her/ his MT is the language that her/his families or communities belong to, although, the child may not communicate in that language. The argument is likely to continue, as on one hand '. . . nearly one-fourth of Nepalese languages are viable to be threatened due to reasons such as lack of inter-generational language transmission . . .' (Yadava, n.d., 12). And, on the other, for activists, MLE, 'sometimes means teaching in a community language that children may not speak.' (Weinberg, 2010) Likewise often elites of languages with no writing system or that have multiple forms tend to impose their system and form rather than the one that a child brings with her/him to the classroom making it more difficult to teach and learn.

INTERFACE BETWEEN IMPLEMENTATION MODALITY AND BUREAUCRACY

Particularly, in the case of the MLE pilot project, the implementation modality is interfaced with bureaucratic limitations. The modality was innovative, in the sense that it recognized and utilized local people's knowledge employing participatory processes. However, such a modality was difficult to fit into a bureaucratic system. Bureaucracy by nature is bound by structure and is required to follow certain pathways on one hand and on the other it has to cover a larger territory than that of the pilot projects. Therefore, the structure, extent of financial, and technical supports that the pilot project dispensed was not immediately possible for the government. In this situation, sustaining the inputs and effects of the pilot was a challenge.

The Curriculum Development Centre (CDC), an apex agency of the Ministry of Education, has long been engaged in textbook translation and development in local languages. This was a response to the MLE related policies and legal provisions that emerged after the 1990s political change. But instead of collaborating with CDC and building on what had already been done, the project adopted a completely new modality. Although, at later stage, the project began to recognize the work done by CDC, the initial resentment left a lasting effect in the relationship between bureaucracy and the project.

The pilot project was designed to test different modalities of MLE in Grades I to III. School-based and community-based Early Childhood Education and Development (ECED) programmes, and non-formal primary education programmes known as alternative schools were two sources from where children came to enrol in these grades in pilot schools. Therefore, graduates of these programmes who joined pilot schools had no MLE exposure and adjusting to new classroom processes at the later stage was likely to create problems in student learning.

CONTESTING PERSPECTIVES

Different and contesting viewpoints regarding MLE exist. Some believe that MLE is needed but teaching/learning in MT is not a sensible idea. People with this viewpoint believe that small children have the ability to learn multiple languages simultaneously, therefore they can be taught through different languages. Thus, children only need to be familiar with different ways of saying the same thing. How this is possible pedagogically and how cognitive development of such children can be ensured, is not clear in their argument. Often this group of intellectuals is more inclined towards a language transfer technique than cognitive development of non-Nepali speaking children. For some people, MLE is the traditionally used semi or full translation method which they believe was doing fine and should be continued. There are another set of people who view MLE purely from linguistic point of view and their drive is towards the use of 'standard' form of MT/s. Yet another set of people believe that MLE is about conserving one's language and culture thereby protecting the group identity and giving continuity to traditional customs. All types of mindsets influence school education in one way or another (European Commission, 2001).

Weinberg (2009a) in her research of MLE in five different local MTs hardly found anyone from teachers to school management committees to parents understanding MLE as a way to enhance teaching and learning for non Nepali-speaking children. For almost all of them, MLE was a tool for preservation of their respective languages and cultures. For example, an Athpariya Rai parent from a hill district and a Sherpa teacher from a mountain district whose child was also learning in Sherpa language both saw teaching in MT as a vehicle to ensure continuity to traditional customs and rituals (MLE Research & Expert Team, 2009; Weinberg, 2009b).

Unaware of the pedagogical value, some activists were even found pursuing their conservation objective alone in the MLE project (MLE Research & Expert Team, 2009). Hence, most MLE programmes seemed to be operating without a clear vision and understanding of educational benefit of teaching—learning in MT.

With no or very little consideration to the distinction between the Basic Interpersonal Communication Skill (BICS) and Cognitive Academic Language Proficiency (CALP), all these perspectives are influencing the MLE programmes. Lack of this distinction puts non Nepali-speaking children in a disadvantaged position (Awasthi, 2004). In the midst of this reality, a small group of people who believe that MLE is teaching/learning in MT with a gradual transition to other language are found advocating for pedagogical reform through MLE.

SYSTEMIC AND INDIVIDUAL CAPACITY

A shortfall in systemic and individual capacities and an over ambitious design affected the implementation as well as outcome of the MLE pilot project. The project intended to reform curriculum, textbook, and to capacitate different levels of stakeholders with focus on language issues. But it encountered other issues, which hindered the effective use of MT. For example, in one MLE pilot school where Grades II and III students belonged to one mother tongue were grouped together and taught in their MT. The project team named it as multi-grade teaching. However, neither the curricular materials used to deliver the lessons were designed for multi-grade teaching nor were the teachers trained in multi-grade teaching. The students were receiving half of the teacher's time as she took turns to deliver the lessons from grade-specific textbooks (MLE Research & Expert Team, 2009).

A meaningful classroom interaction could not occur. In this situation, in spite of the use of MT, it was unlikely that the students' learning would improve. Besides, in a system that functions with under-qualified teachers especially at the primary level, inadequate teacher support, inappropriate and uneven teacher student ratio, lack of adequate reading materials in MT, poor financial management system, dearth of human resources in local MTs for curricular material development, and inadequate monitoring sustenance and effect of MLE activities for better student outcome has always been a challenge.

Additionally, multiple language settings of Nepal required schools to apply multiple teaching and learning techniques and create multiple arrangements. Moreover, internal migration is likely to keep on changing the language dynamics of schools, making it more challenging to manage the diversity. Mostly schools located in the urban and semi urban areas are likely to face this challenge. Schools that are already facing financial and technical resource constraint for MLE the changes add more pressure.

One of the main factors that influence MLE is the teacher. Teachers' competence, commitment, attitude, and behaviour to a larger extent influence the quality of education, particularly of those students who come with MT other than the existing medium of instruction. Teachers belonging to MTs other than Nepali are fewer in number. Those available are unevenly distributed across districts. Not all of the teachers belonging to local MTs are well versed in their own MTs either. With few exceptions teachers belonging to Nepali MT or MT other than that of students often lack the language skills of local languages; see no benefit of teaching in MT; find it more time and resource consuming business; and show little or no interest in learning and using local language in classroom teaching (Weinberg, n.d.). If teachers are not competent or believe in multilingual and multicultural diversity as resources, MLE programmes are not likely to be implemented appropriately.

A highly politicized teaching force makes it harder to redeploy on one hand and appraise their performance on the other. Trends to hire untrained and under qualified teachers for special purposes like MLE further short-change the students who are already disadvantaged. Therefore, the recommendation to 'get the best teachers; get the best out of teachers; and step in when pupils start to lag behind' proposed by the McKinsey Report on the basis of PISA 2006 findings (*The Economist*, 2007) is remotely possible in the education system of Nepal at present.

The government's female teacher policy, which requires the presence of a female in a primary school, is a double-edged sword when it comes to MLE. For gender equality and role models for girls, the female teacher policy is a desired measure but the majority of the female teachers belong to Nepali MT and many married female teachers end up teaching in new localities where they moved to either due to their husbands' work or due to the rule of patrilocality (bride moving to groom's residence). In this situation, they are often found unable to use the local language of the area (MLE Research & Expert Team, 2009).

INFLUENCE OF SOCIAL CONTEXT AND LABOUR MARKET

The response to MLE programmes varies across districts. Primarily, differences in occupational scope and social contexts influenced the responses. Most parents and communities search for occupational and economic value of the languages that are used in their children's classrooms. Unaware of the long-term educational value of MT teaching, they often view MT as limiting their children's mobility.

In Rasuwa as in other mountain districts of Nepal people move to upper grasslands (hills) with their cattle during summer. This kind of seasonal migration mostly among Tamangs, dominant ethnic group of Rasuwa affects children's schooling, which cannot be addressed only through MLE. On the other hand, some parents and communities from the MLE pilot project started to pressurize in favour of Nepali and English languages because, with popular trekking routes and conservation park tourism is the main occupation there. Whereas in the western district of Kanchanpur where there is less scope of interaction with outsiders, and the community is quite homogenous, with farming as their main occupation, parents were happy with the use of MT in classroom. A MLE pilot school in Jhapa, a district that borders Darjeeling, India's famous town for private English medium boarding schools, has been struggling to prevent children from transferring to private schools. Moreover, many adults move to Kathmandu seeking better opportunities or send their children to private boarding schools in Kathmandu. Often these children do not speak their local MTs. In this situation, the MLE programmes 'do not reach the people most likely to abandon the language.' (Weinberg, 2010)

PARENTAL PREFERENCE FOR ENGLISH AND PRIVATE SCHOOLS

Additionally, parents' growing preference for English language and style promoted by private schools threaten the efforts made in MLE (MLE Research & Expert Team, 2009; Weinberg, n.d.-b). As in most developing countries, in Nepal English language has become synonymous with quality education. Most private schools have been able to use this perception in their favour. Related studies of Acharya and Giri (2009) and of the MLE Research and Expert Team (2009) reveal that private schools' focus on English language, neatness, tidiness, and strict management helped attract parents and students. While the MLE pilot project was still operating in twenty government aided schools from Eastern Nepal where three of the pilot schools were located, they decided to apply neck-tie, belt, and English medium in order to increase the student enrolment which otherwise would further decline. (Adhikari, 2009, 20) For instance, a mother from an indigenous community said, 'my child would not come here if wearing neck-tie was not made a rule this year.

This has given relief to those of us who cannot send their children to private schools.' (Adhikari, 2009)

Weinberg (2009a) in her visit to one of the pilot schools located in Eastern Nepal, where there were children from three languages—Rajbanshi, Santhal, and Nepali heard that the management committee of that school also decided to start English as a medium of instruction from Grade I and discontinue teaching in mother tongues. Weinberg (n.d.-c) encountered a similar situation in one of the *Tharu* MLE programme supported by the non-government sector in Dang district in Western Nepal. Parents preferred English and Nepali as a medium because they feared that their children's mobility and marketability would be limited if they were taught only in MT. The government schools cannot take the risk by losing students. Language communities and concerned agencies on the other hand have no evidence within Nepal to demonstrate the benefits of teaching children in their MTs in early years of their education. MLE programme school personnel are also dubious about the future move due to lack of concrete examples of positive impacts of MT education. (Weinberg, 2009a) In Weinberg's (2010) observation: 'In an educational system with limited resources, they do not want to devote money and effort to something that seems as frivolous as changing the language of instruction.'

INCONSISTENT PROVISIONS

Many policies and legal provisions related to MLE were developed and adapted at different times to respond to domestic issues and international instruments related to the indigenous people's rights. Since those policies and provisions were developed, framed, or adapted at different times and to address particular needs or demands, they remained detached from each other. For example, the Education Act 1971 (5th Amendment) has provision for primary education in MT. Primary education according to the Act are Grades I–V. Whereas, the Interim Constitution of Nepal (2007) has ensured MT Teaching up to basic level, which are Grades I–VIII (Nepal, Ministry of Education and Sports, 2008a, 2008b; and Nepal, Ministry of Education and Sports, Curriculum Development Centre, 2007). Education Regulation 2002, which has been amended for the sixth time in 2010, does not speak about medium of instruction. This situation has also created tension in the understanding and implementation of MLE.

Partial Fulfilment of Policy Objectives

Particularly, in relation to the government MLE initiatives, full utilization of available policies/strategies has been an issue. For example, the policy related to the decentralized curriculum and textbook development has not been implemented fully. It only started under the MLE pilot project in a limited scope. The fund available through the local governments is hardly utilized in MT or in any other quality related aspects.[2] The fund has rather been utilized for construction and hiring more teachers, oftentimes to expand grades/level. It is challenging to efficiently decentralize curriculum/textbook related activities and utilize locally available funds in a system, which has been functioning through centralized approaches for long and where there is minimal level of political commitment towards quality education.

Yet another part, which the available policy and strategy hardly touches upon, is the MLE in the context of private schools. With high priority given to English language, the local MTs are not of concern to private schools. As suggested by a UNESCO (2008) study in relation to Peru, unless the programme and policy move beyond indigenous community, Nepal's MLE will also develop as a compensatory education and education that cannot make 'an asset of linguistic and cultural diversity.' (p. 40) Example of Solukumbu district where trend of out migration among Sherpas have left only those who could not afford to migrate and have been speaking Sherpa, with MLE programme, is a case in point (Weinberg, 2009b).

CONCLUSION

In an effort to utilize the benefit of MLE, the country has placed various rules and regulations in place along with developing materials and translating textbooks. In order to further promote the quality of education, a pilot project was launched in 2007 by the government and development partner. Several other MLE programmes have also been launched through the efforts of non-government organizations. The implementation of the pilot project and other MLE programmes has led to some insightful observations and understandings of the way the MLE interacts with different aspects of education system and with larger social and economic situations. The key insights derived below recognize the many forces associated with the design and implementation of MLE.

The historical review of modern education indicates that preferential treatment to one language and attempts to establish a *one language and one culture* system was a deliberate choice. The legacy of this choice is still reflected in people's attitude and practice, and policies/strategies. Nevertheless, the fact that multilingual classrooms are a reality and not an exception has been established. Many children with local language MTs falling behind in education, political changes, language and cultural rights movement, and evidence from international studies gradually influenced both policies and practices related to MLE. As a result, at present, available policies/strategies are more liberal in adopting and expanding MLE. However, the international and domestic experiences show that MLE does not work alone. Low quality of most of the government-aided schools affects every student in one way or the other. This has established that teaching in MT does not automatically improve student learning and thus MLE cannot be isolated from other pedagogical and learning aspects that influence children's education. Here, capacity of the system and individuals involved in MLE come in the way because their capacities largely determine the successful implementation of MLE programmes.

Language hierarchy has been firmly established. In the hierarchy, English is at the top and local MT is at the bottom, whereas, Nepali is somewhere in the middle. In this situation, teaching in MT has been difficult to implement. Parents are always looking for education that equips their children to earn a living in and beyond their immediate localities. This is a reasonable expectation given the size of the country, topographic and ecologic variation, urban centred employment opportunities and urban centred services. Internal and out-migration is thus unavoidable for time unknown. Therefore, community and parents are unlikely to support MLE unless they are sure about their children's prospects of higher education and economic mobility.

Along with parental choices, politicization of language issue has also challenged MLE. Different stakeholders interpret MLE from different perspectives, which influence not only the implementation modality but identification of children's MT as well. When MLE is viewed as a means to preserve one's language and cultural identity, and liberation from oppression there is always a danger of pedagogical aspect of MLE being submerged. Teachers' attitude and resentment further weakens the implementation processes.

Lack of researchers, particularly in the area of medium of instruction (MOI), classroom practice and student outcomes have left many MLE practitioners to dwell in confusion. The market force, which pushes for English and Nepali languages and confusion at the implementation level, has put MLE at risk. In this situation, lack of evidence to argue in favour of MT teaching has made the advocates and educationists difficult to push the agenda further.

RECOMMENDATIONS

Mother Tongue (MT) teaching is associated with various ingredients of the education system. Therefore, making suggestions only tailored towards MLE is not viable. However, in order to minimize the challenges mentioned in this chapter some immediate and long-term measures have been suggested.

POLICY CONSISTENCY AND CONNECTION TO OVERALL QUALITY ASPECTS

Keeping in view the effect of multiple factors, the immediate need is to review and revise MT/MLE related provisions for consistency and cohesiveness, and at the same time connect them with other quality components at the implementation level.

LOCAL RESOURCE MOBILIZATION: EMPOWERING COMMUNITY, SUPPORTING MLE

Communities can be both implementing partners and resources. Community members can be involved in teaching as they can help in connecting local knowledge, values and skills with modern knowledge, values, and skills. This empowers the community as well as motivate children conserve their heritage. Therefore, a community language and culture resource centre established in community ownership is necessary. Such centres can also help create need of MT by providing venue for teacher training, student research, and tourist attraction. Funds available at local governments for MLE can be utilized to enrich and expand such centres. Linking MT teaching with governance can also enhance MT's marketability. For it, both micro- and macro-level intervention are necessary. Options could be: use of MT in official transactions, including hospitals and courts. Expansion of market of MT then creates need of MLE in private schools as well.

BRIDGING POLICY AND PRACTICE

Often policies inadequately communicated with the beneficiaries are likely to fall short. Therefore, it is important to keep in mind that community and parents will not support MLE if they were kept unknown about their children's prospect of higher education and economic mobility. In this situation, it is necessary to have continuous interaction with parents and communities about the intent of the programme and language transition plan.

DIVERSITY IN CAPACITY DEVELOPMENT

While technical knowledge and skills are fundamentals for the implementation of MLE, positive attitude and behaviours are equally essential at all levels of the education system. Perception makes attitude. Attitude guides behaviour and determines one's commitment towards the cause. Therefore, an overarching capacity development framework with follows up plans and technical backstopping especially for teachers is necessary.

LINKING PRACTICE WITH RESEARCH

Focused studies help to address many issues associated with MLE implementation. Therefore, micro as well as macro level research initiatives are necessary. Practitioners' research at local level will help generate useful information to resolve the issues at practice level. Whereas, a higher level education institution or university is essential for systematic language and culture related academic, research, development, and innovative works. Established research and development activities linked with classroom practice help expand market for MT as well as regularly provide human and technical support to teaching/learning. Moreover, research help produce evidence to demonstrate the benefits of MLE.

COLLABORATIVE INTERVENTION

All the above directions clearly indicate that for a successful MLE programme, collaboration among different actors are unavoidable. Within the education sector, functional collaboration between institutions and/or units are very essential. Role of the leaders of language communities is more important as they are the ones who can demonstrate and convince parents about teaching and learning in MT and its role in their children's quality education.

REFERENCES

Acharya, Sushan, and Giri, D. (2009), 'Measuring learning achievement of Nepali and non-Nepali speaking students of Dang district', (Kathmandu: Save the Children Japan).

Adhikari, C. (2009), 'Tie, belt to increase student', (In Nepali), *Kantipur,* 20.

Awasthi, L. D. (2004), 'Exploring Monolingual School Practices in Multilingual Nepal (Doctoral dissertation)', (Danish University of Education, Copenhagen).

Cause, L. (2010), 'Bernstein's code theory and the educational researcher', *Asian Social Science,* 6(5), 3–9.

Cummins, J. (2009), 'Basic interpersonal communicative skills and cognitive academic language proficiency'.

Cummins, Jim (2001), 'Bilingual children's mother tongue: Why is it important for education', *Sprogforum,* 7(19), 15–20.

D' Emilio, A. L. (2009), 'Indigenous languages: A view from UNICEF', *State of the World's Minorities and Indigenous People 2009.* www.minorityrights.org/download.php?id=664

European Commission (2001), 'European report on the quality of school education, Sixteen quality indicators', http://ec.europa.eu/education/policies/educ/indic/rapinen.pdf

Finland Ministry for Foreign Affairs (2006), 'Project document for Finnish technical assistance to the implementation of the bilingual education programme for all non-Nepali speaking students of primary schools of Nepal (Final)', (Kathmandu: Government of Nepal).

Karki, V. (2002), 'School effectiveness in Nepal: A synthesis of indicators', (Kathmandu: Research Centre for Educational Innovation and Development).

KC, D. (2009), 'Tharu language stops school dropout rate', *The Kathmandu Post,* 5.

Khanal, C. (2003), Education Act Regulation (main text with comments in Nepali), (Kathmandu: Pairavi).

Luykx, A., Lee, O., Mahotiere, M., Lester, B., Hart, J., and Deaktor, R. (2007), 'Cultural and home language influences on children's responses to science assessments', *Teachers College Record*, 109(4), 897–926.

MLE Research, & Expert Team (2009), Review of policies and strategies of MLE in Nepal (in Nepali), (Sanothimi: DOE/MLE Programme).

Nepal, Ministry of Education and Sports (2008a), SSR Core Document, (Kathmandu: Government of Nepal).

Nepal, Ministry of Education and Sports (2008b), SSR Plan 2009–2015, (Kathmandu: Government of Nepal).

Nepal, Ministry of Education and Sports, Curriculum Development Centre (2007), 'National Curriculum Framework for School Education of Nepal', (Kathmandu: Government of Nepal).

Nepal, National Education Planning Commission (1955), Report of the National Education Planning Commission (National Education Plan), Kathmandu, Nepal.

Nepal, National Language Policy Recommendation Commission (1994), Report of National Language Policy Recommendation Commission, Kathmandu.

Nepal, Parliament (1999), Local Self Governance Act 1999, (Kathmandu: Government of Nepal).

Nepal, Parliament (2000), Local Self Governance Regulation 2000, (Kathmandu: Government of Nepal).

Nepal, Parliament (2007), Interim Constitution of Nepal, 2007, (Kathmandu: Government of Nepal). Retrieved from www. peace.gov.np

Panda, Minati and Mohanty, Ajit K. (2009), 'Language matters, so does culture: Beyond the rhetoric of culture in multilingual education', in M. Panda, A. K. Mohanty, R. Phillipson & T.

Skutnabb-Kangas, eds., *Multilingual Education for Social Justice: Globalizing the Local* (New Delhi: Orient Blackswan), 295–312.

Sadovnik, A. R. (2001), Basil Bernstein (1924–2000), *Prospects: The Quarterly Review of Comparative Education*, XXXI(4), 687–703. Retrieved from http://unesdoc.unesco.org/images/0012/001256/125636e.pdf

Sharma, G. (2002), Reports of Education Commissions of Nepal (in Nepali), (Kathmandu: Makalu Books).

The Economist (2007), 'How to be top. What works in education: The lessons according to Mckinsey', Retrieved from www.economist.com/PrinterFriendly.cfm?story_id=9989914

UNESCO (2003), 'Education in a multilingual world', (Paris: UNESCO).

UNESCO (2005), 'Mother tongue-based teaching and education for girls', Advocacy brief, (Bangkok: UNESCO).

UNESCO (2008), 'Mother tongue matters: Local languages as key to effective learning', (Paris: UNESCO).

Weinberg, M. (2009a), 'Multilingual Education in Nepal: Experiences from the field', Paper presented at the Talk Programme on 9 July 2010, Centre for Nepal and Asian Studies, Tribhuvan University.

Weinberg, M. (2009b), 'Sherpa language education in Khumbu and Pharak: Some observations'.

Weinberg, M. (2010), 'Multilingual Education in Nepal: Facing Challenges and Challenging Definitions', Paper presented at the Fulbright Forum Presentation 8 July 2010, Fulbright Commission, Kathmandu.

Weinberg, M. (n.d.-a), Newa pre-primary schools.

Weinberg, M. (n.d.-b), Thangmi language programme summary.

Weinberg, M. (n.d.-c), Tharu multilingual education programme.

World Bank (2005), Education Notes. Retrieved from http://site resources.worldbank.org/EDUCATION/Resources/Education-Notes/EdNotes_Lang_of_Instruct.pdf

Yadav, Y. P, and Turin, M. (2005), 'Indigenous languages of Nepal: A critical analysis of the linguistic situation and contemporary issues', In Y. P. Yadav and P. L. Bajracharya, eds., *The Indigenous Languages of Nepal (ILN): Situation, Policy Planning and Coordination* (Kathmandu: National Foundation for Development of Indigenous Nationalities), 6–46.

Yadava, Y. P. (n.d.), 'Proposing use of language in primary education in federal Nepal', a paper prepared for discussion initiated by the Support Group for Education and Federalism.

Yonjan-Tamang, A. (2006), 'Identity, current situation and language development plan of languages of Nepal (Nepalka bhasaharuko pahichan, sthiti, ra bhasabikash yojana)', (Kathmandu: Indigenous Linguistic Society).

Yonjan-Tamang, A. (2009), 'Linguistic Heritage of Nepal: Multilingualism for Social Justice, Harmony and Peace', (MPhil/PhD Presentation) (Kathmandu University: Kathmandu).

NOTES

1. In 1990, one-party system ended and a multiparty political system was restored.
2. Local Self-Governance Act 1999 and Regulation 2000 have provision to fund MT teaching at primary level in respective constituencies.

9

W(h)ither the Teaching Profession in India

—*Ajay Sharma*

INTRODUCTION

Fundamental changes are afoot in the provision of schooling in India. Through the Right to Education (RTE) Act of 2010, the Indian central government has committed itself to achieving the laudable goal of providing free and compulsory education to every Indian child between the ages of six to fourteen years by the Millennium Development Goals (MDG) mandated deadline of 2015 (Hoyle, 1995; India, Planning Commission, 2009; Joshi, 2006). At the same time, however, the twin discourses of neo-liberalism and free-market capitalism have become dominant in Indian policy-making. Over the past two decades, the Indian government has consistently lowered barriers to corporatization of nation's economy while simultaneously curbing its support for the social sector (Bagchi, 2006; Patnaik, 2006). Consequently, the Indian state finds itself in a difficult position where, on one hand, it has to expand the public education system in order to achieve MDG goals in education, while on the other hand it remains in thrall of neo-liberal ideas.

This contradiction is being partly resolved by transforming the teaching profession. This chapter explains this transformation and highlight its implications for teaching as well as learning in India's schools. As elementary schools are at the core of ongoing efforts to universalize education, this chapter focuses on elementary school teachers, particularly those working in public schools.[1] I believe that it is not just teachers but just about everyone who should worry about what is happening to their profession. As India's national educational policies have consistently emphasized, and as research has also shown, teachers are central to education and are the most noteworthy determinant of the quality of education offered to students in schools (Darling-Hammond, 2000; India, Ministry of Human Resource Development, 1968, 1998; Stronge, Ward, Tucker, & Hindman, 2007). Thus, any changes in the nature and conditions of their work can be expected to impact student learning in significant ways. Also, as more and more under-privileged and poor students get ghettoized in India's government-run schools (Harma, 2010), who teaches these children and under what conditions will have significant implications for educational justice in the sense of access to quality education for all.

Written as an integrative review of research literature and policy documents, this chapter begins with a section on Universalization of Elementary Education (UEE) in India, wherein I first analyze the nature of government support to education as a public good, and then provide a summary of ongoing efforts by the central and state governments to achieve MDG goals in education. This section, thus, situates the teaching profession in the larger institutional and discursive context and prepares us to understand the likely impact of current government policies and actions on the teaching profession in India—a task I attempt in the next section. My analysis indicates that the way the goal of universalization of elementary education is being pursued in India, a grievous harm is being done to the teaching profession. The chapter ends with some thoughts on the implications of these changes for the cause of educational justice for all and a plea to researchers, educators, and concerned citizens for a higher priority to the de-professionalization of teaching in India.

UNIVERSALIZATION OF ELEMENTARY EDUCATION (UEE) IN NEO-LIBERAL TIMES

In the early 1990s, the Indian central government agreed to implement the World Bank and International Monetary Fund-promoted structural adjustment programme to remain financially solvent and put the nation on a trajectory of high growth rate (Joshi, 2006). By doing so, the state basically agreed to follow neo-liberal principles of corporatization of the nation's economy, transfer of public assets and commons into private hands, and reduction in social sector spending (Jha, 2005). This commitment to neo-liberal principles was renewed in 2003 by the passage of the Fiscal Responsibility and Budget Management Act (FRBMA) by the Indian parliament that obligated the central government to reduce the national fiscal deficit to 3 per cent by 2007–8 (Patnaik, 2006). Let me begin by first outlining the implications of such fiscal austerity on the state support for public education.

Later, I will discuss what this means for the state's efforts to universalize elementary education.

STATE'S SUPPORT FOR PUBLIC EDUCATION

State has always expressed strong support for public education in its policy documents. However, there is often a gap between its rhetoric and its actual commitment as reflected in the level of financial support it provides to public education. This gap has widened in the two decades. For instance, according to an analysis of government expenditure on education at an all-India level in the decade (1980–1990) before Indian state adopted neo-liberal prescriptions, the education expenditure rose from 3.2 per cent to a peak of 4.1 per cent of GDP (Joshi, 2006). However, since then, even though Indian state is rapidly expanding the public education system to meet its Universalization of Elementary Education (UEE) mission, we do not see a corresponding increase in public expenditure on education. In the last ten years, expenditure on education both as a percentage of total public expenditure and GDP has remained remarkably stable and low (see Table 1). In fact, according to De and Endow (2008), there is marked decline in expenditure on education at constant prices in per capita terms, and 'while aggregate expenditure on education is increasing, the rate of increase is not necessarily keeping pace with budgetary expenditure, GDP growth, or rate of inflation.' (p. 9) On paper, the central government committed itself to increasing expenditure on education up to 6 per cent of GDP in the ongoing eleventh 5-year plan (India, Planning Commission, 2009). However, actual budgetary allocations show that there is still quite a gap between rhetoric and reality.

An important reason for the stagnation of public expenditure on education lies in the structural adjustment programmes and accompanying economic reforms imposed upon India under pressure by global finance capital and multilateral funding agencies since early 1990s (Bhaduri, 2006; De & Endow, 2008; Patnaik, 2006). As mentioned earlier, these reforms forced the Indian government to reduce its fiscal deficit and enact the FRBMA. Expenditure on education (and other social sectors) is clubbed as an expenditure in revenue account for budgeting purposes in India. Thus, expenditure on education adds to the national fiscal deficit. This has straitjacketed the state in terms of its planning for the social sector. In fact, even the National Planning Commission in one of its reports (GoI, 2006) admitted that because of FRBMA, 'far from any increase in fiscal deficit as a means of mobilising resources we are constrained to work with a reduction of the fiscal deficit of around 1 percentage point of GDP to be achieved in the first two years of the Plan.' (pp. 67–8) Several economists, such as De and Endow (2008) and Bagchi (2006), concur and have made the case that the central government and state governments have tried to rein in their respective fiscal deficits by reducing expenditure in education and other social sectors.

Of course, this is an aggregate picture, and some state governments are doing better than others in terms of financing primary education. However, what has also happened over the last two decades is that autonomy of the states in terms of implementation has narrowed. This is because the central government has started playing an increasingly important role in state education finance, thanks to centrally sponsored schemes, such as *Sarva Shiksha Abhiyan* (SSA)—the umbrella programme for UEE (De & Endow, 2008). The central government provides 75 per cent of the funds for implementation of SSA to states. Thus, the imprint of the central government, and indirectly of the international funding agencies, on implementation strategies followed by the state is quite prominent.

Table 1: Public Expenditure on Education—Recent Trends

Year	Expenditure on Education by Education & other Departments as % of Public Expenditure	Expenditure on Education by Education Department as % of GDP	Expenditure on Education by Education & other Departments as % of GDP
1999–00	14.60	3.43	4.19
2000–01	14.42	3.25	4.28
2001–02	12.89	3.09	3.81
2002–03	12.60	3.03	3.78
2003–04	11.98	2.88	3.51
2004–05	12.13	2.82	3.36
2005–06	12.73	2.88	3.45
2006–07 (P)	13.29	2.92	3.64
2007–08 (P)	13.32	3.02	3.74
2008–09 (P)	13.63	3.13	3.78

P = Provisional Estimate.
Source: India, Ministry of Human Resource Development, 2010.

Investment in education was supposedly an important part of the safety net envisaged by the World Bank to off-set the adverse consequences of the structural adjustment programme in the social sector (Jandhyala B. G. Tilak, 2008). Ironically, despite the high profile nature of the World Bank involvement in elementary education, public schools in India remain largely funded by Indian taxpayers. As De and Endow (2008) point out, despite the fact that the Indian government keeps doors open for foreign aid, it has always remained quite low, as a proportion of aggregate, public expenditure on education. For instance, they point out that 'in 2002–03 when external aid was at its maximum level it was equivalent only to 1.5 per cent of education expenditure and 3 per cent of expenditure on elementary education.' (p. 28) However, it is interesting to note that in spite of their limited financial contribution to public education, the World Bank's impact at the educational policy level has been rather significant (Govinda & Josephine, 2005).

The financial picture for India's public education, therefore, raises a remarkable quandary. And that is, all educational data clearly indicate that public education is expanding. The central as well as the state governments are making tremendous efforts to provide students with more classrooms and more teachers. So how can that be possible if public expenditure on education is not rising? To answer this question, I turn next to the issue of implementation of the Universalization of Elementary Education (UEE) mission.

STATE'S EFFORTS TO UNIVERSALIZE ELEMENTARY EDUCATION (UEE)

Indian policymakers have long proclaimed their commitment towards education for all. As early as 1950, free and compulsory education was adopted as one of the directive principles of state policy in the Indian constitution. The first National Policy on Education (India, Ministry of Human Resource Development, 1968) too declared the Indian government's resolve to promote the development of education by advocating that 'strenuous efforts should be made for the early fulfilment of the directive principle under Article 45 of the constitution seeking to provide free and compulsory education for all children up to the age of fourteen.' (p. 39) However, as far as expansion of elementary education is concerned, nothing much really happened in terms of changes in the realities on the ground (Goldman, Kumar, Liu, & Corporation, 2008; Prakash, 2008). The resolve for universal access to free primary education was again reiterated in the second National Policy on Education (NPE) that came out in 1986. The second NPE somewhat shook up things as a slew of government programmes aimed at elementary education, such as the Operation Blackboard (1987–1988) and the Restructuring and Reorganization of Teacher Education (1987) were initiated. Spurred by foreign funding agencies, the pace of change quickened with the initiation of the District Primary Education Programme (DPEP) in 1993—a programme that also signalled the entry of foreign funds and policy agendas in the arena of school education in India. The commitment for universalizing elementary education was put on a firmer footing in 2002 with the amendment of the nation's constitution to include free and compulsory education as a fundamental right. Alongside and perhaps in anticipation of a constitutional amendment, in 2001, DPEP and other elementary education programmes were merged into Sarva Shiksha Abhiyan (SSA)—a national flagship programme for universalization of elementary education in a time-bound manner.

The role of SSA in achieving universal elementary education became central and vitally important with the passage of Right to Education Act (RTE) by the Indian Parliament in 2009, and its enactment in 2010. Specifically, the RTE act makes it mandatory for central and state governments to provide free and compulsory education by 2013 to every child between the ages of six to fourteen. As is obvious, with this act, the Indian state has compelled itself to match its policy proclamations with commensurate action on the ground. As I elaborate ahead, such a time-bound commitment portends significant short-term benefits with equally momentous long-term costs and potential dangers, especially inasmuch as the fates of the teaching profession and educational justice are concerned.

Thus, for the last few decades, the Indian state has strenuously attempted to universalize elementary (Grades 1 to 8) education. The seventh India education survey (India, National Council for Teacher Education, 2002) shows that between 1993 and 2002, enrolment in primary (1–5) and upper primary (6–8) grades increased by 26.15 per cent and 37.49 per cent respectively. In case of girls, the increase was

36.85 per cent and 52.46 per cent respectively. The gross enrolment ratio at the primary stage increased in this period from 81.85 per cent to 93.32 per cent. Similar improvements were made at an infrastructural level, such as the availability of schooling facilities. For instance, the percentage of rural human habitations with a primary schooling facility within a distance of 1 km increased from 83 per cent in 1993 to 87 per cent in 2002. The corresponding increase at the upper-primary level was from 76 per cent to 78 per cent. According to the latest figures available (for the year 2008–2009), the gross enrolment ratio at the primary level is now 115.3 (India. National University of Educational Planning and Administration, 2010b).

The next all-India education survey will tell us how the nation is doing in terms of access to primary and upper-primary schooling facilities. But other related recent figures tell us a story of rapid increase in availability of schools at both primary and upper-primary levels, and a corresponding improvement in school infrastructure (see Table 2). For instance, there are now about 3.3 primary and 1.45 upper-primary schools per 10 sq. km (India. National University of Educational Planning and Administration, 2010a, 2010b).[2] According to an analysis (Mehta, 2010), 'Of the total schools that impart elementary education in the country in 2007–08, 15.13 per cent are opened since 2002–03.' (p. 23) According to the Central Ministry of Human Resources Development (2010), India needs another 780,000 classrooms to meet the challenge of UEE. Thus, in two decades, the Indian state has reached within a hair's breadth of providing universal access

to primary education for all its children, and further progress
is afoot.

Table 2: Improvements in School Availability and Infrastructure

Select Indicators	2003–04	2008–09
Density of primary schools (per 10 sq. km)	n.a.	3.3
Density of upper-primary schools (per 10 sq. km)	n.a.	1.45
Ratio of primary to upper-primary schools/ sections	2.87	2.27
Percentage of schools having pucca building	69.29	73.44
Percentage of schools having drinking water facility	77.89	87.77
Percentage of schools having girls' toilet in school	28.24	53.6

Source: India, National University of Educational Planning and
Administration, 2010a, 2010b.

As can be expected, the rapid expansion of government-
provided schooling has led to a huge demand for elementary
teachers. In a recent meeting of state education secretaries, it
was admitted that there was an already existing need to fill
523,000 vacant teacher posts in government primary and
upper-primary schools. In addition, the state governments
have still to fill a remaining balance of 225,000 teaching
positions already sanctioned under SSA. It was further
recognized in this meeting that on top of all these shortages,
the demand for teachers has been further exacerbated by
the RTE Act as it requires a Pupil-Teacher Ratio (PTR) of

30:1 at primary level[3] and 35:1 at upper-primary level in all schools. Thus, the state governments will have to hire another 510,000 teachers (India, Ministry of Human Resource Development, 2010). In all, there is a commitment to recruit more than a million teachers in the next three years. All over the country, states are launching large recruiting drives. For instance, Bihar and Bengal plan to recruit 111,000 and 60,000 teachers respectively before the academic session of 2010–11 (India, Ministry of Human Resource Development, 2010). This massive recruitment drive will be accompanied by equally large scale 'professional training' of existing 760,000 untrained teachers in primary and upper-primary schools and 'inducting training' of freshly recruited 1.33 million teachers (India, Ministry of Human Resource Development, 2010). It is now time to revisit the all-important question: How is it possible to recruit so many teachers and train them if public expenditure on education is not rising?

To answer this question, we need to remind ourselves that the largest budget item in a school system is always teacher salaries. In a 2010 meeting of state education secretaries in Delhi, it was estimated that to implement RTE Act, the total public expenditure for the whole nation would amount to about 1.8 trillion rupees over a period of three years. Of this, about 28 per cent would go in teacher salaries (India, Ministry of Human Resource Development, 2010). Any savings made in this budget item would be substantial and can go a long way in funding expansion of the public education system in terms of building more schools, providing more child entitlements and teaching-learning materials, and even hiring more teachers.

And this is exactly what has happened over the last two decades. Infrastructure development comes out of plan expenditure and teacher salaries out of non-plan expenditure on education. If we look at Table 3, that highlights the plan and non-plan expenditure on education since early 1990s, it is clear that the ratio of non-plan expenditure has been going down over the years. Thus, states, with the support of the central government have tried to rein in their fiscal deficits, as required by the FRBMA Act, by reducing inter alia their expenditure on teacher salaries (Sankar, 2007). But, since they still have to meet their UEE goals, the states are using funds provided by the central government under the SSA programme to recruit a sizeable segment of new teachers as low-paid contract workers. The influence of the World Bank on India's educational policy is indicated by the fact that the idea of hiring contract teachers first began with the World Bank funded District Primary Education Programme (DPEP) in 1995 (Govinda & Josephine, 2005).

Desperate for some solution to their budgetary constraints and unmindful for the long-term damage, this strategy may cause to the teaching profession and public education, the states readily adopted contractualization of teaching as a preferred way to achieve universalization of elementary education. For instance, of the 111,000 teachers Bihar plans to recruit in 2010, 75,000 will be recruited as contract teachers on a fixed pay basis (India. Ministry of Human Resource Development, 2010). The state of Madhya Pradesh is a leader in this respect as it not only stopped recruiting teachers on regular salaries way back in 1998, it has also mainstreamed contractualization of teaching by recruiting all new teachers into a freshly minted cadre of contract teachers, called Samvida Shikshak. Upon satisfactory completion of three years in this position, these contract teachers are employed as teachers (*adhyapaks*) with some salary raise by the local district (Zilla or Janpad) government. Even after employment as *adhyapaks*, the salary of these teachers are far below that of existing 'regular' teachers who are still paid regular salaries recommended by the pay commissions.

Table 3: Plan and Non-Plan Expenditure on Education (Revenue Account)

Financial Year	At Current Prices (Rs. Crores)			% Distribution	
	Plan	Non-Plan	Total	Plan	Non-Plan
1990–91	3,247.9	17,243.3	20,491.0	15.85	84.15
1991–92	3,746.9	18,846.9	22,594.0	16.58	83.42
1992–93	4,009.0	21,021.3	25,030.0	16.02	83.98
1993–94	5,181.1	23,098.6	28,280.0	18.32	81.68
1994–95	6,538.7	26,067.6	32,606.0	20.05	79.95
1995–96	8,383.1	29,795.0	38,178.0	21.96	78.04
1996–97	10,305.0	33,591.1	43,897.0	23.48	76.52
1997–98	10,388.0	38,164.6	48,552.0	21.40	78.61
1998–99	13,280.0	48,298.6	61,579.0	21.57	78.43
1999–00	13,864.9	60,951.2	74,816.1	18.53	81.47
2000–01	13,274.3	69,212.2	82,486.5	16.09	83.91
2001–02	17,902.6	61,963.1	79,865.7	22.42	77.58
2002–03	18,627.5	66,879.8	85,507.3	21.78	78.22
2003–04	19,092.3	69,986.9	89,079.3	21.43	78.57
2004–05(RE)	27,350.0	77,216.0	104,566.0	26.16	73.84
2005–06 (BE)	37,320.2	81,709.6	119,029.8	31.35	68.65

Source: De and Endow (2008).

Thus, under the twin pressure of budgetary constraints and a mandate for rapid expansion of elementary education, state bureaucracies are increasingly resorting to a relatively easy solution of funding UEE through reduction of teacher salaries and by making their work contractual. The central government, though very prescriptive on other aspects of UEE, has conveniently washed its hands of this matter, claiming that, 'salaries of teachers under SSA are contingent on state specific norms.' (India, Ministry of Human Resource Development, 2010) Further savings in expenditure are made by giving these freshly recruited contract teachers a pared-down and piece-meal in-service orientation to teaching that has been found grossly inadequate and quality-deficient by both the National Council of Teacher Education (2009) and the National Council for Educational Research and Training (2009). As can be expected, these momentous changes have profound implications for the future of school teaching profession in India. The next section delves into these implications.

W(H)ITHER THE TEACHING PROFESSION?

According to Hoyle (1995), 'professions are those occupations whose members bring a high degree of knowledge and skill to those social functions which are most central to the well-being of society.' (p. 12) In addition, Hoyle's (1995) criteria for professions postulate that professions also possess a high level of practitioner and collective autonomy as well as a distinct set of professional values. The school teaching profession may not rank high on these criteria, as compared to 'true' professions such as medicine and law, and is generally seen as a 'semi', 'partial', 'lesser' or 'truncated' profession (Sykes, 1999). However, teacher-educators, researchers, and policymakers, both in India and abroad, have always seen increasing professionalization of teaching as central to quality teaching and teacher empowerment (Govinda & Josephine, 2005; India. Ministry of Human Resource Development, 1998). As I explain ahead, the ongoing universalization of elementary education under budgetary constraints is undermining this agenda, and the future of teaching as an empowered, intellectually vigorous, and esteemed profession is much at risk.

CONTRACTUALIZATION OF TEACHING

As discussed in the previous section, one direct consequence of ongoing structural changes in elementary school education in India has been large-scale contractualization of teaching. From a reasonably well-paid professional career, teaching is transforming into low-paid, deskilled contractual work. Unlike regular teachers, contract teachers are paid at levels low enough to be comparable to minimum wages for unskilled, semi-skilled and skilled workers in many industries, such as brick kilns, food products, handloom industry, lime kilns, and oil mills. For instance, in Madhya Pradesh a Grade I Samvida Shikshak is paid a monthly remuneration of only Rs. 4,500. This salary is at par with minimum wages in many sectors, and is much lower than the Rs. 13,042 recommended for school teachers in the latest sixth National Pay Commission (2008).

Though contract teachers are generally referred to as para-teachers in India, there is considerable confusion over their nomenclature and status in official records. In different states and in different kinds of public schools, they are given different names, such as *guruji*, *samvida-shikshak*, *shikshakarmi*, *shikshamitra*, *vidyaupasak*, and *vidya volunteer*.[4] This proliferation of labels has resulted in some level of misrepresentation of the extent of contract teaching in data on school teachers in India. For instance, in 2007, the state government of Madhya Pradesh reclassified all para-teachers, *shikshakarmis*, in regular public schools as *adhyapaks* on employment with local district authorities, and were shown as regular teachers in government records even though they were paid far less than regular teachers. As a result, in official statistics the number of schools employing contract teachers reduced drastically from 7,423 in 2006–07 to 898 in 2007–08 (India, National University of Educational Planning and Administration, 2010b). Still, records show that in the year 2007–08, para-teachers constituted 14.10 per cent of total teachers in public schools in India (India, National University of Educational Planning and Administration, 2010a). The proportion of contract teachers is relatively high in many states such as Uttar Pradesh, Jammu & Kashmir, and Jharkhand. For instance, in the state of Jharkhand, 53.5 per cent of all public school teachers are para-teachers (India, National University of Educational Planning and Administration, 2010a). This figure looks more alarming from an educational justice perspective because when these data are disaggregated, it is revealed that as many as 92.60 per cent of para-teachers were employed in rural public schools

(India, National University of Educational Planning and Administration, 2010a; NUEPA, 2010).

For more than a decade, in a bid to reduce social expenditure governments in Europe have been gradually withdrawing from the direct responsibility of providing services in the social sector, such as medicine, social security, and education (Gerhard, Knijn, & Lewis, 2002; Knijn & Selten, 2009). This is done primarily by modifying secure jobs and careers into terminable, short-term contracts.

Univeralization of elementary education has enabled such forms of contractual governance to cross-national boundaries and reach India—a striking illustration of erosion of states as sites of political, economic, and cultural sovereignty in the age of global capitalism (Appadurai, 2000). Further, private schools, especially Low Fee Private (LFP) Schools, generally employ teachers at far lower salaries and offer more adverse working conditions than public schools (Jain & Dholakia, 2010). With private schools becoming the model for public school system, conditions for teacher employment that obtain in private schools are fast becoming the norm for all schools—public and private. This is tantamount to privatization of public schooling—not in the sense of ownership and existence of profit motive, but as normalization of a discourse on teaching and education within the public sector that hitherto existed only in the private arena.

According to Knijn and Selten (2009), contractualization of social services represents a shift in trust placed on professionals in these services. This change tells professionals and the society at large that professionals are not to be trusted on the basis of their training, expertise, and professional ethics, but on the basis of a contract in which 'all of the tasks, goods, and services are described, calculated, and settled.' (Knijn & Selten, 2009, 26) Knijn and Selten (2009) call this a calculus-based trust wherein the guiding assumption is that these professionals are not as much motivated by their professional honour and ethics as they are by economic-based rational motives and old fashioned carrots-and-sticks methods. In India, this shift in trust on teachers has been much aided by influential reports that showed public school teachers in extremely unfavourable light and showcased them as prime suspects for the poor state of public education (Chaudhury, Hammer, Kremer, Muralidharan, & Rogers, 2006; De et al., 1999; De, Dreze, Samson, & Kumar, 2009). These reports feed the current dominant neo-liberal discourse that equates public sector with bad and private sector with good. As a result, the contractualization of teaching, according to Saxena (2006) has come to acquire middleclass sanction, and the general impression is that public school teachers do not work.

Expectedly, the contractualization of teaching is resulting in progressive loss of social status for school teachers (Sadgopal, 2006). According to Batra (2005), 'school teaching has declined to the status of a least favoured profession.' (p. 43–7) That may be somewhat of an exaggeration, but it is evidently clear that contractualization of teaching, as it is happening in public schools all over India, does not auger well for the social status that society accords to school teachers and their profession. In addition, because the contract is between an individual (the teacher) and the state, contractualization fragments teachers by transforming them from members of professionalized cadre into individual contractees. Thus atomized, these individual actors are then managed from above and made individually responsible for the achievement of unilaterally imposed goals on which they possess little authorship. As is obvious, this process is debilitating for the collective and individual agency of teachers. If research on contractualization in other sectors is to be followed, see for instance (Duyvendak, Knijn, & Kremer, 2009; Gregory, 2001; Sommerlad & Sanderson, 2004), this sort of individualization of work, as entailed by contractualization of teaching, is most likely to be disempowering for school teachers.

Continued disempowerment at the workplace is bound to have serious repercussions for Indian school teachers. Ever since Marx first commented upon alienation of the worker arising from lack of control over his own labour, many sociologists have studied people's alienation from their work in different job settings. For instance, in a sociological study of more than a thousand employees representing seven different occupational groups, it was found that, 'job conditions are significantly more important than background factors for explaining feelings of self-estrangement. In particular, lack of control over task activities (powerlessness) and lack of meaningful work (meaninglessness) are found to be the most powerful indicators across all occupational groups'(Mottaz, 1981). Similar conclusions were reached in a study of teacher burnout in United States (LeCompte & Dworkin, 1991).

Research indicates that public school teachers all over India are already quite demotivated (India, National Knowledge Commission, 2007; Mooij, 2008; Ramchandran, 2005), and teacher burnout appears to be a widespread phenomenon in government schools (Kudva, 1999; Shukla & Trivedi, 2008).[5] According to LeCompte and Dworkin (1991), burnout among teachers can be seen as a coping mechanism as it makes their work less stressful by allowing them to care less about the quality of their teaching (p. 94). Indifferent quality of teaching can then be seen as an extremely unfortunate and troublesome outcome of the demotivating working conditions. It is clear then that as Govinda and Josephine (2004) have argued, further disempowerment of schoolteachers through contractualization of teaching only foreshadows further deterioration in this regard.

DE-PROFESSIONALIZATION OF TEACHING

Like many other professions, teachers perform a social function that is quite central to the well-being of the society. As Cochran-Smith (2003) once remarked, 'teaching is unforgivingly complex.' (p. 4) Good teaching requires understanding of a complex body of knowledge, deep intellectual work, and understanding of and love for students (Nieto, 2003; Shulman, 1987). It is not a simple matter of administering predetermined procedures—that is something that technicians do. Teachers are not technicians; they like other professionals deal with complex, ill-defined work situations that need creativity, improvisation, and quick on-the-feet thinking. Some educators, such as Batra (2005) and

J. B. G. Tilak (2004) argue that underlying state's efforts towards UEE is an assumption that anybody can teach with just a little bit of training. However, as anyone who has done teacher professional development will tell you teachers need rigorous, high quality, and sustained professional preparation and support in order to teach well. Recognizing this need, the latest curriculum framework for teacher education has also recommended an enhancement in duration and rigor of teacher professional preparation (India, National Council for Teacher Education, 2009).

As was indicated earlier, state governments in India are rushing to recruit about one million school teachers for elementary public schools in order to achieve universalization of elementary education and *Pupil-Teacher* ratio mandated under RTE Act of 2010. A very large proportion of these teachers would be entering their classrooms without any professional preparation. The states are gearing up to provide in-service professional preparation to 760,000 already serving but untrained elementary school teachers and about 1.33 million freshly recruited teachers (India, Ministry of Human Resource Development, 2010). These teachers need rigorous professional preparation and consistent professional support if we expect them to do what is expected of them. However, as the government agencies have clearly admitted, such training is of extremely poor quality (India, National Council for Teacher Education, 2009; National Council of Educational Research and Training, 2009; Planning Commission, 2006). As a result, most school teachers are ill-prepared to teach the kind of classrooms that are the norm in most government elementary schools—highly diverse and multigrade (Pratham, 2010; Ramchandran, 2005).

It is clear that in light of the huge numbers involved, preparing teachers to teach well would require a much higher level of financial commitment from the state. But as we saw earlier, that level of support from the state is conspicuously absent. In this way, the state is effectively setting up most of these teachers for professional failure—an outcome that is likely to further dampen their motivation at work, and depress already low social and professional status of their career.

As I said earlier, most professions are distinguished by a distinct set of professional ethos. This shared set of professional values arises from long periods of professional preparation that socializes them into the profession. The long duration of apprenticeship also enables beginning practitioners to imbibe a core repertoire of professional practices and knowledge, that, along with shared professional ethos, helps maintain necessary and distinct professional standards. Recruitment of professionally underprepared teachers who, contrary to NCTE (2009) recommendations, come to the job without spending such intensive and prolonged periods of socialization in university-based teacher education programmes, works against the development of a shared professional ethos among school teachers. Recognizing the dangers of this trend, the report of the working group on elementary education and literacy for the nation's eleventh 5-Year Plan (2007–2012) bemoaned the 'increasing informalisation of the school system' because of 'an indiscriminate increase of the under-qualified cadre of para-teachers' in the 'primary stage—the most crucial stage of education.' (India. Planning Commission, 2006, 181) The report admitted that in the current drive for UEE, 'teacher training and motivation were the weakest links of elementary education schemes.' (India, Planning Commission, 2006, 12)

The cause of the professionalization of teaching is further harmed by the ways these newly recruited teachers are being prepared for teaching in public schools. Under the current Universalization of Elementary Education (UEE) mission, the in-service trainings for these teachers are offered by district level governmental bodies, such as District Institute of Educational Training (DIET), Block Resource Center (BRC), and Cluster Resource Center (CRC). These bodies were set up to meet 'the challenge of ever increasing demand of teachers for achieving universal elementary education.' (India. National Council of Educational Research and Training, 2009, 68) The teachers are trained at DIETs or BRCs for duration of 10 days. According to the guidelines for the UEE mission, a 'split up' model of teacher training is followed during which in the beginning a 6–8 days training is provided at the DIET/BRC level that includes 2 days training in actual classrooms. After this training session, teachers return to their schools for 2–3 months to try out the teaching ideas and practices recommended to them. At the end of this in-school period, the teachers return again to DIET/BRC for a 2-day session of sharing and reflection. Clearly, a training experience of 10 days is too short for the development of any shared professional ethos and/or professional standards among teachers being currently recruited for nation's public elementary schools.[6]

Further, as a recent comprehensive review of teacher preparation programmes in the nation NCERT (2009) showed, these trainings are generally of very poor quality. For example, according to this review, 'in-service programmes are generally not planned based on field observations or any need assessment studies. . . . The programmes planned reflect the top-down model. The in-service programmes usually are not conducted using any innovative methodologies or practices.' (p. 23) The NCERT Report (2009) further states, 'Since the programmes are neither need-based nor oriented towards extending the training received, the in-service programmes seemed to be usually very sporadic, without any direction or a purpose.' (p. 24) In a similar vein, Ramchandran and Bhattacharjea (2009) commenting on existing in-service teacher training programmes, lament that, 'Training is thus rarely based on teachers' everyday practice, experiences, problems or needs and nor is it linked to student learning.' (Ramchandran & Bhattacharjea, 2009) This may well be because as a NCERT Report (2009) points out: 'Most teacher educators, training pre-primary and elementary school teachers for example, are themselves trained in secondary education.' (p. 7) It is safe to conclude then that in the current UEE drive owing to (a) massive recruitment of undertrained and under-prepared teachers, and (b) extremely short and poor in-service professional preparation, school teaching is at a great risk of losing its professional character and is poised to degenerate into a low-paid, semi-skilled wage labour.

The point here is not that these professional training institutions have been negligent of their responsibilities, and improvements would happen just on account of better monitoring and enforcement of accountability. The point is that the Indian state has shown that it can run world class professional training institutions like the venerable Indian Institutes of Technology. Thus, if it really deems it important, the state can surely create high quality professional development programmes for teachers recruited for public elementary schools. Clearly then, what is at stake is the willingness of the state to give teaching profession and public elementary education such a high priority that it is willing to fund such programmes for the nation's public schools. The poor and underprivileged who send their children to public schools do not carry a strong political voice in Indian democracy on most matters crucial to their survival. It is not surprising then that in a bid to universalize elementary education, the Indian state is more focused on providing adults to teach these children than ensuring that these adults are well-prepared teaching professionals.

Indian states' efforts to meet UEE goals through contractualization of teaching have caused another important debilitating impact on teaching profession that doesn't get talked about much: the ensuing fragmentation among teachers as a professional group. As mentioned earlier, state governments have recruited contract teachers under a variety of job titles. Regardless of their official title, they all do the same work, but are administered under different service rules and salary structures. As a result, each of these groups of teachers have come to have a different set of work-related grievances, demands, and agendas—an outcome that has in-turn led them to organize themselves separately and sometimes even in antagonism with each other. Govinda and Josephine (2004) argue that, 'Creating multiple layers of teachers with different salary structure and qualifications but doing exactly similar work is likely to lead to divisions and dissatisfaction on the one hand and make the profession vulnerable to arbitrary actions at local level by those who have no professional training or authority, on the other.' (p. 9) Clearly then, such a splintering of the teaching profession doesn't auger well for their collective professional empowerment and autonomy—a characteristic considered important for survival of any profession (Hoyle, 1995).

So when one wonders where the school teaching profession in India is headed, it gets difficult to be optimistic about its future. Straitjacketed by the ruling neo-liberal discourse that discourages state activism in social sector, the Indian state has opted to universalize elementary education on the cheap and at the expense of de-professionalization of teaching. As a result, what was once a respected profession is fast becoming a low-skilled part-time work—a last resort for educated unemployed youth on the lookout for a temporary fall-back option than a formal career choice (Batra, 2005; India. National Council of Educational Research and Training, 2009).

CONCLUSION

From the analysis presented in this chapter it is clear that the Indian state is attempting to square a circle by attempting to reduce its social sector expenditure while still committing to offer universal and free access to quality elementary education for all in a time-bound manner. A likely outcome of this apparent contradiction would be the progressive deskilling and de-professionalization of school teaching in India. Like all professions, schoolteachers perform an important social function. It is imperative that we realize what social function a deskilled and de-professionalized cadre of part-time education workers is most likely to perform.

As mentioned earlier, teachers matter the most in determining the quality of education offered to students (Darling-Hammond, 2000; Stronge et al., 2007). Any adverse changes in the nature and conditions of their work are likely to negatively affect student learning in significant ways. Available data clearly show that public schools in hard-to-reach and sparsely populated rural and tribal areas are being staffed by under-prepared and under-qualified contract-teachers (Govinda & Bandyopadhyay, 2008). Under such conditions, public schools 'become a ghettoised option of last resort for the poorest and most marginalised in society.' (Harma, 2010, 38) It is fair to assume then, that de-professionalization of school teaching is bound to have significant negative implications for educational justice in the sense of access to quality education for all.

An extremely unfortunate and quite likely outcome of de-professionalization of school teaching will be an 'institutionalized dualism in the schooling system'. (Govinda & Bandyopadhyay, 2008, 25) While pledging to offer quality elementary education for all, the Indian state has all but given up on redeeming this promise for the poor and marginalized sections of Indian society. Increasingly, students attending rural public schools will find that the best they can aspire to learn are some rudimentary functional literacy and numeracy skills taught by a demoralized, semi-skilled, under-prepared, and overwhelmed cadre of part-time educational workers. Such an impoverished education can at best prepare the poor and marginalized to enter the global capitalist productive apparatus as a compliant, exploitable work force. It will certainly be woefully deficient in offering them a better future and grooming them as active citizens for nation's democracy.

Schools have always been suspected of playing an important role in social and cultural reproduction, i.e. of maintaining the existing social, economic and cultural inequities in a society (Bourdieu & Passeron, 2000). The way universalization of elementary education is being pursued in India, it is likely that public school teachers will find themselves positioned to perform the social function of further exacerbating these inequities in Indian society. This is not something they sign up for, and certainly not a role that society, especially the poor and marginalized, expects them to perform. India has to take care of its school teachers first if it really wishes to translate its lofty educational goals as lived reality. I am not convinced that India is so poor that it cannot be fair to its teachers and still fulfil its promise of free quality education for all. When Indian government can plan on sending a manned mission to moon by 2015 at a cost of Rs. 120 billion, I believe it can certainly find ways to increase social sector spending and fund free quality education for all its citizens (IANS, 2008).

In summary, the overriding issue then is definitely the one of national priorities. Currently, educational justice seems rather low on law and policymakers' priorities. This needs to change. However, for that to happen, researchers especially those active in the field of education, have to do their part first. Great strides in research related to Indian education have been made in the recent past, and researchers have explored different aspects of school teaching in both public and private school settings. However, we still do not have in depth investigations of how large structural changes such as those outlined in this chapter are affecting teachers and students in poorer, marginalized regions of the country. There is scant research on teachers' and students' own perceptions of what is happening in their schools. For greater educational justice, we need research that not only communicates the voices of these teachers and students, but is also forceful and persuasive enough to make these voices matter in the mainstream discourses on education. On a larger plane, we need intensive and public critique of the forces that shape government's intent and policies in India today. Such a critical assessment does happen, but it is largely limited to a few small groups of researchers, activists, and concerned citizens. We need to widen this process to make it accessible and participatory for all. Hopefully, such an open discussion would engender a shared appreciation of the critical importance of preserving school teaching as an honoured profession and the need to strive for educational justice for all.

REFERENCES

Appadurai, A. (2000), 'Grassroots globalization and the research imagination', *Public Culture*, 12(1), 1–19.

Bagchi, A. (2006), 'India's fiscal management post-liberalization', *Economic and Political Weekly*, 41(39), 4117–21.

Batra, P. (2005), 'Voice and agency of teachers', *Economic and Political Weekly*, 40(40), 4347–56.

Bhaduri, A. (2006), 'The politics of "sound finance",' *Economic and Political Weekly*, 41(43–44), 4569–71.

Bourdieu, P., and Passeron, J. C. (2000), *Reproduction in Education, Society and Culture* (Thousand Oaks, CA: Sage).

Chaudhury, N., Hammer, J., Kremer, M., Muralidharan, K., and Rogers, F. H. (2006), 'Missing in action: Teacher and health worker absence in developing countries', *Journal of Economic Perspectives*, 20(1), 91–116.

Cochran-Smith, M. (2003), 'The unforgiving complexity of teaching: Avoiding simplicity in the age of accountability', *Journal of Teacher Education*, 54(1), 3–5.

Darling-Hammond, L. (2000), 'How teacher education matters', *Journal of Teacher Education*, 51(3), 166–73.

De, A., Dreze, J., Noronha, C., Pushpendra, Rampal, A., Samson, M., Kumar, S. (1999), *Public Report on Basic Education in India* (New Delhi: Oxford University Press).

De, A., Dreze, J., Samson, M., and Kumar, A. K. S. (2009), 'School education: struggling to learn', *The Hindu*. Retrieved from http://www.hindu.com/2009/02/20/stories/2009022052911000.htm

De, A., and Endow, T. (2008), 'Public expenditure on education in India: Recent trends and outcomes', RECOUP working paper No. 18 (New Delhi: Research Consortium on Educational Outcomes and Poverty).

Duyvendak, J. W., Knijn, T., and Kremer, M. (2009), 'Policy, people, and the new professional: An introduction', in J. W. Duyvendak, T. Knijn and M. Kremer, eds., *Policy, People, and the New Professional* (Amsterdam: Amsterdam University), 7–16.

Gerhard, U., Knijn, T., and Lewis, J. (2002), 'Contractualization', in B. Hobson, J. Lewis & B. Siim, eds., *Contested Concepts in Gender and Social Politics* (Edward Elgar Publishing Limited), 105–40.

GoI (2006), Report of the working group on elementary education and literacy for the 11th five year plan. Retrieved from http://planningcommission.nic.in/plans/planrel/11thf.htm

Goldman, C. A., Kumar, K. B., Liu, Y., and Corporation, R. (2008), 'Education and the Asian Surge: A Comparison of the Education Systems in India and China' (Occasional Paper: RAND Corporation).

Govinda, R., and Bandyopadhyay, M. (2008), 'Access to elementary education in India: Country analytic review'. Retrieved from www.create-rpc.org/pdf_documents/India_CAR.pdf

Govinda, R., and Josephine, Y. (2004), 'Para-teachers in India: A review'. Retrieved from http://www.unesco.org/iiep/eng/research/basic/PDF/teachers5.pdf

Govinda, R., and Josephine, Y. (2005), 'Para-teachers in India: A Review', *Contemporary Education Dialogue*, 2(2), 193–224.

Gregory, R. (2001), 'Getting better but feeling worse? Public sector reform in New Zealand', in L. Jones, J. Guthrie and P. Steane (eds.), *Learning from International Public Management Forum* (Oxford, UK: Elsevier Science Ltd), 211–31.

Harma, J. (2010), 'School choice for the poor? The limits of marketisation of primary education in rural India'. Retrieved from www.create-rpc.org/pdf_documents/PTA23-Harma-finalforweb.pdf

Hoyle, E. (1995), 'Teachers as professionals', in L. Anderson' ed., *International Encyclopedia of Teaching and Teacher Education* (London: Pergamon Press), 11–15.

IANS, (2008), 'India's manned moon mission by 2015', *The Times of India*. Retrieved from http://timesofindia.indiatimes. com/India/Indias_manned_moon_mission_by_2015_ISRO/rss articleshow/3627577.cms

India, Ministry of Human Resource Development (1968), 'National Policy on Education', New Delhi: Government of India. Retrieved from http://www.education.nic.in/natpol.asp

India, Ministry of Human Resource Development (1998), 'National Policy on Education 1986 (as modified in 1992)', New Delhi: Government of India. Retrieved from http://www. education.nic.in/natpol.asp

India, Ministry of Human Resource Development (2010), Minutes of the meeting of state education secretaries held on 28th Jan.–30th Jan., 2010, New Delhi: Government of India. Retrieved from http://education.nic.in/Elementary/ Consolidated_Minutes_Education_Secretaries_28–30_Jan_2010 .pdf

India, National Council for Teacher Education (2002), Seventh India Education Survey, New Delhi: Government of India. Retrieved from http://www.7thsurvey.ncert.nic.in/

India, National Council for Teacher Education (2009), 'National Curriculum Framework for Teacher Education: Towards Preparing Professional and Humane Teacher', (New Delhi: Government of India).

India, National Council of Educational Research and Training (2009), 'Comprehensive Evaluation of Centrally Sponsored Scheme on Restructuring and Reorganization of Teacher Education', (New Delhi: Government of India).

India, National Knowledge Commission (2007), 'Recommendations on School Education', (New Delhi: Government of India).

India, National University of Educational Planning and Administration (2010a), 'Teacher Related Indicators (2007–08)', New Delhi: Government of India. Retrieved from http://www.dise. in/AR.htm

India, National University of Educational Planning and Administration (2010b), 'Elementary Education in India: Progress Towards UEE—Flash Statistics 2008–9, (New Delhi: Government of India).

India, Planning Commission (2006), Report of the Working Group on Elementary Education and Literacy for the 11th Five year Plan. New Delhi: Government of India. Retrieved from http:// planningcommission.nic.in/plans/planrel/11thf.htm

India, Planning Commission (2009), Report of the Steering Committee on Elementary Education & Literacy for the Eleventh Five-Year Plan (2007–12), (New Delhi: Government of India). Retrieved from http://planningcommission.nic.in/plans/ planrel/11thf.htm

Jain, P. S., and Dholakia, R. H. (2010), 'Right to education and public-private partnership', *Economic and Political Weekly*, 45(8), 78–80.

Jha, P. (2005), 'Withering commitments and weakening progress: State and education in the era of neo-liberal reforms', *Economic and Political Weekly*, 40(33), 3677–84.

Joshi, S. (2006), 'Impact of economic reforms on social sector expenditure in India', *Economic and Political Weekly*, 41(4), 358–65.

Knijn, T., and Selten, P. (2009), 'The rise of contractualisation in public services', in J. W. Duyvendak, T. Knijn & M. Kremer, eds., *Policy, People, and the New Professional* (Amsterdam: Amsterdam University), 19–33.

Kudva, P. (1999), 'Impact of Selected Professional Aspects on Teacher Burnout'.

LeCompte, M. D., and Dworkin, A. G. (1991), *Giving Up on School: Student Dropouts and Teacher Burnouts* (Newbury Park, CA: Corwin Press).

Mehta, A. C. (2010), 'Elementary education in India: Progress towards UEE' (Analytical report 2007–08) (58), (New Delhi: National University of Educational Planning and Administration).

Mooij, J. (2008), 'Primary Education, Teachers' Professionalism and Social Class about Motivation and Demotivation of Government School Teachers in India', *International Journal of Educational Development*, 28(5), 508–23.

Mottaz, C. J. (1981), 'Some Determinants of Work Alienation', *The Sociological Quarterly*, 22(4), 515–29.

Nieto, S. (2003), 'Challenging current notions of "highly qualified teachers" through work in a teachers' inquiry group', *Journal of Teacher Education*, 54(5), 386–98.

NUEPA, (2010), Teacher related indicators (2007–08), New Delhi: National University of Educational Planning and Administration.

Patnaik, P. (2006), 'What is wrong with "sound finance",' *Economic and Political Weekly*, 41(43–4), 4560–64.

Prakash, V. (2008), 'Directions in educational planning: Changing landscape of educational planning in India', (Paris: International Institute for Educational Planning).

Pratham (2010), 'ASER 2009—Annual Status of Education Report (Rural)', Retrieved from www.asercentre.org

Ramchandran, V. (2005), 'Why school teachers are demotivated and disheartened', *Economic and Political Weekly*, 40(21), 2141–44.

Ramchandran, V., and Bhattacharjea, S. (2009), 'Attend to primary schoolteachers!' *Economic and Political Weekly*, 44(31), 17–20.

Sadgopal, A. (2006), 'A post-Jomtien reflection on the education policy' In R. Kumar, ed., *The Crisis of Elementary Education in India* (New Delhi: Sage), 92–136.

Sankar, D. (2007), 'Financing Elementary Education in India through Sarva Shiksha Abhiyan', (Washington DC: World Bank).

Saxena, S. (2006), 'Marginalization of the equity agenda', in R. Kumar, ed., *The Crisis of Elementary Education in India* (New Delhi: Sage), 176–99.

Shukla, A., and Trivedi, T. (2008), 'Burnout in Indian Teachers', *Asia Pacific Education Review*, 9(3), 320–34.

Shulman, L. S. (1987), 'Knowledge and Teaching: Foundations of the new reform', *Harvard Educational Review*, 57, 1–22.

Sommerlad, H., and Sanderson, P. (2004), 'Cultures of professional knowledge and competence: issues in the training and regulation of legal advice providers in the U.K'. Paper presented at the Association Internationale de Sociologie, 4ème Conférence Intermédiaire: Savoirs, Travail et Organization, Versailles, France. Retrieved from http://eprints.hud.ac.uk/5569/

Stronge, J. H., Ward, T. J., Tucker, P. D., and Hindman, J. L. (2007), 'What is the Relationship between Teacher Quality and Student Achievement? An Exploratory Study', *Journal of Personnel Evaluation in Education*, 20, 165–84.

Sykes, G. (1999), 'The "new professionalism" in education: An appraisal', in J. Murphy and K. S. Louis, eds., *Handbook of Research on Educational Administration* (San Francisco: Jossey-Bass), 227–49.

Tilak, J. B. G. (2004), 'Education in UPA government common minimum programme', *Economic and Political Weekly*, 39(43), 4717–21.

Tilak, J. B. G. (2008), Political economy of external aid for education in India, *Journal of Asian Public Policy*, 1(1), 32–51.

NOTES

1. *Public school* refers to any school run by a government body at the local, state, or national level.
2. Of course, these figures are for government schools alone. Total number of schools is much greater because of the increasing presence of private schools in all areas—rural or urban. For instance, about percentage enrollment at the primary level in private schools is about 26% (NEUPA, 2010).
3. For schools with more than 200 students, PTR should not exceed 40:1 (excluding head-teacher).
4. Though, as (Sadgopal, 2006) points out, care is always taken to not label contract-teachers as just *teachers*.
5. Such findings correlate quite well with my own experiences with government school teachers in the state of Madhya Pradesh in India.
6. As a comparison it is instructive to remind ourselves that in India aspiring doctors undergo about 6 to 7 years of intensive and continuous apprenticeship before being allowed to practice their chosen profession.

10

Teacher Education Continuum: A Case for Continuing Professional Development
—Anjum Halai

INTRODUCTION

Since the Partition of India and the creation of Pakistan in 1947 that marked the independence of the subcontinent from British rule there has been rapid and massive expansion in the system of formal education leading to an increase in the number of schools and teachers in the country.

A major impetus to expansion came immediately after the independence when primary education (Grades I–V) was recognized as the right of citizens. Since then, the size of school education system has shown a massive increase. Subsequently, global policy focus on Education for All (EFA)[1] and Millennium Development Goals (MDGs) also led to increased awareness and spending on provision of basic education. According to the official education statistics, it is estimated that 1.35 million teachers[2] are working in government schools from primary to higher education. Expansion in coverage of schooling has led to the creation of a massive education bureaucracy and an exponential increase in number of teachers with implications for education quality in general and for teacher quality in particular.

This chapter takes into account issues related to teacher quality and its implications for teacher education in the wake of rapid expansion of school system. It provides an overview of perspectives on teacher education as a continuum of teacher learning, from preparation to induction and beyond, with a specific focus on issues related to provision and quality of continuing professional development. Through illustrative examples of continuing professional development programmes for teachers in Pakistan it provides insights into issues and processes of implementation of programmes on the ground and raises questions for policy, practice and research in teacher education. In order to situate the discussion in context, a brief description of the policy context of teacher education in Pakistan is provided below.

CONTEXT OF TEACHER EDUCATION IN PAKISTAN: A BRIEF OVERVIEW

In Pakistan policymaking, including Education Policy and setting the strategic direction is the responsibility of the federal government.[3] Implementation is mostly carried out by the provincial governments and more recently from provincial to districts level. Initial and in-service teacher education is primarily a provincial subject. While, there are commonalities in the curriculum and accreditation of teacher education programmes across the four provinces there are several structural differences in the organizational structure of teacher educational institutions in the public sector. Besides the public sector institutions there has been a major influx of private sector in teacher education. The influx of private sector in teacher education is relatively a new phenomenon. Among other institutions it includes the setting up of the Institute for Educational Development (henceforth the Institute) of a premier private university in Karachi. The Institute also has satellite campuses in Gilgit and Chitral in the northern mountainous region of Pakistan. Since its establishment in 1993 the Institute has gained a reputation for innovative, contextual programmes for in-service teacher education in the country and more broadly in the developing world. Including the public and the private sector, there is an estimated 275 teacher training institutions providing pre-service training (certificates, diplomas, and degrees). In addition, there are 300 teacher training resource centres in the districts.[4]

The initial teacher preparation for primary and secondary school teachers in Pakistan, until recently had three main programmes each of a one year duration: (a) Primary Teaching Certificate (PTC);[5] (b) Certificate in Teaching (CT);[6] (c) Bachelor of Education (BEd).[7] However, it was recognized that the duration of pre-service teacher education programmes was too short and curricula were of theoretical nature, outdated and not relevant to the current global and local context (H. M. Iqbal, 2007; Social Policy Development Centre, 2003). Over the decade 2001–11, several large-scale programmes for reform in pre-service teacher education have been launched. For example the Pre-Step[8] Programme is a multimillion US$ initiative undertaken by the government agencies in collaboration with bilateral donors. A key purpose of the initiative is to bring reform in the policies, development of national professional standards for teachers and development of a national framework for the accreditation and licensing of teachers. In line with these reforms, the National Education Policy (2009) has upgraded the entry requirements for all elementary and secondary teachers and states:

> A Bachelors degree, with a B.Ed., shall be the requirement for teaching at the elementary level. A Masters level for the secondary and higher secondary, with a B.Ed., shall be ensured by 2018. PTC and CT shall be phased out through encouraging the present set of teachers to improve their qualifications, while new hiring shall be based on the advanced criteria. Exceptions shall be made in case of less developed areas where teachers with relevant qualifications are not available. Diploma in Education (D.Ed.) may be used as an intermediate qualification till B.Ed. teachers are available universally. (Pakistan, Ministry of Education, 2009, 33)

As can be seen from the discussion so far a major thrust of the reform is in pre-service or initial teacher preparation. Typically continuing professional development has been the purview of the Provincial Institute for Teacher Education (PITE).[9] However, the various PITEs in the absence of a regular and systematic source of funding have provided sporadic in-service programmes without a coherent framework that linked to the initial teacher preparation or provided a systematic coverage to all teachers. Moreover, most of the large teacher training projects undertaken by the various PITE's were usually external donor funded and did not necessarily build in sustainability and continuity of reform. However, in the National Education Policy (2009) there is provision for continuing professional development for teachers.

> All teachers shall have opportunities for professional development through a programme organized on a three-year cyclic basis. Progress in career shall be linked to such professional development. (Pakistan, Ministry of Education, 2009, 33)

While the policy initiatives in improving the quality of teacher education are laudable the implementation is yet to be seen. Until the time that strategic implementation programmes are rolled out with strong monitoring and quality assurance frameworks, it is difficult to see how the policy would effect change in the ground realities of the quality of teacher education and teacher within the country. What is more significant is that there is continued provision in the policy for recruitment of teachers who might not necessarily meet the minimum criteria. These issues have implications for continuing teacher professional development and will be discussed in the ensuing section.

TEACHER EDUCATION CONTINUUM

It is widely recognized that teacher is the single most important variable that affects quality of the classroom process and is strongly related to student achievement than other kinds of educational investments such as reduced class size, overall spending in education, and teacher salaries

(Govinda, 2008; Halai, 2007; H. M. Iqbal, 2007; Reimers, 2003). There is an increasing recognition of the vital role of provision of teacher education during the course of a teacher's career and not just at the initial stage of teacher preparation. (Darling-Hammond, 2000; Feiman-Nemser, 2001; Reimers, 2003)

Historically, stages of teachers' career development and its implications for teacher professional development are well documented. For example, Burden (1982) identified three stages of teachers' career development, with different developmental characteristics at each stage. According to Burden (1982), the first year of teaching corresponds to the survival stage where the teacher is mainly concerned with meeting the professional responsibilities and adjusting to the school climate. The next three years of teaching are years of increasing confidence alongside adjustment. From fifth year onwards is third stage which is the mature stage where teachers feel professionally secure. (Burden, 1982, 19) Along similar lines Christensen, Burke, Fessler, and Hagstrom (1983) suggest that effective teacher professional development programmes show sensitivity to the stages of early, mid and late stages in a teacher's career. More recently, Steffy and Wolfe (2001) recognize several stages of a teacher's career including the 'novice stage' which extends to 2–3 years of joining the profession, followed by the 'professional stage' where the teacher is growing in confidence about his or her teaching ability. The professional stage is further sub-divided into other stages and finally the 'expert/master stage' of the teaching profession, where teachers are at the height of their career in that they are excellent practitioners of their craft (Steffy & Wolfe, 2001, 16–19). Needs and nature of professional development required at each stage of the career is different with implications for the kind of support and infrastructure made available to the individual teachers.

The stages of teachers' career provide a sense of progression of teachers' professional journey but they do not necessarily build on each other explicitly or implicitly in terms of identifying and addressing teachers' developmental needs. As a consequence, typically, teacher education provision at the different stages has been fragmented, not coherent in its approach and underpinning philosophy. Hence, there is a felt need for a coherent framework for provision of teacher education at the various stages of a teacher's career so that learning from initial stage leads to development and growth in subsequent stages. In the influential and in depth document 'World Education Report on Teachers and Teaching' by UNESCO it is recognized that teaching like other professions is a 'learning' occupation and teachers need to have opportunities for updating their knowledge skills and capabilities through the course of their careers and not just at the stage of initial preparation (UNESCO, 1998, 69).

Along similar lines in a UNESCO supported publication with wide outreach and significance Schwille, Dembélé, and Schubert (2007) maintain that teacher preparation commences with the apprenticeship of observation (Lortie, 1975) which refers to what teachers learn about teaching by observing their own teachers during the course of their own schooling. They maintain that the apprenticeship of observation has a significant influence on learning to become a teacher but is often not recognized as teacher preparation. Moving on from there teachers commence their education in initial teacher preparation programmes. However, teacher learning does not end with the programme, rather it continues throughout the course of the teachers' career and is therefore named as *continuum of teacher learning* (Schwille et al., 2007, 30).

The chapter goes on to make recommendations for policy and provision of teacher education that it should take into account all the stages along the continuum.

Teacher education within the framework of a continuum of teacher learning has gained currency more widely. For example, in a major nine-country comparative study of teacher education, Conway, Murphy, Rath, and Hall (2009) have found that the continuum of teacher education has become the key policy focus for decision makers and key stakeholders in education including government and bilateral donor agencies. This focus is evident in the increasing emphasis on teacher education over the professional life cycle of a teacher and not just initial teacher education. Similar views are also found elsewhere (Feiman-Nemser, 2001; Musset, 2010; Plessis & Muzaffar, 2010).

Perspective of teacher education on a continuum of teacher learning across the career span puts forward a view of teaching as a profession which requires continuous renewal and is different from the view where initial teacher education with sporadic and infrequent in-service training was considered adequate for the teachers. More significantly continuum of teacher learning includes within it notion of formal programmes and structures such as mentoring schemes, and communities of learning which are in practice. Within this change in perspective, there are some salient features which have emerged for teacher education of quality. These are discussed below especially with reference to the conditions and constraints of teacher preparation in the developing world countries.

Initial teacher preparation is the first stage in the journey to become a teacher. In most technologically advanced countries there are policies, provisions, and practices which ensure that an individual cannot enter the teaching profession without a basic minimum academic and professional qualification. However, in the context of rapidly expanding school systems, such as those in Pakistan, innovative and accelerated programmes for recruitment of teachers are put in place, which lead to recruitment of teachers who do not necessarily meet the minimum criteria for qualifications to enter into the teaching profession. For example, the employment of untrained teachers or employment of inadequately prepared teachers in the increasingly large private schools sector in Pakistan especially in the case of girls'[10] schools in remote rural areas or contract teachers within government aided schools. Recruitment of teachers who do not meet the minimum qualification implies that potential deficiencies would be somehow addressed as the teachers move along the continuum of teacher education. A consequence is that continuing teacher education programmes are expected to provide input in areas which would traditionally be provided academic and initial teacher preparation courses.

The nature, duration, and quality of initial teacher preparation provide the foundation on which subsequent teacher development is built. Coherence and alignment of perspectives at the different stages of the continuum would be important to ensure that teachers can move effectively from one phase of their career to another. A related issue is that teachers who have had no teacher preparation or a very brief teacher preparation tend to model their teaching on their own experience of having been taught. While, learning to teach through your own experience of being taught is not a bad practice per se, it is problematic in contexts where traditional views of teaching prevail with concomitant notions of teacher as an expert, transmitting knowledge to students who are passive recipients. Until the time that inadequately prepared teachers with no exposure to *alternate* models of teaching continue to enter the school systems, interventions would be required to break the vicious cycle of routine transmission of knowledge to passive learners. Re-conceptualization of the role of a teacher is a complex process requiring questioning of some deep-rooted assumptions about what it means to be a teacher. Strong professional development programmes would need to be in place to support teachers in the process of reconceptualization of their practice (Halai, 2011, 2013)

The gap in academic knowledge that teachers exhibit is an issue that is more prominent in the developing countries primarily because of the low quality of the higher education compounded with the fact that many teachers do not meet the minimum education criteria that would enable the teachers to provide quality teaching. For example, H. M. Iqbal (2007) draws from the results of National Education Assessment System (NEAS) which was on a sample of about 12,000 students randomly selected from schools all over Pakistan to show consistent low student achievement in core school curriculum subjects like mathematics, science, and language (Urdu). (pp. 48–50) H. M. Iqbal (2007) goes on to compare the results from more than a decade of studies[11] which relate teacher effectiveness to student achievement. He maintains that poor performance of students across different subjects and across studies spread over a period of time correlates with the low level of competencies that teachers have in terms of their knowledge and pedagogical skills. An implication of this knowledge deficit is that in-service teacher development is expected to fill in the gaps. On the same issue of knowledge gap, Halai (1998) and A. Halai (2006) presents the work of school-based mentors who worked with mid-career teachers. She maintains, 'issues of inadequate teacher preparation and development albeit not of direct pertinence to in-service education had to be addressed in the setting of in-service education. A consequence was that mentors found that strategies for promoting a questioning stance towards own practice was not enough, something more was needed in terms of exposure to new ideas, new knowledge, and understandings to enable teacher growth through reflection.' (A. Halai, 2006, 708). These observations raise important questions for teacher professional development. Surely teacher professional development programmes cannot be expected to provide everything that academic and initial preparation left out? If not what are the alternatives?

Induction into teaching practice is a crucial stage in the professional journey as it is here that early career teachers make sense of the theoretical knowledge in the real world of schools and classrooms. This is a difficult stage even when teachers have entered into the profession with strong academic and professional education. Hence, field-based mentorship programmes are put in place to support the newly qualified teachers. Field-based mentorship to promote reflection on practice, and focused peer coaching cycles are deemed effective in enabling newly qualified teachers to gain confidence by identifying their needs and working towards their resolution (Hagger & McIntyre, 2006). In cases where teacher preparation curricula are highly theoretical with insufficient attention to issues of practice in the real world of schools and classroom, the stage of induction into teaching practice is even more crucial.

Beyond induction is the longest phase of the teachers' career and requires continuous teacher professional development. New directions in continuing professional development suggest approaches and strategies such as *Inquiry into Practice* which prepares teachers to look critically at problems arising out of practice as the basis for professional judgment and growth (Darling-Hammond & Richardson, 2009; Dean, 2005; N. Halai, 2006). Action research where teachers in collaboration with peers engage in cycles of needs analysis, planning, action, and reflection (Halai, 2004; Kemmis, McTagart, & Retallick, 2004). Inquiry and action research approaches are aimed at improving the practice and the social situation within which the teaching practice is located. These are wide approaches which often employ techniques and methods such as working with a critical friend or a mentor in a peer-coaching cycle, analysis of critical incidents in own classrooms, developing teaching portfolios to document growth and provide a basis for action and analysis. These approaches and strategies recognize that routines of practice need to be questioned and underpinning assumptions need to be challenged on an ongoing basis so that the teacher is not a mere cog in the large machinery of education but is an agent of change. They bring a substantively different orientation to teacher development from the traditional staff development or raining workshops. However, the place of expert input in the form of a workshop or training programme mounted by a regional or national authority is not ruled out. It is clear that there might be limits to what can be learnt through inquiry into practice and there is place for input from external sources. This is especially the case in the current climate of knowledge explosion and technology revolution. Teachers need to reinvent themselves as they are faced with learners who are 'digital natives' often have a vast amount of knowledge at their finger tips just a mouse-click away. In such situations the teachers need training and upgrading of their knowledge and skills of innovations in education.

An important feature of teacher education at all stages but most significant at the continuing professional development stage is that it promotes collaborative learning among teachers through building networks of learning (Lieberman, 2000) or communities of practice (Lave & Wenger, 1991), or school as a learning community (Retallick & Farah, 2005), or professional learning communities (DuFour, 2004; Plessis & Muzaffar, 2010). Assumption is that agency of teacher has greater potential of being realized if teachers have shared goals towards improvement of their practice and work collegially to achieve the shared goals by creating networks to connect institutions and individuals.

Finally, and perhaps most significantly the focus in teacher education has shifted from inputs and processes to outcomes and accountability. Increasingly teachers are held accountable for learners' improved achievement. Philosophically, there are issues in linking teacher education directly with improved learner outcomes as it could potentially lead to a narrow and reductionist conception of teacher education. However, an advantage of focus on outcomes and achievement is that it keeps the teachers and teacher educators focused on evidence on whether or not their practice is measuring up to standards of excellence in teaching.

In summary, key features for continuing professional development include: coherence in terms of linkage with initial preparation and long term goals; recognizing the agency of the teacher in bringing about change and improvement in his/her practice; reconceptualization of teacher's role as a learner who learns by inquiry into practice; collaborative nature of teachers' engagement (Halai, 2011, forthcoming 2013).

The discussion so far was on the perspective of teacher education on a continuum of teacher learning and its implications in the context of developing world settings with large education infrastructures and a weak initial teacher preparation provision. In the forthcoming section, exemplars of two programmes of continuing teacher professional development are provided to illustrate key issues of implementation at the level of teachers and schools. Purpose of the presentation is not to provide prescriptive or definitive solutions to issues of continuing teacher professional development. Rather the salient features of the two cases are analyzed for lessons learnt for policy and practice of teacher education.

CONTINUING PROFESSIONAL DEVELOPMENT IN PRACTICE: ILLUSTRATIVE EXAMPLES

The first of the two programmes the 'Cluster-Based Mentoring Programme (CBMP)' was a programme for continuing professional development for teachers in rural settings in provinces of Sindh and Balochistan which have some of the most poverty stricken regions in the country. CBMP was led by the Institute of a private university mentioned earlier in the paper, within the framework of the external donor funded Education Sector Reform Assistance Programme (ESRA), in selected districts of Sindh and Balochistan (Hussain & Ali, 2010). Between 2004 and 2006, CBMP trained more than 300 mentor teachers who went on to mentor around 8,000 teachers. The basis of the programme was prior experience on part of the Institute in launching innovative and successful field-based programmes and emerging international evidence of the effectiveness of field-based in-service programmes which utilize the devolved education structures for programme delivery and quality assurance (Leu, 2004; Memon, Lalwani, & Meher, 2006). The box below provides a brief statement of the objectives and outcomes of the CBMP.

CLUSTER-BASED MENTORING PROGRAMME (CBMP)

Box 1: Cluster-Based Mentoring Programme (CBMP)

Objectives of the Cluster-Based Monitoring Programme (CBMP) were to prepare school-based mentors who would: (a) enhance teachers' content knowledge in the curriculum areas; (b) develop skills for curriculum integration; (c) develop child-centred learning methods; (d) enable teachers to develop resources from locally available material; and (e) enable teachers to take an inquiry approach to teaching.

The CBMP was evaluated externally by ESRA and showed the evidence of improvement in teachers' skills and students' achievement (ESRA-Pakistan,12 2005a; ESRA-Pakistan,13 2006). The CBMP was also studied systematically by the faculty of the private university (Hussain & Ali, 2010; Hussain, Rahim, & Ali, 2007). Their findings showed that mentor teachers reported that the mixed mode training gave them the confidence to deliver training within their clusters. The mentee teachers maintained that an advantage of using practicing teachers as mentors was that colleagues were inspired by their improved practice and transformed attitudes. Classroom observations revealed improvements in learning environment, teachers' competency, and students' engagement in learning. Challenges encountered by CBMP include: large numbers of teachers in some clusters, political meddling and frequent transfers, unavailability of substitutes when teachers of single-teacher schools attended workshops, and lack of coordination with components of the broader education reform.

The process of CBMP as implemented in the field had the following main elements:

Creating Clusters and Networks: The Cluster-Based Monitoring Programme (CBMP) attempted to develop a model of systemic reform by creating clusters of 15–20 primary within a reasonable radius. The central school of each cluster served as an open Learning Resource Centre and the process was monitored by the field-based coordinators of CBMP. The coordinators were in the district education office but were supervised and supported by the staff of the Institute.

Selection and Training of School-Based Mentors: Mentors were carefully selected from more experienced teachers and provided in the first phase a total of ten weeks of training including face to face seminars at the Institute and field training in the reality of schools and classrooms. Face to face sessions focused on developing critical thinking to enable participants to conceptualize their new roles as mentors and teachers. Input was given on subject knowledge and methodology. Specific needs were also addressed including preparation of training manuals and development of low cost instructional material. During the two-week field-based sessions trainee mentors started mentoring other teachers within their cluster, supervised by CBMP coordinators. However, the posts of mentors were not regularized within the education bureaucracy and were limited to the duration of the programme.

Field Support: Once trained, the mentors in the second phase of CBMP conducted weekly workshops for teachers in their clusters over forty-eight weeks. They also visited teachers in their classrooms where they co-planned and co-taught the lessons and issues emerging were analyzed collaboratively.

The CBMP raises several issues for discussion and analyses and these are taken up after the presentation of the second programme in continuing professional development, the Whole School Improvement Programme. It is believed that a collective discussion would provide comparative insights into the merits and demerits of the two programmes.

THE WHOLE SCHOOL IMPROVEMENT PROGRAMME (WSIP)

Situated in the extreme north-east are the Northern Areas of Pakistan with Gilgit as the capital. Educational history of the Northern Areas of Pakistan does not go back very far. However, the Gilgit district does have the basic infrastructure of teacher education in the public sector offering the PTC, CT and B.Ed courses in teacher education. In addition to the government agencies, a network of private schools from a non government organization also plays a significant role in the promotion of education in the region. A key feature of this network is that it trains Field Education Officers to provide field-based teacher development to the teachers in its more than 123 primary and secondary school in region (Beiges & Shafa, 2011).

The WSIP is a one-year programme offered by the Professional Development Centre North (PDCN) in Gilgit to schools in the Northern Areas of Pakistan including those in the private and in the government sector. The PDCN of the Institute has been in field for about a decade and has offered CPD to several hundred teachers in the mountain region without standing success stories. WSIP is its flagship programme and continues to date.

Box 2: The Whole School Improvement Programme

Objectives of the Whole School Improvement Programme (WSIP) include development in six major components of school improvement: (1) teaching and learning; (2) leadership, management and administration; (3) curriculum enrichment and staff development; (4) community participation; (5) building, accommodation, and resources; and (6) social and moral development, and health education.

Systematic research into the process and outcomes of the WSIP programme showed that classrooms were more participatory, learner centred, and less didactic. Teachers appeared to be skilful in developing resource materials to improve the learning environment in their classrooms. Students were more confident and engaged in the process of learning. Head teachers' role was broader to include instructional leadership and not just administration and management. Field support and seminars conducted by the PDCN appeared to be providing much needed input in pedagogy and subject knowledge.

A holistic approach to school improvement had led to a positive and constructive role played by the community through village education committees which were organic in nature. However, the nature of assessment and examination tended to be narrow and limited to the confines of the official textbooks. Difficult terrain and spread meant that field visits in some schools were not as frequent as planned.

Source: Beiges and Shafa (2011), and Campaign for Quality Education (2007).

The process of implementation of WSIP included the following key elements.

Holistic Approach: The focus of WSIP was broader than improvement in academic learning and included social and moral development. Likewise, human resource development in WSIP targeted teacher professional development and head teacher training and development. Finally, along with the learning environment, improvement of the physical environment was also focused upon.

School Clusters and Networks: The programme was built to create a model systemic reform. This was through creating clusters of schools, linking clusters vertically with the PDCN in Gilgit, which was in turn linked to the Institute in Karachi. In addition the school clusters collaborated through horizontal linkages with the local education offices in the public and the private sector.

Seminars and Field-Based Training: WSIP spreads over a year with intensive face to face seminars for teachers during summer and winter break on improving pedagogic and content knowledge, and developing curriculum materials. Field visits twice a month would take place for co-planning, co-teaching, observation and feedback. Needs-based workshops and seminars are offered at the PDCN or at one of the cluster schools.

Mentors and Field Education Officers: For the field support, WSIP utilized the services of field education officers from the private network of schools, of education officials some members of its own staff known as 'Professional Development

Tutors' and where necessary staff from the district education office. In each case, the individuals were provided training and education through participation in certificate courses at the PDCN. Designated positions with appropriate career ladders were created for the Field Education Officers and/or the Professional Development Tutors.

Community Mobilization: The Village Education Committee (VEC) mobilized as part of the WSIP programme worked *with* the school in a variety of ways, hiring teachers for vacant positions, monitoring teacher regularity and punctuality, mobilizing resources for the school.

DISCUSSION

The two programmes CBMP and WSIP in continuing professional development noted above have certain key features, which could potentially provide an approach for coherent input within the framing of teacher education as a continuum of teacher learning. First, the programmes were rooted in the context and focused on teaching and learning processes in the classroom. Second, through structured and trained field support they potentially addressed the academic and professional needs of the teachers in rural disadvantaged classrooms. Third, they were philosophically oriented towards the role of a teacher as a lifelong learner. Fourth, both made attempts to reach out to wide geographical spread and large numbers by creating clusters of schools in turn connected strategically to institutors of higher education. Finally, community support was drawn in to complement the programmatic efforts. However, this was more the case in

WSIP. Provided below is a discussion of the issues that arose in the course of implementation of the programmes and the lessons learnt.

Rootedness in the field and focus on teaching and learning was a significant feature of the CPD in both the programmes noted above. For example, teachers developed lesson plans, which incorporated new ideas introduced in the formal seminars. Lessons were observed by the facilitators in the WSIP and the mentors in the CBMP project. In post observation conference, these lessons were analyzed and critiqued for further development and improvement. For example, through analysis of their practice, teachers recognized the need to engage learners and created low-cost or no-cost teaching materials to support active learning. Spaces were created in the teaching and learning process for students to explain their thinking to their peers and to the teacher. These may appear to be small changes but reflect a major shift from the traditional practice where teacher is the expert and transmitter of knowledge and the student is expected to receive the wisdom (Halai, forthcoming 2013). However, several issues emerged in the process and had to be woven into the fabric of the CPD being offered. A key issue was that learning from inquiry into practice is a slow process and required raising questions. This is a difficult process given that most of the teachers themselves come from a tradition of being passive recipients of knowledge received from experts. Mentors and facilitators had to scaffold the process of critique through judicious questioning. There was evidence that the process of critique and questioning of practice had started. A teacher of CBMP said:

> I am so ashamed of what I had been doing over a number of years. I never realized that I was not teaching but I was cheating (Hussain & Ali, 2010).

Classroom support was carefully structured and provided over a period of time in both the programmes. Evidence showed that not only did the classroom visits support the process of teacher development but also the school because the lesson observations over a period of time identified the needs for further inputs. In CBMP, the coordinators were professionally qualified individuals, in most cases teachers in the local schools, whose potential for leadership was recognized by the concerned authorities and nurtured through various means such as nomination for being the mentors in the CBMP Project and participation in leadership training workshops. Likewise, the field education officers employed in WSIP were also experienced teachers carefully selected and trained for the purpose. This process was a shift from the usual supervisory practices where teachers were observed by expert supervisors and informed about what improvement to make in their teaching practice. The teacher was a *participant* in the change process and not a recipient of reform. However, given the large scale of the programme and the number of mentors involved there was variation in the quality and frequency of classroom support provided. For example, one teacher said of her head teacher who was supposed to observe and provide classroom support:

She observes classes of some teachers but cannot observe every teacher. She randomly selects teachers for observations. There is no schedule for her observation. For example, she observes three classes of one teacher but none of the others. Neither she gives any feedback nor does she keep any record of it, and it is just useless. (WSIP Teachers' Interview, 05/05/06)

Both the programmes had a carefully designed system of school clusters, connected to nodes vertically to provide input in specific areas of need and ensure quality. In WSIP the schools clusters were linked to a Cluster Centre and the PDCN which in turn was a satellite of the Institute and would draw support from there. In CBMP, the clusters were linked to a central school or a Learning Resource Centre, which was responsible to provide expertise and opportunities not available at the level of the schools. The Learning Resource Centres or central schools formed nodes which were in turn connected to a provincial centre in this case the Private University.

This was significant arrangement for schools in remote disadvantaged settings such as interior Sindh, Balochistan, or northern areas of Pakistan, which are isolated so that teachers and other education stakeholders do not have the opportunities to upgrade their knowledge and skills on a regular basis. More significantly, the creation of networks linked vertically to an institute of higher education worked towards providing coherence to the content and process of the CPD being offered. For example, qualified research informed facilitators played a key role in design and development of the programme so that there were opportunities for addressing the 'knowledge gap' especially in science and mathematics. There was also space and provision in the programme for teachers to be exposed to new technology and methods in education. These clusters and networks provided the teachers with opportunity and scope to link up with resources, which they would not have access to on an individual basis. For example, a teacher in the WSIP states:

> Before WSIP there was no any concept of meeting and interacting with the teachers of other schools but WSIP developed a network of the schools where the same project was running. Those exposures and interschool workshops developed an environment of a positive competition. (WSIP Teachers' Interview, 04/05/2006)

However, there were issues in connecting schools with each other. For example, a majority of the schools in CBMP were 'single teacher' schools. This meant that they could not attend workshops and seminars unless scheduled during the school vacation. More difficult mountainous terrain in the Northern Areas and vast geographical spread also created challenges in school maintaining regular contact with the cluster centres.

Community support was seen as an important resource for supporting the reform efforts locally. Collaboration and involvement of the community in resource mobilization, monitoring and quality assurance was a prominent feature especially in the case of the WSIP programme.

> Without the involvement of community it is very difficult to achieve success. We tried our best to involve parents in the affairs of the school through inviting them in various programmes.

The parents have to play a vital role in the development of their children so their involvement is extremely important. A school that enjoys support and cooperation of community has a better chance of success. (Interview, 18/06/2010)

In the CBMP, the involvement of the community was through the School Management Committees, which were not necessarily organically developed as in the case of WSIP. Possibly because of this the involvement of community was not necessarily beneficial or supportive to the efforts of the CBMP. For example, Hussain et al. (2007) report that political meddling from the community and frequent transfers based on decision taken beyond the education stakeholders interfered with the process of teacher development because of loss and dissipation of effort.

Philosophically and methodologically, it is problematic to show a direct link between inputs in teacher development and student learning outcomes. However, students examined as part of the evaluation of ESRA showed that they were performing better in mathematics and language as compared to their baseline performance. Observational data showed that the students were more confident and the environment in the classroom conducive to student participation. Likewise, WSIP programme evaluations tested students in numeracy and language (Urdu) and found the achievement scores higher than those in the non-WSIP schools. However, student outcomes from end of the year school examination over a period of time were not tracked to note trends in improvements in achievement scores if any, nor was achievement data compared with student achievement in national examinations such as NEAS.

CONCLUDING REFLECTIONS

Should the 'continuum of teacher professional development' be considered as a framework for national policy, the implication is that all teachers are provided with the opportunity to participate in quality continuing professional development programmes. This is easier said than done in a context where scale of operation is large, and the building blocks of CPD i.e. teachers' academic and professional preparation is mostly weak and inadequate. However, CBMP and WSIP have reached out to a large number of teachers and have demonstrated their potential to be taken to scale. These programmes are resource intensive but given the millions of US dollars spent over the last few decades on 'external project driven reform' in the country the issue is not necessarily that of scarce funding but of judicious and informed decision-making in utilization of funds. Similarly for human resource, particularly under the devolved governance structure in which the implementation of education is devolved to the level of the district there is the possibility of creating clusters at the level of districts or tehsils/talukas for teachers to network and support each other in this process. Teacher education officials from the district office could potentially provide the human resource infrastructure for monitoring, evaluation, and supporting the teachers. The nodes in the district could in turn be connected strategically to the vertical infrastructure of teacher education such as the Provincial Institute of Teacher

Education or the Institute of Educational Research in public sector universities in the country.

However, three major issues would need to be taken into account for a programme like CBMP or WSIP to be taken to scale at the national level. One, the orientation of the visiting education officials should not be that of supervision and policing. Experience has shown that visiting education officers from the department of education or district education office are often ill trained and unaware of their role in educational leadership. Hence, they see the purpose of their visit as policing the school and evaluating the teacher. There is little evidence of their role in monitoring the extent to which teachers are able to implement reform in the classroom, identify the emerging needs, and support development of the teacher in the classroom. An implication is that programmes in teacher development should have a complementary focus on educational leadership including skills and attributes for mentorship development. This component should be offered to head teachers or district education officers who would be expected to support teachers on a regular basis. Second, creation of networks that support development and improvement requires a relationship of trust between the various stakeholders. This in turn requires a core group or a critical mass of change agents to be created at the level of the cluster. This process is impeded if frequent transfers and political meddling takes place. Across the level of the education ministry an ethos of meritocracy would need to be created so that transfers, appointments and promotions are not on the basis of political motivation and recommendation.

Third, the cluster centres or Learning Resource Centres would need to be recognized in terms of policy space, adequate resource allocation, and an incentives scheme would be required to serve as motivating factors to sustain the momentum of change in the clusters. A career ladder along with policies and procedures for merit-based selection and promotion of cluster-based mentors would be important to build a critical mass at the nodes of the network. In the presence of a regularized career ladder and an incentives scheme it is possible to transform classrooms through a philosophical shift in orientation of the teacher as a learner.

Pakistan, Academy of Educational Planning and Management (2004), (Pakistan, Education Sector Reform Assistance Programme, 2005a); Pakistan, Education Sector Reform Assistance Programme (2005b), UNESCO (2001); UNESCO (2002); Mirza, Hameed, and Iqbal (1995); Mirza, Iqbal, Abdullah, Nosheen, and Rehman (1999); H. M. Iqbal and Mahmood (2000).

REFERENCES

Beiges, and Shafa, M. D. (2011), 'The influence of Whole School Improvement Programme on the value orientation of a head teacher in the mountainous region of Gilgit-Baltistan, Pakistan', *Journal of Authentic Leadership In Education*, 1(2).

Burden, P. (1982), 'Implications of Teacher Career Development: New Roles for Teachers, Administrators, and Professors', Paper presented at the Annual Workshop of the Association of Teacher Educators, August 1982, Slippery Rock, PA.

Campaign for Quality Education (2007), 'Education in Pakistan: What works & why?' (Lahore: CQE).

Christensen, Judith C, Burke, Peter, Fessler, Ralph, and Hagstrom, David (1983), *Stages of Teachers' Careers: Implications for Staff*

Development, Washington, DC: ERIC Clearinghouse on Teacher Education.

Conway, P, Murphy, R, Rath, A, and Hall, K. (2009), 'Learning to teach and its implications for the continuum of teacher education: A nine-country cross national study Dublin', Teaching Council Ireland.

Darling-Hammond, L. (2000), 'How teacher education matters', *Journal of Teacher Education*, 51(3), 166–73.

Darling-Hammond, L., and Richardson, N. (2009), 'Teacher learning: What matters?' *Educational Leadership*, 66(5).

Dean, B. (2005), 'Citizenship education in Pakistani Schools: Problems and possibilities', *International Journal of Citizenship and Teacher Education*, 1(2), 36–55.

DuFour, R. (2004), 'What is a Professional learning community?', *Educational Leadership*, 61(8), 6–11.

Feiman-Nemser, S. (2001), 'From preparation to practice: designing a continuum to strengthen and sustain teaching', Teachers College Record, 103(6), 1013–15.

Govinda, R. (2008), 'Education for all in India: Assessing progress towards Dakar goals', *Prospects*, 38(3), 431–44. doi: 10.1007/s11125-009-9101-6

Hagger, H., and McIntyre, D. (2006), *Learn Teaching from Teachers: Realizing the Potential of School-based Teacher Education* (Milton Keynes: Open University Press).

Halai, Anjum (1998), 'Mentor, mentee, and mathematics: A story of professional development', *Journal of Mathematics Teacher Education*, 1(3), 295–315.

Halai, Anjum (2004), 'Action research to study impact: Is it possible?' *International Journal Educational Action Research*, 12(6), 515–34.

Halai, Anjum (2006), 'Mentoring in-service teachers: issues of role diversity', *Teaching and Teacher Education*, 22(6), 700–10.

Halai, Anjum (2007), 'Status of teachers and teaching: Conclusions, implications and recommendations', in H. Anjum, ed., *Teacher Status in Pakistan* (Karachi: AKU-IED).

Halai, Anjum (2011), 'Equality or equity: Gender awareness issues in secondary schools in Pakistan', *International Journal of Educational Development*, 3(1), 44–9.

Halai, Anjum (forthcoming 2013), 'Implementing curriculum change in classrooms: Small steps towards a big change', in L. Tikly & A. Barrett, eds., *Education Quality and Social Justice in the Global South: Challenges for Policy, Practice and Research* (London: Routledge).

Halai, Nelofar (2006), 'Learning to use innovative pedagogy: The experience of a primaryscience teacher', *Science Education International*, 17(2), 123–32.

Hussain, R, & Ali, S, (2010), 'Improving public school teachers in Pakistan: Challenges and opportunities', *Improving Schools*, 13(1), 70–80.

Hussain, R, Rahim, H, and Ali, S. (2007), Evaluation of cluster-based mentoring programme for teachers' professional development in Sindh and Baluchistan (Karachi: AKU-IED).

Iqbal, H. M. (2007), 'Teachers' content knowledge and pedagogical competence: Issues for teacher status in Pakistan', in A. Halai, ed., *Teacher Status in Pakistan,* Karachi: AKU-IED, 42–64.

Iqbal, H. M., and Mahmood, N. (2000), 'Teacher education in Pakistan: Policies and practices'. In S. K. Abell, ed., *Science Teacher Education: An International Perspective* (The Netherlands: Kluwer Academic Publisher), 75–92.

Kemmis, S., McTagart, R., and Retallick, R. (2004), 'The action research planner' (Karachi: Aga Khan University).

Lave, Jean, and Wenger, Etienne (1991), *Situated Learning: Legitimate Peripheral Participation* (Cambridge: Cambridge University Press).

Leu, E. (2004), 'The patterns and purposes of school-based and cluster-based teacher professional development programmes', Working Paper No. 2 EQUIP 1.

Lieberman, A. (2000), 'Networks as learning communities, shaping future of teacher development', *Journal of Teacher Education*, 51, 221–27. doi: 10.1177/0022487100051003010

Lortie, D. (1975), *Schoolteacher* (Chicago: University of Chicago Press).

Memon, M, Lalwani, F, and Meher, R. (2006), 'Mentoring as an alternative approach to in service teacher education in Baluchistan: Some successes and challenges', in I. Farah and B. Jaworski, eds., *Partnerships in Educational Development* (London: Symposium Books), 103–19.

Mirza, S. M., Hameed, A., and Iqbal, H. M. (1995), 'Teacher Competency, the Curriculum and Student Achievement' (A study conducted under World Bank-Primary Education Project III), (Lahore: Institute of Education and Research University of the Punjab).

Mirza, S. M., Iqbal, H. M., Abdullah, M., Nosheen, M., and Rehman, S. (1999), 'Baseline survey of Grade 8 student achievement in middle schools (A study contracted under DFID Punjab Middle School Project)', (Lahore: Institute of Education and Research, University of the Punjab).

Musset, P. (2010), 'Initial teacher education and continuing training policies in a comparative perspective: Current practices in OECD countries and a literature', OECD Education Working Papers, No. 48, OECD Publishing.

Pakistan, Academy of Educational Planning and Management, (2004), 'Study on comparing school performance to understand which schools are doing better by assessing and comparing quality of education' (Islamabad: Government of Pakistan).

Pakistan, Education Sector Reform Assistance Programme (2005a), Technical report on teacher behavior and student achievement: Balochistan Cycle 1 (Islamabad: USAID).

Pakistan, Education Sector Reform Assistance Programme (2005b), Technical report on the teacher behaviour, student achievement and head-teacher performance (Islamabad: USAID).

Pakistan, Ministry of Education (2009), 'National Education Policy 2009', Islamabad: Government of Pakistan. Retrieved from http://www.moe.gov.pk/nepr/NEP_2009.PDF

Plessis, Joy, and Muzaffar, Irfan (2010), 'Professional learning communities in the teachers college: A resource for teacher educators', Washington, DC: Educational Quality Improvement Programme 1 (EQUIP1).

Reimers, E. (2003), 'Teacher professional development: An international review of literature', (Paris: UNESCO International Institute for Educational Planning).

Retallick, J. and Farah, I. (2005), *Transforming Schools in Pakistan, Towards a Learning Community* (Karachi: Oxford University Press).

Schwille, J., Dembélé, M., and Schubert, J. (2007), 'Global perspectives on teacher learning: Improving policy and practice'. (Paris: UNESCO, International Institute for Educational Planning).

Social Policy Development Centre (2003), 'Social development in Pakistan: The state of education', *Annual Review 2002–3* (Karachi: SPDC).

Steffy, B. E. and Wolfe, M. P. (2001), 'A life cycle model for career teachers', *Kappa Delta Pi Record*, 38(1), 16–19.

UNESCO (1998), 'World education report: Teachers and teaching in a changing world' (Paris: UNESCO).

UNESCO (2001), 'Learning Achievement in Primary Schools of Pakistan: A quest for quality education' (Islamabad: UNESCO).

UNESCO (2002), 'Monitoring Learning Achievement', (Islamabad: UNESCO).

NOTES

1. Education for All (EFA) is an international commitment first launched in Jomtien, Thailand in 1990 to bring the benefits of education to 'every citizen in every society'. EFA has six major goals (for details see http://www.unesco.org/education/efa/ed_for_all/).
2. Information available at the website by UNESCO Islamabad (http://www.teachereducation.net.pk/).
3. This has changed after the 18th Amendment to the Constitution, which devolves education almost in its entirety to the provinces. Pakistan is a federation with four provinces i.e. Punjab, Sindh, Balochistan, and North-West Frontier Province (NWFP or as it is now called Khyber Pakhtunkhwa (KPK); Federally-Administered Areas, Azad Jammu & Kashmir, and the federal capital Islamabad. Sindh and Balochistan include some of the most poverty stricken regions in the country.
4. Teacher education in Pakistan see http://www.teachereducation.net.pk/
5. Primary school teachers for Grades I–V were required to complete a minimum of a one-year teacher-training programme leading to a PTC. Admission was based on completion of Grade X.
6. Elementary/Middle School Teachers for Grades VI–VIII had to have twelve years of schooling before being admitted to a one-year teacher-training programme leading to the award of a CT.
7. Teachers for secondary education Grades IX–X were required to complete a one-year teacher-training programme for which the admission requirement is a 4-year Bachelor of Arts or Bachelor of Science. The credential awarded was a B.Ed.
8. Further information is available at http://www.prestep.org/
9. There are provincial variations in the infrastructure of in-service education. For example in Punjab the Department of Staff

Development was also responsible for in-service education for teachers in the province.

10. School education especially beyond primary (Grades I–V) is segregated along lines of gender. Students in the girls' schools are taught by female teachers and in the boys' school by male teachers.

11. See for example, Pakistan, Academy of Educational Planning and Management (2004), (Pakistan, Education Sector Reform Assistance Programme, 2005a), Pakistan, Education Sector Reform Assistance Programme (2005b), UNESCO (2001); UNESCO (2002); Mirza, Hameed, and Iqbal (1995); Mirza, Iqbal, Abdullah, Nosheen, and Rehman (1999); Iqbal and Mahmood (2000).

12. Referred to as Gilgit-Baltistan in the light of the Ordinance, 2009.

11

A Conceptual Framework for Measuring the Quality of Pakistan's Higher Education System*

—Pervez Hoodbhoy

INTRODUCTION

Common wisdom everywhere is that increased funding can solve all—or at least most—systemic problems that bedevil higher education. But Pakistan offers an instructive counter example: a manifold increase in university funding from 2002–08 resulted in only marginal improvements in some parts of the higher education sector. One can, in fact, also point to deterioration in other areas from the existence of excess monies. This violation of 'commonsense' points to the need for some fresh thinking.

This chapter will analyze the progression of Pakistan's higher education system. It divides naturally into three parts:

i. First, a brief background on the history of higher education in Pakistan will serve as an introduction. From a single university in 1947, the number has

---

*A brief version drawn from this chapter is available at http://pide.org.pk/pdr/index.php/pdr/article/viewFile/2643/2610

increased to well over one hundred (Pakistan, Ministry of Finance, 2010). This impressive expansion has still not changed the fact that, relative to other countries of South Asia, only a small proportion of Pakistanis are enrolled in higher education (World Bank, 2010). The cost of rapid expansion has been a significant deterioration of quality.

ii. Second, I shall attempt an objective definition of quality that goes beyond personal and subjective opinions. How is one to assess the quality and usefulness of individual institutions? A 'quality factor index', tailored to the Pakistani situation, will be proposed here. Hopefully, it shall have relevance to other countries as well. Large international organizations, such as the World Bank and United States Agency for International Development (USAID), which have loaned billions to Pakistan, may actually want to invest in making meaningful assessments of quality, to be defined here, for a wide range of Pakistani colleges and universities before they commit further resources. This would help develop policies that could address actual needs and put brakes on wasteful spending.

iii. Third, I shall ask what must be done to arrest the manifest decline in academic standards. It will be argued that solutions must be sought at three distinct levels: re-apportioning resources towards immediate and urgent needs, efficient and responsible implementation of approved plans and projects, and, most importantly, inducing appropriate attitudinal changes towards education and its values.

HIGHER EDUCATION ENROLMENT AND GROWTH

In the early twentieth century, Muslims of the Indian sub-continent were, in general, poorly educated relative to Hindus. This was both because of British prejudice against Muslims, as well as resistance by orthodox Muslims to modern scientific ideas and to the English language. Poor education made it difficult for Muslims to get high-level government jobs. This was historically one of the most important reasons that led to the demand for Pakistan.

Compared with much of India, the areas that currently constitute Pakistan were educationally backward. In 1947, Pakistan had only one teaching university, Punjab University in Lahore, with a student enrolment of 644. It lost its best faculty members, who were mostly Hindus, to the migration following the Partition. Although the University of Sindh also formally existed at this time, it was only an examining body and began its role as a teaching university after relocating from Karachi to Hyderabad in 1951. Karachi University was established in 1950. University level education in Pakistan clearly had a very modest beginning.

The first private Pakistani universities were the elite Lahore University of Management Sciences (LUMS) established in 1984, followed by the Aga Khan University Hospital in 1985. The tally on the Higher Education Commission (HEC) website[1] in 2010 was as follows:

- 60 public universities (several upgraded from college status)

- 13 public Degree Awarding Institutes (DAIs)
- 42 private HEC recognized universities
- 17 private Degree Awarding Institutes

This makes a grand total of 132 universities and DAI's, an apparently impressive achievement given the low starting point. Student enrolment increased correspondingly.[2]

First, let us briefly take up the issue of access. Apart from the absolute numbers that are denied education, a significant feature of the situation here is the inter-provincial as well as intra-provincial inequity. The populations in Punjab, Sindh, Khyber Pakhtunkhwa, and Balochistan are roughly 55 per cent, 23 per cent, 16 per cent and 5 per cent of the total population respectively. In the context of enrolment, if Balochistan had the same population as Punjab the enrolment there would be only 63,591 instead of Punjab's 102,781, showing that this province has much lower access. Sindh, by comparison, appears to have far greater access—it would have 190,802 for equal population with Punjab. But this is deceptive because the city of Karachi, with a population of nearly 16 million, has the overwhelming number of higher education institutions in the province of Sindh.

To put these figures in context: the university enrolment of Khyber Pakhtunkhwa and Balochistan put together is less than the enrolment at a single large US university. The University of Maryland, for example, has over 50,000 students. Pakistan does not compare favourably even in comparison with its neighbours—Iran and India. Iran with a population of about 65 million in 2004 had over 2.2 million students in its universities (Iran, Ministry of Knowledge, n.d.). India has approximately twice as much of its eligible population enrolled in comparison to Pakistan. Such comparisons put pressure upon policy makers to show fast results.

In a nutshell, the Pakistani situation is as follows:

i. Enrolment in higher education has increased manifold over the last six decades;
ii. Access is still limited to only a small fraction of the eligible population;
iii. Provincial disparities are substantial;
iv. The number of formally qualified teachers is low; and
v. Funding for universities has increased enormously since 2002.

But the real problem—higher education quality—has so far not entered the national discourse on education in a significant way. To address this will be our central task.

MEASURING UNIVERSITY QUALITY

Every country wants universities, and the more the better. There is a clear utilitarian goal behind this: universities have become the engines of progress for knowledge-driven economies in the age of rapid globalization. They are the fountainheads of modern science, and of technologies that have changed the world more in the past fifty years than the previous ten thousand years.

But higher education requires much more than just building structures and calling them universities or colleges. There is little to be gained from a department of English where the department's head cannot speak or write a grammatically correct non-trivial sentence of English; a physics department where the head is confused about the operation of an incandescent light bulb; a mathematics department where graduate students have problems with elementary surds and roots; or a biology department where evolution is thought to be newfangled and quite unnecessary to teach as part of modern biology. Nor does putting a big signboard advertising a 'centre of excellence' make it one.

There are many colleges and universities in Pakistan where the above is literally true. On the other hand, there are also examples of high quality such as a world-class medical university and business school, and some good quality engineering and fine-arts colleges.

It is clearly essential to define 'quality' of higher education. Equivalently, how may one differentiate between higher education institutions on the basis of quality? Of course, judging quality is always controversial. Comparing universities across countries, or even within a country, is fraught with difficulties. And yet, it is a task that must be attempted if we are to genuinely move our institutions towards quality and excellence.

THE IDEAL UNIVERSITY

As a tool that could help us frame the issues properly, let us create for ourselves a hypothetical *ideal university*. Freed from practical constraints, this allows us to imagine all that a university should be and hence provides a datum against which actual universities can be assessed (Hoodbhoy, 2007).

First, the ideal university is a bastion of critical inquiry covering every conceivable field of human endeavour. It has first-rate faculty that does first-rate research on let's say super-massive black holes and discovers new extra-solar planets, figures out quantum computation and the folding of proteins, documents the mating habits of macaws and tarantulas, and deciphers the extinct languages of Sumeria and Mesopotamia. The professors are widely cited and known for important discoveries. Their fame attracts talented researchers and students from across the world.

Our (imagined) university also spawns high-tech companies that create more powerful computers and data compression techniques. It generates products and ideas upon which civilizations' progress and survival depend, such as new crop varieties and renewable energy sources. It also does a splendid job at training engineers, doctors, economists, business managers, and other professionals.

Most importantly—this ideal university creates a modern citizenry capable of responsible and reasoned decision-making. Its graduates can think independently and scientifically, have an understanding of history and culture, can create discourses on social and political issues, and are capable of coherent expression in speech and writing. They are in demand everywhere—both in academia and industry—nationally and internationally. A tall order indeed! Harvard, Massachusetts Institute of Technology (MIT), Cambridge,

Oxford, Sorbonne are considered among the world's best universities. But even these are poor approximations to an impossibly high ideal.

Coming down to earth: one would like to know what constitutes a reasonable expectation from a public university in Pakistan. If, for example, Khairpur University, deep in the backwaters of Sindh, or Quaid-i-Azam University (QAU), in the heart of Pakistan's capital, are to be called real universities, then by what criteria should they be evaluated?

A perfectly objective assessment is simply impossible. Value judgments are inevitably involved. Even more fundamentally, ideology and purpose play a crucial role. For example, Soviet and Chinese universities concentrated largely on utilitarian goals whereas western universities—or at least the better ones among them—seek a balance between scholarship and utilitarian needs. Nonetheless, the need to judge and assess is one that cannot be avoided.

Why does quality have to be reflected in numbers? The fact is that resources and finances are always finite. The world we live in demands that hard choices be made. If you are a planner in a high position, finances have to be allocated in a manner according to some rational policy. This means one simply must have numbers. The thoughtful educational planner is inevitably presented with a dilemma: hard numbers reflecting a sufficient measure of truth are essential for decision-making. But at the same time, he or she is aware that behind these numbers can be hidden subjective judgments.

Let us therefore invent a new quantitative measure and call it the 'Institutional Teaching Quality Factor' (ITQF). ITQF is based upon five key determinants:

a. Quality of teaching and teachers
b. Quality of student body
c. Adequacy of basics
d. Governance and ethics
e. General ambience

A numerical calculation of ITQF goes like this:

$$
\begin{aligned}
(ITQF)_{total} \quad = \quad & W_{teachers} \quad \times \quad (QF)_{teachers} \\
+ \ & W_{student} \quad \times \quad (QF)_{students} \\
+ \ & W_{basics} \quad \times \quad (QF)_{basics} \\
+ \ & W_{governance} \ \times \quad (QF)_{governance} \\
+ \ & W_{ambience} \quad \times \quad (QF)_{ambience}
\end{aligned}
$$

The weight W of each Quality Factor (QF) component is a number between zero and one. W assigns importance to each determining factor. The sum of all weights is, of course, one. An ITQF of one means that all enrolled students in that institution have full and proper access to higher education. Conversely, a non-functional university would have an ITQF equal to zero—enrolling any number of students does not amount to any real access at all.

The W's cannot be mechanically generated by a computer—they reflect the individual judgment of those who have been tasked with planning. How much importance should one give to having good teachers as compared to, for example, good administrators? There can never be an answer that is fully satisfactory and one might end up by saying they should given equal importance, or perhaps that teaching is twice as important as administration, etc.

Since individual opinions and judgments are inevitably involved, is it worth the effort to compute numbers requiring so much detailed knowledge? The answer is yes. The very fact that one must work through details makes individual whim less important. And what about research? Should it not be part of the figure-of-merit of a teaching institution? If so, why has it been excluded from the above formula? We shall return to this important matter later.

Here is what a hypothetical calculation of the ITQF for a particular university might look like:

$$(ITQF)_{total} = \frac{1}{5} \times (QF)_{teachers} + \frac{1}{5} \times (QF)_{students}$$

$$+ \frac{1}{5} \times (QF)_{basics} + \frac{1}{5} \times (QF)_{governance}$$

$$+ \frac{1}{5} \times (QF)_{ambience}$$

The weights are chosen as: $W_{teachers} = W_{students} = W_{basics} = W_{governance} = W_{ambience} = 1/5$. This gives equal importance to these five factors. Numbers, hypothetically reported by researchers who thoroughly investigated and evaluated the institution, give:

$$(ITQF)_{total} = \frac{1}{5} \times 0.40 + \frac{1}{5} \times 0.64$$
$$+ \frac{1}{5} \times 0.30 + \frac{1}{5} \times 0.80$$
$$+ \frac{1}{5} \times 0.60$$
$$(ITQF)_{total} = 0.55$$

In this imagined evaluation, governance is found to be very good (0.8) but basics are rather poor (0.3) because of limited space, facilities, internet connectivity, etc.

In the following, we shall take up the considerations that are needed for giving a numerical value to each constituent of the overall ITQF.

QUALITY OF TEACHERS AND THEIR TEACHING

The ignorant must not teach the ignorant. It is not our intent here to discuss philosophical questions of what constitutes ignorance or wisdom. Instead, there is a practical question: how can one decide whether an individual is adequately knowledgeable, or perhaps unacceptably ignorant, to function as a university or college teacher?

Requiring formal qualifications is the first step. It is sensible to assume that an individual with a higher university degree possesses a higher degree of knowledge, and, hence, is relatively more suitable as a teacher in a higher education institution. In much of the world this works. But the premise is valid only when an educational system has sufficient integrity. After it is sufficiently corrupted, the correlation between university degrees and the quantum of subject knowledge could be lost. Examples are not hard to find. Nothing can be done about a fifty-year-old English professor who speaks or writes ungrammatical English, or a physics professor unable to solve a simple quadratic equation. Does such basic incompetence exist at the 20, 50, or 70 per cent level? Higher or lower?

These questions are unanswerable unless one creates yard-sticks, and then proceeds to use them for performing measurements.

At least in the sciences, criteria are possible to devise. One measure of a college or university teacher's adequacy would be if he or she can solve at least a certain percentage of the problems and exercises at the end of the book chapter. Textbook writers and experts strongly recommend, and even require, problem solving. This encourages analytical thinking and requires the student to acquire a certain minimum understanding. One can imagine more stringent tests.

A second possibility for assessing the competence of a college or university science teacher is to use some standardized subject test. Such tests are frequently used for entrance into US universities. The Graduate Record Examination

(GRE), administered by the Educational Testing Service (ETS) in Princeton, is the most commonly used one. Subject areas include a number of scientific disciplines: biology, biochemistry, cell and molecular biology, chemistry, physics, mathematics, and computer science. In 2006, the GRE subject test was officially declared mandatory for obtaining admission into a PhD programme in Pakistani universities. Unfortunately, under the pressure of students and their supervisors, this condition was withdrawn in 2010.

A locally devised so-called GRE substitute also exists in Pakistan. A private company, the National Testing Service (NTS),[3] offers specialized subject testing in ten areas: agriculture sciences, computer engineering, economics, electronics, electrical engineering, education, geography, Islamic studies, management sciences, and veterinary/ animal sciences. Unfortunately, the Pakistani clone is marred by substandard scholarship. One hopes that professional management of the company, and oversight by suitably capable academics, will eventually change the situation.

In the humanities and social sciences, assessment of a university teacher's adequacy or otherwise is harder and more controversial. One must resort to such criteria as whether the teacher is capable of holding an intelligent discussion in the subject he or she is teaching; has adequate verbal and quantitative skills; is reasonably fluent in oral and written expression; and has adequate capacity to think analytically and abstractly. In principle, one would like such abilities of a general academic nature, which are independent of specialization, to be measured by some kind of standardized test. The general part of the GRE is one such test that is widely used.

Standardized subjects tests could also be used to either screen new applicants for college and university teaching positions at the lecturer or assistant professor level, or determine the quality of existing faculty, or both. In every case, one expects that there will be resistance from a substantial portion of the existing teaching community, as well as aspiring teachers. One must be conscious, however, that some of this resistance has legitimate cause. The difficult and unfamiliar English language terms puts test-takers from an Urdu-medium educational background at a disadvantage. Another critique of the general GRE is that the quantitative part is unfamiliar to all but a minority, which has studied in the O–A level system. The importance of quantitative reasoning for disciplines like history, anthropology, international relations, etc. is questionable.

Standardized tests do offer a possible means of discriminating on the basis of ability and scholarship—provided they are designed for the local environment. The low performance in these tests is worrisome. Many government scholarships for foreign study have been offered to in-service university teachers provided they achieve reasonable scores in the GRE but only a few have succeeded.

Other important determinants of teaching quality are:

- *The extent to which teachers teach concepts rather than use rote learning.* Rote learning is the dominant learning mode at the high school and intermediate levels, and remains so in all except the very best departments of universities.[4] A possible way to quantitatively research this would require a scrutiny of past examination papers in order to identify the frequency of questions that are:

(a) Repeated from past exam papers
(b) Lifted directly from the prescribed text
(c) Simply demand repetition of materials contained in the text

- *The extent to which teachers use modern textbooks rather than old notes.* Most university and college teachers in Pakistan teach from notes taken when they were students. In earlier years, only a small minority used some modern textbook published internationally. This was either because suitable textbooks were not available or expensive, or because they were unfamiliar and difficult to follow. To an extent, this has changed because of the ready availability of e-books and printed textbooks, mostly by Western authors, published in India as cheap South Asian editions.[5]

- *The time that teachers of a particular institution spend on their jobs rather than moonlight.* Many college and university teachers, usually secretly and illegally, have jobs that are unrelated to their main occupational position. Some teach at private institutes, others give tuitions to students. A few look after family businesses. In 2003–04 out of a total of 37,428 university and DAI teachers, 22,812 were part-time only. Most of these were probably moonlighting from their parent institutions.

Financial needs, as well as lax institutional rules, have contributed to this phenomenon. This is a major reason why teachers generally spend little time on the campuses.

- *The frequency with which new courses are introduced, old ones updated, term papers and problem sets regularly assigned, and class or individual projects given.* Only in a handful of university departments— and almost never in colleges—is regular student work handed out and then marked. This is in spite of the fact that the current student-to-teacher ratio of 19:1 in Pakistani universities is fairly reasonable, although in colleges this is higher.

- *Adherence to basic principles of teaching, grading, and fairness.* Two outstanding questions need to be researched and quantified:

  (a) To what extent do teachers encourage, tolerate, or discourage class participation and questions asked in class?

  (b) How often do teachers allow their grades to be checked and challenged by students?

The situation is relatively better in the more progressive American-type 'semester system', as compared to the more common British-type 'annual system'. Both systems operate in Pakistan. College and university authorities should make it mandatory for all semester tests to be returned to students, and establish the right of students to view their examination answer sheets. This reduces the chances of abuse considerably, and allows students to understand where they might have gone wrong. In the 'annual system' it is next to impossible for a student to view the marked exam paper; at most the marks obtained in individual questions can be re-totalled.

To summarize this point: assigning roughly equal numerical weights to each, 'teacher quality' can be estimated using the categories suggested below:

1. Whether teachers actually teach concepts rather than use rote learning.
2. The extent to which teachers use modern textbooks rather than old notes.
3. The time that teachers of a particular institution spend on their jobs, rather than moonlight.
4. The frequency with which new courses are introduced, old ones updated, term papers and problem sets assigned, and class or individual projects given.
5. Adherence to basic principles of teaching, grading, and fairness.

A hypothetical numerical evaluation of an individual teacher is shown below. The $(QF)_{teachers}$ for the entire college or university could be obtained by averaging over a sufficiently large representative group of teachers spread over different departments.

A Typical Teacher Evaluation

$$(QF)_{teacher} = \frac{3}{10} \times (QF)_{understanding} + \frac{1}{10} \times (QF)_{books\ used}$$

$$+ \frac{1}{5} \times (QF)_{time\ on\ job} + \frac{1}{5} \times (QF)_{innovation}$$

$$+ \frac{1}{5} \times (QF)_{ethical\ behaviour}$$

The weights are chosen to give the greatest weight to the teacher's understanding of the subject and pedagogy (3/10), quality of textbooks used (1/10), time on job (2/10), the degree of innovation shown in teaching (2/10), and indifference to extraneous—ethnic, religious, and political factors (2/10).

$$(QF)_{teacher} = \frac{3}{10} \times 0.9 + \frac{1}{10} \times 0.8$$

$$+ \frac{1}{5} \times 0.75 + \frac{1}{5} \times 0.8$$

$$+ \frac{1}{5} \times 1.0$$

$$(QF)_{teacher} = 0.86$$

This teacher, hypothetically evaluated, is rated perfectly for ethically grading papers and being fair to students, but is not very highly rated for introducing new courses or introducing innovative approaches to teaching.

QUALITY OF STUDENT BODY

Student admission into higher education institutions determines the quality of the student body. Countries with a properly functioning higher education system take this very seriously. US universities admit students on the basis of their grades, recommendations, and SAT/GRE scores; British universities place heavy emphasis on O–A level scores; the well-known Indian Institutes of Technology have fiercely contested national competitive examinations; Iranian universities require a centralized nationwide university entrance examination and select roughly 150,000 out of 1.4 million high school graduates who take a tough 4.5 hours multiple-choice exam. (Iran, Ministry of Knowledge, n.d.).

Student quality is fundamental to the success of a university. But how is this to be defined? Traditional societies educate their young to be replicators and reproducers of existing wisdom. This was as true for traditional Islamic societies as for classical education of Victorian times in England. But creating a modern citizenry capable of responsible and reasoned decision-making imposes very different demands.

Critical inquiry is fundamental. This attitudinal trait is essential for generating new knowledge of the physical world, as well as of human societies. The traditional concept of knowledge will simply not do. Knowledge is not something to be acquired because of a divine command nor can it be acquired once and for all; rather it is the result of an incremental process and the outcome of exercising critical intelligence.

From this standpoint, there has probably been significant deterioration in the student quality of Pakistani public higher education institutions, and perhaps in private ones as well. But there is no 'smoking gun' proof of this, just partial indicators.

A hint that standards are falling comes from the number of Pakistani students studying in the US. Generally, only students with sufficient academic background succeed in getting admission to a US university because, in contrast to some European universities, many require credible proof of academic achievement. However, the situation is complicated by the fact that visas for studying in the US are relatively hard to get, and expenses are greater as well. Nevertheless, it is interesting to look at some current trends. From the International Institute for Education (IIE), which publishes a year-wise report for every country, one learns that in academic year 2009–10, from Pakistan 5,222 students were studying in the United States; down 1.4 per cent from the previous year; in the same year there were 104,897 Indian students (Institute of International Education, 2009). The majority of Pakistani students study at the undergraduate level. In 2008–09, their breakdown was as follows:

- 48.5%   undergraduate
- 41.8%   graduate students
- 1.7%   other
- 8.0%   OPT (Optional Practical Training)

According to the Institute of International Education (2009), following a period of decline in the 1990s, Pakistan experienced significant growth in the first two years of the 2000s. Since, 2001–02, the number of Pakistani students in the US has dropped significantly, pushing Pakistan out of the top 20 sending places of origin in 2006–07 (Institute of International Education, 2009). The number of students from Pakistan continued to decline, by 1 per cent in 2007–08 and again by 0.9 per cent in 2008–09. Politics and profiling in admission policies may provide a partial explanation but the factor of declining educational standards here also appears to be in play.

Table 1: Foreign Students in United States Universities from Different Countries

Country	No. of Students in USA (2006–2007)
India	83,883
Turkey	11,506
Indonesia	7,338
Nigeria	5,943
Nepal	7,754
Pakistan	5,401

Source: Institute of International Education (2009).

Most students in the US from Pakistan study at the undergraduate level, which indicates that they mostly come from elite Pakistani private high-schools and not public higher education institutions, where the student body is manifestly of poorer academic quality. Countries with stronger universities have a greater fraction of students in United States graduate programmes: compare India (73.7%) and Turkey (59%) with Pakistan (37.1%).

Let us now return to the question: how should one seek to determine student quality at a particular institution? A combination of all four determinants below with appropriately chosen weights could provide an adequate gauge.

- *Quality of the standardized test that checks reading, writing, and math skills for selecting incoming students.* Ideally, one would like to know how the typical student entering a Pakistani college or university institution compares in reading, writing, reasoning, general knowledge, and mathematical skills relative to a student of equal age in other institutions within Pakistan, as well as in other countries. Standardized nationally administered tests offer the best hope of improving student intake. This task must be undertaken but it is not easy. There are two difficulties: First, as mentioned earlier, the US-centred SAT is expensive and unsuitable for the ordinary Pakistani student while the local equivalent—the NTS test—is of poor academic quality and currently not sufficiently credible. Secondly, strong political will is needed because there is strong opposition to standardized tests. In Khyber Pakhtunkhwa, street demonstrations in 2005 demanded scrapping a proposed test for university admissions because students from tribal areas would suffer a disadvantage if they had to compete against students from urban areas. Similar protests have taken place at various times in the interior of Sindh. The Punjab Law Department has already opposed a proposal to declare the NTS test as mandatory for admissions to public sector universities in Punjab (*Daily Times*, 2007).

At the graduate level, the Graduate Record Examination (GRE), administered by the Educational Testing Service in Princeton, is considered a relatively reliable tool for testing basic subject competence. Subject areas include a number of scientific disciplines: biology, biochemistry, cell and molecular biology, chemistry, physics, mathematics, and computer science. GRE results for Pakistani students are fragmentary. Nevertheless, there is reason to be disturbed. In 2007, as an experiment, 54 students in the best physics department in Pakistan (at Quaid-i-Azam University), took the GRE physics subject test. The best individual score obtained was 63 percentile— meaning that that student had done better than 63 per cent of all students worldwide. Most scores ranged in the 15–30 per cent range. US graduate schools rarely accept students with scores below 70 per cent. However, results have rapidly improved with time. In 2010, three students from the same department achieved scores exceeding 80 percentile.

The attention to the GRE was a consequence of the HEC having made GRE subject tests mandatory in 2005 for the award of a PhD degree from every public university. Of course, the passing mark set was ludicrously low (40 percentile). But performance was steadily improving. About 15 physics students from the physics department at Quaid-i-Azam University (QAU) cleared this hurdle in the first three years. Students were suddenly confronted head-on with a hard fact: science is about problem solving and they will have to shape up if they want to play ball. The fact that students could not simply cheat or cram did a huge amount of good. The withdrawal of the GRE requirement is a serious setback to higher education quality.

- *The quality of the student selection mechanism used in a particular institution.* The more an institution worries about how it will select its students, the better the rating it deserves in this regard. In Pakistan, elite private universities—LUMS, AKU, GIKI, NUST, etc.—either conduct their own entrance tests or require the Scholastic Aptitude Test (SAT). But in public higher education institutions, with the exception of a few scattered departments, the selection of students is done using rigid mechanical rules based on 'merit'. This term is a misnomer because it is only determined by marks obtained in local board examinations where rote memorization, predictable exam papers, massive cheating, and poor marking practices are rampant. Reform of these boards has been much discussed but little progress has actually been made (Greaney & Hasan, 1998).

- *Employer satisfaction with graduates.* Graduates from higher education institutions are ultimately absorbed into businesses, industry, and government jobs. Do they perform well? This is a hard question to answer: landing any of these jobs often means using patronage, family or political connections, and religious or ethnic affiliations. However, employee competence and merit are given high priority in large organizations. Among these are Pakistan International Airlines, Pakistan Atomic Energy Commission, Kahuta Research Laboratories, Pakistan Telecommunications Corporation, Public Services Commission, etc. These organizations have selection tests and exams, and do not consider college or university grades sufficiently reliable. It would be significant to check the correlation between the results of their selection exams and formal grades. A possibly significant indicator is that the pass rate on the Federal Public Service Commission examinations has declined from 33 per cent to 7.5 per cent over a period of fifteen years.

- *Student intellectual activities outside the classroom.* Ideally one would also like to include student participation in the nation's intellectual life. This includes production of campus newspapers, academic journals, dramas, and films as well as dancing, music, poetry, participation in cultural events, etc.

A Typical Student Quality Evaluation

$$(QF)_{\text{student body}} = \frac{4}{10} \times (QF)_{\text{test quality}}$$

$$+ \frac{2}{10} \times (QF)_{\text{selection mechanism}}$$

$$+ \frac{3}{10} \times (QF)_{\text{employer satisfaction}}$$

$$+ \frac{1}{10} \times (QF)_{\text{extracurricular}}$$

The selection test quality has been given the highest importance (4/10), followed by employer satisfaction with the university of college graduates (3/10), the adequacy of the admissions process (2/10), and extracurricular activities (1/10).

$$(QF)_{\text{student body}} = \frac{4}{10} \times 0.9$$

$$+ \frac{2}{10} \times 0.7$$

$$+ \frac{3}{10} \times 0.7$$

$$+ \frac{1}{10} \times 0.5$$

$$(QF)_{\text{student body}} = 0.76$$

In the above, the test quality was good but students were insufficiently engaged in work outside of the classrooms. However, the small weightage given to the latter made the impact of the latter rather small.

ADEQUACY OF BASICS

Every college or university has certain basic infrastructural and operational requirements. An assessment should involve the following key factors.

- **Land and buildings:** It is impossible to lay down hard and fast rules as to what is adequate. Functionality must suffice as the bare-bones criterion. Rural land is relatively cheap whereas land is extremely expensive in crowded urban environments. Most public universities were given large amounts of land in earlier decades by the government. Today, these assets are under threat from encroachers, profiteers, and even that university's own faculty. Quaid-i-Azam University, Punjab University, and Karachi University are examples.

- **Period of actual university operation:** How many days of the year and how many hours of a working day does a given university actually function? Is there a schedule that is adhered to? A survey could uncover unknown, but easily knowable, facts. University working hours are generally short with many breaks during the day (lunch, prayer, unscheduled). There are many unscheduled holidays—typically a semester's teaching begins 1–2 weeks after the announced date, 3-day Eid holidays actually mean 8–12 days, various disturbances and unscheduled holidays add to non-working days. During evenings, most campuses have unutilized building capacity. Universities do not publish an operating schedule. Only a few private universities announce in advance student application deadlines, dates for start of the next academic session, courses to be offered etc.

- **Adequacy of library facilities:** As a crude measure, it may be enough to know the total number of books in a university library and the library budget. A finer measure would consider library organization, adequacy of shelving and lending records, fraction of new books purchased yearly, etc.

- **Adequacy of science teaching laboratories:** While this is an important element, it is difficult to assess except through field visits by trusted experts. Anecdotal evidence indicates that experimental methodology is poorly taught even where adequate equipment and supplies exist.

- **Internet access and average number of computers per student:** This may be the easiest parameter to estimate. Usage would certainly be a useful but difficult quantity to know. It could presumably be estimated by looking at downloads of academic materials.

INSTITUTIONAL GOVERNANCE AND ETHICS

Universities are microcosms of the society in which they exist. As such they necessarily reflect values and practices in the rest of society. The successful functioning of a higher education institution depends critically upon adherence to basic norms of academic values and behaviour. Conversely, any institution that violates its own rules is unlikely to have collective self-respect.

When rating a university, one must seek answers to questions such as those below:

- **Are faculty appointments and promotions done by subject experts, fairly, and transparently on academic grounds alone?** The traditional Pakistani public university recruitment system relies upon a selection board appointed by the university's highest body, the syndicate. Apart from the department's chairperson, this board has minimal representation by subject experts. Starting in the early 1980s, and continuing for over twenty years, prospective faculty were often required to answer questions completely unrelated to their subject, such as various Quranic prayers on the ideology of Pakistan, their political preferences, etc. In some universities, this practice was never discontinued. Candidates would often lobby fiercely, seeking political and personal connections by which to influence the selection board members. Comparatively speaking, the Tenure Track System (TTS) offers better protection against political tampering. It requires that applications be sent for review to subject experts outside Pakistan. While TTS has been partially implemented in a few universities, it has been rejected by most because of opposition by their faculty. Many teachers feel threatened and insecure at the thought of being judged by experts over whom they have no control.

- **Is the university head chosen by a credible process or a political appointee?** All public university vice chancellors are political appointees. Some are well-chosen, but most are poorly equipped in terms of intellectual and administrative capability. Having military officers as university heads was a disaster. Some attempt has been made to address this issue, but until a more stable national political system comes about, it is likely that university heads will not be well chosen.

- **Is the reward and punishment structure for faculty helpful in creating a better academic body?** The old system was time-bound and had no challenges or incentives. Promotions and regularizations were more or less automatic; with time everyone rose together. There is no known case of a Pakistani academic who has been fired for not knowing his or her subject. The new TTS system is better in this regard. But it has been implemented in a way that has generated new problems: even trivial research is rewarded with cash and promotions, creating a plagiarism pandemic on campuses. The arrival of the internet has raised the problem to new levels of complexity.

- **How common is unethical behaviour among students, faculty, and administrators?** Institutional ethics are essential to successful performance. In the university context, the key issues are:

a) Cheating by students in examinations
b) Plagiarism by students and teachers
c) Fake or forged degrees
d) Unfair grading where a student is either favoured or victimized for ethnic, religious, or political reasons

There is little doubt that these issues are of grave importance in Pakistan, but they need quantitative investigation for every individual institution that is to be considered. It has been estimated that 30–40 per cent of students cheat in one way or the other at the matriculation and intermediate levels; plagiarism is tolerated and results in penalties only in exceptional situations; fake degrees are common to the point, where even members of the National Assembly are well-known for having these dubious credentials; and grading abuse is common because the teacher wields enormous authority.

- **Does there exist a community of scholars reasonably familiar with the work of other colleagues, respectful of the other's professional accomplishment, and able to self-govern?** A university is not a factory where each worker performs a narrow specialized task about which others have little or no idea. By virtue of his or her education in a university, a university teacher is well rounded and able to understand at least the broad outlines of the work carried out by colleagues. This is crucial for creating an environment where academic work receives the level of recognition it deserves, new programmes can be sensibly discussed, courses prescribed, etc. Collegiality is essential for the successful performance of university departments and academic bodies. Conversely, adversarial politics—which is all too common on campuses—can be severely detrimental if it exists to an extreme degree. Therefore, in assessing university quality, a qualitative estimate of this factor is needed.

CAMPUS AMBIENCE

The learning environment matters in an educational institution. The 'feel' of a campus is necessarily subjective—different individuals will assess the ambience differently, and different kinds of institutions create different environments. The atmospherics of a well performing technical training school are unlikely to be suitable for a liberal arts college, etc. Hence, weights for the criteria below must be adjusted appropriately.

- **How much academic and personal freedom is permitted?** While students study at a university primarily to get a degree, they need to have the right to question, to raise unpopular issues, or to put forward controversial views without being penalized. In Pakistan, the restrictions on thought, speech, and actions are imposed both by the state as well as the cultural milieu. The authority of the teacher is so dominating that few students dare ask questions in class. Most students often have an impoverished view of their genuine academic rights. The amount of personal freedom varies from place to place. This reflects in how students may dress, whether they may listen to music or see films, meet or talk to members of the opposite sex, etc. In conservative parts of the country, the choice for women is between the *Burqa* and *Hijab*—exposing their face is not an option on many campuses.

- **How common are campus colloquia, seminars, workshops, etc?** *Do international visitors come to the* *campus? Are there research collaborations with foreign universities?* For a university, mere classroom teaching is insufficient. Intellectual variety and diversity are critical to the growth of ideas, and regular academic activities are important. A university that is capable of absorbing inputs from the world at large has much to gain. The more common situation in Pakistan is where foreign visitors are rare, and even visitors from other Pakistani institutions are few.

- **Is the campus law-and-order adequate? Are professors and students reasonably secure in physical terms?** Contrary to popular perception, most universities have not been closed for extended periods. However, some campuses are run by gangs of hoodlums and harbour known criminals, while others have Rangers with machine guns on continuous patrol. On occasion, student wolf packs attack each other with sticks, stones, pistols, and automatic weapons. Student gangs organize mostly on ethnic lines, but also sometimes on the Shia–Sunni divide. The student groups associated with the Jamaat-i-Islami (JI) and Muttahida Quami Movement (MQM) are known for their strong-arm tactics. A survey is needed to reveal correct facts.

Well-functioning universities are the products of a complex organic and evolutionary process that is internal to a society. Facilities matter, but it is much more important for a university to have a forward looking worldview, an open environment, high ethical standards, a sense of collegiality and shared sense of purpose, and good governance practices.

Finally, let us ask: should university research be counted in assessing university quality? In principle, the answer is: yes. There are excellent reasons for this. A university should be the place where new knowledge grows, new questions are asked, and curiosity is encouraged as a matter of principle. The best teachers are often those who have created new concepts and worked at the cutting edge of their field. They can create a genuine sense of excitement in their students.

COUNTING RESEARCH PAPERS IS A BAD CRITERION

For Pakistani public universities—at least in their present condition—a culture of wholesale corruption has made the value of research doubtful. Research is a seriously misunderstood concept in much of Pakistan's academia, and the criteria for assessing its worth are often wrong.

A unique and precise definition for genuine research in an academic field—mathematics or physics, molecular biology or engineering, economics or archaeology—does not exist. An exploratory definition might be that research is the discovery of new and interesting phenomena, creation of concepts that have explanatory or predictive power, making of new and useful inventions and processes, etc. The researcher must certainly do something original, not merely repeat what is already known. But merely doing something for the first time is not good enough to qualify as research. So, for example, one does not do meaningful research by gathering all kinds of butterflies and listing the number caught of each kind in a particular place at a particular time, etc. Nor is it 'research' if one finds the spectrum of one kind of atom after another, or merely categorizes the compounds found in certain plants, or note wind speeds at different geographical locations. Unless there is a valid and interesting reason for doing so, to gather data is essentially valueless. It is not research—even if it is published in some journal, whether national or international.

The success of research is judged by its importance. For research of an applied nature, the impact can be measured by its effect upon industrial or academic production, jobs created, rise in company stock, etc. The number and type of patents that follow from the research give an important indication of success.

For academic research, only the specialist in that exact field can be entrusted with the evaluation. Of all imperfect measures, the least imperfect one is to count the number of citations in refereed journals. However, this ignores the contribution of university faculty to specific national needs, as judged from the importance given by decision-makers in government or industry. Clearly, judging research quality involves many different criteria.

Nonetheless, one cannot abandon the task of judging research quality, importance, and impact. Counting journal publications, and rewarding individuals proportionately, has worsened the state of corruption. An environment, where unethical behaviour was regrettably common to begin with, has been made yet unhealthier.

Although research quality is always difficult to exactly evaluate, numbers related to academic research in Pakistan are, like research elsewhere, relatively easy to obtain in the age of the internet. Below, Pakistan, together with the seven most productive Muslim countries, is compared against some other countries. The results are not flattering.

Table 2: Comparison of Research Papers/ Citations across Countries (2007)

Country	Physics Papers	Physics Citations	All Science Papers	All Science Citations
Malaysia	690	1,685	11,287	40,925
Pakistan	846	2,952	7,934	26,958
Saudi Arabia	836	2,220	14,538	49,654
Morocco	1,518	5,332	9,979	35,011
Iran	2,408	9,385	25,400	76,467
Egypt	3,064	11,211	26,276	90,056
Turkey	5,036	21,798	88,438	299,808
Brazil	18,571	104,245	128,687	642,745
India	26,241	136,993	202,727	793,946
China	75,318	298,227	431,859	1,637,287
USA	201,062	2,332,789	2,732,816	35,678,385

Source: Philadelphia-based science information specialist, Thomson ISI.

In 2005–06 research funding totalled Rs. 0.342 billion— an enormous sum considering how badly the colleges are funded. The policy of monetary rewards for publishing research papers, given by the Pakistan Council for Science and Technology (PCST) and Higher Education Commission (HEC), led to an outbreak of plagiarism without improving the quality of the research. Research projects need to be evaluated much more carefully than at the present time. Unfortunately, this is easier said than done.

In the current state of Pakistan's universities, throwing money on equipment is easily done but achieves little. There is a fervent plea to acquire the latest equipment, no matter what it costs. One might think that this price to be paid for excellence. Are not the thousands of 'research' papers proof of public money well spent?

The answer is no. One can point to some significant papers here and there. But an overwhelming number of Pakistani publications are largely based upon routine aspects of data collection. These have zero or few citations, as may be verified by accessing free database or still more comprehensive databases.

My point is not to denigrate academic research in Pakistan, but to make the case that such research is consuming a disproportionate amount of resources at the cost of our desperately impoverished educational system. The real problem is that Pakistani students in government schools, colleges, and universities—as well as their teachers—are far below internationally acceptable levels in terms of basic subject understanding.

Setting aside a small minority of good professionals, the poor state of subject knowledge that public university teachers currently have simply does not warrant the current government strategy of hugely rewarding research. It leads, on the contrary, to distorted priorities and immense wastage. Today, what goes under the name of 'research' is largely done to increase publication numbers of individual teachers. It adds little to the stock of existing knowledge. Nor does this reflect in new inventions, patents, etc.

To summarize: a concept for evaluating university quality has been presented here. The primacy of faculty and student quality has been stressed. Although gathering data calls for considerable effort, an attempt at measurement would, at the very least, focus on the key elements needed for creating universities that actually work. Else one will continue to shoot in the dark.

THE PATH TO REAL REFORM

A key challenge for every government in Pakistan will be to sort out (in all the areas of public policy) the facts on the ground from the intricate fictions offered over the eight years of General Pervez Musharraf's regime that paraded for success. This means going beyond the standard blame game. Governments have come and gone without setting Pakistan on a clear way forward. So what sets it apart from the developed world, or even India? At the deepest level, it is the value system that shapes modern education and a modern mindset built upon critical thinking. Pakistan's educational system, shaped by deeply conservative social and cultural values, discourages questioning and stresses obedience. Progress demands that ultimately the dead hand of tradition be cast aside.

More specifically, in seeking change of values, it will be important to break the absolute tyranny of the teacher, a relic of pre modern social values. Closed minds cannot innovate, create art and literature, or do science. Modern education is all about individual liberty, willingness to accept change, intellectual honesty, and constructive rebellion. Critical thought allows individuals to make a revolutionary difference and to invent the future. Else they will merely repeat the dysfunction of the past. But Pakistani students memorize an arbitrary set of rules and an endless number of facts and say that 'X' is true and 'Y' is false because that's what the textbook says (I grind my teeth whenever a master's or PhD student in my university class gives me this argument!). The key point is that minds must be opened.

To develop thinking minds, change must begin at the school level. Good pedagogy requires encouraging the spirit of healthy questioning in the classroom. It should therefore be normal practice for teachers to raise such questions as: How do we know? What is important to measure? How to check the correctness of measurements? What is the evidence? How to make sense of your results? Is there a counter explanation, or perhaps a simpler one? The aim should be to get students into the habit of posing such critical questions and framing reasoned answers.

On a more practical level, there is urgent need for better academic planning and management at the national level. This will be amplified upon below.

REVISE SPENDING PRIORITIES

Currently these are the haphazard expressions of individual whims, not actual needs. For example, most Pakistani students in higher education (about 0.8 million) study in about 800 colleges. These colleges receive pitifully small funding compared to universities. The spending per college student is only one-sixth that for a university student. This is absurd. It is no surprise then that public colleges are in desperate shape with dilapidated buildings, broken furniture, and laboratory and library facilities that exist only in name.

The beggarly treatment of colleges compared to universities is often justified on grounds that universities perform research while colleges do not. But, notwithstanding a few honourable exceptions, this 'research' has added little to the stock of existing knowledge as judged by the international community of scholars. Nevertheless, in 2005–06 university research funding totalled a whopping PKR 0.342 billion. Past experience shows that much of the money will be used to buy expensive research equipment that will find little if any real use.

Public universities in the Musharraf–Atta-ur-Rehman era were awash in funds. They went on a shopping binge for all kinds of gadgetry—fax machines, fancy multimedia projectors, and electricity-guzzling air-conditioners. But this did not improve teaching quality, even marginally. Worse, the availability of 'free money' led to the pursuit of expensive but unworkable projects. False claims of bringing in hundreds of European university professors to teach in Pakistan ultimately foundered. Given suicide bombings and the general environment of instability, was this ever a realistic project? Or was it always meant as a public relation exercise?

CONCENTRATE UPON FACULTY DEVELOPMENT

Because bad teaching quality largely comes from having teachers with insufficient knowledge of their subject, it is important both to have better teacher selection mechanisms and to create large-scale teacher-training academies focused on specific disciplines or areas in every province. Established with international help, these academies should bring in the best teachers as trainers from across the country and from our neighbours.

A proposal in 2003, authored by Pakistanis at the Massachusetts Institute of Technology, floated the idea of a National Faculty Academy. The abstract read as follows:

> In the short-term, the academy will seek to enhance basic competencies in teaching of the core sciences—physics, chemistry, biology, mathematics, computer sciences, and functional English—at the Bachelor and Masters levels in Pakistani universities and colleges. It will offer training programmes for junior faculty at the level of lecturers and assistant professors. Master trainers with excellent professional and pedagogical skills will train junior faculty to assure a satisfactory level of basic subject competency, encourage a problem-solving approach, and make available new methods for teaching and demonstrations. The scale of operation for the academy will achieve significant impact on the national higher education system within 5–10 years.

Unfortunately, this proposal was rejected by the HEC. This effort will cost money and take time—perhaps on the order of a billion dollars over five years. However, such efforts must not be abandoned. High-quality teacher training institutions should have a clear philosophy aimed at equipping teachers to teach through concepts rather than rote learning, use modern textbooks, use distance-learning materials effectively, and emphasize basic principles of pedagogy, grading, and fairness. They should award degrees to create an incentive for teachers to enrol and to do well. Until a sufficiently large number of adequate university teachers can be generated by the above (and various other) means, the practice of making new universities must be discontinued.

INSTITUTE NATIONAL LEVEL UNIVERSITY ENTRANCE EXAMINATIONS

These would separate students who can benefit from higher education from those who cannot.

Qualifying tests for university faculty must be made mandatory. The system has remained fractured for so long that written entrance tests for junior faculty, standardized at a central facility, are essential.[6] Teachers will surely resist this but without such tests, universities will continue to hire teachers who freely convey their confusion and ignorance to students. No teacher has ever been fired for demonstrating incompetence.

Be harsh and uncompromising. Academic crime flourishes in Pakistan's universities because it is almost never punished. Even when media publicity makes action unavoidable, the punishment amounts to little more than a slap on the wrist. The discovery that dozens of Pakistani parliamentarians have fake degrees has, at the time of this writing, not resulted in their resignation or dismissal.

IMPLEMENT TRANSPARENT AND ACCOUNTABLE WAYS TO RECRUIT ADMINISTRATORS

Pakistan has a patronage system that appoints unqualified and unsuitable bureaucrats or military men as vice chancellors, and that staffs universities with corrupt and incompetent administrators. Fortunately, there seems to be some indications of positive change and, at least for the appointment of a number of vice chancellors, search committees were set up.

PERMIT STUDENTS TO SELF-ORGANIZE

It is crucial to bring back on to the campuses meaningful discussions on social, cultural, and political issues. To create the culture of civilized debate, student unions must be restored, with elections for student representatives. They will be the next generation of political leaders. Such a step will not be free from problems—religious extremists rule many Pakistani campuses although all unions are banned. They would surely try to take advantage of the new opportunities offered once the ban is lifted. Political parties have also been less than responsible in their conduct on campus. However, the reinstatement of unions—subject to their elected leaders making a pledge to abjure violence and the disruption of academic activity—is the only way forward towards creating a university culture on campus. Ultimately, reasonable voices, too, will become heard. As an interim step, the government should allow and encourage limited activities such as community work, science popularization by students, etc. To condemn Pakistani students as fundamentally incapable of responsible behaviour amounts to a condemnation of the Pakistani nation itself. If students in neighbouring countries can successfully study, as well as unionize and engage in larger issues, then surely Pakistan's can do so as well.

REMOVE NATIONALITY RESTRICTIONS ON FOREIGN FACULTY HIRING

It is a positive step that the Higher Education Commission (HEC) has initiated a programme for hiring foreign faculty with attractive salaries. There are simply not enough qualified persons within the country to adequately staff the departments. But the success of this programme is uncertain, and programme management is poor. Jealousy at salary differentials, and a fear that local incompetence will be exposed, has led local teachers and university administrations to effectively block the hiring of faculty from abroad.

Pakistan's image as a violent country deters most foreigners from wanting to come and live in Pakistan for any considerable period. Therefore, westerners are almost totally absent from the list of those who have applied under the foreign faculty-hiring programme. Apart from Pakistani expatriates in the Middle East, the bulk of applicants are Russian speakers from the former Soviet Union countries. One wishes it could be otherwise. It would be a major breakthrough if Indian and Iranian teachers could be brought to Pakistan. Indians, in particular, would find it much easier to adapt to local ways and customs than others and also have smaller salary expectations. The huge pool of strong Indian candidates could be used to Pakistan's advantage—it could pick the best teachers and researchers, and those most likely to make a positive impact on the system. In the present mood of rapprochement, it is hard to think of a more meaningful confidence-building measure.

Pakistani higher education will turn around only if Pakistan can be turned around. This cannot happen while maniacal terrorists constantly attack its cities, towns, army, and police. Winning peace is therefore critically needed for uplifting higher education.

REFERENCES

Daily Times (2007), No decisions made in meeting on NTS, *Daily Times*. Retrieved from http://www.dailytimes.com.pk/default.as p?page=2007%5C06%5C05%5Cstory_5-6-2007_pg7_26

Greaney, V., and Hasan, P. (1998), Public examinations in Pakistan: A system in need of reform, In P. Hoodbhoy ed., *Education and the State—Fifty Years of Pakistan*. Karachi: Oxford University Press.

Hoodbhoy, P. (2007), World-class universities: a new holy grail, *SciDev.Net*. Retrieved from http://www.scidev.net/opinions/ index.cfm?fuseaction=printarticle&itemid=617&language=1

Institute of International Education (2009), Retrieved from http:// opendoors.iienetwork.org/

Iran, Ministry of Knowledge, R., and Education (n.d.). Statistics. Retrieved from http://www.irphe.ir/fa/statistics/Statictics%20 Forms/w-br.bruoshoor83-84.pdf

Pakistan, Ministry of Finance (2010), *Economic Survey*. Islamabad: Government of Pakistan.

World Bank (2010), Brief on Education in South Asia, 2009. Retrieved from http://go.worldbank.org/G22NKEQZP0

NOTES

1. Pakistan. Higher Education Commission. http://www.hec.gov.pk/new/QualityAssurance/Statistics.htm
2. Ibid.
3. Pakistan. National Testing Service (2009). http://www.nts.org.pk/
4. The well-known English chemist, J. B. S. Haldane ('Is Science a Misnomer', *The Hindu Weekly Review*, 31 Aug. 1959) recounts an instance that particularly impressed upon him the manner in which science is generally taught and learned in Pakistan: 'I was walking near my house one Sunday afternoon when I heard a male voice raised in a monotonous chant. I supposed that I was listening to some mantras, and asked if my companion could identify them. The practice of repeating religious formulae is, of course, about as common in Europe as in Pakistan. But my companion stated that the language of the chant was English and the subject organic chemistry. We returned and I found he was right. The subject of the chant was aliphatic amines, with special reference to various precautions.'
5. The Indian edition of a typical textbook published in North America listed at US$60–70 (PKR 3,600–4,200) can be bought in Islamabad for as little as Rs. 400–500.
6. In Italy, passing the centrally administered 'concorso' examinations is necessary for the appointment of junior faculty. A sample lecture must also be delivered on a topic given to the candidate a day earlier.

12

The Missing Dimension:
Adult Literacy in South Asia
—Amita Chudgar and Seher Ahmad

Adult literacy rates in South Asia are among the worst in the world. Close to four hundred million adults in the region, continue to be denied the right to basic education and literacy.[1] Almost two-thirds of these illiterate individuals are women. While reducing adult literacy is recognized as an important goal in the Education For All (EFA) framework, unfortunately, both in policy and research dialogues this problem receives limited attention. In light of this background, in this chapter we discuss the prevalence of adult illiteracy in South Asia, the consequences of illiteracy and the policy responses to this massive challenge.

According to the most recent UNESCO (2007) report, 84 per cent of adults (age 15 and over) in the world are literate. Looking at developing countries only, the rates of adult literacy are lower at 79 per cent. Among developing countries, when we focus on South and West Asia we find that only 63.6 per cent of adults in these countries are literate. Within South Asia, Sri Lanka is an exception with adult literacy rates close to 91 per cent. However, outside of Sri Lanka the literacy rates in other South Asian countries are dismal with Bangladesh (52.5%), Bhutan (54.3%), India (65.2%), Nepal (55.2%), and Pakistan (54.2%).[2]

In this, we will focus on Bangladesh, India, Nepal, and Pakistan because obtaining comparable data on Bhutan has proved challenging.[3] Literacy rates have been low historically in these countries. While there have been some variations in the trajectory (most notably in the case of Bangladesh) for the most part in these four countries, the progress in literacy rate has also been slow and marginal.[4]

Not only are literacy rates low overall, a close inspection reveals significant inequities/disparities in literacy rates depending on individual characteristics. For instance, in each of these countries women, individuals living in rural areas, and individuals between ages twenty-five and over are more likely to be illiterate.

Female literacy rates are the lowest in Pakistan with less than 40 per cent adult female literacy, followed by 42 per cent in Nepal, close to 47 per cent in Bangladesh, and there are 53 per cent adult literate women in India. Not only are women less likely to be literate compared to men, the extent of gender disparity in literacy has remained practically unchanged in South Asia (Stromquist, 1992). For example, in Pakistan, for over almost ten years there was no change in the literacy gap between male and female adults. In Nepal, this gap actually worsened over time. Also, India and Bangladesh too have been able to make only marginal gains in terms of bridging the gender gap.[5]

In terms of rural prevalence of adult illiteracy, the Indian census reports states that while urban literacy rates were 80 per cent in 2001, in rural areas the literacy rates were 59 per cent.[6] Similarly in Pakistan, urban literacy rates in 1998 was 64.7 per cent and in rural areas this rate was as low as 34.4 per cent (Bano, 2007).

The third important dimension of inequity is age. Younger adults tend to experience higher literacy rates compared to older adults. A UNESCO report points out that in almost every country of the world, older cohorts are less educated than younger cohorts because education is concentrated in the younger age groups and most education systems have expanded over time (UNESCO. Institute for Statistics, 2006). Indeed in the four countries we study here, we find that the literacy rates among 'youths' (age 15–24) are significantly higher ranging from 69 per cent in Pakistan to 81 per cent in India.

Once again, however, young women tend to be less likely to be literate compared to young men. While this is of course, a positive sign going forward, to the extent that a large number of individuals in the age group of twenty-five and above are illiterate should be a serious cause for concern in its own right.

This brief overview of historical and contemporary trends underscores that adult illiteracy has been and continues to remain a widespread problem in South Asia that disproportionately affects individuals over the age of twenty-four, women, and rural populations. What are the consequences of adult illiteracy and why should these high rates of illiteracy be a cause for concern for policymakers?

CONSEQUENCES OF ADULT ILLITERACY, WHY IS THIS AN IMPORTANT PROBLEM?

The ability to read and write with comprehension is central to many activities in the modern society. Everything from post offices, banks, transport systems, government offices, their children's school systems, and good parenting in general requires a basic comprehension of the written word from an average adult. Not being able to read often means navigating important decisions without basic information that is available routinely to the literate individual. Not surprisingly, adult literacy is one of the key components of the United Nation's measure of human development the 'Human Development Index' (UNDP, 1999, 2007). It seems highly plausible that adult literacy may be strongly associated with economic productivity, access to information and as a result health and educational outcomes. Also, because this an attribute of an 'adult' who may typically be responsible for other individuals in the family, most likely their children, it is also highly likely to benefit not just the adult herself or himself but also their children and family members as well as others who are in close proximity. In economic terms, adult literacy is likely to have neighbourhood effects that contribute to the common good.

Few empirical studies have focused on investigating the relationships between adult literacy and development outcomes systematically. This paucity of literature may be explained in part due to the lack of availability of good data on literacy levels. As such, then, adult literacy in South Asia remains an open area of investigation with a lot of room for policy relevant research. For the purpose of this chapter, we first investigate some of the key evidence from the existing literature. Then utilizing highly relevant and recently collected data from four study countries, we conduct some preliminary empirical analysis to provide additional evidence to support the association between adult literacy and development outcomes.

EVIDENCE FROM THE LITERATURE

A significant amount of existing literature has focused on adult females in particular. Given their more direct responsibilities for child rearing, it is not surprising to find studies, arguing for a stronger relationship between adult female literacy and children's health and educational outcomes.

In Nepal, the adult literacy levels in the household were found as the strongest 'mutable' determinants of their children participating in formal schools. Similarly, utilizing nationally representative datasets, Chudgar (2009) found that a child's likelihood of school enrolment and school completion were significantly higher even in a barely literate household versus being in a completely illiterate household. These relationships were especially strong when looking at improvement in literacy levels of mothers. The study also showed that the benefits of adult literacy in fact far outweighed the benefits derived even from reducing the family's poverty level. Additionally, Chudgar (2009) and Chudgar (2007) showed that improvement in adult literacy levels at the community level also has strong positive associations with improved schooling outcomes of children.

Some studies have similarly shown the linkages between adult literacy and economic prosperity that extend beyond the adult. In Nepal, Shrestha et al. (1986) note a negative association between adult literacy and poverty levels in the community. Chowdhury (1995) makes a similar observation while noting that literate adults are likely to be more self-confident and better prepared to engage in economic activities beyond the subsistence sector. Basu, Narayan, and Ravallion (2001) provide some fascinating evidence from Bangladesh. Using household survey data from Bangladesh they find that in the non-farm economy, an illiterate adult earns significantly more when living with at least one literate family member. In particularly, they find that illiterate women compared to illiterate men tend to especially benefit from living in a household with at least one literate member.

Several authors have more broadly and sometimes specifically in the South Asian context noted the importance of adult literacy training for improved self-confidence, self-esteem, empowerment, autonomy and greater access to information resulting in more active citizens, and more active civil societies (Abdazi, 2003; Lauglo, 2001; Stromquist, 2005). An especially large amount of evidence on the linkages between literacy, especially adult female literacy, and development outcomes has focused on health. The general argument tends to be that literate mothers engage in better parenting practices and make better (more informed) decisions about their children than do illiterate mothers. Children of these mothers enjoy better nutrition and are less likely to succumb to infant mortality (Chowdhury, 1995; Lauglo, 2001; Sandiford, Cassel, Montenegro, & Sanchez, 1995; Street, 2003).

In Nepal, Comings, Shreshtha, and Smith (1992), for instance noted remarkable gains in the women's knowledge about child rearing including the benefits of smaller families and approaches to care of sick children at the end of literacy training. Also in Nepal, Levine, Rowe, and Schnell-Anzola (2004) argue that literacy skills are in fact the pathway through which schooling is associated with health outcomes. They administered literacy tests to a select sample of women. They found that women's higher literacy skills as measured by their study were associated with greater ability to comprehend health messages in print, over the radio, comprehend medical instructions and tell 'an organized health narrative' (Levine et al., 2004, 874). In India, McNay, Cassen, and Arokiasamy (2003) argue that one reason why women that are more uneducated may be using contraceptives may be the 'spill-over' benefits of having more educated and knowledgeable women around them.

This brief overview of the existing literature reveals that greater levels of adult literacy may be associated with several benefits for the individuals themselves ranging from higher self-confidence to being better informed. In addition, the existing evidence shows that higher levels of adult literacy both within the family and even within the community are associated with higher educational attainment of children residing in such families and better economic and health outcomes for adults and children residing in such families and communities.

EMPIRICAL ANALYSES

While this existing evidence supporting linkages between the adult literacy and various human development indicators, including education is compelling, it is not available consistently for all the four countries we are studying. Also, likely for these studies is to use slightly different measures of literacy (some may work with self-reported measure, some use actual tests etc). Therefore, we decided to use the Demographic and Health Survey (DHS) data available for each of the four countries and produce additional empirical evidence where we looked at the same outcomes across all the four countries.

DATA

We used the 2007 Demographic and Health Survey (DHS) data for Bangladesh, 2005–06 DHS data from India, 2006 DHS data from Nepal and 2006–07 DHS data from Pakistan. Apart from the regency of these data, there are three advantages of using these dataset for our purposes.

i. First, these data are collected in a consistent manner across different countries, allowing us to observe similar or the same outcome in our four countries of interest.

ii. Second, while the larger data collection is conducted at the household level, these data also have a specific module that focuses on females and males (except

Pakistan where only female data are available). Within these specific modules, literacy data are collected from female and male survey respondents by actually testing their ability to read a pre-designed brief text. Based on this the respondents are categorized into: cannot read at all, can read parts of sentence, or can read whole sentence. This test allows for fairly accurate and nuanced measure of adult literacy as it is often argued that self-reports[7] on adult literacy levels can be inaccurate.

iii. Third, because these data are collected to be nationally representative, the data-set provides a weight along with each observation, and appropriately using these weights allows for generating nationally representative analysis.

The limitation of using these pre-existing secondary data is that not all the variables of interest are available. For example, children's education data are not available in these separate female/male files, and would require several additional steps to retrieve from the larger household data-set. Also, while fairly consistent, not all the information is available for all the four countries.

FINDINGS

Table 1: Literacy Rates and Sample Sizes in the Countries Studied (Female and Male)

	Country	Sample size	Cannot read (%)	Read parts of a sentence (%)	Can read (%)
Female	Bangladesh	10,996	45.41	6.74	47.48
	India	124,385	44.54	4.93	50.19
	Nepal	10,793	45.73	8.88	45.65
	Pakistan	10,023	64.32	6.70	28.8
Male	Bangladesh	3,771	43.51	6.82	49.62
	India	74,369	22.21	5.47	72.11
	Nepal	4,397	21.17	7.66	71.06

Note:
1. The numbers do not add to a 100 because two categories, which include 'no card with required language' and 'blind/visually impaired' are not reported. However, these numbers are negligibly small in most cases.
2. Male data from Pakistan are not available.
Source: DHS data, Bangladesh (2007), India (2005–2006), Nepal (2006), Pakistan (2006–2007).

The differences in the sample sizes for males and females in Table 1 reflect DHS's primary focus on female health and fertility issues. Also, India, owing to its size has a significantly larger sample size compared to the other countries. Furthermore, as noted earlier Pakistan has no literacy data available for males.

The available data are worrisome. These figures are more recent than any of the national statistics cited at the beginning of this chapter. Yet, they are not much different from those older numbers. Now, as was the case earlier, less than 50 per cent women in any of these countries can read a simple sentence. In Pakistan, the number is even lower with only 29 per cent women able to read a sentence. Male literacy rates are higher, especially in India and Nepal but still as many as 30 per cent to 50 per cent (in Bangladesh) men also were not able to read a simple sentence when tested by the DHS survey team.

How the ability to read is associated with different development outcomes? Tables 2 and 3 provide a preliminary answer to that question separately for male and female survey respondents.[8] Again, as is evident from the table, there are variations across countries in terms of variables on which information is available for males and females. Not all data are available for all the four countries.

Table 2: Association between Literacy Rates and Various Outcomes (Female Data)

Country	Cannot read	Read parts of sentence	Can read
	Does not read newspapers		
Bangladesh	100	96.30	71.45
India	100	71.5	30.40
Nepal	100	90.31	32.91
	Never heard of TB		
Bangladesh	4.75	1.88	0.54
India	24.15	14.68	6.27
Nepal	6.24	2.46	0.66
Pakistan	16.20	12.18	3.32

	Never heard of AIDS		
Bangladesh	54.37	30.92	12.15
Nepal	51.24	22.51	4.78
Pakistan	73.77	46.18	17.86
	Wife beating justified if she argues with husband		
Bangladesh	22.94	20.99	20.20
India	37.95	34.10	23.25
Nepal	11.41	8.93	4.82
	The woman gets to decide how to spend money in the household		
Bangladesh	25.86	33.00	35.75
India	22.83	26.99	28.09
Nepal	23.34	34.02	40.63
	Average number of male children died since birth		
Bangladesh	0.28	0.18	0.08
India	0.23	0.10	0.04
Nepal	0.28	0.16	0.04
Pakistan	0.26	0.19	0.11
	Ideal number of desired children		
Bangladesh	2.40	2.35	2.16
India	2.63	2.29	1.99
Nepal	2.69	2.27	1.99
Pakistan	4.4	4.0	3.44

Source: DHS data, Bangladesh (2007), India (2005–6), Nepal (2006), Pakistan (2006–2007).

Table 2, which focuses on the relationship between female literacy and selected development outcomes, provides an opportunity for several interesting observations on cross-national differences as well. However, here we will maintain our focus on the relationship between these outcomes and literacy as the primary area of discussion.

The first three questions in the table (reading newspaper, knowledge of TB and AIDS) can all be seen as indicators of 'access to information'. It is amply evident that women who cannot read at all are deprived of information. They naturally do not read newspapers at all in any of the countries for which data are available.

Even women who read only parts of a sentence are much less likely to read newspapers. However, close to 70 per cent women who can read, especially those in India and Nepal read newspapers. In Bangladesh, for some reason, in spite of the ability to read, women simply do not read newspapers in general.

With respect to information about TB, the numbers in India followed by Pakistan are the worst in terms of illiterate women, they are far less likely to be aware of tuberculosis (TB) compared to even women who can read just parts of a sentence, and certainly far less likely to be informed than those who can read. These general patterns hold in Bangladesh and Nepal too, but in these countries, overall, awareness about TB is higher regardless of literacy levels.

With respect to AIDS, the numbers are alarming in each country where data are available. More than half the illiterate women have no idea what AIDS is. Again, it is striking that even with the ability to read a few words out of a sentence, the knowledge of AIDS improves significantly. Say in Nepal while 51 per cent illiterate women do not know about AIDS, far fewer 22 per cent women who can at least read parts of a sentence do not know about AIDS.

The next two questions (wife beating justified if she argues with husband and the woman gets to decide how to spend money in her household) can both be seen as indicators of women's autonomy. Again, these variables in isolation can only tell part of the story since we do not know for instance if these women are currently married, or they are married to the household head (in which case they may be more likely to make financial decisions at home).

However, once again a few patterns are hard to ignore. First off, overall the data seem to indicate that women in Nepal are much better off and women in India are worse off in terms of these questions. Once again, women who are illiterate tend to be more likely to agree that wife beating is okay for arguing with her husband, and they seem to be less likely to be in control of the finances in their houses. In general, women who are literate tend to be less agreeable to the statement that domestic violence is acceptable. Though notably in Bangladesh women regardless of their literacy levels do not seem to have widely divergent view on that question (where 20–23 per cent women agree that domestic violence is justified). Similarly, literate women in general tend to be more likely to control household finances, but once again, in India these differences are marginal across the literacy levels (where only 23–28 per cent women have control over household finances).

The final two panels in the table can be thought to represent awareness of health and fertility practices (average number of male child mortality and ideal number of desired children) where a lower number would represent greater awareness.

First, looking at the mortality of the male child (where presumably in all of these male-dominant cultures, that is a prized child) on average mortality rates for male children are alarmingly high for illiterate women. An illiterate woman is likely to lose 1 in 3 to 1 in 4 male children. These rates decline drastically with marginal improvements in literacy levels and decline more sharply when a woman is literate. With respect to ideal number of children we once again notice that illiterate women are more likely to suggest wanting more children than literate women do.

Table 3: Association between Literacy Rates and Various Outcomes (Male Data)

Country	Cannot read	Read parts of sentence	Can read
Never heard of TB			
Bangladesh	2.16	0.24	0.24
India	19.04	12.55	4.58
Nepal	2.89	3.14	0.31
Never heard of AIDS			
Bangladesh	28.04	9.93	4.59
India	48.17	27.38	6.68
Nepal	35.80	21.0	2.29
Wife beating justified if she argues with husband			
Bangladesh	32.35	26.53	17.96
India	33.82	33.42	22.54
Nepal	16.32	14.63	6.31

Source: DHS data, Bangladesh (2007), India (2005–2006), Nepal (2006), Pakistan (2006–2007).

Table 3 provides a similar analysis for the male data. In general, the patterns that we observe in the female data continue to persist here as well. In India, overall TB awareness is lower and specifically within India, and also in Nepal and Bangladesh illiterate men are least likely to know about TB. A similar pattern remerges with AIDS, with close to 50 per cent illiterate men in India being unaware of AIDS.

Once again, lack of awareness about AIDS reduces drastically even when the individual can read only marginally. Finally, we notice that in Nepal men in general are far less agreeable to domestic violence against their wives being acceptable. However, having said that men who are literate are less likely in all the three countries to agree that domestic violence is acceptable.

In summary these findings amply demonstrate the importance of adult literacy, and sometimes just being able to merely read parts of a sentence in ensuring that these adults, especially women would be well-informed, empowered in their homes and able to make better health and fertility related decisions.

In conjunction with the existing research summarized earlier and the findings from this descriptive analysis based on recent and nationally representative data from all four countries, one conclusion becomes obvious. Adult illiteracy in South Asia, especially adult female illiteracy, is associated with some of the worst forms of deprivations. It may deprive an individual (and as a result their dependents) from information, empowerment, and even health.

The present rates of massive adult illiteracy in South Asia are simply not acceptable in their own right and because what they mean for several other basic development outcomes. What has been the national response to this massive challenge? This is the question we turn to next.

ADULT LITERACY POLICIES[9]

In preparation for the Sixth International Conference on Adult Education in December 2009, in October 2009, Bangladesh, India, Pakistan and six other countries, which together constitute 85 per cent of the world's non-literate population, came together in Beijing, China, 'to promote the collaborative implementation of UNESCO's Literacy Initiative for Empowerment (LIFE) and develop capacities of these countries.'[10] While there are several such attempts and deliberations to address adult illiteracy within and across nations, in general adult literacy remains neglected in educational dialogues.

In 2006, the Education For All (EFA) report identified literacy as 'one of the most neglected' EFA goals (UNESCO, 2005, 27). The report notes that literacy is 'not prominent in most education plans and typically accounts for only 1 per cent of public spending on education.' (UNESCO, 2005, 248). The EFA report from 2008 adds, 'Illiteracy is receiving minimal political attention and remains a global disgrace.' (UNESCO, 2007, 1). Perhaps reflecting this limited attention to adult literacy in country budgets, the UNESCO Institute of Statistics, country education profiles which provide detailed information on expenditure on pre-primary, primary, secondary, and tertiary levels does not even provide a separate column of information to indicate the funding allocated to adult literacy activities.

This broader global neglect is reflected in our brief overview of country policies as well. It is beyond the scope of this chapter to investigate the long and complicated history of adult literacy policies in each of these four countries. Instead, here we will aim to provide a brief overview and highlight only the most salient observations in each case.

While each country has adopted its own set of adult literacy programmes, with a varying degree of emphasis on various issues, there are several similarities across the countries that are worth noting. Since, as noted earlier too, adult illiteracy has been a long-standing problem in each of the four countries, their policy rhetoric responds to this issue through statements of commitment to address the illiteracy challenge by eliminating adult literacy.

While Bangladesh, India, and Pakistan began their adult literacy programmes only soon after their independence, Nepal, where adult literacy rates in 1950 were also extremely low (as low as 2 per cent according to one report), serious interventions began only in 1956 (Nepal, Ministry of Education, 2000; Pakistan, Ministry of Education, 2000), and it was the intervention of NGOs and INGOs in 1980s that literacy activities gained real momentum, most notable with the National Literacy Programme in 1984 (Tuladhar, 1997).

In Bangladesh, it was the creation of the Directorate of Non Formal Education in 1995 that invigorated the drive towards adult education (Owusu-Boampong, 2007). In India, it was the launching of the National Literacy Mission (NLM) in 1988 followed by a decidedly mixed performance of 1978 National Adult Education Programme that brought a renewed sense of urgency to the adult illiteracy issues (India, Planning Commission, 2002). In Pakistan, the adult basic education society was established in 1971.

Many of these adult literacy programmes had additional focus on gender issues, mainly women's empowerment (such as in India), or imparting life-skills and improving livelihood opportunities (such as in Nepal). Additionally, in Bangladesh and Nepal a vast majority of their literacy interventions have actually been led or supported either by external donors or by NGOs. As a UNESCO report on non-formal education (NFE)—of which adult literacy is a part—the funding for NFE in Bangladesh has mainly been external (Owusu-Boampong, 2007).

In general, the scholars from within these countries have tended to view the government's efforts in relatively poor light. The experts from these countries note that government adult literacy efforts show a lack of political will see for example, India (Bhola, 1988; Mathew, 2002), Pakistan (Bano, 2007), and Nepal (Nepal, Ministry of Education, 2000).

In Bangladesh, a study from a nationwide survey of almost 20,000 adults in the year 2000 revealed that less than 4 per cent respondents relied exclusively on government provided Total Literacy Mission (TLM) interventions for literacy training. Of those that relied on TLM only 1.3 per cent were actually literate (Ahmed, Nath, & Ahmed, 2003). The author thus concluded that based on this analysis, the national adult literacy programmes in Bangladesh including TLM have had no impact on literacy rates (Ahmed et al., 2003).

In India TLM was pronounced only a marginal success story. This was due to lack of political commitment and mobilization, incentives to misreport numbers, natural disasters, limited availability of infrastructure and the lack of systematic conceptualization of literacy itself (Dighe, 2002; Ghosh, 1994). In Pakistan, the recent Pakistan county report by Bano (2007) cites Dr J. H. Aly who notes that '. . . almost 15 major literacy programmes/projects have been launched in the country since independence. However, most were terminated before completion.'

Similarly, in case of Nepal the country report notes that literacy programmes have made limited (only 3%) contribution to improving literacy rates in Nepal (Chitrakar, 2007; Nath & Raj, 2005).

These reviews are by no means glowing, and perhaps the single most important question with regard to these policies may boil down to what kind of financial resources have these governments committed to the adult illiteracy challenge? Without a substantial and sustained financial commitment, it is hard to envision how policy rhetoric can be turn to reality.

In case of Bangladesh, we were unable to obtain the relevant budget allocation data, but as already noted, NGOs and international partners run a large portion of Bangladesh's adult literacy programme. In India, Nepal, and Pakistan, where data are available, the budget allocation to adult illiteracy is extremely limited.

In India, adult literacy has always been underfunded. In absolute terms there may have been a decline or stagnation in the budget allocated to adult education over time. The 2.34 billion rupees allocated to adult education in the 1995–96 education budget increased very slightly, to 2.63 billion for 2005–06 (India, Ministry of Finance, 1997; India, Ministry of Human Resource Development, Planning, and Monitoring Unit, 2006). Accounting for inflation over the decade, this represents an actual decline in expenditure on adult education.

In more recent terms, in 2005–06 adult education accounted for 0.42 per cent of total expenditure on education (Chudgar, 2009; India, Ministry of Human Resource Development, Planning and Monitoring Unit, 2006). Between 2003 and 2006, adult education expenditure only increased about 13 per cent compared to a more than 100 per cent increase in the elementary education expenditure.

Similarly in Nepal, the country report indicates that in all the phases of adult literacy intervention (from the mid-50s), the interventions have been underfunded. The most recent budgetary provisions over three years ranged from 0.50 to 0.67 per cent of the education budget. In fact, in Nepal too historically literacy education over the years has received less than 1 per cent of the education budget. And while in Nepal non-governmental actors do play an important role. To these ends, no systematic data are available to account for their contribution (Nath & Raj, 2005). Plus, as observers note, working with international funding has its own limitations as the donors are often interested in 'products and outputs' rather than 'sustainable processes' (Tuladhar, 1997).

The budget allocations in Pakistan are no different. In fact, according to the country assessment report, provinces as such do not allocate any budget for literacy, and the programme runs only on federal funding which is itself limited (Pakistan, Ministry of Education, 2000). In Pakistan too, over the years, adult literacy allocation was barely 1 per cent and that money too was not always provided on time.

CONCLUSION

This chapter highlights a few important patterns. Adult illiteracy is widespread in South Asia, especially among South Asian females. Adult illiteracy is associated with several forms of deprivation. While it has received a prominent place in national rhetoric, historically it has received neither the political commitment nor the financial resources that would be adequate to address large levels of adult illiteracy.[11]

As we make a case of greater investment and attention to adult literacy we must acknowledge that it is a complex problem plagued with many challenges. Some of these challenges are unique due to its adult audience. For instance, due to lack of avenues to practice, adult literates are at risk of relapsing into illiteracy, due to regular work commitment participation in structured programmes is harder for these learners, it is important that the learning material and the programme structure are relevant to their daily lives. Together these constraints often result in learner apathy and lack of commitment on part of the adult student which policymakers may not be able to address easily. The other set of challenges are associated with the implementation of any large-scale government project in developing countries. These programmes often suffer from poor management, lack of accountability, corruption, teacher absence, and apathy. These challenges must be acknowledged and addressed by any adult literacy intervention that hopes to be successful.

These problems notwithstanding, for now, the large numbers of adult illiterate and the small amounts of resources traditionally allocated to this problem is enough to remind us that as countries we are yet to address this important problem with complete dedication and with all our might.

REFERENCES

Abdazi, H. (2003), 'Adult literacy: A review of implementation experience', (Washington DC: The World Bank Operations Evolution Department).

Ahmed, M., Nath, S. R., and Ahmed, K. S. (2003), 'Literacy in Bangladesh: Need for a new vision, Overview of the main report', Education Watch 2002: Campaign for Popular Education.

Bano, M. (2007), Progress since Dakar: Pakistan country review, Background paper for EFA Global Monitoring Report 2008.

Basu, K., Narayan, A., and Ravallion, M. (2001), 'Is literacy shared within households? Theory and evidence for Bangladesh', *Labour Economics*, 8(6), 649–65.

Bhola, H. S. (1988), 'A policy analysis of adult literacy education in India: Across the two national policy reviews of 1968 and 1986',

Paper presented at the Comparative and International Education Society (CIES), Atlanta, GA.

Chitrakar, R. (2007), 'Nepal non-formal education country profile', Background paper for EFA Global Monitoring Report 2008.

Chowdhury, K. P. (1995), 'Literacy and primary education', Human Resources Development and Operations Policy.

Chudgar, A. (2007), 'Looking beyond the household: The importance of community-level factors in understanding under-representation of girls in Indian education', in M. A. Maslak ed., *The Structure and Agency of Women's Education* (Albany: State University of New York Press), 201–8.

Chudgar, A. (2009), 'Does adult literacy have a role to play in addressing the Universal Elementary Education challenge in India?' *Comparative Education Review*, 53(4).

Comings, J. P., Shreshtha, C. K., and Smith, C. (1992), 'A secondary analysis of a Nepalese national literacy programme', *Comparative Education Review*, 36(2), 212–26.

Dighe, A. (2002), 'Social mobilization and total literacy campaign', in R. Govinda ed., *India Education Report* (New Delhi: Oxford University Press), 242–50.

Ghosh, A. (1994), 'Evaluation of literacy campaign in India: Report of expert group', (New Delhi: Ministry of Human Resource Development).

India, Ministry of Finance (1997), *Economic Survey* (New Delhi: Government of India).

India, Ministry of Human Resource Development, Department of School Education and Literacy (2009); *Saakshar Bharat* (New Delhi: Government of India).

India, Ministry of Human Resource Development, Planning and Monitoring Unit (2006), 'Analysis of Budgeted Expenditure on Education 2003–4 to 2005–6', (New Delhi: Government of India).

India. Planning Commission (2002), 10th Five-Year Plan (2002–2007) (New Delhi: Government of India).

Lauglo, J. (2001), 'Engaging with adults: The case for increased support to basic adult education in Sub-Saharan Africa', Africa Region Human Development Working Paper Series.

Levine, R. A., Levine, S. E., Rowe, M. L., and Schnell-Anzola, B. (2004), 'Maternal literacy and health behavior: A Nepalese case study'. *Social Science and Medicine*, 58(4), 863–77.

Mathew, A. (2002), 'Indian engagement with adult education and literacy', in R. Govinda ed., *India Education Report* (New Delhi: Oxford University Press), 221–32.

McNay, K., Cassen, R. H., and Arokiasamy, P. (2003), 'Why are uneducated women in India using contraception?' A multilevel analysis Population Investigation Committee.

Nath, K. B., and Raj, A. B. (2005), 'Real options for policy and practice in Nepal'. Background paper prepared for the Education for All Global Monitoring Report 2006.

Nepal, Ministry of Education (2000), 'Education for All: The Year 2000 Assessment Country Report' (Kathmandu: Government of Nepal).

Owusu-Boampong, A. (2007), 'Compilation of data on non-formal education provision and policies', Background paper for EFA Global Monitoring Report 2008.

Pakistan, Ministry of Education (2000), 'Education for All: The Year 2000 Assessment Country Report' (Islamabad: Government of Pakistan).

Sandiford, P., Cassel, J., Montenegro, M., and Sanchez, G. (1995), 'The impact of women's literacy on child health and its interaction with access to health services', Population Investigation Committee.

Shrestha, G. M., Lamichhane, S. R., Thapa, B. K., Chitrakar, R., Useem, M., and Comings, J. P. (1986), 'Determinants of educational participation in rural Nepal'. *Comparative Education Review*, 30(4), 508–22.

Street, B. (2003), What's 'new' in new literacy studies? Critical approaches to literacy in theory and practice, *Current Issues in Comparative Education*, 5(2), 77–91.

Stromquist, N. P. (1992), 'Women and literacy: Promises and constraints', *Annals of the American Academy of Political and Social Science*, 54–65.

Stromquist, N. P. (2005), 'The political benefits of adult literacy'. Paper commissioned for the EFA Global Monitoring Report 2006.

Tuladhar, S. K. (1997), Litearcy in Nepal: The CERID/CIE project. Kathmandu: Tribhuvan University, Research Center for Educational Innovation and Development.

UNDP (1999), Human Development Report 1999 (New York: UNDP).

UNDP (2007), Human Development Report 2007 (New York: UNDP).

UNESCO (2005), 'Literacy for Life', EFA Global Monitoring Report 2006 (Paris: UNESCO).

UNESCO (2007), EFA Global Monitoring Report 2008 (Paris: UNESCO).

UNESCO Institute for Statistics (2006), 'Global Age-specific Literacy Projections Model (GALP): Rationale, Methodology and Software', L. Wolfgang, and Sergei, Scherbov. eds. Montréal (Québec), Canada.

NOTES

1. Definitions of literacy used in various countries studied, obtained from the Asia-Pacific Literacy Database.

   Bangladesh: A person is literate who has attained skill in reading and writing simple text and numeracy.

India: A person is literate who has attained skill in reading and writing simple text and numeracy.

Nepal: A person who is able to read and write short and simple sentences related to daily life in his/her mother tongue or national language with understanding and who is able to communicate with others and perform simple tasks of calculation.

Pakistan: A person is literate who can read and write a paragraph (3 lines) in national/regional language with comprehension.

2. http://www.unesco.org/en/efareport/resources/statistics/statistical-tables/

3. It must be noted that 'adult literacy' is a complex concept with multiple definitions. Scholars also debate if literacy should be tied so narrowly to an individual's ability to read and write and if such a concept is limiting? (for instance Street 2003 or UNESCO 2006). We acknowledge these debates but for the purposes of this chapter, we work with the 'functional' definition of literacy in our empirical analysis, and we use the pre-existing nationally representative data for our descriptive analysis.

4. Trends in Literacy Rates http://www.accu.or.jp/litdbase/efa/progress.htm

5. Ibid.

6. http://www.censusindia.gov.in/Census_Data_2001/India_at_glance/literates1.aspx

7. Self-reporting or reporting by the informant is the standard method to collect information on various household variables in most household surveys.

8. The analysis presented here should be only viewed as a simple description. A more systematic analysis to establish cause-and-effect would require an extensive quantitative modelling. At the very least such an advanced quantitative model would account for regional differences, age differences, wealth differences etc. in understanding the relationship between adult literacy and development outcomes.

9. This section especially benefited from the excellent online data source on adult literacy in Asia http://www.accu.or.jp/litdbase/index.htm

10. http://www.unescobkk.org/en/education/efa/efanews/news-details/
    article/e-9-countries-strengthen-collaboration-to-tackle-illiteracy-in-
    rural-areas/

11. At the time of writing this chapter, we learned about the Indian
    governments newest adult literacy programme launched in October
    2009 called 'Saakshar Bharat' (literally meaning, a literate India).
    The programme document available online actually provides a
    fair appraisal of the government's literacy efforts so far when it
    notes that prior efforts have suffered from inadequacies in design,
    implementation, management, lack of community support,
    and inadequate funding (India, Ministry of Human Resource
    Development, Department of School Education and Literacy, 2009).
    In this background, this new programme with a specific focus on
    women is launched to replace the National Literacy Mission. In
    financial terms at PKR 6502.70 crores the programme has a greater
    budgetary allocation than similar programmes in the past. The
    programme proposes several departures from earlier practices and on
    an optimistic note this may finally initiate the country's much needed
    progress towards adult literacy.

13

Quality, Relevance, and Equity: Negotiating an Educational Development Strategy in Bangladesh[1]

—Manzoor Ahmed and James H. Williams

AN OVERVIEW OF THE EDUCATION SITUATION

With independence in 1971, Bangladesh inherited an education system composed of a small number of elite schools and a larger number of lower quality institutions—public, private and organized by religious organizations. Still, the majority of the population received little or no education. In working to educate its people, the Bangladesh government greatly expanded education in terms of both the numbers of institutions and enrolments at all levels, especially in the last two decades. In addition, the country has overcome a substantial gender gap in primary and secondary school participation. Girls are now as likely as boys to enrol at those levels.

However, the key considerations in understanding and assessing the role of education in poverty alleviation and enhancement of human development and human dignity are: (a) access to education, (b) quality and relevance of education, and (c) equity in access and participation so that the poor and the disadvantaged are indeed the beneficiaries.

The education system in Bangladesh, as will be seen below, is not equitable and the quality and content of education do not effectively serve the goals of human development and poverty reduction. Despite rhetoric since the colonial days and the constitutional pledge of an independent Bangladesh, effective participation in basic education—primary education for children and functional literacy and continuing education for youth and adults—remains beyond the reach of a large proportion of the population. The numbers of institutions and enrolments have grown at all levels, but it is generally agreed that quality of education has deteriorated and remains seriously deficient, especially in institutions in which the children of the poor predominate. Even in the public sector in education, equity, and service to the poor are not explicit criteria in financial provisions and budget allocations. The education system has failed to make the grade in respect to access with quality and equity.

The linkages between education and human development and poverty reduction can be examined in light of three broad policy domains: the state of *access with equity and quality*, the effects of *education governance*, and *the provision and use of resources in education.*

ACCESS WITH EQUITY AND QUALITY

Access to universal primary education is the right of every citizen, under the constitution and international human rights treaties. This is also a national development imperative. However, realities of today's world relentlessly demand wider access to increasingly higher levels of education. These realities include rising expectations of people, need for an increasingly broader and higher base of knowledge and skills in a technology-driven economy, and competitiveness in the global market. Secondary level of education is now regarded as a part of basic and compulsory education in many developing countries. Other imperatives include relevant vocational/technical skills, better access to quality tertiary and professional education, and expanded opportunities for lifelong learning.

PRIMARY EDUCATION

There have been two positive aspects of primary education development in the past decade: slowing down of population growth rate from around 2.5 per cent in 1990 to about 1.6 per cent in 2003 (Bangladesh, Bureau of Statistics, 2003a); and gender equality i.e. an increase in girls' enrolment at twice the rate of boys. Still, at the primary level, one in eight children do not enrol in school, and nearly one in two of those enrolled do not complete primary education. This adds up to more than half of the children not having the benefit of a full cycle of primary education. This does not take into account what is actually learned by those who complete primary education. One-third of children after completing five years of schooling are reported to be without functional skills of literacy and numeracy (Ahmed, Nath, & Ahmed, 2003). The explanation lies in the low average attendance in class by enrolled students, crowded classrooms, lack of learning materials, untrained and often unenthusiastic teachers, and short contact hours in schools which mostly operate in two shifts.

While enrolment has increased, serious problems of access to primary education remain. Access is often narrowly defined only as initial enrolment but given the realities of the system, this could be revised. A meaningful definition needs to take into account exclusions such as non-access at the age of entry and not being ever enrolled, dropout before completion of the particular stage, nominal enrolment but non-engagement in learning, therefore vulnerability to drop out, and failure to progress to the secondary level after completion of primary education (Ahmed, Ahmed, Khan, & Ahmed, 2007).

It is generally agreed that poverty hinders participation in education. The proportion of population in poverty is estimated to be around forty, half of whom can be categorized as hardcore poor (Bangladesh. Ministry of Finance, 2007). The number of primary school-age children in the hardcore poor category (about 4 million) is more than double of the number of children who never enrolled (about 1.5 million). Available information suggests, expectedly, that poverty overlaps and interacts with other conditions of disadvantage and vulnerability and becomes an obstacle to children's enrolment in school as well as their continuation and effective participation in education. This includes poor children from female-headed households, children who are working, children with special needs who suffer from mild to severe disabilities, ethnic/language minorities, and inhabitants of remote and inaccessible areas.

Access to and participation in primary education, especially of the poor, is not simply a matter of providing schools within physical reach. In fact, with nearly 80,000 primary level institutions in the country, almost every village has a primary school. Yet, as the demand for non-formal primary education and attendance of at least 1.3 million children show, the functioning of the school has to be responsive to the specific needs of children. This includes not just regular features of a school such as a daily timetable, annual calendar, affordable costs of exercise books and pencils etc. but also the assurance to parents that the teacher is present every day on time and that the children indeed learn.

The primary education centres of NGOs, which serve the poor population—dropouts from regular schools and the 'never-enrolled'—have demonstrated that children from poor families do not drop out, even without the incentives of stipends offered in formal schools. This is because the NGO schools ensure that there is no cash cost to families to send their children to school, unlike in government schools where parents usually have to bear unofficial payments of various kinds (for sports, transport of government-supplied textbooks, terminal examination fees etc.).

SECONDARY EDUCATION

Transition from primary to secondary level (defined as proportion of Grade V students enrolled in Grade VI in the following year) was estimated at 83 per cent in 2004 (Ahmed et al., 2007). This relatively high transition rate does not mean a high enrolment ratio at the secondary level because of the high cohort dropout in primary school. Thus, while progress has been made in expanding enrolment, net enrolment is still at 45 per cent.

There are four major types of provisions in secondary education—general *Bangla* medium schools, government-assisted madrasas (religious seminaries), vocational/technical institutions, and different types of private and government-assisted English medium schools. The system lacks a unified approach to curricular standards and quality of educational provision and outcomes, and thus reinforces existing divisions and inequities in society.

Enrolment in government-assisted madrasas has almost doubled in the decade since 1995, whereas in the mainstream schools the increase has been under 50 per cent (Bangladesh, Bureau of Educational Information and Statistics, 2006). The *qaumi* madrasas run privately, and the government exercises no oversight over them. Reliable data are not available, and are thus not included in these madrasa statistics. This raises the policy question about whether public preferential funding should support a large educational programme of questionable value, quality, and relevance.

At the secondary level, 80 per cent of the children starting Class 6 do not pass the SSC examination (Bangladesh, Bureau of Educational Information and Statistics, 2006). The same problems of inequity and quality as in primary education plague secondary education. Education Watch 2005, which focused on secondary education, found that those who do not enrol in school or do not complete secondary education are largely the poor, extreme poor or other disadvantaged groups. There is irregular attendance in schools and there is also a widespread practice of silent or virtual exclusion i.e. children who attend classes irregularly and do not learn anything. Additionally, the public examinations like: Secondary School Certificate and Higher Secondary School Certificates, pass rates have shown large variations from year to year, which raises questions about reliability of the tests and whether these properly measure competence and knowledge of students (Ahmed, Nath, Hossain, & Kalam, 2006).

Currently, secondary schooling serves essentially as a screening device for disqualifying a large majority of young people and selecting a small minority for tertiary education, rather than having an educational purpose of its own. The curriculum and teaching are geared to preparation for higher education, to which only a fraction of students can aspire. Secondary schooling currently offers students little in relation to prospects for gainful employment, entrepreneurship or practical skills—none of which, of course, need be a disqualification for further education (Asian Development Bank, 1998).

As at the primary level, the closing of the gender gap in secondary school enrolment is a positive development, in spite of overall inequities. Incentives such as stipends and elimination of tuition for girls in rural areas have made a difference but this outcome does not compensate for the structure of inequity that characterizes the system. More girls, in absolute numbers, are benefiting from education, but girls from the poorest families, remote rural areas, urban slums, and ethnic minorities remain deprived as do their male counterparts.

Most developed countries and an increasing number of developing countries count at least ten years of education as compulsory education. Clearly, Bangladesh must greatly increase access and participation rates in secondary education to raise the basic level of education of the population. To be meaningful, this has to be done by increasing access with quality and equity, keeping a balance among the different major streams of post-primary education.

VOCATIONAL AND TECHNICAL EDUCATION (VTE)

The Vocational and Technical Education (VTE) subsector is characterized by very limited opportunities for systematic development of vocational and technical skills for Bangladesh's vast population.

A recent survey showed that for each person in the workforce with VTE, there were 104 graduates of secondary school and 34 college or university graduates (Bangladesh, Bureau of Statistics, 2003b). Does this mean that there are too few workers with vocational-technical qualifications? Should secondary students be encouraged to move in large numbers to VTE? There are no simple answers, but one thing is certain: these measures would improve learning and reduce inequalities only with a major overhaul of the system.

The overall education and skill level of the workforce is very low. There is, at the same time, a mismatch between skill training offered, especially in the public sector, and the skill demands of the employers. For example, less than 10 per cent of the graduates of VTE institutions are employed in their areas of training soon after graduation. The rest are divided equally between unemployed and enrolled in other education or training courses (World Bank, 2006). It should also be noted that 80 per cent of the workforce in Bangladesh is employed in the informal sector, to which the VTE has little link with.

Traditional informal apprenticeship and on-the-job experience create most of the skills that keep the bulk of the economy and production running. A master craftsman, himself inheriting the skill from his father or another 'master', trains his assistants in exchange for free labour or a reduced wage in such skills as welding, turning, bricklaying, etc. Gaining an understanding of the informal system and considering how the more formal training programmes of the government and the private sector can complement and supplement the informal system could be beneficial in enhancing the effectiveness of the nation's capacity to generate skills.

Stated government policies and goals are to increase substantially the proportion of post-primary students enrolling in

VTE. The equity effect of this expansion is dependent on the extent to which the programmes are accessed by the disadvantaged and poor, and their impact on increasing employment opportunities.

The impact of public sector VTE on poverty alleviation is undermined in two ways. It serves mainly *young males* who have completed at least the eighth grade. This rules out those who do not survive in the education system up to Grade IX, mostly the poor as well as the majority of girls. Secondly, failure to diversify its clientele and to make the programme more flexible, adaptable and responsive to market needs and geared to the informal economy means that VTE is failing to help the poor improve their income and employment prospects.

NON-FORMAL EDUCATION (NFE)

In the early 1990s a broadly conceived non-formal education programme known as the Integrated Non-Formal Education Programme (INFEP) was initiated to serve the diverse learning needs of the population. It envisaged extensive involvement of NGOs in developing and carrying out NFE activities. Since the mid-1990s, however, the government has chosen to concentrate on a narrowly conceived non-formal education programme confined to basic literacy courses carried out through a campaign approach (called the Total Literacy Movement or TLM) managed by the government administrative machinery in each district. TLM was initiated in 1994 with the ambitious aim of eliminating illiteracy from the country within a decade. According to the now-defunct Directorate of Non-Formal Education (DNFE), closed down in the face of complaints about widespread mismanagement and corruption, seventeen million people participated in literacy programmes between 1994 and 2002. It was claimed that, as a result of all these activities, two thirds of all adults in the country acquired literacy skills. However, independent observers were sceptical about the literacy outcome and its functionality. Various independent studies indicated that the adult literacy rate was in the range of 40 to 50 per cent with a high degree of gender disparity (Ahmed et al., 2003; Bangladesh, Bureau of Statistics, 2003a).

Currently, the main public-sector NFE activity under the Ministry of Primary and Mass Education is the Post-Literacy and Continuing Education (PLCE) project funded by a group of donors including the World Bank and ADB. It aims to serve 1.3 million adults who went through the TLM course. The content focuses on consolidating literacy skills and short trainings to teach income-earning skills.

Other than the PLCE projects, there are no substantial adult literacy efforts at present. This is in part due to lack of a workable strategy and a clearly defined national goal. To avoid falling back into the shortcomings and difficulties that characterized earlier literacy and NFE efforts, it is essential that lessons learned from past failures be fully taken into account.

A comprehensive vision for non-formal education has to be a major component of building a learning society. Despite the existing policy framework for NFE, adopted in 2005, there is a vacuum in respect of an appropriate mechanism with oversight and overall responsibility for NFE in the public sector.

Box 1: Status of Progress on Six EFA Goals

Goal 1. Expanding and improving comprehensive early childhood care and education, especially for the most vulnerable and disadvantaged children.

Status: *Roughly 25% of eligible children, not necessarily the most disadvantaged, have access to preschools. A national plan, objectives, targets, policy framework and quality standards need to be developed.*

Goal 2. Ensuring that by 2015 all children, particularly girls, children in difficult circumstances and those belonging to ethnic minorities, have access to, and complete, free and compulsory primary education of good quality.

Status: *Fulfilment of goal is unlikely at present rate of progress. A specific and targeted plan has to be adopted and implemented seriously.*

Goal 3. Ensuring that the learning needs of all young people and adults are met through equitable access to appropriate learning and life-skills programmes.

Status: *An overall operational plan has not been adopted. The draft NPA based on Dakar Goals has not been finalized.*

Goal 4. Achieving a 50 per cent improvement in levels of adult literacy by 2015, especially for women, and equitable access to basic and continuing education for all adults.

Status: *Not on track. Debate about the baseline for literacy level and appropriate definition and measurement of literacy skills has not been resolved. Independent research suggests that there has been insignificant progress in literacy level since 2000. There is a wide gap in literacy level between rural and urban populations and between men and women.*

Goal 5. Eliminating gender disparities in primary and secondary education by 2005, and achieving gender equality in education by 2015, with a focus on ensuring girls' full and equal access to and achievement in basic education of good quality.

Status: *Gender disparity in enrolment by 2005 has been achieved. Full gender equality with 'full and equal access . . . and achievement in basic education of good quality' by 2015 calls for effective strategies with a workable implementation mechanism.*

Goal 6. Improving all aspects of the quality of education and ensuring excellence of all so that recognised and measurable learning outcomes are achieved by all, especially in literacy, numeracy, and essential life skills.

Status: *A comprehensive plan, strategy, and programme with objectives and targets are not in place.*

Source: BRAC University-Institute of Educational Development (BU-IED), 2007; UNESCO, 2005.

TERTIARY EDUCATION

In 2005, the major components of tertiary education network were 21 public, general, and specialized universities, 53 private universities, 1,597 colleges of different kinds affiliated with the National University as well as the Bangladesh Open University. Just over a million students were enrolled in higher education, which was 4 per cent between the age-group of 17–23 years. The equivalent proportion for India is 12 per cent, 29 per cent in Malaysia, and 37 per cent in Thailand (Bangladesh, University Grants Commission, 2006). The University Grants Commission (UGC) is the regulatory body for university level institutions.

Historically, the University of Dhaka and degree colleges in the old district centres of the eastern part of Bengal had earned a reputation for high academic standards and as centres of intellectual pursuit. A massive expansion of the system and the demands of time have altered the character of Bangladeshi higher education over the last half century. In numbers of institutions and enrolment, tertiary education has recorded over five-fold growth since independence in 1971. Yet, participation of only 7 out of every 1,000 persons in higher education in today's 'knowledge economy' and 'information society' has to be considered meagre.

Table 1: Students and Teachers in Higher Education (2004–2005)

No.	Enrolment	Numbers	(% Share)
1.	Public Universities	112,430	(10.9%)
2.	Private universities	62,856	(6.1%)
3.	Colleges under National University	773,492	(74.9%)
4.	Bangladesh Open University	84,271	(8.1%)
	Total	1,033,049	(100.0%)

Source: Bangladesh, University Grants Commission (2006).

The government has followed an expansionist approach in liberally approving the charters for private universities. These universities have grown rapidly in number since the Private Universities Act was adopted in 1992 and the number of students and institutions has increased more than seven times. However, there are concerns about quality and protecting consumers from unscrupulous 'entrepreneurship'. Colleges under the National University cater to over three-quarters of the higher education students. They largely supply the teachers for primary and secondary schools. This change could be critical for reversing the decline in the entire education system.

The main issues regarding access to tertiary education are the equity of access to prestigious institutions leading to potentially high private returns from higher education, and the balance of enrolment in different fields.

A highly inequitable system of higher education results from two processes: the culling-out process in secondary education, which allows only a small proportion of students to complete the secondary stage, and the diversion of a large majority of higher education aspirants, often the ones from poor and lower middle class families in rural areas, to low quality degree colleges. Selectivity based on merit is not the issue. The problem arises when general colleges become an expedient way of meeting social and political pressures rather than offering a credible education programme.

Inequity is compounded by high public subsidy for higher education. This is multiplied progressively through higher stages of education, reflected in selectivity which is urban and wealth-biased.

Gender disparity also persists in higher education, despite progress at the primary and the secondary levels. About a third of the students in degree colleges are girls and less than a quarter are girls in universities. The ratio of girls is lower in most specialized professional institutions (Japan Bank for International Cooperation, 2002, 53–4).

Balance among disciplines in tertiary education as a whole remains tilted towards humanities and social sciences at the cost of science, technology, and applied subjects, mainly because of lower costs of offering instruction in the humanities.

Over 80 per cent of the students in public universities are enrolled in general studies rather than in applied sciences or specialized professional courses. A hard formula cannot be prescribed for distribution among disciplines, but the present balance would be generally regarded as inappropriate (Japan Bank for International Cooperation, 2002, 54).

GOVERNANCE AND MANAGEMENT OF EDUCATION

All of the major problems of the education system can be attributed directly or indirectly to governance and management of the system, which is ruled by regulations and practices based on tradition, custom, and precedence rather than responsiveness to changing needs and conditions.

Concern has been expressed in the Education Commission Reports of 2000 and 2003 about rampant lack of discipline, student unrest and other adverse influences of the politicization of education decision-making (Bangladesh, Ministry of Education, 2003c). The related problems of corruption and mismanagement, spawned and nurtured by partisan politics, when disciplinary and remedial action cannot be taken, have become the most serious obstacle to educational reform and change. The poor mostly suffer from a failure of the system, because the rich and the elite can opt out of the system and go to private institutions or abroad (Bangladesh, Planning Commission, 2006).

OVERALL SECTORAL POLICYMAKING, COORDINATION AND OVERSIGHT

An important systemic concern is how the education system as a whole and its sub-sectors function to help meet key social goals.

The overall organization and management of education, for example, show critical disjunctions and discontinuities. For instance, all levels of education operate with differing learning objectives and academic standards, with little opportunity for horizontal movement of students, and no interaction among organizational authorities running these different streams.

These concerns point to the need for rethinking the organizational structures, functions and roles in the education system. A systemic approach has to contribute to an overall education system goal defined by society's overarching priorities, such as poverty alleviation. India, for example, has opted for a super-ministry for human resource development, which coordinates the work of different ministry and department level agencies and organizations involved in various aspects of building human resource capacity. Thailand and Indonesia have permanent statutory commissions with similar functions.

The Education Commission Report (2003c) has suggested a permanent and independent National Education Commission as an institutional mechanism for public debate and scrutiny of educational policies and priorities and for protecting education from undue political interference. The need has been expressed for a strong and autonomous body, replacing the weak UGC (University Grants Commission), for coordination of higher education, serving national development needs, setting and maintaining standards in higher education (Bangladesh, University Grants Commission, 2006).

Allocation of authorities and functions at the central level: The distribution of authority, functions and capacities among central entities—ministries, directorates and other support institutions—has been identified as a serious management issue. A need expressed by many is to redefine the division of roles and responsibilities between the Secretariat of Ministry of Education (MOE) and Ministry of Primary and Mass Education (MOPME) and the Directorates, ceding more of the responsibilities for planning, initiating policy reforms and overseeing policy implementation to the professional staff of the Directorates (Ahmed, Ali, & Khan, 2004a).

DECENTRALIZATION AND DEVOLUTION OF RESPONSIBILITY AND AUTHORITY

The centralized structure of management of both government and government-assisted institutions has not changed over the years despite the rhetoric about decentralization. In recent years, increased politicization of education management has led to greater centralization. Many small and large decisions, which should be disposed of at the Directorate, district or Upazila level, end up at the highest level in the central ministry. Salary subvention and ad hoc grants paid to non-government institutions by the government, and enforcement of compliance to regulations for this purpose, have provided an avenue for exercising various forms of central control over these institutions (Ahmed & Nath, 2004b).

At the primary education level, the Primary Education Development Programme (PEDP)-II Macro Plan states:

> Fundamental to the process of quality improvement in primary education is the principle of decentralization and devolution of authority and responsibility to middle and local levels of the education system. . . . A distinctive thrust of the PEDP II is to increase authority and accountability, and enhance resources at school level to achieve quality improvement in learning with equitable access. In line with this approach, key outreach support mechanisms will be developed at the upazila level . . . additional functions will be assigned to schools and upazilas, which will be strengthened in terms of infrastructure and staff. It is important to ensure that these promises are actually fulfilled (Bangladesh, Ministry of Primary and Mass Education, 2003, 48–9).

The quality of education can be enhanced and schools can be held accountable for performance when individual institutions take responsibility for managing their own learning programmes. Even in the current general bleak picture, exceptional institutions which have earned a good reputation actually take greater responsibility for their own management, usually through good leadership of the head of the institution and support of an enlightened managing committee. These can serve as the model for a gradual move towards greater institutional responsibility and accountability.

EDUCATION FINANCING

An anomaly of both under-resourcing and waste characterizes the financing of education in Bangladesh.

It is a *low-cost and low-yield system*. Per student primary education expenditure is about US$13 and for non-government secondary education it is US$16 (Bangladesh, Bureau of Educational Information and Statistics, 2006). The low per capita and low overall costs are no reason for satisfaction, because educational quality—judged in terms of learning outcomes, the pedagogic process and essential inputs—is clearly the victim of this situation.

There is a *mismatch of financing and objectives*. Total national education expenditures, especially the public budget allocation, which is currently around 2 per cent of GNP, has to increase substantially in the medium-term to meet national goals and priorities regarding expansion and quality improvement of education. The share of government budget for the education sector would need to rise under one scenario from under 15 per cent in 2000 to 26 per cent in 2008 in order to achieve essential quality improvement (World Bank, 2000, Vol. I, 58–108).

Staff compensation dominates the recurrent budget (97% of the total) in primary education and comparably high at other levels. This leaves very little funding for other essential quality inputs such as learning materials, upgrading of teachers and academic supervision.

There are *high incentive expenditures* in primary and secondary education such as development expenditure which is dominated by incentive payments in the form of stipends. The important policy question that has arisen is whether the benefits in terms of participation, equity and quality improvement would not be better achieved by spending the funds directly on improving inputs and performance in school (Knowles, 2001).

Experience with NGOs, NFPE programme shows that the problem is one of supply—offering quality schooling at the right time and place and in the right way without a direct cost burden on families for unofficial fees—rather than one of creating demand by offering stipends. Stipends may, in fact, defeat the purpose of increasing learning, if resources cannot be provided for essential quality inputs.

The *significant household contribution for education* is not taken into account in government public financing strategy for advancing policy objectives such as equity and quality improvement. Education finance arrangements reinforce *the pattern of inequity* in the education system. The share of benefits from public spending in education enjoyed by households rises with income levels of households at all stages of education, but especially in secondary and tertiary education (World Bank, 1998). In primary education, the expenditure roughly corresponded with the income distribution of the population. But considering actual effective spending and benefits, counting who actually completes the primary stage, it is clear that the distribution is far from equitable.

COMMENTARY ON THE BANGLADESH EDUCATION SCENE

As discussed, the great achievements of expansion of access and gender parity in Bangladesh have not translated into substantially greater social equality. Rural children have lower secondary pass rates than urban children. Girls have lower pass rates than boys, and pass rates in non-government secondary schools are lower than in government secondary schools. The poor tend to predominate in non-government secondary schools and in rural areas. Higher Socio-Economic Status (SES) children are better prepared for university, and again predominate, especially in the more prestigious fields and in Dhaka University. Even so, unemployment rates are growing among degree holders, while employers in some fields cannot fill available positions. Thus, while the education system has greatly expanded, it continues to manifest, reinforce, even create, great inequalities in access to high quality schooling as well as to higher levels of education. Expansion of education has not yet played the transformative role in national development as promised by what might be called the 'optimistic view of education and development'.

THE ROLE OF EDUCATION: HUMAN CAPITAL FORMATION OR SOCIAL REPRODUCTION?

What we are calling the 'optimistic view of education and development' sees expansion of education as fostering economic and national (and individual) development. Increases in human capital should lead to economic growth, help individuals to improve their economic status and reduce social inequality.

In this view, as the population increases its knowledge, attitudes, and skills—its stock of human capital increase—enlarging the economic pie and increasing the per capita income. As meritorious individuals from disadvantaged backgrounds increase their human capital, they should improve their economic standing, and inequality should decrease. 'Wise' education policies would be paralleled by wise economic decisions—in the neo-liberal economic view, liberalization of markets, opening of the economy, and so forth. Strong proponents of human capital theory tend to find sympathetic ground with neo-liberal approaches to economic development.

While few would disagree with the importance of education and skills in economic development, critics see a much less deterministic role for education. Patterns of inequality and unequal power relationships frustrate the workings of meritocracy. Differences in the quality and availability of schooling, which often vary along socio-economic lines, result in unequal accumulation of human capital. Social reproduction theorists claim that education serves primarily to reproduce the social order, including existing inequalities and power relationships. In many cases schooling plays an active role in (re)creating inequality, by claiming to allocate socio-economic opportunities on the basis of merit (meritocracy), while actually doing so primarily on the basis of social background. The children of those with means start out ahead of the children of the poor, and their resources help them maintain a more favourable place in line. Rather than certifying the skills of individuals, credentials signal an individual's place.

All but the most fervent social reproductionists reject a deterministic view of education as social reproduction.

Instead, they would claim, some individuals do manage to overcome the handicap of poor background and do well. Such individuals, however, are generally exceptions, and do not obviate the larger processes at work. Proponents of social reproduction emphasize the persistence of inequalities and the failures of schooling to overcome them, and tend to support critical theories of economic development.

Empirical evidence is mixed. Considering the role of human capital in national development, it is clear that high-income countries have high levels of human capital. Indeed, a number of national-level studies have found that educational participation rates and stocks of human capital are positively associated with higher rates of economic growth (Barro, 1991; Petrakis & Stamkis, 2002). Investment in education as measured by prior educational expenditures is also positively associated with economic growth rates (Poot, 2000; Sylvester, 2002).

However, associations cannot determine the direction of causality. It may be that causality moves in the other direction—that growth in national income leads to increases in educational investment and participation. Alternately, some third factor may be involved, causing both expansion of education and economic growth. Indeed, the causal mechanisms and factors underlying national economic growth are complex and not well understood. Finally, some research has questioned the empirical link between education and economic growth (Krueger & Lindhall, 2000; Levine & Reneld, 1992).

The research provides no definitive basis for deciding between competing theories. Human capital theory could account for weak correlations between education and economic growth if the school system failed to convey the knowledge and skills needed for economic growth, either through mismatch between the knowledge acquired and needs of the economy or low quality of schooling. On the one hand, social reproductionists could claim that countries where educational expansion has been followed by economic growth are advantaged in other ways that are ultimately more determinative, their core or peripheral status in the world economy, for example.

Counter-intuitively, if labour markets do not grow, educational expansion may be associated with increases in educated unemployment and deflation in the value of credentials. Similarly, expansion of education may not result in economic growth to the extent that significant segments of the population lack access to the wage economy, e.g. rural poor, women, and ethnic minorities. It may also be the case that the national returns to educational investments are long-term, measured in decades rather than years (Krueger & Lindhall, 2000). Finally, technological change may shift the relationship between the quantities or qualities of education and economic growth, tightening the linkage between some types of education and economic growth, while loosening the linkage in other cases (Hannum & Buchmann, 2006).

In terms of the second claim—that educational expansion permits individuals to improve their economic status—there is strong evidence at the individual level supporting the importance of education as a determinant of occupational outcomes. Education is associated with higher wages even when statistical controls are used to account for the effects of ability and social background (Brint, 1993). Most rate of return analyses suggest positive returns to education at the individual, and often, social levels (Psacharopoulos & Patrinos, 2002).

At the same time, there are substantial variations within and between countries in the linkages between schooling and occupational attainment and the rates of return to various levels of education in different times and locales. These differences suggest the substantial role of context (or at least other factors) in mediating educational outcomes. Returns to education are often lower in areas of high poverty and may also vary according to local economic conditions. Returns are generally higher where technology and market conditions support innovation. Moreover, the value of a given set of credentials appears to vary to some extent on the credentials held by others in the area. The greater the credentials possessed by peers, the less the relative value of a given level of credentials.

In a context such as Bangladesh, where growth in the number of credentials is outpacing growth in labour markets, and where there are substantial variations in the relative value of credentials from different institutions, credential inflation has its greatest albeit negative effect on individuals at less prestigious institutions, primarily the already disadvantaged. The question posed by 'credentialism' remains: does schooling actually increase the productivity of educated individuals, or does it simply select some individuals to be first in line?

The large body of research findings suggests to the extent that schooling is valued for its scarcity rather than content—whether scarcity is defined by years of education or institution—that schooling is likely to play a greater sorting function (Shavit & Mueller, 1998). We conclude that in many contexts, education does add value, doing more than simply sorting individuals into queues. At the same time, the economic and educational playing fields are not level. Initial advantages give a substantial lead but the extent to which education improves economic opportunities and economic welfare is variable and context-dependent.

The third proposition, that educational expansion reduces social inequalities, can be understood in terms of traditionally disadvantaged groups such as the poor, women, and people living in rural areas. Considerable research suggests that expansion of education does little to change the relative status of different groups (Brint, 1993; Hannum & Buchmann, 2006; Shavit & Blossfeld, 1993). As educational opportunities expand, higher socio-economic groups tend to capture the most advantageous types and levels of schooling.

Increased participation of girls in education may result in gender parity at lower levels of education, while higher levels of education remain predominately male. Increasing gender participation in schooling does not necessarily translate into increased occupational opportunities, which depend in a large part on labour market conditions of supply and demand and cultural norms (Brinton, Lee, & Parish, 1995; Cameron, Dowling, & Worswick, 2001).

Indeed in Bangladesh, expansion of education has permitted greater numbers of disadvantaged groups—the poor, women, and rural dwellers—to attain schooling. However, the differentiations of schools by quality and at higher levels by type and quality closely follow the larger societal patterns of disadvantage.

HUMAN RESOURCE-ORIENTED DEVELOPMENT STRATEGIES IN PRACTICE

Independent of theoretical debates on the effects of education, some countries, poor in natural resources, have relied substantially on their human resources to develop economically and socially. The experience of these countries suggests some of the elements in what might be termed a human resource-oriented development strategy. These countries, we would argue, adopted a pragmatic strategy, combining prescriptions arising from both human capital/neo-liberal and social reproduction/critical analyses of development.

The objection could be raised that conditions in the countries briefly considered here—Japan, Korea, Singapore, and Finland—are hardly representative of those in developing countries and substantially different from conditions in Bangladesh. While none of these countries represent Bangladesh's current conditions, none was predicted to develop as they did. While strategies developed in one context should be applied very carefully if at all to another, the comparison is interesting.

First each country is discussed in a brief case study. Then, suggestive elements of a human resource-oriented development strategy are laid out in a series of somewhat speculative propositions. The intent is to provoke discussion and lay an initial groundwork for empirical work.

JAPAN

Closed until forced by armed US ships to open itself to international trade in 1853, Japan modernized rapidly, transforming what had been a largely feudal society into an industrial competitor of the West in less than sixty years. Though lacking a modern school system prior to opening, Japan began with relatively high rates of literacy as a result of temple schools, with the Meiji government realizing that education was a powerful means of national unification and competing with more powerful countries in the West. In part to avoid the colonial fate of China and later as part of its modernization process, a national system of formal education was rapidly developed in the second half of the 1800s. By 1900, Japan had achieved nearly universal primary education and universal literacy, with the government playing a guiding role in the development of secondary and tertiary education.

After World War II, the US occupation led reform of the education system, resulting in a structure modelled on the American system and the teaching of democratic values. Demand for secondary and higher education increased dramatically as the country grew economically, and as employment in white collar jobs became tightly linked with education. To meet excess demand, government allowed the proliferation of private schools, but regulated the private system closely. The Japanese economy grew rapidly up to the early 1990s, by which time it was among the largest economies in the world.

This rapid growth can be attributed to a number of factors, including and beyond human capital: high rates of savings; strong institutions and (mostly) wise governance; high levels of literacy and skills in the workforce; a highly disciplined and cohesive people; conditions and policies that fostered cohesiveness; broad distribution of economic benefits of development; ethno-linguistic homogeneity (though arguably less so than was emphasized during the formative period). Finally, Japan had both good luck and the capacity to maximize on the opportunities.

SOUTH KOREA[2]

Since the end of the Japanese occupation and the Korean War, the Republic of Korea has adopted a strong state-centered education development strategy as part of its nation building efforts. Much of its rapid development has been attributed to the supply of well-educated workers. The education system linked national and economic development by introducing an ideology of modernization, national spirit, patriotism-imbued workforce preparation, and education. As a result of the government's economic policy and international market conditions, South Korea has transformed itself from a developing nation into the world's 11th largest economy within the last four decades (Brender & Jeong, 2006; Sorenson, 1994).

In the 1960s, the Park Chung-Hee administration initiated a series of five-year economic plans which emphasized an export-orientated strategy well-suited to Korea's abundance of manpower and limited domestic market. The rate of economic growth, however, placed considerable pressure on both the Korean government and industry to prepare a workforce equipped to handle increasingly sophisticated jobs. The education system grew concomitantly with Korea's industrialization needs: after the initial state-driven policy of primary and then secondary education development, increased demands for higher education followed. Moreover, as the education level of parents increased, so did expectations for increased educational opportunities, leading the government to expand tertiary education by establishing private colleges. In the late 1980s and early 1990s, government education policy expanded technical high schools and occupation training institutes. However, given its higher prestige, students and parents (and employers) have opted to pursue the traditional academic track (Morris, 1996).

Socio-cultural forces within Korea enabled the education system to take root. After reconstruction, education became the key mechanism for upward mobility, which has resulted in Korea becoming an educational 'testocracy'. Parental support for education has prompted parents to sacrifice their own resources to pay for additional educational opportunities, often contributing as much as two-thirds of their child's educational costs. This has enabled the Korean government to devote a relatively small amount of its national budget to education, roughly 4.5 per cent of GNP (Sorenson, 1994).

SINGAPORE[3]

With independence in 1965, Singapore found itself poor in natural resources and with a large low-skilled population. The People's Action Party (PAP) government initiated an ambitious development strategy focused on foreign investment and the accumulation of human capital through skills formation. This strategy became one of the world's most successfully managed development efforts. Human resource development in Singapore can be understood as paralleling four stages of economic development.

During Stage 1, basic manufacturing (1965–1979), PAP economic strategy focused on developing 'cheap and disciplined labour' along with a 'strong and stable political system' to attract foreign investment. The work was labour rather than skills intensive, and so the primary education level of most workers was not inhibiting. However, in order to create a more skilled workforce, training programmes were developed and workers' skills systematically linked to economic development (Sung, 2006).

The education system followed in this period was the British model, producing a highly trained, university educated elite and a much larger percentage of secondary school completers with limited labour force skills. At the same time, development of streaming and technical training helped ensure that workers had the skills needed by international and national firms.

Stage 2 (1979 to 1991) involved skill upgrading. In the 1980s, Singapore, facing increased competition from other countries with lower labour costs and protectionist policies, launched its 'second industrialization', focusing on value-added manufactured goods. This required a more skilled labour force, in response to which the government made substantial investments in education and industrial training.

Stage 3 (1991–1999) focused on high value-manufacturing. In the 1990s, Singapore set out to achieve 'the Swiss standard of living' by 2020–30. To remain competitive, the country needed to move Singaporean companies to markets with lower labour costs. At the same time, the government worked to further upgrade skills in three areas: core skills required to participate in an advanced industrial society, enhancement of intermediate level technical skills, and expansion of higher education.

Stage 4 refers to participation in globalization and a knowledge-based economy (from 1999 to present). The focus now is on developing a workforce with knowledge-based, conceptual and adaptive skills to allow Singapore to compete in the knowledge economy and globalized markets (Sung, 2006).

A critical part of Singapore's economic success was formation of the development worker: 'A developmental worker is any worker who, by virtue of his/her participation, helps to deliver the economic vision of the developmental state whilst their continuing participation is maintained in exchange for current, but more importantly future, benefits for themselves and their family.' (Sung, 2006, 47) The PAP was able to link education to individual economic success as well as other social programmes to increase the individual worker's stake in success of economic reforms.

Also critical were the linkages between education systems and the economy: the role of education in developing skills; a technology transfer model that used foreign expertise to train local workers; inducements to the private sector in partnership with government to assume a key role in skills training; and incentives to firms to invest in training of their workforce. A high human capital base and a trained, disciplined bureaucracy were essential (Kuruvilla, Erickson, & Hwang, 2002).

Singapore benefited from broad acceptance of government policies, continuity of policy and consequent macro-economic stability, relatively low levels of corruption, and the (authoritarian) government's ability to implement policies conducive to growth. The government was also relatively free of influence from special interest groups. Interestingly, the country is now at a point where economic development is necessary to legitimize and perpetuate the government (Huff, 1995).

FINLAND[4]

Prior to the 1990s, Finland was highly dependent on the Soviet Union. With the collapse of the Soviet economy, Finland's economy fell as well. In the early 1990s, unemployment rose from 2 per cent to more than 15 per cent, government debt rose to over 60 per cent of GDP, inflation pushed up interest rates and the collapse of the Soviet Union took away 15 per cent of Finland's foreign trade. Finland's real GDP dropped more than 10 per cent between 1991 and 1993. Forestry was Finland's main export.

During the 1990s, Finland's economy transformed itself from a resource-driven economy to one driven by knowledge and innovation. Since 2000, Finland has ranked No. 1 in the World Economic Forum's competitiveness index; top in the OECD's Programme for International Student Assessment studies of learning skills and educational attainment; and consistently among the highest scoring countries on the Knowledge Economy Index (Dahlman, Routti, & Yla-Antilla, 2007).

Finland grew its economy through diversification of exports and growth of knowledge-based industry. Finland based its social and industrial policy on the principle that knowledge and expertise are the basis of economic competitiveness. The country knew it had to raise the education level of the population and of the labour force. Accordingly, emphasis was placed on general, secondary, vocational, adult, and higher education. Education is free through university level and has a strong focus on equality. In these ways, the education system played a crucial role in economic restructuring.

Finland increased its investment in research and development, which now accounts for 3.5 per cent of GDP, third highest in the world. When the government liberalized trade and capital in the 1990s, privately-funded research and development increased rapidly, significantly driven by Nokia.

An extensive adult vocational and technical education system was expanded and upgraded, with Finnish companies focusing on training. In the latter half of the 1990s, Finnish companies invested about 3 per cent of their personnel budgets in training.

By expanding higher education and increasing higher education's capacity for research and development, the government sought to increase ties between higher education institutions and the industry, decreasing the time for innovation transfer between researchers and industry. The number of Finns with PhDs has doubled since 1985. Around 35 per cent of higher degrees are in science and technology.

Planned in the 1980s, adult education became a focus of Finland's national educational policy and planning in the 1990s. Adult education is now available in over 1,000 institutions, universities, polytechnics, public and private vocational institutions, adult education centres, summer universities, adult upper secondary schools, study centres, sports institutes and music institutes. The 2000 Adult Education Survey found that 41 per cent of the population aged 18–64 participated in adult education related to their job or vocation.

Some of the elements of Finland's success are: a strong rule of law; strong governance and accountability; stable macroeconomic policy and strong financial sector; openness to outside ideas and a free trade regime; domestic competition; strong welfare state, particularly a very strong focus on education; coordination of policies among key government agencies, and between government and the productive sector; a focus on R&D and innovation; a new type of industrial policy, and an 'independent spirit of self-reliance and a "can-do" mindset.' (Dahlman et al., 2007, 1)

IMPLICATIONS FOR POVERTY REDUCTION AND IMPROVEMENTS IN HUMAN WELFARE

These cases suggest some of the ways development of human resources has played a central role in economic and social transformation in several countries. Of course, definitive conclusions cannot be drawn from short description of select cases. Still, it may be useful to articulate some of the patterns seen here and contrast them with the situation in Bangladesh.

PROPOSITIONS ON THE ROLE OF HUMAN RESOURCES IN COUNTRY CASES

- In all these cases, human resources were placed at the centre of national development strategy and most of these strategic decisions were made before global consensus had coalesced around its importance. National decisions were made by 'enlightened leaders' to do what was necessary to develop, and to rely on human resources as a core element.
- There was nothing inevitable about development in any of the countries examined. However, local policy

elites did not rely on international conventional wisdom regarding their prospects for growth.

- Prior to economic expansion, each country had developed a strong human capital base of broadly-based literacy and skills.
- This literacy and skills base was subsequently developed and enhanced in parallel with economic developments in the countries.
- Less clearly, social institutions (family/community, business, and/or public social welfare institutions) provided good health and a social safety net. The fruits of development were broadly shared, giving workers a stake in the national project. Economic opportunities were broadly distributed as the economy grew—new jobs, higher wages, increased educational opportunities, expanded housing, and health care programmes.
- Ways were found to link educational provision with larger needs of the economy. Generally, government took the lead in designing policies aimed at upgrading the breadth and depth of skills in the workforce, fostering expansion of increasingly higher levels of education, and focusing attention on needs of the economy, in parallel with economic expansion.

Despite its centrality, the human capital and skill base was regarded as necessary but not sufficient for sustained economic development. 'Sound' economic policies, 'strong institutions', and 'good' if not always democratic governance were also emphasized. More specifically in terms of education:

- Provision of high quality basic education for all children was made a priority.
- Ways were found to expand opportunities for higher level training in secondary and tertiary institutions. In Japan and Korea, government provided a select number of public institutions, at least one in each region, and permitted development of private institutions under government regulation, to meet public demand. In Finland and Singapore, government took the lead in provision of secondary, vocational/technical, tertiary, and adult education systems.
- Mechanisms for selection of students for higher levels of education have been widely regarded as tough but fair. By and large, the legitimacy of selection mechanisms has not been widely questioned.
- Expertise in science and technology has been emphasized whether through specialized schooling at secondary and tertiary levels, or high levels of training by large firms.
- Schools teach values more or less explicitly with an emphasis on national identity, loyalty, hierarchy, hard work, and a future orientation highly compatible with the needs of a cohesive nation and a growing economy.
- Education is associated with upward mobility. In East Asia, there is a perception that individual effort can overcome disadvantage (Cummings & Altbach, 1997; Rotberg, 2004).
- A strong role has been emphasized for actors at three levels of the education system—parents/community, school teachers and school leaders, and central education authorities. Parents have largely supported the work

of schools, reinforcing the importance of study and covering many private costs associated with support and direct costs (Bray, 1996). Central education authorities have tended to play a strong guiding role in setting of strategic directions for the system. The state is responsible for the framework. At the same time, teachers and school directors are recognized as important implementers, highly professionalized, and empowered to play a strong role in instructional leadership (Cummings, 2008).

- Initially, in Asia at least, substantial bodies of knowledge were 'imported'. Over time, the knowledge was adopted, localized and adapted to 'local' national contexts.

In all of these cases, global conditions have permitted development of export industries. Even so, it seems the countries were prepared to take advantage of opportunities that arose and adopted a pragmatic approach, following principles rather than a template. In hindsight, this process is likely to appear much more systematic and planned than at the time.

In contrast, Bangladesh has not placed education and human resources at the forefront of development strategy in budgetary or political terms. Education, like other areas of public activity, has become mired in politics. Despite expansion of number of enrolments and educational institutions, Bangladesh still has a weak human capital base of literacy and skill, science and technology are not emphasized, and poverty, though reduced, is still pervasive. Expansion of education has not led to large-scale changes in patterns of inequality. In some ways, inequity has been strengthened as selection mechanisms and disparities in quality reinforce social inequalities. Decision-making is highly centralized, sub-sectors within education are poorly coordinated, and there is weak articulation among different providers of education.

ELEMENTS OF A STRATEGY

In working to realize the potential, a good starting point for the journey to 2030 and beyond are ten recommendations called 'a framework for action on education governance' adopted in a national conference held in March 2008 to achieve better outcomes in education. These are listed below (Governance in Education Conference, 2008a, 2008b).

DECENTRALIZATION OF AUTHORITY WITH ACCOUNTABILITY IN EDUCATIONAL MANAGEMENT TO LOCAL LEVEL AND INDIVIDUAL INSTITUTIONS

A structure of decentralization of education management should be developed which will assign central authorities such as the ministry, directorates, and boards, with broad policy and regulatory responsibilities, while empowering zilla (district) and upazilla (sub-district) education offices, training institutes and schools to make decisions regarding activities, institutions, and personnel.

To do this effectively and to strengthen the capacity and resources at the local level, development and trial should be undertaken in a number of districts, before introducing it nationally.

POLICYMAKING AND COORDINATION STRUCTURES

A permanent National Commission on Education for pre-tertiary education composed of distinguished and respected representatives of major stakeholders—the civil society, the academic community, and the government education establishment—answerable directly to the National Parliament should be established. The Commission should be a statutory body with functions and status specified in a national education law. It should have a secretariat with technical capacity for policy review and evaluation of the performance of the education system. The Commission may provide an overall report on the national education system and a specific aspect or sub-sector of the system in alternate years.

Quality parameters need to be redefined for primary, secondary, technical, and vocational education levels. Recruitment and promotion rules need to be revisited for education administration, teachers, and members of management committees, and enforced transparently and objectively.

A COMPREHENSIVE LAW FOR NATIONAL EDUCATION

A National Education Law should be enacted as a comprehensive legal framework for implementing the constitutional provision of providing free and compulsory education to all. It should spell out rights, responsibilities, and obligations of citizens and government agencies at different levels, principles of decentralization and accountability, regulatory framework for different types of education programmes and institutions, and principles of defining and protecting public interest in education. The Citizen's Charter initiative, espoused by the Chief Adviser, may be enforced through this law for all educational administrative and service provider institutions.

ADEQUATE RESOURCES FOR EDUCATION WITH QUALITY AND EQUITY

Measures should be taken to double the share of GNP and of government budget for education in the next ten years. Medium-term budgetary framework (3 to 5 years) needs to be developed for both development and recurrent expenditures in education in order to achieve the target for ensuring adequate resources. Public subvention and incentives to educational institutions should be linked to commitment and fulfilment of agreed performance criteria and targets; greater autonomy and control of resources can be offered to institutions that prove their capability to use resources effectively. Schools may be given incentives to generate local funds.

EDUCATION GOVERNANCE FREED FROM PARTISAN POLITICS

A consensus has to be built regarding political parties restraining themselves from involving teachers and teachers' organizations in partisan politics; educational decision-making including those on appointments, transfers, and promotions should be protected from extraneous political influence;

appropriate legal provisions and rules for election for the parliament and other people's representative bodies should help protect education institutions from undue political influence. Codes of conduct for teachers and students should be developed and enforced.

SCHOOL AS THE LOCUS OF ACTION

The locus of action for purposeful governance to address issues of quality and equity in education should be the school alone. Parents and the teachers can work out appropriate measures to act upon specific circumstances of disadvantage.

Strategy to promote greater authority with accountability at school level. Schools which perform well, based on Key Performance Indicators (KPIs) that are localized to the specific needs of the community, can be rewarded, exempted from control and allowed to develop and follow their own higher standards, as the incentive for nurturing self-regulation and greater school-level responsibility with accountability.

Making managing committees responsive and accountable. Modification of regulations, awareness raising, and active encouragement on the part of political and education authorities are needed to make the selection of the chairperson and members of the managing committees less beholden to local political personalities and more a genuine choice of the community so that this key responsibility is given to those genuinely interested in education.

Gender balance in managing committees. The School Managing Committees should have better gender balance with more than symbolic participation of women.

SUPPORTING DEVELOPMENT AND USE OF PROFESSIONAL CAPACITY

Human resource policy and practices in education including career structure should allow and facilitate professional development so that the staff can rise to management and decision-making level. Institutions including IER of Dhaka University, IED of BRAC University, NAPE, NAEM, and NCTB should be supported to work together on developing strategy and plans for professional capacity development in primary and secondary education. The elements of this effort should include institutional and organizational analysis of primary and secondary education management, establishment of a primary education cadre, development of short and longer specialised training and professional development courses, rethinking and redesigning pre-service and in-service training for teachers and members of school management committee, including refresher training, and action research to cope with huge needs in terms of quality and quantity.

Information and Communication Technologies for Development (ICT) tools such as TV, VCD, mobile phone, and computer may be leveraged for 'anytime-anywhere' training thereby saving time and cost and allowing flexible learner-centred schedules. A dedicated educational BTV channel for interactive educational programmes should be a reality without delay, as suggested by the Chief Adviser.

CAREER GROWTH AND BETTER REMUNERATION FOR TEACHERS

A workable approach to increase remuneration for teaching and linking it with performance is to design remuneration structures to allow for more differentiation in teaching positions (for example, entry-level assistant teachers, teachers, senior/master teachers/team leaders/assistant headmaster and headmaster) with promotion and salary raise tied to clearly established and enforced performance criteria. Special rewards or bonuses can be tied to group performance at the institution. The key role of the head master of the primary and secondary school as an educational leader and manager with enhanced authority should be recognized and commensurate status and salary granted.

A GREATER VOICE OF STAKEHOLDERS AT ALL LEVELS

Openness and sharing of information and dialogue in public forums (including posting the 'Citizen's Charter' publicly) should be the norm at school, zilla parishad (district council) and upazilla education offices regarding objectives, plans and progress, and budgetary allocations in the school, and for the upazilla. Monitored results of the Citizen's Charter should also be posted publicly in the form of Citizen's Report Cards.

Participatory planning process at the school and zilla parishad levels yearly and evaluation of execution based on Key Performance Indicators on a half-yearly basis need to be instituted.

PARTNERSHIP BUILDING

In local-level planning and management, formulating goals and strategies at national and local levels, and monitoring and reviewing progress, genuine partnerships have to be built for the government authorities and the non-governmental bodies to work together. Initiatives are needed on both sides to change the mindset, perceptions, and attitudes in order to foster the spirit of genuine partnership for working towards the common goals in education.

These priorities for action in fact encapsulated ideas which emerged from recent educational discourse involving education practitioners, policymakers, academics, researchers, and civil society representatives. These indeed can be the starting point if the education authorities and the political leadership choose to pursue the proposed action points purposefully.

REFERENCES

Ahmed, M., Ahmed, K. S., Khan, N. I., and Ahmed, R. (2007), Access to education in Bangladesh (Country analytic review prepared for the Consortium for Research on Educational Access, Transitions and Equity), BRAC University Institute of Educational Development (BU-IED).

Ahmed, M., Ali, K. S., and Khan, K. K. (2004a), 'Bangladesh education sector mapping', (Report prepared for CIDA), Dhaka.

Ahmed, M., Nath, S. R., and Ahmed, K. S. (2003), 'Literacy in Bangladesh: Need for a new vision', *Education Watch 2002* (Dhaka: Campaign for Popular Education [CAMPE]).

Ahmed, M., and Nath, S. R., et al. (2004b), 'Quality with equity: The primary education agenda', Education Watch 2003–2004 (Dhaka: Campaign for Popular Education [CAMPE]).

Ahmed, M., Nath, S. R., Hossain, A., and Kalam, M. A. (2006), 'The State of Secondary Education: Progress and Challenges', Education Watch 2005 (Dhaka: Campaign for Popular Education [CAMPE]).

Asian Development Bank (1998), Secondary Education Sector Development Plan (Bangladesh) 2000–10 (Manila: ADB).

Bangladesh, Bureau of Educational Information and Statistics (2006), Bangladesh Educational Statistics 2006 (Dhaka: Government of Bangladesh).

Bangladesh Bureau of Statistics (2003a), Population Census 2001 (Dhaka: Government of Bangladesh).

Bangladesh Bureau of Statistics (2003b), National Labour Force Survey 2002 (Dhaka: Government of Bangladesh).

Bangladesh Ministry of Education (2003c), Report of the National Education Commission 2003 (Dhaka: Government of Bangladesh).

Bangladesh Ministry of Finance (2007), Bangladesh Economic Review (Dhaka: Government of Bangladesh).

Bangladesh Ministry of Primary and Mass Education (2003), Second Primary Education Development Programme: PEDP II Final Plan (Dhaka: Government of Bangladesh).

Bangladesh, Planning Commission (2006), 'Unlocking the Potential: National Strategy for Accelerated Poverty Reduction', (Dhaka: Government of Bangladesh).

Bangladesh University Grants Commission (2006), 'Strategic Plan for Higher Education in Bangladesh: 2006–2026', (Dhaka: Government of Bangladesh).

Barro, R. J. (1991), 'Economic growth in a cross-section of countries', Quarterly Journal of Economics, 106, 407–43.

BRAC University-Institute of Educational Development (BU-IED) (2007), 'Brief on Literacy and Non-Formal Education, Dhaka', (Bangladesh: BRAC University).

Bray, M. (1996), 'Counting the full cost: Parental and community financing of education in East Asia', (Washington DC: World Bank/UNICEF).

Brender, A., and Jeong, B. (2006), 'South Korea overhauls higher education', *Chronicle of Higher Education*, 52(28), A50–A53.

Brint, S. G. (1993), *Schools and Societies* (Thousand Oaks, CA: Pine Forge Press).

Brinton, M. C., Lee, Y. J., and Parish, W. (1995), 'Married women's employment in rapidly industrializing societies: Examples from East Asia', *American Journal of Sociology*, 100, 1099–1132.

Cameron, L. A., Dowling, J. M., and Worswick, C. (2001), 'Education and labor market participation of women in Asia: Evidence from five countries', *Economic Development and Cultural Change*, 49, 460–77.

Cummings, W. K. (2008), 'Towards national strategies to support human resource development', in W. K. Cummings and J. H. Williams, eds., *Policy-making for Education Reform in Developing Countries: Policy Options and Strategies* (Lanham, MD: Rowman & Littlefield), 309–32.

Cummings, W. K., and Altbach, P. (1997), *The Challenge of Eastern Asian Education: Implications for America* (Albany: State University of New York Press).

Dahlman, C., Routti, J., and Yla-Antilla, P., eds. (2007), 'Finland as a Knowledge Economy: Elements of Success and Lessons Learned', (Washington DC: World Bank).

Governance in Education Conference (2008a), 'Chief Adviser's Inaugural Address', Paper presented at the Governance in Education (organized by UNESCO in cooperation with

Ministries of Education and Primary and Mass Education) 2–4 March 2008, Dhaka.

Governance in Education Conference (2008b), 'Conclusions and Recommendations', Paper presented at the Governance in Education (organized by UNESCO in cooperation with Ministries of Education and Primary and Mass Education) 2–4 March 2008, Dhaka.

Hannum, E., and Buchmann, C. (2006), 'Global educational expansion and socio-economic development: An assessment of findings from the social sciences', in J. E. Cohen, D. E. Bloom and M. B. Malin, eds., *Educating All Children: A Global Agenda* (Cambridge, MA: Amercian Academy of Sciences), 495–534.

Huff, W. (1995), 'The developmental state, government, and Singapore's economic development since 1960', *World Development*, 23(8), 1421–38.

Japan Bank for International Cooperation (2002), Bangladesh education sector overview, Dhaka: JBIC.

Knowles, J. (2001), Bangladesh public expenditure review. Education sector draft (Prepared for ADB and World Bank), Dhaka.

Krueger, A., and Lindhall, M. (2000), 'Education for growth: Why and for whom?' NBER Working Paper 7591.

Kuruvilla, S., Erickson, C. L., and Hwang, A. (2002), 'An assessment of the Singapore skills development system: Does it constitute a viable model for other developing countries?' *World Development*, 30(8), 1461–76.

Levine, R., and Reneld, D. (1992), 'A sensitivity analysis of cross-country growth regressions', *American Economic Review*, 82, 942–63.

Morris, P. (1996), Asia's four little tigers: A comparison of the role of education in their development, *Comparative Education*, 32(1), 95–110.

Petrakis, P., and Stamkis, D. (2002), 'Growth and education levels: A comparative analysis', *Economics of Education Review*, 21, 513–52.

Poot, J. (2000), 'A synthesis of empirical research on the impact of government on long-run growth', *Growth and Change*, 31, 516–47.

Psacharopoulos, G., and Patrinos, H. (2002), 'Returns to investment in education: A further update', World Bank Policy Research Working Paper 2881 (Washington DC: World Bank).

Rotberg, I. C. (2004), *Balancing Change and Tradition in Global Education Reform* (Lanham, MD: Scarecrow Press).

Shavit, Y., and Blossfeld, H. (1993), *Persistent Inequality: Changing Educational Attainment in Thirteen Countries* (Boulder, CO: Westview Press).

Shavit, Y., and Mueller, W. (1998), *From School to Work: A Comparative Study of Educational Qualifications and Occupational Destinations*, (New York: Oxford University Press).

Sorenson, C. (1994), 'Success and education in South Korea', *Comparative Education Review*, 38(1), 10–29.

Sung, J. (2006), *Explaining the Economic Success of Singapore* (Cheltenham, UK and Northampton, MA: Edward Elgar).

Sylvester, K. (2002), 'Can educational expenditures reduce income inequality?' *Economics of Education Review*, 21, 43–52.

UNESCO (2005), 'Literacy for Life', EFA Global Monitoring Report 2006, Paris: UNESCO.

World Bank (1998), 'From counting the poor to making the poor count' (Dhaka: World Bank).

World Bank (2000), Education Sector Review, Vols. I, II, and III, (Dhaka: University Press Ltd).

World Bank (2006), 'The Bangladesh vocational education and training system: An assessment', (Dhaka: World Bank).

NOTES

1. This chapter is based on a paper presented at the conference 'Bangladesh in the 21st Century, 13–14 June 2008' jointly organized by the Bangladesh Development Initiative (BDI), the Democracy and Development in Bangladesh Forum (DDBF) and the Ash Institute for Democratic Governance & Innovation—John F. Kennedy School of Government, Harvard University.

2. We are grateful in this section to Jamie Oberlander, who researched the material presented here.

3. Here we acknowledge with gratitude the research assistance of Sarah Palacio-Wilhelm.

4. In this section, we are indebted to Kaylea Happell for her research assistance.

Appendix:
Country Profiles

Bangladesh

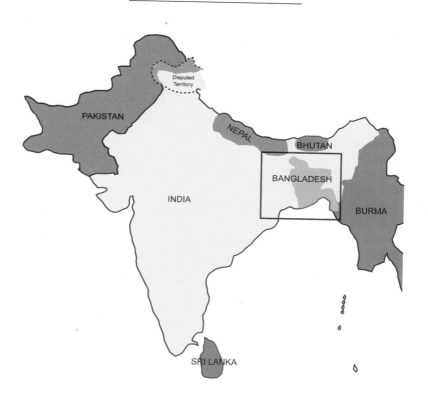

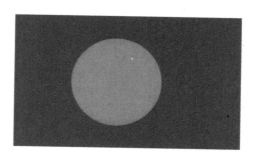

EDUCATION AT A GLANCE

Education Access, Coverage, and Efficiency	Most Recent Estimates	Year
Adult Literacy Ratio (%) [Male/Female]	56.77 [61.3/52.2]	2010–11
Primary Gross Enrolment Ratio (%) [5 years]	M: 93.2 F: 97.2 Total: 95.1	2010–11
Secondary Gross Enrolment Ratio (%)	M: 41.4 F: 45.8 Total: 43.5	2010–11
Primary Dropout Rate (%)	M:38.1 F: 29.4 Total: 33.8	2009–10
Primary Completion Rate (%)	M: 52.0 F: 57.0 Total: 54.5	2011–12
Gender Inequality Index (GII) [Rank]	0.55 [112]	2011–12
Ratio of girls to boys in primary education	1.08	2011–12
Pupil-Teacher Ratio at primary level (%)	43	2010–11
Trained Primary School Teachers (%)	58.4	2011–12
Enrolment in Private Schools at Primary Level (%)	40.9	2009–10
Education Financing		
Public Sector Spending (% of GDP)	2.23[1]	2009–10
Public Sector Spending (% of government expenditure)	14.1	2009–10
Education System		
Primary School Starting Age [Years]	6	2011–12
Secondary School Starting Age [Years]	11	2011–12
Compulsory Education [age group]	6–10	2011–12
Definition of Literacy	A person who is able to write a letter in any language has been considered as literate.	

CONTEXTUAL INFORMATION

Area	Most Recent Estimates	Year
Area (Sq. Kilometer)	143,998	2011–12

Population		
Total (million) [Urban/Rural]	150.493 [42.7/109.7]	2011–12
Density (per square kilometer)	1061	2011–12
Population Growth Rate (%) [Annual]	1.2	2011–12

Social Development Indicators		
Life Expectancy at Birth (in years) [Male/ Female]	69 [68/70]	2011–12
Under 5 Mortality Rate (per 1000 live births)	46	2011–12
Population Ages 0–14 (% of Total)	31	2011–12
National Poverty Line (%)	31.5	2010–11
Population living below 1.25$ a day (%)	43.3	2010–11
Human Development Index (HDI)	0.500	2011–12

Labour Force		
Total (millions)	72.32	2010–11
Annual Growth in Labour Force (%)	2.4	2010–11
Labour force participation rate (% of 15 years & above) [Male/Female]	84/57	2010–11
Employment to population ratio (% of 15 years & above)	68	2011–12
Unemployed [000] (% of Labour Force)	2700 (5.0)	2009–10
Unemployment (% of youth)	9.3	2009–10

Economy		
GDP Growth Rate (%)	6.2	2011–12
Sectoral Share in GDP		
Agriculture (%)	18.6	2010–11
Industry (%)	28.5	2010–11
Services (%)	53.0	2010–11
GDP per capita (PPP) [US$]	1569	2011–12
GNI per capita (PPP) [US$]	1940	2011–12

India

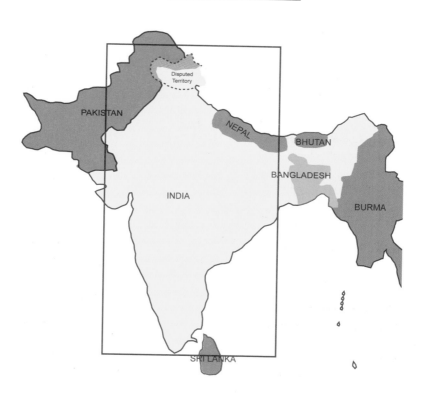

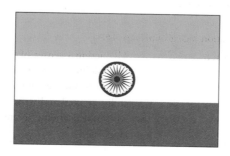

EDUCATION AT A GLANCE

Education Access, Coverage, and Efficiency	Most Recent Estimates	Year
Adult Literacy Ratio (%) [Male/Female]	74 [82/65]	2011–12
Primary Gross Enrolment Ratio (%) [5 years]	M: 116 F: 116 Total:116	2008–09
Secondary Gross Enrolment Ratio (%)	M: 64.4 F: 58.9 Total: 61.8	2010–11
Primary Dropout Rate (%)	M:33.8 F: 34.7 Total: 34.2	2008–09
Primary Completion Rate (%)	M: 92 F: 89 Total: 91	2011–12
Gender Inequality Index (GII) [Rank]	0.617 [129]	2011–12
Ratio of girls to boys in primary education	0.96	2011–12
Pupil-Teacher Ratio at Primary level (%)	32	2010–11
Trained Primary School Teachers (%)	–	2011–12
Enrolment in Private Schools at Primary Level (%)	28.3[ii]	2011–12
Education Financing		
Public Sector Spending (% of GDP)	3.3	2010–11
Public Sector Spending (% of government expenditure)	10.5	2010–11
Education System		
Primary School Starting Age [Years]	6	2010–11
Secondary School Starting Age [Years]	11	2010–11
Compulsory Education [age group]	6–14	2011
Definition of Literacy	The national census of India defines a 'literate' person as one having the ability to read and write with understanding in any language.	

CONTEXTUAL INFORMATION

Area	Most Recent Estimates	Year
Area (Sq. Kilometer)	3,287,263	2011–12

Population		
Total (million) [Urban/Rural]	1241.491 [623.7/586.5]	2011–12
Density (per square kilometer)	384	2011–12
Population Growth Rate (%) [Annual]	1.4	2011–12

Social Development Indicators		
Life Expectancy at Birth (in years) [Male/ Female]	65 [64/67]	2011–12
Under 5 Mortality Rate (per 1000 live births)	61	2011–12
Population Ages 0–14 (% of Total)	30	2011–12
National Poverty Line (%)	29.8	2010–11
Population living below $1.25 a day (%)	32.7	2010–11
Human Development Index (HDI)	0.547	2011–12

Labour Force		
Total (millions)	473	2010–11
Annual Growth in Labour Force (%)	1.4	2010–11
Labour force participation rate (% of 15 years & above) [Male/Female]	81/29	2010–11
Employment to population ratio (% of 15 years & above)	54	2011–12
Unemployed [000] (% of Labour Force)	17,134 (4.4)	2009–10
Unemployment (% of youth)	10.5	2009–10

Economy		
GDP Growth Rate (%)	8.7	2011–12
Sectoral Share in GDP		
Agriculture (%)	19.0	2010–11
Industry (%)	26.3	2010–11
Services (%)	54.7	2010–11
GDP per capita (PPP) [US$]	3203	2011–12
GNI per capita (PPP) [US$]	3590	2011–12

Nepal

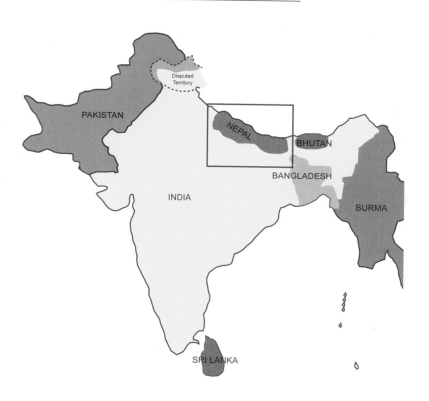

EDUCATION AT A GLANCE

Education Access, Coverage, and Efficiency	Most Recent Estimates	Year
Adult Literacy Ratio (%) [Male/Female]	60.31 [73.0/48.3]	2010–11
Primary Gross Enrolment Ratio (%) [5 years]	M: 127 F: 126 Total: 126	2008–09
Secondary Gross Enrolment Ratio (%)	M: 49.9 F: 48.7 Total: 49.3	2010–11
Primary Dropout Rate (%)	M: 40.3 F: 36.4 Total: 38.4	2009–10
Primary Completion Rate (%)	M: 85 F: 91 Total: 88	2011–12
Gender Inequality Index (GII) [Rank]	0.558 [113]	2011–12
Ratio of girls to boys in primary education	0.82	2011–12
Pupil-Teacher Ratio (%)	30	2010–11
Trained Primary School Teachers (%)	80.7	2011–12
Enrolment in Private Schools at Primary Level (%)	11.88	2011–12

Education Financing		
Public Sector Spending (% of GDP)	4.7	2010–11
Public Sector Spending (% of government expenditure)	20.2	2010–11

Education System		
Primary School Starting Age [Years]	5	2009–10
Secondary School Starting Age [Years]	10	2009–10
Compulsory Education [age group]	–	2011–12
Definition of Literacy	Literacy is defined as the ability of a person (age 6 years and above), who can read and write a simple letter with understanding in any language and perform simple arithmetic calculations.	

CONTEXTUAL INFORMATION

Area	Most Recent Estimates	Year
Area (Sq. Kilometer)	147,181	2011–12

Population		
Total (million) [Urban/Rural]	30.485 [5.2/24.1]	2011–12
Density (per square kilometer)	212	2011–12
Population Growth Rate (%) [Annual]	1.7	2011–12

Social Development Indicators		
Life Expectancy at Birth (in years) [Male/ Female]	69 [68/70]	2011–12
Under 5 Mortality Rate (per 1000)	48	2011–12
Population Ages 0–14 (% of Total)	36	2011–12
National Poverty Line (%)	25.2	2010–11
Population living below $1.25 a day (%)	24.8	2010–11
Human Development Index (HDI)	0.458	2011–12

Labour Force		
Total (millions)	16	2010–11
Annual Growth in Labour Force (%)	2.6	2010–11
Labour force participation rate (% of 15 years & above) [Male/Female]	88/80	2010–11
Employment to population ratio (% of 15 years & above)	82	2011–12
Unemployed [000] (% of Labour Force)	323 (2.7)	2009–10
Unemployment (% of youth)	–	2009–10

Economy		
GDP Growth Rate (%)	4.0	2011–12
Sectoral Share in GDP		
Agriculture (%)	36.1	2010–11
Industry (%)	15.4	2010–11
Services (%)	48.5	2010–11
GDP per capita (PPP) [US$]	1,106	2011–12
GNI per capita (PPP) [US$]	1,260	2011–12

Pakistan

EDUCATION AT A GLANCE

Education Access, Coverage, and Efficiency	Most Recent Estimates	Year
Adult Literacy Ratio (%) [Male/Female]	58 [69/46]	2011–12
Primary Gross Enrolment Ratio (%) [5 years]	M: 101 F: 83 Total: 92	2008–09
Secondary Gross Enrolment Ratio (%)	M: 38.6 F: 29.6 Total: 34.2	2010–11
Primary Dropout Rate (%)	M: 46.8 F: 49.0 Total: 47.8	2010–11
Primary Completion Rate (%)	M: 77 F: 68 Total: 73	2011–12
Gender Inequality Index (GII) [Rank]	0.573 [115]	2011–12
Ratio of girls to boys in primary education	0.84	2011–12
Pupil-Teacher Ratio (%)	41	2011–12
Trained Teachers in Primary Education (%)	84.2	2011–12
Enrolment in Private Schools at Primary Level (%)	32.3	2011–12
Education Financing		
Public Sector Spending (% of GDP)	2.4	2010–11
Public Sector Spending (% of government expenditure)	9.9	2010–11
School Going Age		
Primary School Starting Age [Years]	5	2011–12
Secondary School Starting Age [Years]	10	2011–12
Compulsory Education [age group]	5–16	2011–12
Definition of Literacy	A person (age 10 years & above), who can read a newspaper and write a simple letter in any language.	

CONTEXTUAL INFORMATION

Area	Most Recent Estimates	Year
Area (Sq. Kilometer)	796,095	2011–12

Population		
Total (million) [Urban/Rural]	176.745 [65.3/111.8]	2011–12
Density (per square kilometer)	227	2011–12
Population Growth Rate (%) [Annual]	1.8	2011–12

Social Development Indicators		
Life Expectancy at Birth (in years) [Male/ Female]	65 [64/66]	2011–12
Under 5 Mortality Rate (per 1000)	72	2011–12
Population Ages 0–14 (% of Total)	35	2011–12
National Poverty Line (%)	32.6	2010–11
Population living below $1.25 a day (%)	22.6	2010–11
Human Development Index (HDI)	0.504	2011–12

Labour Force		
Total (millions)	60	2010–11
Annual Growth in Labour Force (%)	3.3	2010–11
Labour force participation rate (% of 15 years & above) [Male/Female]	83/22	2010–11
Employment to population ratio (% of 15 years & above)	51	2011–12
Unemployed [000] (% of Labour Force)	2,430 (5.0)	2009–10
Unemployment (% of youth)	7.7	2009–10

Economy		
GDP Growth Rate (%)	2.8	2011–12
Sectoral Share in GDP		
Agriculture (%)	21.2	2010–11
Industry (%)	25.4	2010–11
Services (%)	53.4	2010–11
GDP per capita (PPP) [US$]	2,424	2011–12
GNI per capita (PPP) [US$]	2,870	2011–12

Sri Lanka

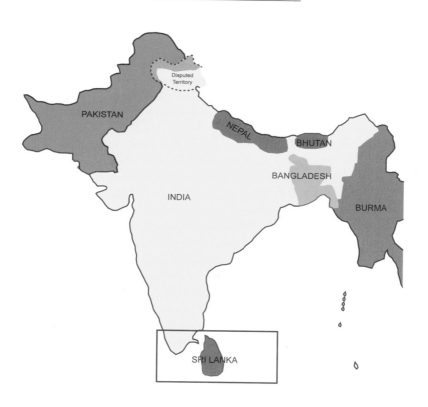

EDUCATION AT A GLANCE

Education Access, Coverage, and Efficiency	Most Recent Estimates	Year
Adult Literacy Ratio (%) [Male/ Female]	91.2 [92.6/89.9]	2010–11
Primary Gross Enrolment Ratio (%) [5 years]	M:101.3 F:101.5 Total: 101	2008–09
Secondary Gross Enrolment Ratio (%)	Total: 87	2010–11
Primary Dropout Rate (%)	M: 6.8 F: 6.4 Total: 6.6	2008–09
Primary Completion Rate (%)	M: 97.9 F: 98.9 Total: 98.4	2011–12
Gender Inequality Index (GII) [Rank]	0.419 [74]	2011–12
Ratio of girls to boys in primary education	1.01	2011–12
Pupil-Teacher Ratio (%)	24	2011–12
Trained Teachers in Primary Education (%)	–	2011–12
Enrolment in Private Schools at Primary Level (%)	2.8	2010–11

Education Financing		
Public Sector Spending (% of GDP)	1.97	2010–11
Public Sector Spending (% of government expenditure)	8.6	2010–11

School Going Age		
Primary School Starting Age [Years]	5	2010–11
Secondary School Starting Age [Years]	10	2010–11
Compulsory Education [age group]	5–14	2011–12
Definition of Literacy	There are two components: 1. One who can both read and write with understanding a short statement is considered literate. 2. A person who can read and write only his or her name, figures or memorized phrases should not be considered literate.	

CONTEXTUAL INFORMATION

Area	Most Recent Estimates	Year
Area (Sq. Kilometer)	65,610	2011–12

Population		
Total (million) [Urban/Rural]	20.869 [3.07/17.24]	2011–12
Density (per square kilometer)	324	2011–12
Population Growth Rate (%) [Annual]	1.0	2011–12

Social Development Indicators		
Life Expectancy at Birth (in years) [Male/ Female]	75 [72/78]	2010–11
	12	2011–12
Under 5 Mortality Rate (per 1000)	25	2011–12
Population Ages 0–14 (% of Total)	8.9	2010–11
National Poverty Line (%)	7.0	2010–11
Population living below $1.25 a day (%)	0.522	2011–12
Human Development Index (HDI)		

Labour Force		
Total (millions)	9	2010–11
Annual Growth in Labour Force (%)	0.9	2010–11
Labour force participation rate (% of 15 years & above) [Male/Female]	76/35	2010–11
	53	2011–12
Employment to population ratio (% of 15 years & above)	975 (7.6)	2009–10
	21.3	2009–10
Unemployed [000] (% of Labour Force)		
Unemployment (% of youth)		

Economy		
GDP Growth Rate (%)	7.0	2011–12
Sectoral Share in GDP		
Agriculture (%)	12.8	2010–11
Industry (%)	29.4	2010–11
Services (%)	57.8	2010–11
GDP per capita (PPP) [US$]	4929	2011–12
GNI per capita (PPP) [US$]	5520	2011–12

REFERENCES

India. Online Pages (2013), Literacy Rate in India. Retrieved 30 April 2013, from http://www.indiaonlinepages.com/population/literacy-rate-in-india.html

Mahbub ul Haq Human Development Centre, (2012). 'Human Development in South Asia: Governance of People's Empowerment', in M. Haq. and K. Haq, eds. (Lahore: Lahore University of Management Sciences [LUMS]).

Pakistan, Ministry of Education (2007), 'Literacy Initiative for Empowerment: Pakistan' (Islamabad: Government of Pakistan).

Pakistan, Ministry of Finance (2012), Economic Survey of Pakistan (2011–12). Islamabad: Government of Pakistan Retrieved from www.finance.gov.pk

UNDESA (2011), Revision of World Population Prospects from United Nations. Retrieved from http://esa.un.org/wpp/unpp/panel_population.htm

UNESCO (2005), 'Literacy: Real Options for policy and practice in India, Background Paper prepare for Education for All Global Monitoring Report 2006', in A. Mathew, ed. (India).

UNESCO (2009), Institute of Statistics, 2012. Retrieved from from http://stats.uis.unesco.org

UNESCO (2012), Institute of Statistics. Retrieved 15 October 2012, from http://stats.uis.unesco.org

UNFPA (2012), State of the World Population, Population Projections by Planning Commission's Working Group on Population Sector, New York.

United Nations (2012), Development Indicators Unit, Statistic Division, New York, Retrieved from http://mdgs.un.org/unsd/mdg/SeriesDetail.aspx?srid=611

World Bank (2012a), Education Statistics (EdStats), Retrieved 2012, from The World Bank http://web.worldbank.org/WBSITE/EXTERNAL/TOPICS/EXTEDUCATION/

EXTDATASTATISTICS/EXTEDSTATS/0,,menuPK:3232818 ~pagePK:64168427~piPK:64168435~theSitePK:3232764,00. html

World Bank. (2012b), 'World Development Indicators', The World Bank, Washington. Retrieved from http://data.worldbank.org/ topic/education?display=default

NOTES

1. Most recent data available on education financing.
2. Enrolment for age group (6–14).

Index

Controller and Auditor General (CAG) of India 38

Convention on the Elimination of all forms of Discrimination against Women (CEDAW) 221

Corporatization 310, 312

Corruption 38, 415–16, 424, 450, 466, 471, 489

Cost-effective 258, 261, 276

Credentials 47, 412, 478, 480–1; Credentialism 481

Crime 183, 423; Crimes 213; Criminal 176; Criminals 414

Cross-national 327, 439

Culture 46, 110, 165, 167–70, 191, 193, 211, 213, 219, 276, 287–8, 292, 301, 303, 305, 388, 415, 424; Cultural 48–9, 90, 125, 144, 148, 153–6, 161–2, 169, 173, 176, 181, 185, 190–1, 200–1, 217, 225, 281–2, 300–2, 327, 338, 406, 413, 419, 424, 483, 486; Cultures 168, 280, 289, 292, 442

Curriculum 7, 13, 43, 61, 63, 110, 117–19, 125, 135, 141, 149, 160, 169, 173, 180, 192–3, 199, 204–5, 215, 219, 225, 240, 277, 281, 283, 285, 291, 293, 299, 331, 348, 357, 362, 365–6, 462; Curricula 10, 12–13, 17, 126–7, 219, 349, 358; Curricular 141, 260, 282–3, 293–4, 461

Curriculum Development Centre (CDC) 291

D

Dalit 43

Daltonganj 38

Dang (district) 288, 298, 305

Danuwar 277

Darjeeling 297

De-professionalization 19, 312, 336–8

Debt 490

Decentralization 12, 93, 96, 98, 111, 120, 125, 169, 192, 299, 473–4, 496, 498; Delegated 89, 128, 130, 135; Delegation 101, 140

Deflation 480

Dehovita Zone 124

Delhi 42, 48, 321

Democracy 50–1, 92, 107, 169–70, 335, 338; Democracies 59, 70; Democratic 5, 11, 33, 39, 45, 50, 59, 68, 78, 86, 90, 98, 110, 118, 168–9, 484, 493; Democratization 92–3, 111–12, 226

Democracy and Development in Bangladesh Forum (DDBF) 507

Demographic and Health Survey (DHS) 35, 435, 437–9, 442

Denationalization 57

Devanagari (script) 288

Dhaka University 477, 500; University of Dhaka 468

Discrimination 12, 14, 160, 177, 180–2, 192–3, 211, 214, 217, 221, 395